I0028091

The
Power of Ideas

The Rising Influence of Thinkers and Think Tanks in China

The
Power of Ideas

The Rising Influence of Thinkers and Think Tanks in China

Cheng Li

Brookings Institution, USA

World Scientific

NEW JERSEY · LONDON · SINGAPORE · BEIJING · SHANGHAI · HONG KONG · TAIPEI · CHENNAI · TOKYO

Published by

World Scientific Publishing Co. Pte. Ltd.

5 Toh Tuck Link, Singapore 596224

USA office: 27 Warren Street, Suite 401-402, Hackensack, NJ 07601

UK office: 57 Shelton Street, Covent Garden, London WC2H 9HE

Library of Congress Cataloging-in-Publication Data
Names: Li, Cheng, 1956–   author.
Title: The power of ideas : the rising influence of thinkers and think tanks in China /
    Cheng Li, John L. Thornton China Center, Brookings Institution.
Description: Singapore ; New Jersey : World Scientific, 2017. |
    Includes bibliographical references and index.
Identifiers: LCCN 2016048665 | ISBN 9789813100220 (hc)
Subjects: LCSH: Political planning--China. | Policy sciences--China. |
    Research institutes--China.
Classification: LCC JQ1509.5.P64 L52 2017 | DDC 320.60951--dc23
LC record available at https://lccn.loc.gov/2016048665

British Library Cataloguing-in-Publication Data
A catalogue record for this book is available from the British Library.

First published 2017 (Hardcover)
Reprinted 2017 (in paperback edition)
ISBN 978-981-3232-18-1

Copyright © 2017 by World Scientific Publishing Co. Pte. Ltd.

All rights reserved. This book, or parts thereof, may not be reproduced in any form or by any means, electronic or mechanical, including photocopying, recording or any information storage and retrieval system now known or to be invented, without written permission from the publisher.

For photocopying of material in this volume, please pay a copying fee through the Copyright Clearance Center, Inc., 222 Rosewood Drive, Danvers, MA 01923, USA. In this case permission to photocopy is not required from the publisher.

Desk Editor: Sharon Khoo

Typeset by Stallion Press
Email: enquiries@stallionpress.com

Dedicated to

John L. Thornton

whose intellectual leadership and foresight have profoundly
contributed to think tank development across the Pacific.

Acknowledgments

Under Xi Jinping's leadership, think tanks have become increasingly important to assessing and crafting domestic and foreign policy in China. New institutions have sprung forth at an unprecedented rate just as older ones have expanded their operations and scopes of research. These major developments underscore the need for overseas China-watchers to study this subject more thoroughly. I hope this volume can serve as a waypoint while this field of inquiry continues to grow and deepen. Naturally, the contents rely on the research and ruminations of many individuals: some whose work is the subject of discussion and others whose assistance and contributions have made this specific volume possible.

Most of the chapters in this volume have appeared either in my English publications or are translations of my Chinese commentaries and interviews — all about think tanks and Chinese thinkers — throughout the past eight years. All chapters have been edited for consistency in style and narrative. Chapters 2–5 are drawn from my comprehensive introductions to each of the four volumes of the Thornton Chinese Thinkers Series, published by the Brookings Institution Press. Both the Brookings Institution Press and the authors of those books — Yu Keping, Hu Angang, He Weifang, and He Huaihong — deserve praise and admiration for the many hours they poured into responding to my comments on their scholarship over these years. In all relevant chapters throughout this volume, a full citation of the original source appears as the first endnote.

Many of the ideas and observations in this book reflect my experience at the Brookings Institution. Having just celebrated its centenary, Brookings owes its continued success to a stellar leadership team that keeps sight of the proverbial forest and yet still finds time to tend to the individual trees. I am indebted to Strobe Talbott, president of Brookings, for his generous trust and confidence; Martin Indyk, executive vice president of Brookings, for his gracious mentorship and friendship; and Bruce Jones, vice president of Brookings and director of its Foreign Policy program, for his judicious counsel and support. The scholars at Brookings make the institution the wellspring that it is. My colleagues are not only the most brilliant individuals from whom I have had the privilege of learning; they are also some of the kindest people I know. For their boundless wisdom and warm friendship, I am grateful to Jeffrey Bader, Kenneth Lieberthal, Jonathan Pollack, Richard Bush, David Dollar, Michael O'Hanlon, Ted Piccone, Katherine H.S. Moon, Mireya Solís, Daniel B. Wright, Charles Freeman, Evan Osnos, and many others.

Often less visible, yet equally important to Brookings's work, is an exceptionally talented team of research assistants and support staff. For their indispensable contributions to this volume, I am grateful to Meara Androphy, Eve Cary, Jordan Lee, Andrew Marble, and Paul Wozniak. Special thanks are due to Ryan McElveen, Lucy Xu, Zach Balin, and Vincent Wang, who did much heavy lifting to get this volume into shape and saw it through to the end. A group of skilled, knowledgeable, and enthusiastic interns also made essential contributions and, collectively, suggest that the future of China research and studies of U.S.–China relations is in good hands: Ming Ching Chai, Kejia Jin, Aubrey Kenton Thibaut, John Langdon, Veronica Li, Yalin Liu, Yingxian Long, Benjamin Tsui, Haiyue Xue, Kevin Wu, Will Zeng, Kun Zhang, Jing Jing Zhang, Yuxin Zhang, Jeffrey Zhao, and Tony Zhao.

This analysis benefitted enormously from the work of thinkers and practitioners on the ground in China. Prominent leaders and thinkers like Zeng Peiyan, Liu He, Tung Chee Hwa, Zheng Bijian, Dai Bingguo, Fu Ying, and the late ambassador Wu Jianmin have immersed themselves in efforts to develop Chinese think tanks into world-class institutions. Their success is a testament to the enormous talent and acumen they have brought to this task. Similarly, I wish to thank and express my admiration for scholars Wang Jisi, Yang Jiemian, Jia Qingguo, Yu Keping, Qu Xing, Su Ge, Hu Angang, Xue Lan, Ni Shixiong, Wu Xingbo, Shen Dingli, Wang Lili, Wang Huiyao, Wang Haiming, and Zhu Xufeng, whose academic contributions have set a very high bar and signal a bright future for Chinese think tanks.

For decades, Tsinghua University has lived on the cutting edge of research and thinking in China. Brookings is fortunate to have a partner that is so committed and engaged, qualities that have been exemplified countless times by former president Chen Jining, former chair of Tsinghua University Council Hu Heping, President Qiu Yong, Chair of Tsinghua University Council Chen Xu, Vice President Yang Bin, and Dean Xue Lan. By the same token, I extend my heartfelt appreciation to members of the Brookings China Council — Michael Ahearn, Anla Cheng, Deng Feng, Ding Jian, Jiang Weiming, Ambassador Jon Huntsman, Shen Nanpeng, Vaughan Smith, Michael Sweeney, Tang Xiaodan, Jerry Yang, Yang Yuanqing, and Zhang Chi — for their interest in think tank work, their recognition of its importance, and their exceedingly generous support in making projects like this possible.

I have had the great pleasure of watching the Brookings–Tsinghua Center, which recently celebrated its 10th anniversary, grow from an ambitious idea into a thriving research institution. I am tremendously grateful to the Center's dedicated director Qi Ye, whose scholarship on climate policy ranks among the best in the world, and its gifted and tenacious staff, including Li Yuan, Pan Zizhu, An Jing, Wang Mengni, and Lu Jiaqi. Thank you, as well, to a superior team of multitalented interns — Rene Ding, Mao Danni, and Eric Liu — for their brilliant work in translating chapters of this volume and their general commitment to excellence.

I am grateful to Qi Xiao, a former editor at the World Scientific Publishing Company, who initiated this important book project. His astute vision, guidance, and patience have been matched only by his colleague, Sharon Khoo, the senior editor who copyedited this entire volume.

I owe thanks beyond measure to my spouse, Yinsheng Li, who contributed to this volume in every way, shape, and form, and whose general support, advice, and encouragement inspire and sustain me.

This book is dedicated to John L. Thornton, co-chair of the board of trustees at Brookings, whose visionary input and personal guidance I have cherished. John personally recruited me to Brookings over a decade ago. I am inexpressibly grateful to him for giving me the opportunity to work in — and now lead — the Thornton China Center at Brookings, as well as for his continued trust and confidence. Truly, this volume could not have been possible without John. Not only has he been instrumental in introducing and promoting Chinese thinkers in the United States — the aforementioned Thornton Chinese Thinkers Series was his brainchild — but for many years he has also worked tirelessly to boost Chinese think tanks and to encourage intellectual exchanges with their U.S. counterparts.

Contents

List of Tables

Abbreviations

AMS	Academy of Military Science
BCG	Boston Consulting Group
BTC	Brookings-Tsinghua Center
CAE	Chinese Academy of Engineering
CAG	Chinese Academy of Governance
CAS	Chinese Academy of Sciences
CASS	Chinese Academy of Social Sciences
CCDI	Central Commission for Discipline Inspection
CCER	China Center for Economic Research
CCG	Center for China and Globalization
CCIEE	China Center for International Economic Exchanges
CCP	Chinese Communist Party
CCPL	Central Commission of Politics and Law
CCS	Center for China Studies
CCTB	Central Compilation and Translation Bureau
CCYL	Chinese Communist Youth League
CDI	China Development Institute
CFR	Council on Foreign Relations
CIC	China Investment Corporation
CICIR	China Institutes of Contemporary International Relations
CISM	China Institute of Strategy and Management
CLGCDR	Central Leading Group for Comprehensively Deepening Reforms
CNCPEC	China National Committee for Pacific Economic Cooperation
CPPCC	Chinese People's Political Consultative Conference
CPS	Central Party School
CSCC	Center for the Study of Contemporary China
CSRC	China Securities Regulatory Commission

CUPSL	China University of Political Science and Law
DRC	Development Research Center (in the State Council)
GFI	Global Financial Integrity
ICBC	Industrial and Commercial Bank of China
IIS	Institute of International Studies
IISD	Institute of International Strategy and Development
IMF	International Monetary Fund
NCER	National Center for Economic Research
NDRC	National Development and Reform Commission
NDU	National Defense University
NGO	Non-governmental Organizations
NIFD	National Institution for Finance and Development
NIIS	National Institute of International Strategy
NPC	National People's Congress
NSC	National Security Commission
NSD	National School of Development
NSF	National Science Foundation
PBOC	People's Bank of China
PLA	People's Liberation Army
PRC	People's Republic of China
PSC	Politburo Standing Committee
SAFE	State Administration of Foreign Exchanges
SARS	Severe Acute Respiratory Syndrome
SASAC	State-Owned Assets Supervision and Administration Commission
SASS	Shanghai Academy of Social Sciences
SOE	State-Owned Enterprises
TTCSP	Think Tanks and Civil Societies Program
UNCTAD	United Nations Conference on Trade and Development
WRSA	Western Returned Scholars Association
WTO	World Trade Organization

I
Introduction

Chapter 1

The Power of Ideas and Ideas of Power: Chinese Think Tanks in Search of Prominence

Thought precedes action as lightning precedes thunder.

— Heinrich Heine

Ideas have consequences.

— Victor C. Ferkiss

In 2005, Qian Xuesen, a 94-year-old, Caltech-educated Chinese scientist known as "the father of China's space program," raised an intriguing question during his meeting with then premier Wen Jiabao. "Why are Chinese schools not able to foster outstanding intellectual giants?" asked Qian.[1] He observed that, in terms of academic achievements, none of China's post-1949 graduates could be compared with the gurus educated during the Republican era.[2]

Qian's question, later dubbed "the Qian Xuesen Question" (钱学森之问, *Qian Xuesen zhiwen*), has brought public attention to some major defects in the education system of the People's Republic of China (PRC), especially its relative disregard for innovation and creativity. To many observers at home and abroad, despite the country's remarkable economic rise on the global stage in the reform era (1978–present), China has not yet produced world-class scientists and thought leaders.[3] Some critics cite the absence of PRC-educated Nobel laureates in the sciences and literature as key evidence supporting Qian's critical observation.[4]

3

Of course, not all observers share this negative assessment of Chinese universities and academia. Yang Zhenning (Chen-Ning Franklin Yang), a Chinese American who received the Nobel Prize in Physics in 1957, stated in July 2012 that Qian Xuesen was too hasty in making such a generalization.[5] Interestingly, only three months later, the Chinese writer Mo Yan received the Nobel Prize in Literature. And three years after that, in 2015, Tu Youyou, a Chinese pharmaceutical chemist who discovered a drug to treat an especially virulent form of malaria, became the first PRC citizen to receive a Nobel Prize in the sciences. Both Mo and Tu received their college educations in the PRC and conducted their intellectual pursuits almost exclusively in their native land.

According to Yang Zhenning, younger generations of Chinese scholars and thinkers are even more likely to excel than the older generation of intellectual sages like Mo and Tu.[6] Yang believes that Deng Xiaoping's open door policy for international educational exchanges has benefited the country intellectually and surely will produce still-greater achievements in the years to come. PRC-born scholars — including those who were trained both at home and abroad and those who currently work in China or elsewhere — are among the most promising candidates for future Nobel Prizes and other globally prestigious awards. In Yang's view, "the development of the sciences in the PRC during the reform era has not been too slow, but actually exceptionally fast."[7]

Contrasting Assessments of China's "Think Tank Fever"

Opinions on the role of the social sciences in the PRC are perhaps even more polarized, particularly in relation to the nature and implications of the leadership's recent emphasis on public policy research and think tank development in the country. In April 2013, when President Xi Jinping remarked that China should regard think tank building as part of its national development strategy, the statement sparked an unprecedentedly high-profile discussion on the role of think tanks. Meanwhile, many institutions across the country — including those within the party apparatus, government ministries, the military establishment, local administrations, universities, research institutions, business enterprises, social organizations, and media outlets — all have ridden the wave of

Xi's pronouncement by establishing so-called "new types of think tanks with Chinese characteristics."[8]

China's New National Strategy on Think Tank Development

According to *Caijing*, a well-respected Chinese magazine focused on finance and economics, the terms "think tank," "Brookings Institution," and "Rand Corporation" are now commonly mentioned in the Chinese media.[9] Some scholars have begun referring to this trend as "think tank fever" (智库热, *zhikure*).[10] This development has been driven largely from the top down, with heavy promotion and endorsement from the Xi administration. The government's recognition of and support for think tank–building is, of course, not entirely new. In 2007, the report of the 17th National Congress of the Chinese Communist Party (CCP) explicitly identified a need to enhance "the role of think tanks."[11] But under the leadership of Xi Jinping, think tank development has become a government-sponsored national strategy (国家战略, *guojia zhanlüe*). A brief chronological review of major events relating to the promotion of Chinese think tanks demonstrates how this objective has become unambiguously pronounced:

- In November 2012, the 18th National Party Congress report called for "the improvement of decision-making mechanisms and procedures, exhibiting a greater role for think tanks."[12]
- At the CCP Central Economic Work Conference held in December 2012, Xi Jinping stated that China should establish high-quality think tanks engaged in forward-looking research and policy consultation.[13]
- In November 2013, the resolution of the Third Plenum of the 18th Central Committee endorsed Xi Jinping's comments made in April 2013 by stating that building new types of think tanks with Chinese characteristics should be part of China's strategic mission.[14]
- In October 2014, at the meeting of the CCP Central Leading Group for Comprehensively Deepening Reforms, Xi Jinping stressed the importance of China's think tank development in enhancing the country's soft power.[15]

- In January 2015, the General Offices of the CCP Central Committee and the State Council jointly issued *Guidelines for Strengthening the New Type of Think Tanks with Chinese Characteristics*, announcing China's effort to promote 50–100 high-end think tanks.[16] The goal was to have "several think tanks wielding major global influence" by 2020.[17]
- In December 2015, the Chinese government announced the first group of 25 high-end think tanks, covering the areas of politics, economics, ideology, science and technology, military, law, and international affairs.[18]
- In April 2016, in an important speech delivered at the Internet and Information Security Work Conference, Xi Jinping proclaimed that China should adopt the "revolving door" (旋转门, *xuanzhuanmen*) mechanism prevalent among think tanks in many foreign countries, whereby political and intellectual elites move fluidly between positions in think tanks, the government, and the private sector.[19]
- In May 2016, Xi Jinping made a detailed speech concerning the development of the social sciences and philosophy in China, in which he called for strengthening international academic exchanges at research institutions, establishing overseas Chinese academic research centers, encouraging China studies in foreign institutions and foundations, and promoting scholarly collaborations between Chinese and foreign think tanks.[20]

The emphasis on building think tanks with Chinese characteristics does not imply that the Chinese leadership is pitting these institutions against their foreign counterparts. On the contrary, collaboration with foreign think tanks has been deemed a necessity. In March 2013, Xi Jinping stated that collaboration in think tank research should be part of the BRIC (Brazil, Russia, India, and China) agenda. On subsequent foreign state visits, President Xi Jinping continued to emphasize the need for bilateral think tank exchanges with countries such as France, Germany, Great Britain, the United States, Indonesia, and Pakistan.[21] Think tank exchanges with foreign counterparts are now considered the primary channel for "second track diplomacy" (二轨外交, *ergui waijiao*).[22]

Nowadays, China's top leaders often choose to deliver foreign policy speeches at think tanks abroad. During his visit to Europe in the spring of 2014, President Xi Jinping made speeches at two think tanks: the Körber

Foundation in Berlin, Germany, and the Collège d'Europe, an independent university think tank for the EU based in Bruges, Belgium. In June 2014, Premier Li Keqiang gave a major speech at a forum organized by two British think tanks, the Royal Institute of International Affairs (Chatham House) and the International Institute for Strategic Studies. Within China, international think tank dialogues have been frequently held not only in major coastal cities such as Beijing, Shanghai, and Shenzhen, but also in inland cities.

Cynicism and Negativity toward Chinese Think Tanks

Critics in China and abroad assert that the urgency to develop Chinese think tanks is driven primarily by the party leadership's desire to augment China's soft power and influence.[23] According to these critics, the old-fashioned bureaucratic mechanisms of this government-led initiative will not lead to a genuinely new era of intellectual ferment and public discourse on government policies. Instead, it may result in problems like waste of financial resources, duplication of low-level research, repetition of thematic topics, and fragmentation of institutional coordination on scholarship. Critics believe that under the current system, think tank scholars are required to "endorse" (背书, *beishu*) government policies rather than critically evaluate policy initiatives and political dissent.[24] As a scholar at the Institute of Policy and Management Science of the Chinese Academy of Sciences recently observed, a large number of well-funded Chinese think tanks, both old and new, seem to be "forum-centric think tanks" (平台型智库, *pingtaixing zhiku*) instead of "research-centric think tanks" (研究型智库, *yanjiuxing zhiku*).[25]

This disparity explains China's shortage of globally recognized social scientists and thinkers. Many critics deride Chinese think tanks as being "tanks without thinkers" (有库无智, *youku wuzhi*) or quip that there are "plenty of tanks but little thinking" (库多智少, *kuduo zhishao*).[26] Wei Jianing, a senior fellow at the Development Research Center of the State Council, recently acknowledged that China urgently needs de-bureaucratization (去官僚化, *qu guanliaohua*) in order to build world-class think tanks and research institutions.[27] Heavy CCP interference and political control in the operations of Chinese think tanks often undermine academic credibility, "therefore limiting [the] ability [of Chinese think tanks] to engage successfully with their Western counterparts."[28] One skeptic of China's think tank fever, Huang Yanzhong, a senior fellow at the Council on Foreign Relations, bluntly protests that "China is experiencing a think-tank 'Great Leap Forward'" — in that the country is wasting a devastating amount of resources.[29]

The recent tightening of political and ideological control over intellectual discourse at Chinese universities, NGOs, and on social media has reinforced negative views of the Chinese government's initiative to promote think tank development. Furthermore, the recent promulgation of the Foreign NGO Law and the National Security Law has severely undermined the credibility of the Chinese leadership's promise to promote independent research at Chinese think tanks.[30] Critics believe that such a rigid political system and today's conservative ideological environment are fundamentally incongruent with official claims of promoting international exchanges between Chinese think tanks and their international counterparts.[31]

Optimism and Positivity about Chinese Think Tanks

Though valid to a great degree, this negativity towards the status of and prospects for Chinese think tanks may overlook several important trends and intriguing phenomena — as some scholars have observed. First, the relationship between the government and think tanks in China is much more complex than many critics have recognized. Zhu Xufeng, a professor of public policy at Tsinghua University and a leading scholar of think tank studies in China, argues that foreign scholars are often biased in their understanding of Chinese think tanks. Zhu believes that some "foreign scholars superficially consider Chinese official think tanks to be government mouthpieces."[32] But in reality, as Zhu observes, "many of these Chinese research institutions themselves may not follow the same ideology. China's official think tanks sometimes openly criticize government policies."[33] Along a similar line of thinking, Silvia Menegazzi, an Italian scholar who specializes in the study of think tanks, argues that Western observers often underestimate Chinese think tanks. The proximity of Chinese policy research institutions to the government apparatus causes them to have "a bad reputation for the quality of their policy recommendations, especially when compared with their Western counterparts."[34] Such a "bad reputation," according to Menegazzi, may not be deserved.

Numerous empirical cases support Zhu Xufeng's and Silvia Menegazzi's arguments. The Central Party School (CPS) has long been a primary think tank for the Chinese Communist Party. But in the late 1970s and the early 1980s, under the leadership of then executive vice president Hu Yaobang, the CPS became a stronghold for challenging Maoist ideological indoctrination and correcting mistakes that were made during the Cultural Revolution.[35] In the mid- and late-1980s, the Institute of Political Science at the Chinese Academy of Social Sciences (CASS) — under the directorship of Yan Jiaqi — and the National Institute of Economic System Reform — under the directorship of Chen Yizi — both served as core think tanks for then premier and general secretary Zhao Ziyang. These think tanks proposed important political and economic reforms, including the abolishment of life tenure for top party and government leaders and the expansion of the rural household contract system.

More recently, when Yu Keping served as director of the China Center for Comparative Politics and Economics in the CCP Central Committee Central Compilation and Translation Bureau (CCTB), this prominent party think tank became a leading advocate for modern governance, inner-party democracy, civil society, and universal values. Chapter 3 profiles the remarkable intellectual pursuits of Yu Keping, a leading liberal theoretician in the Chinese political establishment. At his own initiative, Yu recently stepped down from his vice-minister-rank position in the CCTB and now serves as the dean of the School of Government at Peking University.

Secondly, the paradoxical attitudes of the Chinese leadership and think tanks towards one another further complicate their relationship. For the Chinese authorities, modern governance — including public policy in the areas of finance, trade, investment, taxation, budget, technology, the environment, and energy — requires special knowledge and expertise. China's economic rise on the world stage, its growing integration (and interdependence) with global financial institutions, and its need to improve the country's international image all call for think tanks to take up a larger role in policymaking. At the same time, the increasing influence of think tanks and especially their criticism of government policy mistakes could undermine the political legitimacy of the party leadership. This explains the CCP leadership's ambivalence toward the think tank community.

For the think tank community in China, increasing proximity to and gaining the trust of policymakers in Zhongnanhai is of utmost importance. In large part, PRC scholars share the same aspirations for China as CCP leaders: to achieve great power status in the eyes of the world. Nevertheless, some foreign observers insightfully point out that as "China's research community is increasingly internationalized, increasingly professionalized, and is producing higher quality and diversified research and policy recommendations for a wider range of customers," the think tank community will inevitably challenge the political and ideological control of the CCP and contribute to a more pluralistic political environment for policy discourse and institutional participation.[36] How to reconcile this inherent tension between the CCP leadership and the think tank community is of considerable consequence for China's economic and sociopolitical transformation. This dilemma further highlights the need to study and examine the multifaceted role of Chinese think tanks and the government's policies towards them.

Thirdly, for those who hold more optimistic views of China's think tank development, it is one thing to say that Chinese think tanks significantly lack intellectual freedom or independent thinking, but it is quite another to assume that political repression begets nothing but mediocre scholars. Throughout world history, some of society's greatest thinkers and the most creative minds have emerged from politically hostile circumstances, and even during the dark ages.

Some internationally respected Chinese writers and artists whose formative years occurred during the Cultural Revolution are collectively referred to as the "lost generation," as they missed the opportunity to pursue formal education owing to the decade-long "national madness of anti-intellectualism."[37] Examples include novelists Yu Hua and the aforementioned Mo Yan, movie directors Zhang Yimou and Chen Kaige, avant-garde artists Xu Bing and Cai Guoqiang, and musicians Tan Dun and Tian Haojiang. These exceptional talents have attributed their extraordinary careers to the hardships they endured, the dreams that were broken, and the wisdom they gained during the Cultural Revolution.[38] Many of them only attended college in their late twenties or even early thirties after the Cultural Revolution. Chinese dissident intellectual Wang Juntao (who himself is a member of the lost generation) predicted long ago that "this unique group [would] most likely produce the country's most talented scientists, writers, philosophers, educators, artists as well as statesmen in the future."[39]

Fourthly, like their counterparts in many other countries, Chinese think tanks serve multiple functions: gathering intelligence, analyzing events, assessing risks, drafting laws and regulations, and recommending and evaluating policy.[40] Working with Chinese think tanks offers arguably the best opportunity to glimpse the country's opaque policymaking process. As a German scholar asserts, "by engaging in exchanges with Chinese think tanks and their staff, foreign scholars and officials can take advantage of an unofficial channel in order to transmit their own opinions and concerns to their peers in China, hopefully bringing about increased understanding and coordination."[41]

Finally, of particular interest to foreign observers is China's perception of its role in the new world order, especially because this is where China's major think tanks and chief aides to the top leadership play an increasingly important role. In fact, Chinese thinkers and think tanks often initiate and formulate the governing ideas and policy moves of top leaders. Some of the major policy initiatives associated with a top leader actually can be traced back to brainstorming or discussion that occurred at a specific think tank or in conversation with a prominent thinker. Examples include former Fudan University law professor Wang Huning's contributions to Jiang Zemin's "Theory of the Three Represents," CCP theoretician and former vice president of the Central Party School Zheng Bijian's input into Hu Jintao's "Peaceful Rise of China," and the recommendations that Jin Liqun, an internationally renowned Chinese financial technocrat, made to Xi Jinping regarding the founding of the Asian Infrastructure Investment Bank (AIIB).[42]

More often, prominent Chinese think tanks are directed by top leaders to conduct further studies on certain policy initiatives. For example, after Xi Jinping declared the launch of the "One Belt, One Road" initiative (一带一路, *yidaiyilu*) in Central Asia in September 2013, 10 think tanks were invited to examine various aspects of this undertaking.[43] The research agendas of Chinese think tanks also reflect China's growing presence in Central Asia, which itself is bolstered by the "One Belt, One Road" initiative. In 2014 alone, China established at least nine new think tanks that focus exclusively on Central Asia.[44]

China's military established the China National Security Studies Center in 2015. Located at the National Defense University (NDU) of the People's Liberation Army (PLA), this new think tank claims the following main tasks: (1) to study the major security issues China faces; (2) to provide advice to the Central Military Commission; (3) to formulate the National Security Annual Report of China; and (4) to host a high-end annual forum on national security issues.[45] Retired major general of the PLA Luo Yuan, who currently serves as executive vice chair of the China Strategic Culture Promotion Association, recently stated that his association submitted 24 proposals to the Chinese leadership, among which 10 were adopted, including the establishment of the Special Administrative Region of the South China Sea and the formation of the National Maritime Police.[46] Each of the above efforts demonstrates the increasing influence of Chinese think tanks and prominent thought leaders in present-day China.

Recognizing Prominent Chinese Thinkers

China's momentous socioeconomic transformation is certainly not occurring in an intellectual vacuum. Chinese scholars and public intellectuals are actively engaged in fervent discussions about the country's economic and sociopolitical challenges, demographic constraints, domestic and foreign policies, and its ever-tightening integration into the world community. Therefore, for China watchers, it is incredibly valuable to understand the venues where China's political and policy ideas ferment and, perhaps even more importantly, to grasp how some of China's most prominent thinkers assess and envision China's growing power in the world and the various challenges confronting the country.

In an article entitled "Thinkers are Valuable National Assets," Yu Keping observes:

> China's path to reform and opening up has been a process in which old and new ideas collide — a continuous process where new ideas

overcome the old. Such a great era has not only brought forth great ideas, but the reform and opening up itself is a product of this great liberation of ideas.[47]

Yu further argues that "A great nation in a great age needs great ideas. Or more accurately, a nation and an era is great because it embraces great ideas."[48] Yu believes that a true thought leader exhibits three main traits: foresight (预见性, *yujianxing*), critical thinking (批判性, *pipanxing*), and appreciation for diversity (多样性, *duoyangxing*).[49] According to Yu, there are three ways in which visionary thinkers can change history: (1) by indicating the direction and goals that will progress human society, in accordance with morality and rationality; (2) by addressing critical issues of the day and seeking broad consensus; and (3) by offering suggestions and advice so that the government adopts sound policies.[50] In Yu's view, "throughout China's long history, those who have earned the respect of the Chinese nation are not primarily emperors and ministers, but outstanding thinkers."[51]

Along the same line of thinking, Wang Lili, a professor of public policy at Renmin University and a leading scholar on think tank studies in China, asserts that a country owes its rise to prominence on the world stage — as has occurred in China over the past three decades — to the instrumental role of thinkers. In Wang's words, "Throughout history, great powers have spent a great deal of financial capital to expand their knowledge base and develop intellectual capital."[52] Similarly, two other prominent Chinese scholars who study think tanks, Wang Huiyao and Miao Lü, argue that "A great power's rise in the world must have been accompanied by the establishment of global think tanks in that country."[53] A comprehensive report released by the China Center for International Economic Exchanges (CCIEE) in 2015 states that "A great nation with big ambitions must have great brainpower" (成大事者, 不可不用大谋, *chengdashizhe bukebuyong damou*).[54] The report highlights the relationship between China's emergence as a major power in world affairs and the growing importance of Chinese think tanks.

As Brookings scholar Richard Bush observes, almost all countries "are facing huge policy challenges as populations age, economies mature, technological change accelerates, globalization deepens, external security is more uncertain, and government budgets stagnate or decline. The state in modern societies must reconcile a number of competing objectives with limited resources."[55] Consequently, international learning and collaboration have become particularly essential. Globally-minded think tanks help facilitate international exchanges between great minds. Over the past decade, several dozen Chinese books focusing on overseas think tank development have been published.[56] Meanwhile, numerous volumes by foreign scholars from virtually all academic fields have been translated into Chinese, and many are now required reading for graduate and undergraduate courses at Chinese universities.[57]

Some Chinese analysts argue that never before in the Middle Kingdom's long history has there been such active international exchange and open embrace of teachings from the outside world as in the reform era. For example, China boasts the largest number of students studying abroad in many Western countries, including the United States and United Kingdom. During the 2014–2015 academic year, there were 124,552 PRC students enrolled in U.S. undergraduate programs and 120,331 PRC students enrolled in U.S. graduate programs.[58] Chinese tourists are now virtually everywhere — over the last few years, 100 million Chinese tourists have travelled abroad annually.[59]

Partly due to the status of English as the lingua franca and partly because of the above-mentioned biases against Chinese thinkers, intellectual exchanges between the Chinese scholarly community and its overseas counterparts remain unbalanced. For example, in recent years China has imported ten times as many books as it has exported, reflecting what the Chinese analyst Wang Wen calls an "intellectual deficit" or "thought deficit" (思想的逆差, *sixiang de nicha*).[60] Despite the fact that scholarly communities and the overseas public, particularly in the West, tend to undervalue Chinese intellectual contributions, some Chinese scholars have been recognized on the world stage. Table 1-1 shows the PRC public intellectuals listed among the world's top 100 thinkers or most influential people between 2005 and 2016 according to U.S.-based *Foreign Policy* and *Time* magazines.[61]

The fifteen Chinese thinkers included in the table differ from each other in terms of gender, generation, geographic region, educational background, academic field, ideological perspective, and political stance.

Table 1-1:   Public Intellectuals in the PRC Named the World's Top 100 Thinkers or Most Influential People by *Foreign Policy* and *Time* Magazines, 2005–2016.

Name	Year of Birth	Birth Place	Academic Field	Positions (Previous and Current)	Foreign Policy	Time
Zheng Bijian	1932	Sichuan	International Relations	Former executive vice president of the Central Party School, currently chairman of China Institute for Innovation and Development Strategy	2005	
Wang Jisi	1948	Guangzhou	International Relations	Former dean of the School of International Studies at Peking University, currently president of the Institute of International Strategy at Peking University	2005, 2012, 2014	
Fan Gang	1953	Shanghai	Economics	Former fellow at CASS, currently president of China Development Institute, Shenzhen	2005, 2007, 2008, 2010, 2014	
Ma Jun	1968	Beijing	Environment	Currently director of the Institute of Public & Environmental Affairs (IPE)	2011, 2012	2006
Hu Shuli (f)	1953	Beijing	Journalism	Former editor-in-chief of *Caijing* magazine, currently editor-in-chief of *Caixin* Group	2008, 2009, 2010	2011
Wang Hui	1959	Jiangsu	Literature	Currently professor and executive director of the Center for the Advanced Study of Humanities and Social Sciences at Tsinghua University	2008	

(Continued)

Table 1-1:   *(Continued)*

Name	Year of Birth	Birth Place	Academic Field	Positions (Previous and Current)	Foreign Policy	Time
Yan Xuetong	1952	Tianjin	International Relations	Currently director of the Institute of Modern International Relations at Tsinghua University	2008	
Han Han	1982	Shanghai	Literature	Writer	2010	2010
Liu Xiaobo	1955	Jilin	Literature	Previously lecturer in literature at Beijing Normal University, currently in jail	2010	
Yu Keping	1959	Zhejiang	Political Science	Former deputy director of Central Compilation and Translation Bureau, currently dean of the School of Government at Peking University	2011	
He Weifang	1960	Shandong	Law	Professor of law at Peking University	2011	
Yu Jianrong	1962	Hunan	Law	Currently director of the Research Center on Social Issues at CASS	2012	
Chai Jing (f)	1976	Shanxi	Journalism	Journalist		2015
Tu Youyou (f)	1930	Zhejiang	Science	Fellow at the Academy of Traditional Chinese Medicine		2016
Guo Pei (f)	1967	Beijing	Fashion	Chairman and chief designer of Rose Studio		2016

Source and Notes: The author's research. (f) denotes female.

A majority of them work in the social sciences and humanities. Of these innovative Chinese intellectuals who rank among the world's top thinkers, Tu Youyou is the only scientist and Guo Pei the only fashion designer. Three of these thinkers — namely, Ma Jun, Hu Shuli, and Han Han — were named as top global thinkers in both *Foreign Policy* and *Time* magazines.

The youngest in the list, Han Han, was born in 1982 and is a professional racecar driver, best-selling author, singer, and the most popular blogger in China (or perhaps even the world, with his website having drawn over 300 million visitors). *Time* magazine listed him among the 100 most influential people in the world in 2010, and he was voted the second most influential person in the world in the artists' category of the magazine's Top 100 poll, just after Lady Gaga. In addition, British magazine *New Statesman* ranked Han Han as one of the "World's 50 Most Influential Figures" in 2010.

Wang Jisi, Fan Gang, and Hu Shuli each were named to these lists three or more times. Fan Gang, for example, has not only written eight books and over 100 academic papers on macroeconomics and the economics of transition, with a particular focus on China's market transition in the reform era, but also has served twice as a member of the powerful Monetary Policy Committee of the People's Bank of China (2006–2010 and 2015–present). In 2016, Hu Shuli, who served as editor-in-chief of two of the most influential media outlets focused on economic and financial affairs (first *Caijing* magazine, then *Caixin* magazine), received an honorary degree from Princeton University for her painstaking efforts to promote independent journalism, government accountability, public participation in public policy formation, and media freedom in China.

While some of these thinkers (e.g., Fan Gang, Wang Hui, Yan Xuetong, Liu Xiaobo, Yu Keping, and Yu Jianrong) received doctoral degrees, the writer Han Han did not even graduate high school, having failed seven subject exams. Many of these Chinese thinkers possess experience in foreign studies. Most hold college degrees from Chinese universities and, in their early careers, were visiting scholars at prestigious universities in the United States. For example, Fan Gang, Wang Hui, Yu Keping, He Weifang, and Yu Jianrong all served as visiting scholars at

Harvard University; Ma Jun was a fellow at Yale University; Hu Shuli was a visiting scholar at Stanford University; Liu Xiaobo was a visiting scholar at Columbia University; and Wang Jisi was a visiting professor at both Princeton University and the University of Michigan. In addition, Yan Xuetong received his doctoral degree in political science from the University of California at Berkeley.

With the exception of Liu Xiaobo, who received the Nobel Peace Prize in 2010 for his role in the Chinese democratic movement, none of these thinkers has been labeled a political dissident. Many of them — for example, Zheng Bijian, Wang Jisi, Fan Gang, and Yan Xuetong — are widely perceived to be part of the political establishment, as they all have served as advisors to the CCP leadership. Yet several of these top 15 thinkers have been known for their outspoken criticism of the Chinese authorities in particular areas: for example, Ma Jun and Chai Jing on environmental degradation, He Weifang and Yu Jianrong on the absence of rule of law, Yu Keping on the personality cults of top leaders and the party's resistance to democracy and universal values, and, as mentioned above, Hu Shuli and Han Han on media censorship and the lack of transparency in public policy decisions.

Ma Jun and Chai Jing were instrumental in raising Chinese public awareness of the environmental crises in the country. Both are journalists by training, and both made far-reaching contributions to the environmental protection movement. Ma's 1999 book *China's Water Crisis* was recognized as the country's first major study on the environmental costs and consequences of the reform era.[62] Through his own think tank, the Institute of Public and Environmental Affairs (established in 2006), Ma Jun created the "China Water Pollution Map" (中国水污染地图, *Zhongguo shuiwuran ditu*), the first public database of water pollution information in China.[63] Chai Jing, a journalist who previously worked for CCTV, became a household name virtually overnight when her documentary film on China's disastrous environmental conditions, *Under the Dome* (穹顶之下, *qiongding zhixia*), was released for free online in March 2015. Within two days, the film was viewed more than 150 million times.[64]

Two Chinese thinkers, Wang Hui and Yan Xuetong, are widely regarded as the leading "new left" public intellectuals focused on domestic and foreign policy, respectively. Wang Hui argues that Deng Xiaoping's economic reforms have led to more suffering than progress on the part of workers, farmers, migrants, and other vulnerable social groups in China over the past three decades.[65] He has been similarly critical of Western theories on modernization and globalization. Yan Xuetong has been known for strongly advocating political realism and a zero-sum game perspective in world history and international politics.[66] According to Yan, China should not be so naïve as to believe that existing powers will welcome its rise. Inevitably, in Yan's view, there will be serious tensions and conflicts between existing and emerging powers. Therefore, Yan urges the Chinese leadership to "adopt a more assertive foreign policy" and "change its non-alliance policy, or Non-Aligned Movement principles, that was first adopted in 1982."[67] Yan believes that "China should establish military alliances like the United States does."[68] More specifically, "China should consider having military bases in countries it considers allies" to protect China's national interests.[69] In a way, Yan's view of China's rise mirrors the perspective of hawkish military officers such as Senior Colonel Liu Mingfu, director of the Institute of Military Development of the NDU. In his 2010 best-selling book *The China Dream*, Liu argues that China should pursue a new development strategy of "military rise" (军事崛起, *junshi jueqi*) to secure a global leadership position that will enable it to compete with the United States.[70]

It should be noted that a majority of the Chinese thinkers listed in Table 1-1 are more liberal in their domestic and foreign policy outlooks than either Wang Hui or Yan Xuetong. Also, importantly, four generations of the CCP leadership — Deng Xiaoping's, Jiang Zemin's, Hu Jintao's, and Xi Jinping's — have continually embraced the goals of market reform in domestic development and peaceful cooperation in foreign policy. In the foreign policy domain, the most influential Chinese proponent of China's peaceful rise, or the concept of peaceful development, has undoubtedly been Zheng Bijian. He was included among *Foreign Policy*'s top world thinkers in 2005, the same year that the Brookings Institution Press published his now-famous book, *China's Peaceful Rise*.[71] As the former executive vice president of the Central Party School, Zheng has served as an aide to many top leaders in the PRC, such as Hu Yaobang and Hu Jintao. In the book, Zheng argues that China's rise to major-power status will not, and should not, follow the conventional pattern of hegemonic conflict or war between great powers. Zheng provides four major reasons: (1) a rising China does not intend to pursue ideological warfare with the United States; (2) China neither plans to establish military bases overseas nor seeks a militaristic foreign policy; (3) in light of environmental challenges and resource scarcity, China now has to pursue an industrial development strategy that is more energy efficient; and (4) China will not engage in large-scale emigration, which may cause anxieties and problems for other countries, especially China's neighbors.[72]

Over the past decade or so, Zheng Bijian and other prominent international relations experts, such as Wang Jisi, have argued consistently that economic globalization and the challenges confronting humanity in our time fundamentally have changed world politics.[73] Thus one should reject a Cold War mentality and a 19th-century worldview, which treat international politics as a zero-sum game. The different perspectives of, on the one hand, Zheng Bijian and Wang Jisi and, on the other, Yan Xuetong and Liu Mingfu reflect the increasingly pluralistic thinking that has taken hold in a rapidly changing China throughout the reform era.

This volume includes detailed profiles of four major thinkers in four academic fields, namely: demographer and economist Hu Angang (Chapter 2), political scientist Yu Keping (Chapter 3), legal scholar He Weifang (Chapter 4), and philosopher and ethicist He Huaihong (Chapter 5). They are all influential thinkers who are deeply engaged in intellectual and policy discourse in present-day China. Yu Keping and He Weifang were named among the world's top 100 thinkers in 2011 by *Foreign Policy*. These four chapters not only detail the remarkable intellectual odysseys of these Chinese thinkers, but also highlight dynamic scholarly debates on various critical issues facing the nation and the world.

Differentiating China's Think Tanks

For the Chinese, the term "think tank" is somewhat novel, even if the concept and idea are by no means new. As one Chinese analyst observes, "Though many believe that modern think-tanks were born in the United States, China does have a long-standing partnership between intellectuals and policymakers that could be dated back to ancient dynasties."[74] No less than two thousand years ago, Chinese intellectuals were already essential figures in civic administration, providing emperors with policy recommendations and educating the general public.[75] Emphasizing this link to the past, numerous ancient Chinese terms are often used to describe the role and function of think tanks in the contemporary era, including 智囊 (*zhinang*), 谏官 (*jianguan*), 言官 (*yanguan*), 师爷 (*shiye*), 军师 (*junshi*), and 外脑 (*wainao*).[76] Throughout roughly the first four decades of the PRC's existence, think tanks were usually called research offices (研究室, *yanjiushi* or 调研室, *diaoyanshi*), research institutes (研究所, *yanjiusuo*), policy research departments (政研室, *zhengyanshi*), and academies of social sciences (社科院, *shekeyuan*).

According to the latest annual survey conducted by James G. McGann of the Think Tanks and Civil Societies Program at the University of Pennsylvania, China was home to 435 think tanks in 2015, second only to the United States, which housed 1,835 think tanks.[77] The United Kingdom ranked third with a total of 288 think tanks.[78] But based on Chinese official sources, the total number of Chinese think tanks is actually much higher. According to Li Wei, director of the Development Research Center of the State Council, China now has approximately 2,000 think tanks.[79]

Subcategories of Chinese Think Tanks

Not unlike their foreign counterparts, Chinese think tanks vary significantly in terms of size, degree of political influence, human resources, research interests, institutional objectives, and funding sources. Based on the results of an expansive survey conducted in 2012 by two researchers at the Economics and Management School of the Nanjing University of Aeronautics and Astronautics, in 2012 there were a total of 2,400 think tanks in China, including about 1,500 government-run think tanks (官方智库, *guanfang zhiku*), about 700 university-run think tanks (高校智库, *gaoxiao zhiku*), and about 200 private think tanks (民间智库, *minjian zhiku*).[80]

Among the government-run think tanks, about 40 were institutions at the national level (e.g., the Central Policy Research Office, the Central Compilation and Translation Bureau, the Central Party School, the State Council Development Research Center, the State Council Research

Office, the CASS, and the Chinese Academy of Governance), about 160 were situated under administrations at the provincial level (e.g., the provincial party committee research offices, the provincial government research offices, provincial academies of social sciences, and the provincial party schools), and 1,300 operated at the prefecture and city level (e.g., the municipal party committee research offices, the municipal government research offices, the municipal academies of social sciences, and the municipal party schools).[81] Altogether, these think tanks employ approximately 35,000 researchers and 270,000 supporting staff members.[82] Other Chinese studies split China's think tanks into four categories rather than the aforementioned three. For example, the Research Center on Think Tanks at the Shanghai Academy of Social Sciences divides government-run think tanks into two distinct groups: the first consists of party, government, and military think tanks while the second is composed primarily of social science academies.[83] A newly published Chinese think tank directory lists 1,186 think tanks across six categories: government, party, research institute, university, social organization, and joint venture.[84]

The general consensus of experts is that only about 5–10 percent of all think tanks in the country are private.[85] They are usually small and insufficiently funded, with a limited impact on policy. Private think tanks did not exist in the PRC until the late 1980s, when Cao Siyuan, who drafted China's first bankruptcy law and thus is known as "Bankruptcy Cao," established the Stone Institute of Social Development.[86] After 1989, the organization changed its name to the Siyuan Social Sciences Research Center, thus becoming the first think tank in the PRC to be named after an individual.

Following Deng Xiaoping's famous "southern tour" in 1992, several prominent Chinese intellectuals founded a few reputable private think tanks. For example, three distinguished economists, Mao Yushi, Sheng Hong, and Zhang Shuguang, established the Unirule Institute for Economics in 1993. Yuan Yue, a professionally trained lawyer, established the Horizon Research Consultancy Group in 1992. Other private think tanks and consulting firms (which to a certain extent serve functions similar to think tanks) also came to the fore during that time, such as the Beijing Great Wall Enterprise Institute, the Beijing Dajun Economic Observer

Research Center, the Cathay Institute for Public Affairs, and the Anbound Consulting Firm.[87] Also, Justin Lin's China Center for Economic Research at Peking University, which will be discussed in detail in Chapter 6, was established as a private think tank through funding from the Ford Foundation. In 2004, two internationally renowned scholars, Wu Jinglian and Jiang Ping, founded the Shanghai Institute of Law and Economics. It should be noted that many of these private think tanks have, from time to time, experienced difficulties in terms of their legal status, financial support, and public outreach.[88] These organizations do not rely on the Chinese government, probably because they derive their funding from domestic commercial sources, contributions from private entrepreneurs, or international institutional and commercial sources. This allows them to pursue more-independent research, and thus they also tend to be the institutions most critical of government policy.[89] Chapter 7 and Chapter 8 of this volume discuss the importance of diversity in think tank development and the prospects for China's private think tanks in an increasingly pluralistic society.

By contrast, some government-run think tanks are gigantic institutions with prodigious political, professional, and financial resources. As mentioned above, the Chinese leadership has decided to allocate greater resources in order to promote 100 high-level think tanks in the country. In December 2015, the authorities designated the first 25 of these (see Table 1-2). They are separated into four groups: (1) government-run think tanks; (2) university-hosted think tanks and research institutions; (3) think tanks affiliated with state-owned enterprises (SOEs); and (4) think tanks that are seen as social organizations. CCIEE, which falls into the last category, is not funded by the state budget, but many of its directors are current or former governmental officials and CEOs of major business firms (see Chapter 6). Some of its directors can attend the State Council's executive committee meetings. Owing to high-level government support, CCIEE's research fellows can serve temporarily as deputy heads of national government institutions to gain first-hand experience in policymaking and policy implementation.[90] Not surprisingly, none of the institutions listed is a private or foreign jointly-run think tank. According to *Caijing* magazine, these 25 high-level think tanks are essentially now associated with the Office of Social Science Planning in the Department

Table 1-2:   China's Top 25 National Think Tanks as Designated by the Chinese Government in 2015.

Category	Name	Current Head	Year Founded	Number of Fellows	Location	Homepage
Government	Development Research Center of the State Council, DRC (国务院发展研究中心)	Li Wei	1981	200	Beijing	http://www.drc.gov.cn
	Chinese Academy of Social Sciences, CASS (中国社会科学院)	Wang Weiguang	1977	2,200	Beijing	http://cass.cssn.cn
	Chinese Academy of Sciences, CAS (中国科学院)	Bai Chunli	1949	777	Beijing	http://www.cas.cn
	Chinese Academy of Engineering, CAE (中国工程院)	Zhou Ji	1994	850	Beijing	http://www.cae.cn/cae/html/main/index.html
	Central Party School, CPS (中央党校)	Liu Yunshan	1977	1,100	Beijing	http://www.ccps.gov.cn
	Chinese Academy of Governance, CAG (国家行政学院)	Yang Jing	1994	500	Beijing	http://www.nsa.gov.cn
	Central Compilation and Translation Bureau, CCTB (中央编译局)	Jia Gaojian	1953	N/A	Beijing	http://www.cctb.net
	Xinhua News Agency (新华社)	Cai Mingzhao	1937	N/A	Beijing	http://www.news.cn
	Academy of Military Science, AMS (军事科学研究院)	Liu Chengjun	1958	N/A	Beijing	http://www.ams.ac.cn/main.html
	National Defense University, NDU (国防大学)	Zhang Shibo	1985	N/A	Beijing	N/A

University and Research Institution	CASS National Institution for Finance and Development, NIFD (中国社会科学院国家金融与发展实验室)	Li Yang	2015	N/A	Beijing	http://www.nifd.cn/index.html
	CASS National Institute of International Strategy, NIIS (中国社会科学院亚太与全球战略研究院)	Li Xiangyang	2012	68	Beijing	http://niis.cass.cn
	China Institutes of Contemporary International Relations, CICIR (中国现代国际关系研究院)	Ji Zhiye	1980	175	Beijing	http://www.cicir.ac.cn/chinese/
	Academy of Macroeconomic Research, NDRC (国家发改委宏观经济研究院)	Zhu Zhixin	1995	N/A	Beijing	http://www.amr.gov.cn/web/Default.aspx
	Chinese Academy of International Trade and Economic Cooperation, Ministry of Commerce (商务部国际贸易经济合作研究院)	Gu Xueming	1997	110	Beijing	http://caitec.org.cn
	National School of Development at Peking University, NSD (北京大学国家发展研究院)	Yao Yang	2008	47	Beijing	http://www.nsd.edu.cn
	Institute for Contemporary China Studies, Tsinghua University (清华大学国情研究中心)	Hu Angang	2012	10	Beijing	http://www.sppm.tsinghua.edu.cn

(Continued)

Table 1-2: *(Continued)*

Category	Name	Current Head	Year Founded	Number of Fellows	Location	Homepage
	National Academy of Development and Strategy, Renmin University (中国人民大学国家发展与战略研究院)	Liu Wei	2013	N/A	Beijing	http://nads.ruc.edu.cn
	Institute of Contemporary China Studies, Fudan University (复旦大学中国研究院)	Zhang Weiwei	2015	N/A	Shanghai	N/A
	Wuhan University Institute of International Law (武汉大学国际法研究所)	Xiao Yongping	1980	12	Wuhan	http://translaw.whu.edu.cn/index.html
	Center for Studies of Hong Kong, Macao and Pearl River Delta, Sun Yat-sen University (中山大学粤港澳发展研究中心)	Chen Guanghan	2015	N/A	Guangzhou	http://hkmac.sysu.edu.cn/en/index.htm
	Shanghai Academy of Social Sciences, SASS (上海社会科学院)	Wang Zhan	1958	760	Shanghai	http://www.sass.org.cn
SOE	CNPC Economics & Technology Research Institute (中国石油经济技术研究院)	Li Jianqing	1983	N/A	Beijing	http://etri.cnpc.com.cn
Social Organization	China Center for International Economic Exchanges, CCIEE (中国国际经济交流中心)	Zeng Peiyan	2009	N/A	Beijing	http://www.cciee.org.cn
	China Development Institute, CDI (综合开发研究院)	Fan Gang	1989	83	Shenzhen	http://www.cdi.com.cn/index.aspx

Source: Sha Lu, "25 jigou ruxuan shoupi guojia gaoduan zhiku jianshe shidian danwei han liangjia shehui zhiku" [25 institutions are designated as high-end pilot units in think tank development, including two social organizations], *Xin jingbao* [New Beijing], December 3, 2015, http://www.bjnews.com.cn/news/2015/12/03/386602.html.

of Propaganda of the CCP Central Committee.[91] A majority of these high-level think tanks (20 out of 25) are located in Beijing.

These 25 high-level think tanks were established at different times. Xinhua News Agency, for instance, existed even before the founding of the PRC. The Chinese Academy of Sciences, the Central Compilation and Translation Bureau, the Academy of Military Science, and the Shanghai Academy of Social Sciences all were established in the first decade of the PRC. Interestingly, two of the think tanks are brand new, having been inaugurated in 2015. For example, the Institute of Contemporary China Studies at Fudan University was founded in November 2015, and one month later it was included among China's 25 high-level think tanks.[92] The hasty establishment and promotion of the Institute of Contemporary China Studies at Fudan University largely was motivated by a desire to enhance China's "soft power." The organization's president, Zhang Weiwei, who has been known for his appeals to ultra-nationalism, told the Chinese media at the founding ceremony that the establishment of the institute marked the end of an era in which Chinese academics would serve simply as "amplifiers" (传声筒, *chuanshengtong*) and "wage earners" (打工仔, *dagongzai*) for the West.[93]

Some of these prominent think tanks are quite small. For example, the Institute for Contemporary China Studies at Tsinghua University and the Institute of International Law at Wuhan University each employ only a handful of research staff. The largest think tank in the PRC is, of course, the CASS, which consists of 31 research institutes and 45 research centers, and boasts 4,200 employees, including 2,200 research fellows.[94] The CASS also maintains its own graduate school, which confers advanced degrees. From its founding in 1978 through July 2014, the graduate school had granted 4,154 doctoral degrees and 8,265 master's degrees.[95] Many graduates go on to work in various think tanks and higher education institutions. Several serve as national leaders, several hundred have become provincial and ministerial level leaders, and several thousand are leaders at the departmental and bureau level.[96]

Objectives and Channels of Influence

Notwithstanding some exceptions, scholars at Chinese think tanks typically delineate five main objectives for their work: (1) to provide analysis and advice to policymakers (咨政, *zizheng*); (2) to educate the public (启民, *qimin*); (3) to gather information and propose strategy (伐谋, *famou*); (4) to foster talented people (孕才, *yuncai*); and (5) to promote international exchanges (交流, *jiaoliu*).[97] They tend to overlook the critical role think tanks can play in policy formation, which is a primary function in many other countries. Deng Yuwen, former deputy editor of the Central Party School publication *Study Times*, explained to foreign journalists that his colleagues in the Chinese think tank community tend to "guess what the leaders want to hear" and are "more inclined to deliver their advice privately to leaders, through 'internal reference' channels, personal connections to leaders' secretaries and other means."[98] Quite insightfully, Deng characterizes this long-standing phenomenon as "a defect of Chinese intellectuals — they all want to be the emperor's mentor."[99]

This mentality has profoundly shaped the operation of Chinese think tanks, especially those with close government affiliations. According to Li Yang, former vice president of the CASS and director of the newly established National Institution for Finance and Development, the CASS maintains the privilege of a direct channel through which it can submit reports for circulation among roughly the 40 highest-ranking leaders in the country — presumably members of the Politburo, members of the Secretariat, and members of the executive committee of the State Council.[100]

Similarly, with about 200 highly qualified research fellows, the Development and Research Center (DRC) of the State Council has an impressive capacity to access policymakers. In 2012, for example, the DRC of the State Council submitted 572 reports to policymakers on the CCP Central Committee and the State Council. In return, Chinese leaders provided 271 comments on 145 reports.[101] Similarly, in 2014 the DRC issued 483 reports, and national leaders made 301 comments on 121 reports.[102] As some foreign analysts observe, the "frequency of political leaders' commentaries on think tank reports (批示, *pishi*) almost has become the most important yardstick by which to measure think tank performance."[103]

Not surprisingly, these two Chinese super think tanks enjoy large budgets supported almost entirely by the government. According to Wang Wen, executive dean of the Chongyang Institute for Financial Studies at the Renmin University of China, in 2014 the budget of the CASS was 2.33 billion yuan (about US$358 million), which, as mentioned above, covered the salaries of 4,200 employees, including 2,200 research fellows. The budget for the DRC of the State Council that year was 130 million yuan (about US$20 million). By contrast, the China Institute of Contemporary International Relations (CICIR), the China Institute of International Studies, and the Shanghai Institute for International Studies all operated on budgets under 60 million yuan (less than US$10 million).[104]

In addition to special reports submitted to the leadership, prominent think tanks such as the CASS, DRC, CICIR, and other research offices within the party and the government also regularly publish internal journals or news briefs. These internal journals and news briefs have strictly defined circulation lists. According to Zheng Bijian, *Ideological and Theoretical Internal Reference* (《思想理论内参》, *Sixiang lilun neican*) has a circulation of only 200 people (primarily Politburo members, members of the Secretariat, the General Office of the Central Committee, and the General Office of the State Council).[105] Similarly, *Attached Sheets of Domestic News Proofs* (《国内动态清样附页》, *Guonei dongtai qingyang fuye*) is circulated only among Politburo members. *Domestic News Proofs* (《国内动态清样》, *Guonei dongtai qingyang*) and *International Reference Proofs* (《国际参考清样》, *Guoji cankao qingyang*) are circulated among ministers and provincial chiefs. *Internal Reference* (《内部参考》, *Neibu cankao*) is circulated among prefecture and department level leaders. *Selected Internal Reference* (《内参选编》, *Neican xuanbian*) is a weekly publication and is circulated among county and military regiment level leaders.[106] Allegedly, Mao himself decided to invite the U.S. ping-pong team to visit China after reading an internal news brief that the famous Chinese player Zhuang Zedong and U.S. player Glenn Cowan had a friendly meeting in Nagoya, Japan, during the World Table Tennis Championship in 1971.

Think tank scholars also aim to exert their political influence through lectures and briefings delivered to the national leadership. Since the Hu Jintao era, the CCP Politburo has regularly scheduled study sessions, inviting scholars from universities and think tanks to provide lectures and briefings on specific subjects. Table 1-3 presents the ten think tanks with the highest numbers of scholars who were invited to speak to the Politburo. The CASS has been remarkably well represented. The DRC, the Academy of Macroeconomic Research at the National Development and Reform

Table 1-3: Number of Times Scholars from the Top Ten Institutions Briefed the Politburo at Study Sessions, December 2002–April 2016.

Rank	Institution	16th Politburo	17th Politburo	18th Politburo	Total
1	Chinese Academy of Social Sciences	15	13	4	32
2	Development Research Center of the State Council	7	6	0	13
3	Academy of Macroeconomic Research, NDRC	4	6	1	11
4	Renmin University	6	4	1	11
5	Central Party School	5	3	1	9
6	Academy of Military Science	8	0	1	9
7	Tsinghua University	3	2	3	8
8	Central Party History Research Office	3	3	1	7
9	National Defense University	0	4	1	5
10	Peking University	4	1	0	5

Source: Chinese Communist Party Website, May 26, 2016, http://www.12371.cn/special/lnzzjjtxx/. Calculated and tabulated by Cheng Li.

Commission, and Renmin University also have enjoyed strong representation. All of these institutions are located in Beijing. It is interesting to note that under the Xi administration, no State Council DRC scholar has been invited to brief the Politburo.

Another important function of Chinese think tanks is organizing high-level signature international forums or conferences. The China Development Forum organized by the DRC is arguably the most important annual event of its kind in the country. Table 1-4 provides an overview of China Development Forums from 2000 to 2016. The event is held in Beijing every year in late March. The executive vice premier or one of the vice premiers provides a keynote speech at the forum, while the premier meets with foreign VIPs who are participating in the forum. A large number of State Council ministers and provincial leaders also attend.

As China's economy has occupied an increasingly important position in the global economic landscape over the past decade, the number of foreign participants in the China Development Forum has been

Table 1-4: An Overview of China Development Forums, 2000–2016.

Year	Theme and Main Focus	Dates	Top PRC Leader Attended	Premier Meeting with VIPs	No. of Sessions	Total Speakers	PRC Speakers	Foreign Speakers
2000	China's 2010 Goals, Policy and Perspective	March 27–28	Vice Premier Wen Jiabao	Premier Zhu Rongji	5			
2001	The Role of Government in a Rapidly Globalizing Economy	March 25–26	Vice Premier Wen Jiabao	Premier Zhu Rongji	6			
2002	China after the WTO Accession	March 24–26	Vice Premier Wen Jiabao	Premier Zhu Rongji	7			
2003	China: Building a Well-off Society on All Fronts	March 22–24	Vice Premier Wu Yi	Premier Wen Jiabao	9			
2004	China: Toward a Balanced Development	March 20–22	Vice Premier Zeng Peiyan	Premier Wen Jiabao	9			
2005	China in the World Economy	March 19–21	Vice Premier Zeng Peiyan	Premier Wen Jiabao	10			
2006	China Promoting Economic Development and Social Harmony	March 18–20	Vice Premier Zeng Peiyan	Premier Wen Jiabao	12			
2007	China: Towards New Models of Economic Growth	March 17–19	Vice Premier Zeng Peiyan	Premier Wen Jiabao	12			
2008	2020 Development Goals and Policy Options	March 22–24	Exe. Vice Premier Li Keqiang	Premier Wen Jiabao	12			

(Continued)

Table 1-4:   *(Continued)*

Year	Theme and Main Focus	Dates	Top PRC Leader Attended	Premier Meeting with VIPs	No. of Sessions	Total Speakers	PRC Speakers	Foreign Speakers
2009	China's Development and Reform in the Global Financial Crisis	March 21–23	Exe. Vice Premier Li Keqiang	Premier Wen Jiabao	11			
2010	China and the World Economy: Growth, Restructuring, Cooperation	March 20–22	Exe. Vice Premier Li Keqiang	Premier Wen Jiabao	12			
2011	The Ongoing Transformation of China's Growth Pattern	March 20–22	Exe. Vice Premier Li Keqiang	Premier Wen Jiabao	13			
2012	China and the World: Macro-stabilization and Economic Restructuring	March 17–19	Exe. Vice Premier Li Keqiang	Premier Wen Jiabao	23	140	71	69
2013	China: Deepening Reform and Opening-up for a Well-off Society	March 23–25	Exe. Vice Premier Zhang Gaoli	Premier Li Keqiang	24	160	57	103
2014	China: To Comprehensively Deepen Reform	March 22–24	Exe. Vice Premier Zhang Gaoli	Premier Li Keqiang	26	148	72	76
2015	China's Economy in the "New Normal"	March 21–23	Exe. Vice Premier Zhang Gaoli	Premier Li Keqiang	34	168	91	77
2016	China in the New Five-Year Plan	March 19–21	Exe. Vice Premier Zhang Gaoli	Premier Li Keqiang	37	194	103	91

Notes: Exe. = Executive. The first forum was co-sponsored by the Development Research Center (DRC) of the State Council and Shenzhen Development Bank Co. Ltd., with the aim of building a new mechanism and a new channel for dialogue and exchange among entrepreneurs, scholars, and government officials both at home and abroad. All of the other forums were organized by the DRC.

consistently high. The China Development Forum and other important annual international conferences, such as the Boao Forum for Asia and the World Internet Conference in Wuzhen, provide meaningful opportunities for many Chinese and foreign stakeholders, including representatives of think tanks, to engage in policy discussions, access decision-makers, and exchange ideas and perspectives.

Evaluation and International Rankings

The quality and policy influencing abilities of Chinese think tanks vary widely. Zheng Xinli, permanent vice chairman of the CCIEE and former deputy director of the Central Policy Research Office of the CCP Central Committee, recently noted that many of the more than 2,000 Chinese think tanks that are funded by the state lack any incentive to engage in innovative policy research and are not motivated to compete with and try to outperform other institutions.[107] Other Chinese scholars who study think tank development believe that China's current environment is not conducive to fair competition between the "think tanks in the system" (体制内智库, *tizhinei zhiku*) and "think tanks outside of the system" (体制外智库, *tizhiwai zhiku*).[108] Consequently, the country lacks an institutional framework in which various forms of think tanks can partici-pate in policy consultation in a pluralistic manner.[109]

A recently released comprehensive evaluation, conducted by the Center on the Research of Think Tanks at the Shanghai Academy of Social Sciences, supports the observations of Zheng Xinli and others.[110] The study focuses on six clusters of influence:[111]

- policy impact (决策影响力, *juece yingxiangli*), which refers to the number of instructions and comments from policymakers regarding reports and other research products, the number of times that scholars give consultation and briefings to the leadership and the levels at which these briefings take place, and the ratio of scholars who previously or later served in the government (i.e., the "revolving door" mechanism);
- academic significance (学术影响力, *xueshu yingxiangli*), which refers to the number of publications appearing in core journals in both China

and abroad, the number of citations generated, the number and quality of conferences organized abroad, and the publication of other scholarly papers, monographs, series, and conference proceedings;

- media influence (媒体影响力, *meiti yingxiangli*), which refers to institutional capacity to influence public opinion through the media, the frequency with which think tank experts are interviewed or quoted by the media, and the quality and number of hits on home pages, blogs, and other social media;
- public outreach (公众影响力, *gongzhong yingxiangli*), which refers to the institution's ability to raise public awareness of social justice and common challenges and the needs and concerns of vulnerable groups in society;
- international reputation (国际影响力, *guoji yingxiangli*), which refers to international name recognition, the frequency of international cooperation and exchange with similar foreign institutions, and the capacity to provide sustained attention and in-depth analysis on major international events; and
- growth and market competitiveness (智库成长与营销能力, *zhiku chengzhang yu yingxiao nengli*), which refers to the longevity of institutional existence, the amount of financial investment in research, and the ability to retain top experts and elite scholars.

Based on these comprehensive criteria, this study designates 244 think tanks out of the aforementioned 2,400 Chinese policy research entities as being the "most active" (see Table 1-5). Interestingly, think tanks in the private and social category account for 36.5 percent of these "most active," even though, as mentioned above, private think tanks constitute only about 5–10 percent of all think tanks in the country. Similarly, James G. McGann's global think tank rankings for 2015 includes the new category of "China's top think tanks," and five private or foreign-jointly-run think tanks are included among the top 10, including the Carnegie-Tsinghua Center for Global Policy, the Center for China and Globalization, the Brookings-Tsinghua Center for Public Policy, the Cathay Institute for Public Affairs, and the Unirule Institute for Economics.[112] The Unirule Institute for Economics also made the list of the Global Top 100 for the first time (see Table 1-6).

Table 1-5: Categorical Distribution of the Most Active Think Tanks.

Category	Total Number	Portion of Total (%)
Party, Government, and Military	101	41.3
National Level	15	6.1
Ministerial/Department Level	24	9.8
Provincial Development Research Centers or Policy Research Office	28	11.5
Provincial Party School or Executive Academy	34	13.9
Social Science Academy, Academy of Science, and Academy of Engineering	54	22.1
National Level	3	1.2
Provincial Level	30	12.3
Provincial Capital Level	16	6.6
Prefectural Level	5	2.0
Private and Social	89	36.5
Social Organization (Trade Association)	21	8.6
Non-Governmental Organization	32	13.1
Foundation	3	1.2
Enterprise	20	8.2
Internet and Others	13	5.3
Total	244	100.0

Source: Center on the Research of Think Tanks at the Shanghai Academy of Social Sciences, *2014 nian Zhongguo zhiku baogao* [China's Annual Think Tank Report, 2014], January 2015, 11.

Altogether, a total of seven Chinese think tanks have been included in the Global Top 100 since the rankings were first introduced in 2008. Except for the Unirule Institute for Economics, the think tanks are all government-run and, therefore, well-funded. The CASS and the Shanghai Institute for International Studies have made the list seven and six times, respectively. Excusing the possibility of foreign bias in these rankings, the contrast between the government's support for state-run think tanks, especially its favorable resource allocation to a small number of high-level think tanks on the one hand and the relatively weak international reputations of these think tanks on the other, illuminates the value of

Table 1-6: PRC Think Tanks and Their Rankings among the Global Top 100, 2008–2015.

Name of Think Tank	Ranking							
	2008 *	2009 *	2010 **	2011 ***	2012	2013	2014	2015
Chinese Academy of Social Sciences	25		24	28	17	20	27	31
China Institute of International Studies					38	36	36	35
China Institutes of Contemporary Int'l Relations					48	44	40	39
Development Research Center in the State Council					100	99	48	50
Institute of International and Strategic Studies					63	61	61	64
Shanghai Institute for International Studies	34	34			73	71	71	72
Unirule Institute for Economics							99	

Notes and Sources: *Top 50 non-U.S. think tanks. **Only the top 25 are listed. ***Only the top 30 are listed. James G. McGann, "2015 Global Go To Think Tank Index Report (2016)," Think Tanks and Civil Societies Program, The Lauder Institute, University of Pennsylvania, Global Go To Think Tank Index Reports, Paper 10, http://repository.upenn.edu/think_tanks/10. Also see reports published in previous years.

independence and diversity in think tank development in present-day China. Chapters 7, 9, and 10 of this volume will focus on these issues.

An increasing number of Chinese scholars, including some government officials, have recognized the problems associated with the top-down rather than bottom-up approach to building China's new types of think tanks.[113] Ouyang Wei, a professor and secretary-general of the newly established China National Security Studies Center at the NDU, argues that Chinese think tanks should not be the government's "amplifiers"; instead, they should be engaged in seeking new ideas and policy proposals.[114] The credibility of China's think tanks has become increasingly important as they are "going global" and seeking to promote mutual understanding across the Pacific (for further discussion, see Chapters 11 and 12).

Chinese Think Tank Scholars and Strong Foreign Ties

One significant development in China's think tank community in recent years has been the rapid emergence of think tank scholars who are well-versed in and committed to international affairs. In 2015, the online magazine *Think Tank China* spotlighted a handful of top scholars who represent China's think tank development (see Table 1-7).[115] These representatives were selected based on four criteria: (1) familiarity with the operation of think tanks; (2) systematic observation of foreign think tanks; (3) experience writing about building think tanks in major media outlets; and (4) active participation in forums on think tanks.[116] They represent various generations of PRC scholars (born in the 1940s, 1950s, 1960s, 1970s, and 1980s). All of them have held administrative positions. Li Wei, Chen Yulu, Wei Liqun, Long Guoqiang, and Wang Ronghua are current or former minister or vice-minister level officials. All of them received their educations in the social sciences or humanities, and most studied public administration. More than half of them hold doctoral degrees, and more than half had the experience of studying or working abroad early in their careers.

Xue Lan and Wang Huiyao received their doctoral degrees from foreign universities — Carnegie Mellon University in the United States and the University of Manchester in the United Kingdom, respectively. Both worked overseas for many years before returning to their native country. Xue Lan taught international affairs at George Washington University as a tenure-track professor. Four scholars on the list have professional associations or work experience at the Brookings Institution. Xue Lan is currently a nonresident senior fellow and Long Guoqiang, Wang Lili, and Wang Huiyao were visiting scholars at Brookings. Wang Lili and Wang Huiyao have written books and articles about U.S. think tanks largely based on their experiences as visiting fellows at Brookings.

The youngest scholar on the list, Wang Wen, is a graduate of the Johns Hopkins–Nanjing Center. A former editor of *Global Times*, Wang Wen is a master of public outreach and information dissemination. As executive dean of the newly established Chongyang Institute for Financial Studies at Renmin University (following a 200-million-yuan contribution from Qiu Guogeng, an alumni of Renmin University, in January 2013), Wang has played an instrumental role in publicizing this new think tank in China

Table 1-7: The List of Top Scholars Who Represent China's Think Tank Development, 2014.

Name	Year of Birth	Title and Institution	Research Field	Education (Highest Degree)	Background
Li Wei	1953	President of the Development Research Center of the State Council	Economics and Finance	BA, Shanghai Television University	Assistant to Premier Zhu Rongji
Chen Yulu	1966	President of Renmin University*	Economics and Finance	PhD, Renmin Univ., Fulbright Visiting Professor at Columbia Univ.	Former dean of the National Academy of Development and Strategy, Renmin Univ.
Xue Lan	1959	Dean of the School of Public Policy and Management, Tsinghua Univ.	Engineering and Public Policy	PhD, Carnegie Mellon University	Assistant Professor of International Affairs, George Washington Univ., Nonresident Senior Fellow at Brookings
Wang Huiyao	1958	President of the Center for China and Globalization	Business Management	PhD, University of Manchester	Visiting Scholar at Brookings and Harvard
Wang Wen	1980	Executive Dean of Chongyang Institute for Financial Studies, Renmin Univ.	International Relations	MA, Hopkins-Nanjing Center, Nanjing Univ.	Former editor of *Global Times*
Li Guoqiang	1958?	Deputy Director of the Public Administration and Human Resources Institute of the Development Research Center of the State Council	Economics	MA, Nankai Univ.	Previously worked at the Xinhua Agency Hong Kong office

Name	Birth year	Position	Field	Education	Notes
Wei Liqun	1944	Former executive vice president of the Chinese Academy of Governance	History	BA, Beijing Normal Univ.	Retired in 2012
Long Guoqiang	1966	Vice president of the Development Research Center of the State Council	Economics	PhD, Peking Univ.	Visiting Scholar at Brookings
Wang Ronghua	1946	Former president of the Shanghai Academy of Social Sciences	Marxism-Leninism	MA, Central Party School	Director, Think Tank Research Center of the Shanghai Academy of Social Sciences
Zhu Xufeng	1977?	Professor, School of Public Policy and Management, Tsinghua Univ.	Public Administration	PhD, Tsinghua Univ.	Visiting Scholar at Harvard Yenching Institute
Wang Lili (f)	1976	Deputy Dean of National Academy of Development and Strategy, Renmin University	Public Administration	PhD, Tsinghua Univ.	Visiting Scholar at Brookings
Hu Angang	1953	Director of the Institute for Contemporary China Studies, Tsinghua University	Economics and Demography	PhD, Chinese Academy of Sciences	Post-doctoral fellow at Yale Univ. and visiting scholar at MIT and Harvard
Yu Jin	1970	Executive Director of China Regional Development and Reform Institute	Public Administration and Political Science	MA, Tsinghua Univ.	Editor-in-chief of *China Think Tanks*

Source and Note: "2014 nian Zhongguo zhiku jianshe daibiao renwu bangdan" [The list of top scholars who represent China's think tank development], Zhiku Zhongguo [Think Tank China] Website, February 2, 2015, http://news.china.com.cn/2015-02/02/content_34712363.htm. *Chen Yulu was appointed vice governor of the People's Bank of China in 2015. (f) denotes female.

and abroad. In its first year alone, the Chongyang Institute for Financial Studies published more than 100 reports, organized almost 100 forums and other activities, and submitted 14 reports to the various offices of the CCP Central Committee.[117] In May 2016, Wang Wen was among ten scholars from the social sciences, philosophy, and public policy who were selected to brief President Xi Jinping.[118] The Chongyang Institute was also one of three Chinese think tanks chosen to cohost the T20 ("Think 20" conference) during the G20 summit in Hangzhou in September 2016.[119] In the 2015 global think tank rankings by James G. McGann, Chongyang Institute was ranked number 15 in the new category of "China's top think tanks."

The Chongyang Institute for Financial Studies has been particularly notable for its efforts in international recruitment of full-time fellows and part-time associates. In June 2013, the Institute recruited John Ross as a senior fellow. Ross had served as an economic advisor to Ken Livingstone and as the director of London's economic and business policy while Livingstone was mayor of London. In addition, the Institute has offered nonresident fellow status to 80 former government officials, bankers, and well-known scholars, including the former president of Slovenia, Danilo Türk; the chairman of the Global Alliance of Small and Medium Sized Enterprises (SMEs) and the former director general of the United Nations Industrial Development Organization (UNIDO), Carlos Magariños; and the former secretary general of the Club of Rome, Lees Martin.

Strong foreign influence on Chinese think tanks and the latter's equally strong inclination for international outreach are evident in China Finance 40 Forum (CF40). CF40 is a non-governmental, non-profit, independent think tank dedicated to policy research on economics and finance. CF40 was founded in April 2008 and is a "40 × 40 club," consisting of 40 financial elites who are around 40 years old.[120] Table 1-8 lists CF40 members and their backgrounds.

These individuals make up the generation of technocrats who are usually younger than those who are members of the Chinese Economists 50 Forum (see Chapter 6). A majority of them were born in the 1960s and a few born in the 1970s. Their backgrounds are more or less evenly distributed across three categories: government, business, and academia. Some of them currently serve in vice minister-level leadership

Table 1-8: China Finance 40 Club Members.

Name	Birth Year	Current Occupation	Position	Highest Degree	Foreign Studies
Ba Shusong 巴曙松	1969	Government	Deputy Director, Research Institute of Finance, DRC of the State Council	PhD	Visiting scholar, Columbia Univ.
Bai Chong'en 白重恩	1963	Academics	Vice Dean, School of Economics and Management, Tsinghua University	PhD	PhD in Mathematics, UCSD, and PhD in Economics, Harvard Univ.
Chen Wenhui 陈文辉	1963	Government	Vice Chairman, China Insurance Regulatory Commission	PhD	MPA, Kennedy School of Government, Harvard Univ.
Ding Zhijie 丁志杰	1969	Academics	Assistant President, University of International Business and Economics	PhD	N/A
Fan Wenzhong 范文仲	1972	Government	Director, International Dept., China Regulatory Commission	PhD	PhD in Economics, Yale Univ.
Fang Xinghai 方星海	1968	Government	Vice Chairman, China Securities Regulatory Commission	PhD	PhD in Economics, Stanford Univ.
Gao Shanwen 高善文	1971	Business	Chief Economist, Essence Securities	PhD	MPA, Japan Institute for Policy Studies; visiting scholar, Wharton School
Guan Tao 管涛	1970	Government	Director-General, Balance of Payment Dept., the State Adm. of Foreign Exchange	PhD	MA in Development Economics, Australian National Univ.
Ha Jiming 哈继铭	1962?	Business	Vice Chair of China and Chief Strategist, Dept. of Investment Man't, Goldman Sachs	PhD	PhD in Economics, Univ. of Kansas
Huang Haizhou 黄海洲	1961?	Business	President, China International Capital Corporation	PhD	PhD in Business, Indiana Univ.

(Continued)

Table 1-8: *(Continued)*

Name	Birth Year	Current Occupation	Position	Highest Degree	Foreign Studies
Huang Jinlao 黄金老	1972	Business	Vice President, Huaxia Bank; and Vice President of Suning Group	PhD	N/A
Huang Yiping 黄益平	1964	Academics	Vice Dean, National School of Development, Peking Univ.	PhD	PhD in Economics, Australian National Univ.
Ji Zhihong 纪志宏	?	Government	Director, Financial Market Dept., the People's Bank of China	PhD	N/A
Jia Kang 贾康	1954	Government	Director, Research Institute of Fiscal Science, Ministry of Finance	PhD	Visiting scholar, Univ. of Pittsburgh
Li Bo 李波	1972	Government	Director, Monetary Policy Dept., the People's Bank of China	PhD	PhD in Economics, Stanford Univ.; PhD in Law, Harvard Univ.
Li Daokui 李稻葵	1963	Academics	Director, Schwarzman Scholars at Tsinghua Univ.	PhD	PhD in Economics, Harvard Univ.
Li Fuan 李伏安	1962	Business	Chair, China Bohai Bank	PhD	MBA, Boston Univ.
Lian Peng 连平	1955?	Business	Chief Economist, Bank of Communications	PhD	N/A
Liao Min 廖岷	1968	Government	Director, Shanghai Supervision Bureau, China Banking Regulatory Commission	MA	MBA, Univ. of Cambridge

Name	Birth	Sector	Position	Degree	Education
Liu Chunhang 刘春航	1970?	Government	Director-General, Policy Research Dept., China Banking Regulatory Commission	PhD	MBA, Harvard, and PhD in Economics, Oxford Univ.
Long Guoqiang 隆国强	1966	Government	Deputy Director, Development Research Center, the State Council	PhD	Visiting scholar, Brookings Institution
Lu Lei 陆磊	1970	Government	Director, Research Bureau, the People's Bank of China	PhD	MA in Development Economics, Australian National Univ.
Ma Jun 马骏	1964	Government	Chief Economist, Research Bureau, the People's Bank of China	PhD	PhD in Economics, Georgetown Univ.
Pan Gongsheng 潘功胜	1963	Government	Vice Governor, the People's Bank of China	PhD	Post doctoral fellow at Cambridge Univ. and visiting scholar at Harvard
Qi Bin 祁斌	1968	Government	Director, International Department, China Securities Regulatory Commission	PhD	MBA, Univ. of Chicago, and MS in Biophysics, Univ. of Rochester.
Qu Qiang 瞿强	1966	Academics	Director, Fiscal and Financial Policy Research Center, Renmin Univ.	PhD	Visiting scholar at Hitotsubashi Univ. and Universität Hamburg
Shen Xiaohui 沈晓晖	?	Government	Director, International Dept. Research Office, the State Council	PhD	N/A
Sun Mingchun 孙明春	1971	Business	Chair, Deepwater Capital Co., Ltd	PhD	PhD in Management, Stanford Univ.
Xu Gang 徐刚	1969	Business	Managing Director, CITIC Securities Co. Ltd. (purged)	PhD	N/A
Wei Jianing 魏加宁	1958	Government	Inspector, Dept. of Macroeconomic Research, DRC, the State Council	PhD	Research fellow, Japan External Trade Organization, Univ. of Tokyo

(Continued)

Table 1-8: *(Continued)*

Name	Birth Year	Current Occupation	Position	Highest Degree	Foreign Studies
Wei Shangjin 魏尚进	1964?	Business	Chief Economist, Asian Development Bank	PhD	PhD in Economics, UC Berkeley
Wu Hemao 巫和懋	1952?	Academics	Executive Vice Dean of National School of Development, Peking Univ.	PhD	PhD in Economics, Stanford Univ.
Yan Qingmin 阎庆民	1961	Government	Vice Mayor of Tianjin	PhD	N/A
Yao Yang 姚洋	1964	Academics	Dean, National School of Development, Peking Univ.	PhD	PhD in Applied Economics, Univ. of Wisconsin-Madison
Yin Jianfeng 殷剑峰	1969	Academics	Deputy Director, Institute of Finance, Chinese Academy of Social Science	PhD	N/A
Yuan Li 袁力	1962	Business	Vice President, China Development Bank	PhD	N/A
Zhang Jianhua 张健华	1965	Business	President, Beijing Rural Commercial Bank	PhD	N/A
Zhang Tao 张涛	1963	Government	Deputy Managing Director of IMF, and former vice governor, People's Bank of China	PhD	PhD in International Economics, UC Santa Cruz
Zhang Yujun 张育军	1963	Government	Assistant Chair of China Securities Regulatory Commission (purged)	PhD	N/A
Zhong Wei 钟伟	1969	Academics	Director, Finance Research Center, Beijing Normal University	PhD	N/A

Source and Note: China Finance 40 Forum brochure. Dept. = Department, DRC = Development Research Center, Man't = Management, Univ. = University.

positions, the most noticeable examples being the newly appointed vice chairman of the China Securities Regulatory Commission, Fang Xinghai; the deputy managing director of the IMF, Zhang Tao; the vice governor of the People's Bank of China, Pan Gongsheng; and the vice mayor of Tianjin, Yan Qingmin.

All of these individuals hold doctoral degrees in economics and finance. Almost three-fourths of them studied abroad, and 23 received advanced degrees overseas, especially from top universities in the United States, such as Harvard, Yale, Stanford, Berkeley, and Georgetown. Some of them, including several who currently serve in the government, previously worked at foreign banks. For example, Ma Jun, the chief economist of the Research Bureau of the People's Bank of China, served as chief China economist at Deutsche Bank AG for 15 years (2000 – 2014). Ha Jiming, vice chair of China and chief strategist of the investment management division at Goldman Sachs, currently serves as chief economist of China International Capital Corporation Limited. Foreign-educated Chinese returnees (海归, *haigui*) have not only played a crucial role in China's economic and financial sector; they have also emerged as a distinguished group in China's foreign policy establishment (see Chapter 14).

The presence and expanding roles of Western-educated elites in Chinese think tanks and at various levels of the Chinese leadership will likely increase the diversity of the ruling elite. In fact, some of Xi Jinping's most important aides and advisors have experience at think tanks and Western universities. Xi's two confidants, Liu He (director of the Office of the Central Economic Leading Group of the CCP Central Committee) and Chen Xi (executive deputy-director of the CCP Central Organization Department), are U.S.-educated returnees. Liu received a master's degree in public administration from Harvard's Kennedy School of Government and currently serves as the chief economic advisor to Xi Jinping. Sometimes referred to as "China's Larry Summers," Liu played a crucial role in drafting the pivotal economic reform agenda announced at the Third Plenum of the 18th Central Committee. Chen, who was Xi's roommate in college and who served as a visiting scholar at Stanford University from 1990 to 1992, is now Xi's appointed surrogate in personnel matters.[121]

Xi also likes to consult returnee experts for their views on global economic and financial development. When he was party secretary of Shanghai, Xi came to know the aforementioned Fang Xinghai, then deputy secretary of the Financial Affairs Committee of the Shanghai Municipal Party Committee and director of the Shanghai Financial Services Office. Fang was born in 1964 and attended Tsinghua University's School of Economic Management from 1981 to 1986, majoring in information systems management.[122] He pursued graduate-level education at Stanford University from 1986 to 1993 under the guidance of Joseph Stiglitz, who was awarded the Nobel Prize in Economics in 2001. After receiving his doctoral degree in economics in 1993, Fang worked in the prestigious young professionals program at the World Bank for several years (1993–1998). He returned to China in 1998 and served as director of the coordination department of the China Construction Bank (1998–2000), secretary general of the Galaxy Securities Regulatory Commission (2000–2001), and vice-president of the Shanghai Stock Exchange (2001–2005) before joining the Shanghai municipal government. Fang has developed a close relationship with Xi and often sends him memos regarding financial development in China and around the world.[123] Soon after Xi became general secretary of the CCP, Fang was transferred to Beijing to serve as bureau chief of the General Office of the Central Leading Group for Financial and Economic Affairs. He is now vice-chairman of the China Securities Regulatory Commission.

The above cases of well-positioned returnees shows how this new elite group has not only provided much-needed talent to China's universities and think tanks, particularly in formulating public policy for the leadership, but has also broadened the recruitment channels of Chinese political elites. It remains to be seen whether the number of returnees in the CCP's top leadership will substantially increase at the upcoming 19th Party Congress in the fall of 2017; whether China-educated elites and foreign-trained elites can and will successfully cooperate; whether Western-educated leaders can better communicate China's interests and concerns with the outside world and thus reduce misunderstandings; whether differences in the speeds and trajectories of their career promotions will affect the mechanism of political succession; whether those returnees in the decision-making circle will help propagate international norms and values as a result of their foreign experiences; and whether this development is an accurate indicator of the openness and political transformation of the country.

In their calls for promoting new, diversified, innovative, and globally oriented think tanks, Xi Jinping and other Chinese leaders apparently understand the strategic importance of adapting to the increasingly pluralistic nature of Chinese society. This direction also acknowledges the growing complexity of global geopolitical and economic changes (see Chapters 15 and 16). Never in the six-decade history of the PRC have the Chinese leadership and the general public paid such close attention to interest groups as in recent years. In contrast to the early years of Communist rule, when even the concept of interest groups was politically taboo, China's current leadership has come to recognize the validity of individual and group interests. At the same time, the Chinese people have become more conscious of their own rights and interests (see Chapter 13). This also explains why Xi Jinping has often taken seemingly contradictory stances in responding to the competing policy demands of various socioeconomic groups and public intellectuals who hold different worldviews in both domestic and foreign affairs.

Various interest groups, especially the entrepreneurial class, the middle class, the professional legal community, an increasingly diversified think tank community, a commercial and increasingly pluralistic media, and various new socioeconomic groups — many of whom either did not exist before or were very weak — are now playing important roles in this rapidly changing country.[124] While many of these actors resent the abuse of power and rampant corruption among officials, they also tend to prefer top-down political and legal reform to bottom-up revolution. The intriguing interaction between the political leadership and various social forces — including the complicated relationship between decision-makers and the think tank community — is not, of course, unique to Chinese politics. Analyzing the interplay between these developments not only helps demystify China's modern governance by demonstrating how it is subject to the same pressures as many other systems, but also highlights the significance and potentially far-reaching impact of the rise of Chinese think tanks.

Notes

The author thanks Yinsheng Li, Aubrey Kenton Thibaut, Lucy Xu, Yingxian Long, and Yuxin Zhang for their excellent research and Zach Balin, Ryan McElveen, Rene Ding, Benjamin Tsui, and Lucy Xu for their very helpful comments on earlier versions of this chapter.

1 Li Bin, "Qinqie de jiaotan: Wen Jiabao kanwang Ji Xianlin Qian Xuesen ceji" [A cordial conversation: Highlights of Wen Jiabao's visit to see Ji Xianlin and Qian Xuesen], Xinhua Newsnet, July 30, 2005, http://news. xinhuanet.com/newscenter/2005-07/30/content_3287444.htm; and also Baidu Website, http://baike.baidu.com/view/2978502.htm.

2 Ibid.

3 Didi Kirsten Tatlow, "Education as a Path to Conformity," *New York Times*, January 26, 2010, http://www.nytimes.com/2010/01/27/world/asia/27iht-letter.html; Zheng Yefu, "Dui 'Qian Xuesen zhiwen' de quanmian dafu" [Comprehensive responses to the "Qian Xuesen question"], Consensus Media Net, August 31, 2015, http://www.21ccom.net/articles/culture/ pinglun/20150831128413_all.html; and Wang Huiyao and Miao Lü, *Daguo zhiku* [Global Think Tanks] (Beijing: Renmin chubanshe, 2014), 5.

4 Tatlow, "Education as a Path to Conformity," and Zheng, "Dui 'Qian Xuesen zhiwen' de quanmian dafu."

5 Feng Jie and Deng Hui, "Duihua Yang Zhenning: Jieda Qian Xuesen zhiwen bunengji" [Dialogue with Yang Zhenning: One should not be too hasty in resolving the concerns raised by the "Qian Xuesen question"], *Guangming Daily*, July 5, 2012, http://news.xinhuanet.com/politics/2012-07/05/c_123374326.htm.

6 Zhao Xiuhong, "Yang Zhenning: Jieda Qian Xuesen zhiwen buneng tai zhaoji" [Yang Zhenning: One should not be too hasty in resolving the concerns raised by the "Qian Xuesen question"], *Zhongguo jiaoyu bao* [China Education Daily], April 20, 2015, http://www.jyb.cn/china/gnxw/201504/ t20150420_619528.html.

7 Ibid.

8 In October 2014, at a senior leadership meeting, Xi Jinping claimed that "building new types of think tanks with Chinese characteristics is an important and pressing mission." *China Daily*, October 27, 2014, http://www. chinadaily.com.cn/china/2014-10/27/content_18810882.htm.

9 Zhou Qijun, "Zhongguo zhiku: Zhanzai chuntian, yaowang zhengce" [Chinese Think Tanks: Good timing for favorable policies], Caijing zhoukan [Finance and Economics Weekly], No. 27 (July 13, 2015), http://weekly. caixin.com/2015-07-10/100828042.html.

10 Lin Huihuang, "Jingti zhikure zisheng xinyilun xueshu quanli xunzu" [Think tank fever might create another round of rent-seeking in the Chinese academia], Consensus Media Net, February 29, 2016, http://www.21ccom. net/html/2016/zlwj_0229/1981.html.

11 Nicola Casarini, "The Role of Think Tanks in China," *Short Term Policy Brief*, Vol. 33, June 2012, 4.

12 Shanghai Academy of Social Science, *2014 nian Zhongguo zhiku baogao: yingxiangli yu zhengce jianyi* [2014 Chinese Think Tank Report: Ranking By Influence and Policy Recommendations] (Shanghai: Shanghai Academy of Social Science, 2015), 3.

13 Han Wei, "Zhongguo zhiku jijin" [Fast advance of Chinese think tanks], *Shidai Zaixian Website* [Time Weekly Online], November 3, 2014, http:// www.time-weekly.com/html/20141103/27004_1.html

14 Ibid.

15 Ibid.

16 Xinhua Newsnet, January 21, 2015, http://news.xinhuanet.com/zgjx/2015-01/21/c_133934292.htm.

17 Shannon Tiezzi, "China's Quest for Global Influence: Through Think Tanks," The *Diplomat* Website, January 22, 2015, http://thediplomat. com/2015/01/chinas-quest-for-global-influence-through-think-tanks/.

18 Sha Lu, "25 jigou ruxuan shoupi guojia gaoduan zhiku jianshe shidian danwei han liangjia shehui zhiku" [25 institutions are designated as high-end pilot units in think tank development, including two social organizations], *Xin jingbao* [New Beijing], December 3, 2015, http://www.bjnews.com.cn/ news/2015/12/03/386602.html.

19 Xi Jinping, "Zai wangluo anquan he xinxihua gongzuo zuotanhui shang de jianghua" [Speech at the internet and information security work conference], Xinhua Newsnet, April 25, 2016, http://news.xinhuanet.com/politics/2016-04/25/c_1118731175.htm.

20 Xi Jinping, "Zai zhexue shehui kexue gongzuo zuotanhui shang de jiang-hua" [Speech delivered at the roundtable discussion on the work of social science and philosophy], Xinhua Newsnet, May 18, 2016, http://news. xinhuanet.com/politics/2016-05/18/c_1118891128_4.htm.

21 Wu Jingjing, "Zhiku jianshe zai zongshuji xinzhong you duo zhongyao" [How important is think tank development in the mind of the general secretary of the CCP?], Fenghuang guoji zhiku wang [Phoenix International Think Tank Web], December 30, 2016, http://pit.ifeng.com/a/20151230/46888634_0.shtml.

22 Shanghai Academy of Social Science, *2014 nian Zhongguo zhiku baogao: yingxiangli yu zhengce jianyi*, 4.

23 Tiezzi, "China's Quest for Global Influence: Through Think Tanks."

24 Zhang Yao, "Zhongguo zhiku" [China's think tanks], People's Net, January 29, 2016, http://theory.people.com.cn/n1/2016/0129/c367113-28096295.html.

25 Wan Jingbo, "Zhongguo zhiku de xinshiming yu xinzeren" [The new mission and new responsibilities of Chinese think tanks], *Zhongguo kexuebao* [China Science Times], June 23, 2014, http://news.sciencenet.cn/htmlnews/2014/6/297231.shtm.

26 Wang Simin and Qu Yilin, "Zhiku jianshe ruhe 'quxuhuo qiangjingu'" [How can think tank development avoid a growth bubble and strengthen quality], *Guangming Daily*, June 1, 2016, 15.

27 Zhang Qian, "Zhongguo zhiku mianlin dulixing nanti" [Chinese think tanks confront the perplexity of independence], *Caijing* [Finance and Economy], January 29, 2016, http://www.mycaijing.com/wxshare/244113.html.

28 Silvia Menegazzi, "Building Think Tanks with Chinese Characteristics: Current Debates and Changing Trends," *China Brief*, Vol. 14, No. 24 (December 19, 2014).

29 Huang Yanzhong, "China's Think-Tank Great Leap Forward," Council on Foreign Relations Blog, September 28, 2015, http://blogs.cfr.org/asia/2015/09/28/chinas-think-tank-great-leap-forward/.

30 Chun Han Wong, "China Adopts Sweeping National-Security Law," *The Wall Street Journal*, July 1, 2015.

31 Alessandra Collarizi, "Think Tanks with Chinese Characteristics," Asia Sentinel, November 28, 2014, http://www.asiasentinel.com/society/thinktanks-chinese-characteristics/.

32 Lu Yao, "Qinghua jiaoshou tan Zhongguo minjian zhiku fazhan pingjing" [Tsinghua professor on the development bottleneck in China's private think tanks], *Dongfang liaowang zhoukan* [Oriental Outlook Weekly], February 20, 2014, http://news.sciencenet.cn/htmlnews/2014/2/288798.shtm.

33 Ibid.

34 Silvia Menegazzi, "Building Think Tanks with Chinese Characteristics: Current Debates and Changing Trends," *China Brief*, Vol. 14, No. 24 (December 19, 2014): 14–17, http://www.jamestown.org/single/?tx_ttnews[tt_news]=43214&no_cache=1#.VpgRjPngouM.

35 Shen Baoxiang, "Hu Yaobang yu zhongyang dangxiao de xinsheng" [Hu Yaobang and the rebirth of the Central Party School], *Caixin Magazine*, November 24, 2015, http://opinion.caixin.com/2015-11-24/100877783.html.

36 Menegazzi, "Building Think Tanks with Chinese Characteristics."

37 Cheng Li, *China's Leaders: The New Generation* (Lanham, MD: Rowman & Littlefield Publishers, 2001), 176.

38 Xiao Quan, *Women zheyidai* [Our generation] (Guangzhou: Huacheng chubanshe, 2006).

39 Wang Juntao, "Beida fengyun jiuyou dianping" [Comments about a few distinguished alumni of Peking University], December 25, 2005, www.blogchina.com.

40 Silvia Menegazzi, "China Reinterprets the Liberal Peace," *Istituto Affari Internazionali*, Working Papers, Vol. 12, No. 30 (December 2012): 4; and Kerry Dumbaugh and Michael F. Martin, "Understanding China's Political System," *CRS Report for Congress*, No. R41007 (May 10, 2012), http://www.fas.org/sgp/crs/row/R41007.pdf.

41 Pascal Abb, *China's Foreign Policy Think Tanks: Changing Roles and Structural Conditions,* GIGA Institute of Asian Studies Working Papers, No. 213 (Hamburg: German Institute of Global and Area Studies, 2013).

42 This is based on the author's interviews with Chinese officials and scholars. In a workshop on think tank development held at the Pudong Academy of Executive Leadership on March 27, 2016, Li Junru, former vice president of the Central Party School, provided the detailed account about Zheng Bijian's role in formulating the theory of China's peaceful rise.

43 Jiang Zhengxiang, "Yidaiyilu bairen luntan zhongdian tuijian: 2015 nian yidaiyilu shida zhiku" [Top ten think tanks in 2015 devoted to the study of the "One Belt One Road" initiative], *Guangming Daily* Online, December 31, 2015, http://theory.gmw.cn/2015-12/31/content_18310280.htm.

44 Ruslan Izimov, "Chinese Think Tanks and Central Asia: A New Assessment," *Voices from Central Asia*, No. 23 (November 2015), 5.

45 Li Jian, "Expert: Chinese defense think tanks face enormous challenges," Knowfar Institute for Strategic and Defense Studies, China, July 21, 2015, http://eng.mod.gov.cn/Opinion/2015-07/21/content_4601810.htm.

46 Zhou, "Zhongguo zhiku: Zhanzai chuntian, yaowang zhengce."

47 Yu Keping, "Sixiangjia shi minzu de baogui caifu" [Thinkers are Valuable National Assets], *Zhejiang shehui kexue* [Zhejiang Social Science], No. 8 (2015).

48 Ibid.

49 Ibid.

50 Ibid.

51 Ibid.

52 Wang Lili, *Zhili ziben: Zhongguo zhiku hexin jingzhengli* [Intellectual Capital: The Core Competence of Chinese Think Tanks] (Beijing: Zhongguo renmin daxue chubanshe, 2015), II.

53 Wang Huiyao and Miao Lü, *Daguo zhiku* [Global Think Tanks] (Beijing: Renmin chubanshe, 2014), 6.

54 Jing Chunmei, "Zhongguo tese xinxing zhiku goujian: Xianzhuang, wenti ji duice" [Building of New-Type Think Tanks with Chinese Characteristics: Present Situation, Problems, and Countermeasures], *Quanqiuhua* [Globalization], No. 2, 2015, 107.

55 Richard C. Bush, "Thoughts on Think Tanks and Their Role in Modern Society," paper presented at the conference "Between Power and Knowledge: Think Tanks in Transition," April 10–12, 2013, Institute of International Relations (IIR), National Chengchi University, Taiwan.

56 For a long list of Chinese scholars' studies of foreign think tanks, see Wang Lili, *Zhili ziben: Zhongguo zhiku hexin jingzhengli*, 8.

57 Cheng Li, ed., *Bridging Minds Across the Pacific: U.S.-China Educational Exchanges, 1978–2003* (Lanham: MD: Lexington Press, 2005).

58 China Newsnet, December 26, 2015, http://www.chinanews.com/gn/2015/12-26/7689257.shtml.

59 Wang Wen, *Zhiku miji: yijia Zhongguo tese xinxing zhiku zhixing fuzeren de xinde* [Think Tank Tips: Experiences of An Executive Administrator of a Chinese New-Type of Think Tank], Manuscripts (Beijing: Renmin chubenshe, 2016), 45.

60 Ibid.

61 The table does not include Chinese political leaders in the party and government who also were listed among the most influential people in these two magazines.

62 Ma Jun, *Zhongguo shui weiji* [China's water crisis] (Beijing: Zhongguo huanjing chubanshe, 1999).

63 For the homepage of the Institute of Public and Environmental Affairs, see http://www.ipe.org.cn/en/index.aspx.

64 Gabriel Wildau, "China censors curb discussion of pollution documentary," *Financial Times*, March 5, 2015.

65 Wang Hui, *China's New Order: Society, Politics, and Economy in Transition*, translated by Ted Huters and Rebecca Karl (Cambridge, MA: Harvard University Press, 2003).

66 Yan Xuetong, *Shijie quanli de zhuanyi: Zhengzhi lingdao yu zhanlue jingzheng* [Power shift in world politics: Political leadership and strategic competition] (Beijing: Peking University Press, 2015).

67 Yufan Huang, "Q. and A.: Yan Xuetong Urges China to Adopt a More Assertive Foreign Policy," *New York Times*, February 9, 2016, http://www.nytimes.com/2016/02/10/world/asia/china-foreign-policy-yan-xuetong.

html?_r=0; and also see Heng Li, "Beijing yingpai zhiku: duikang Meiguo Zhongguo bixu jiemeng" [Beijing hawks think tank: China must form an alliance against the United States], Duowei News, February 11, 2016, http://global.dwnews.com/news/2016-02-11/59716996.html.

68 Ibid.

69 Ibid.

70 Liu Mingfu, *Zhongguomeng: hou Meiguo shidai de daguo siwei yu zhanlue dingwei* [The China dream: The great power's mindset and strategic stance in the post–American hegemony era] (Beijing: China Friendship Press, 2010).

71 Zheng Bijian, *China's Peaceful Rise: Speeches of Zheng Bijian, 1997–2005* (Washington, DC: Brookings Institution Press, 2005).

72 Ibid. Also, for more discussion of Zeng's four points, see Chapter 2 of this volume.

73 Wang Jisi, "China's Search for Stability with America," *Foreign Affairs*, September/October 2005.

74 Erdong Chen, "Think-tanks with Chinese characteristics," *Asia Times* Online, July 18, 2009, http://www.atimes.com/atimes/China/KG18Ad03.html.

75 Ibid.

76 "Proceedings of the High-Level Forum of Building New Think-Tanks with Chinese Characteristics," China Executive Leadership Academy Pudong, March 27, 2016.

77 James G. McGann, "2015 Global Go To Think Tank Index Report," TTCSP Global Go To Think Tank Index Reports, 2016, Paper No. 10, 31, http://repository.upenn.edu/think_tanks/10.

78 Ibid.

79 Zhou, "Zhongguo zhiku: Zhanzai chuntian, yaowang zhengce."

80 Xu Xiaohu and Chen Qi, "Zhongguo zhiku de jiben wenti yanjiu" [A study of the basic problems of Chinese think tanks], *Xueshu luntan* [Academic Forum], No. 11 (2012), 180.

81 Ibid.

82 Yu Dong, "Jiang zhiku jiancheng meiyou guding xuesheng de daxue: nanfang fangwu zhiku fazhan zhidao" [Making think tanks serve as universities without students: The development model of the Southern Defense Think Tank], *Nanfang zhoumo* [Southern Weekend], November 20, 2015, http://www.infzm.com/content/105763.

83 Zhang Yao, "Zhongguo zhiku: Mianlin zuihao fazhan jiyu" [China's think tanks: The best opportunities for development], Renmin Website, January 29, 2016, http://theory.people.com.cn/n1/2016/0129/c367113-28096295.html.

84 Xie Shuguang, Cai Jihui, and Shi Xiaolin, comp., *Zhongguo zhiku minglu (2015)* [Chinese Think Tank Directory 2015] (Beijing: Shehui kexue wenxian chubanshe, 2015).

85 Cao Xiaoyang, "Jiema Zhongguo tese xinxing zhiku" [Decoding new think tanks with Chinese characteristics], *Guangzhou ribao* [Guangzhou Daily], November 10, 2014, http://www.gdass.gov.cn/MessageInfo_3327.shtml.

86 For more information about Cao Siyuan and his think tank, see Wei Hongping, "'Zhongguo Lande' meng" ["China's Rand" dream], *Touzijia* [Capitalist], No. 12 (December 2009), 36–37.

87 For more information about these private think tanks, see the special report on "Non-Governmental Think Tanks: China Models," *Touzijia*, No. 12 (December 2009), 31–69.

88 Xu and Chen, "Zhongguo zhiku de jiben wenti yanjiu."

89 Staff writer, "The Role of China's Think Tanks in Policymaking," *US-China Business Review*, July 1, 2009, http://www.chinabusinessreview.com/the-role-of-chinas-think-tanks-in-policymaking/.

90 Zhou, "Zhongguo zhiku: Zhanzai chuntian, yaowang zhengce."

91 Huang, "China's Think-Tank Great Leap Forward."

92 Staff writer, "Fudan daxue Zhongguo yanjiuyuan chengli" [The Institute of Contemporary China Studies at Fudan University has been established], Fudan University Website, November 23, 2015, http://news.fudan.edu.cn/2015/1123/40395.html.

93 Ibid.

94 Zhou, "Zhongguo zhiku: Zhanzai chuntian, yaowang zhengce."

95 See the CASS Graduate School website, http://www.gscass.cn/html/list/201/list1.html.

96 *Diyi wenku* wang [The first library network], http://www.wenku1.com/view/F49633C616FE9FE2.html.

97 Wang, *Zhiku miji*, 28.

98 Staff writer, "The brains of the party," *The Economist*, March 10, 2014, http://www.economist.com/blogs/analects/2014/03/chinese-politics.

99 Ibid.

100 See Li Yang's remarks at the Think Tank Summit organized by the Brookings-Tsinghua Center, April 21, 2015, http://www.brookings.edu/~/media/events/2015/04/21-us-china-think-tank-summit/uschina-think-tank-summit-unedited-transcript.pdf.

101 Liu Yi, "Zhongguo zhiku ruhe canyu gaige juece" [How Chinese think tanks participate in the decision-making regarding reform policies], *Beijing*

qingnian bao [Beijing Youth Daily], November 11, 2013, http://epaper.ynet. com/html/2013-11/11/content_23254.htm?div=-1.

102 Zhou, "Zhongguo zhiku: Zhanzai chuntian, yaowang zhengce."

103 Huang, "China's Think-Tank Great Leap Forward."

104 Wang, *Zhiku miji,* 44.

105 Li Yuting, "Qidi shenmeyang de wenzhang neng zhida Zhongnanhai" [What kind of articles can be submitted directly to Zhongnanhai], Duowei News, January 9, 2015, http://china.dwnews.com/news/2015-01-09/59628999.html.

106 Ibid.

107 Zheng Xinli, "Zhongguo zhiku fazhan cunzaide sida zhuyao wenti" [Four major problems with China's think tank development], *Keji ribao* [S & T Daily], May 4, 2014, http://digitalpaper.stdaily.com/http_www.kjrb.com/ kjrb/html/2014-05/04/content_259765.htm?div=0.

108 Ren Fubing, Bai Yuhan, and Li Danzai, "Dandai Zhongguo zhiku yanjiu xianzhuang, cunzai wenti ji lujing xuanze" [Chinese think tanks: Current status, existing problems, and path selection], *Jingji yu shehui fazhan* [Economy and social development], Vol. 13, No. 5 (October 2015), 116.

109 Ibid.

110 Center on the Research of Think Tanks at the Shanghai Academy of Social Sciences, *2014 nian Zhongguo zhiku baogao* [China's Annual Think Tank Report, 2014], January 2015.

111 Center on the Research of Think Tanks at the Shanghai Academy of Social Sciences, *2014 nian Zhongguo zhiku baogao,* 14.

112 "Zhongguo zhiku shuju quanqiu dier, 4 jia zhiku jingru 100 qiang bangdan" [China has the world's second largest number of think tanks, 4 Chinese think tanks ranked among the global top 100], Global Net, January 27, 2016, http://finance.huanqiu.com/cjrd/2016-01/8460352.html.

113 For example, see Jin Siyu, "Zhuanjia pandian woguo zhiku wuda wenti: zonghe yanpan nengli buzu" [Experts identify five major problems with Chinese think tanks: lack of capacity in comprehensive research and judgment], *Liaowang* [Outlook Weekly], June 15, 2014, http://news.takungpao. com/mainland/focus/2014-06/2538913.html.

114 "Proceedings of the High-Level Forum of Building New Think-Tanks with Chinese Characteristics," China Executive Leadership Academy, Pudong, March 27, 2016.

115 "2014 nian Zhongguo zhiku jianshe daibiao renwu bangdan" [The list of top scholars who represent China's think tank development], *Zhiku Zhongguo* [Think Tank China], February 2, 2015, http://news.china.com.cn/2015-02/ 02/content_34712363.htm.

116 Ibid.

117 Wang, *Zhiku miji*, p. 34.

118 Staff writer, "President Xi holds symposium on philosophy and social sciences," Chongyang Institute of Financial Studies website, June 6, 2016, http://rdcy-sf.ruc.edu.cn/displaynewsen.php?id=21392.

119 Chongyang Institute of Financial Studies website, December 25, 2015, http://www.g20.org/dtxw/201512/t20151225_1716.html.

120 CF40 Secretariat, China Finance 40 Forum Brochure.

121 For more detailed discussion of Xi's close ties with Liu He and Chen Xi, see Cheng Li, *Chinese Politics in the Xi Era: Reassessing Collective Leadership* (Washington DC: Brookings Institution Press, 2016), Chapter 8.

122 For Fang's early career, see Sun Tao, "Guogan Fang Xinghai" [Bold Fang Xinghai]. Also see *Jingrong shijie* [Financial World], August 2012, http://blog.sina.com.cn/s/blog_695557320101d583.html.

123 George Chen and Daniel Ren, "Shanghai Booster Fang Xinghai Lands Beijing Financial Advisory Role," *South China Morning Post*, June 18, 2013.

124 For a more detailed discussion of this argument, see Li, *Chinese Politics in the Xi Era*, Chapter 9.

II
Prominent Chinese Thinkers

Chapter 2

Hu Angang (Demographer and Economist): Championing Chinese Optimism and Exceptionalism

To see ourselves as others see us is a rare and valuable gift, without a doubt. But in international relations what is still rarer and far more useful is to see others as they see themselves.

— Jacques Barzun

China perplexes the world. The country's rapid rise to global economic power poses an important set of questions regarding how one should perceive the transformation of the international system in light of this epochal change:

- Is China on track to become a new superpower? If so, how will this transform the global economic and political landscape?
- Will this ongoing power shift be comparable in scale to the rise of Europe in the 17th century or the rise of America in the late 19th and early 20th centuries?
- Will the world witness increasingly intense competition between the United States, the preexisting superpower, and China, an emerging superpower? Could it even lead to the outbreak of what international relations scholars call a "hegemonic war"?[1]
- Might a new "Cold War" take shape as China, a Leninist one-party state, comes to rival the West in the decades ahead? Will China present a military and ideological challenge to the West, as the Soviet Union did during most of the latter half of the 20th century?

- Conversely, should the rise of the world's most populous country be seen as an auspicious development able to fuel global economic growth and contribute to a more balanced and stable world order?

At this point, there are no definitive answers to these questions, and increasingly sophisticated assessments of China's quest for superpower status have emerged over time.[2] This type of analysis is also difficult, as the real and substantive impact of China's rise on the international system will depend on many factors. To a large extent, China's own economic and political trajectories — as well as the country's popular aspirations and demographic constraints — are crucial factors that will determine the role China adopts. The momentous socioeconomic transformation propelling these changes has not occurred in an intellectual vacuum. In fact, over the past decade, strategic thinkers and public intellectuals in China have engaged in fervent discussions about the nature of China's ever-increasing integration into the world and the country's road ahead.

Unfortunately, English-language studies of present-day China have not adequately informed a Western audience of the dynamism of the debates within China and the diversity of views concerning its own future.[3] In such a rapidly changing and complex world, it would be enormously valuable for the decision-makers of foreign policy and other analysts in the West to broaden their perspective and "see others as they see themselves," as the distinguished historian Jacques Barzun wisely suggests. The international community's discourse on the implications of a rising China will increase in sophistication if it pays greater heed to how Chinese intellectuals perceive and debate the responsibilities that China may assume in the future. In particular, the American China-watching community would be much better informed if it were more familiar with the contemporary strategic discourse of the People's Republic of China (PRC).

The Influence of Hu Angang in the Chinese Discourse on China's Rise

Arguably no scholar in the PRC has been more visionary in forecasting China's ascent to superpower status, more articulate in addressing the daunting demographic challenges that the country faces, or more prolific in proposing policy initiatives designed to advance an innovative and sustainable economic development strategy than Hu Angang. His strong influence on the Chinese intellectual and policy debates concerning the country's future is especially evident in three respects:

- For over two decades, Hu has been forecasting China's socioeconomic and demographic development. He has also established a popular index of comprehensive national power. In his 1991 book, *China: Toward the 21st Century*, Hu accurately forecasted that China would emerge as a global economic giant sometime in the first or second decade of the 21st century, surpassing France, England, and Germany.[4] He was officially involved in drafting the Chinese government's five-year plans, which outline the government's key development goals.
- As a scholar well known for his concerted effort to break down strictly defined academic boundaries, Hu's remarkably broad research interests include demography, ecology, education, public health, environmental protection, anti-corruption, and international relations. As early as 1988, Hu and two of his colleagues at the Chinese Academy of Sciences (CAS) showed great foresight in a well-documented, extensive report arguing that the "ecological deficit [生态赤字, *shengtai chizi*] will be the greatest liability for China's development in the 21st century."[5] Hu was among the first Chinese scholars to call for measuring "green GDP" in regional development.[6]

Hu has not only authored or co-authored nearly 60 books and edited volumes, but he has also published more than 900 *Reports on the China Situation* (国情报告, *guoqing baogao*) through the Center for China Studies (now called the Institute for Contemporary China Studies), an influential think tank that is affiliated with both CAS and Tsinghua University.[7] Hu founded the Center in 2000 and has served as its director ever since. These reports have been primarily circulated among ministerial and provincial leaders and higher authorities.[8] For example, of the 37 reports that were submitted to the State Council from 2007 to 2010, senior leaders of the State Council commented on these reports 39 times.[9]

Hu Angang's active participation in the strategic thinking behind China's development over the past two decades reflects the growing role of public intellectuals and think tanks in the formation of the country's domestic and foreign policies.[10] Economic globalization and China's increasing importance in the world economy, and the technical and specialized knowledge decision-makers therefore require, have understandably resulted in more substantive input from economists and other specialists. Meanwhile, China's booming publishing industry and expanding mass media (both old and new) provide unprecedented opportunities for scholars like Hu Angang to articulate their views, exert their influence, and shape public opinion. While Hu appears to enjoy his role as an informal advisor to senior leaders in the Chinese government, he has maintained his primary role as an independent scholar. Indeed, from time to time, Hu has criticized government policies and voiced concerns about possible policy pitfalls or crises in the making. This combination of close involvement and impartial detachment has afforded Hu Angang a vantage point from which he can exert some influence in decision-making circles, while his refusal to simply toe the party line has helped him establish credibility in the eyes of the Chinese public.

Hu Angang's 2010 book, *China in 2020: A New Type of Superpower*, is partly based on his 2007 Chinese book, *China in 2020: Building a Well-Off Society*.[11] In the more-recent volume, Hu substantially expands the focus and content of the previous book. *China in 2020: A New Type of Superpower* (hereafter referred to as *China in 2020*) covers many broad aspects of China's rise on the world stage, often from a cross-country comparative perspective. In addition to the author's assessment of China's economic transformation, the book examines other important subjects, such as China's demographic trends, public health, education and human resources, science and technology, and approach to climate change, many of which are the focus of Hu's more recent Chinese publications. The volume's rich empirical data, multi-disciplinary nature, explication of indigenous Chinese concepts, and thought-provoking arguments concerning China's rise make it invaluable for understanding China's role in today's world.

The Themes of *China in 2020*: Two Parallel Arguments

In *China in 2020*, two important themes that permeate most of Hu Angang's writings reemerge: *Chinese optimism* and *Chinese exceptionalism*. With respect to the first, Hu Angang has been consistently optimistic about China's socioeconomic transformation and its historic reemergence in the late 20th and early 21st centuries, even during periods when the country was beset by serious challenges, such as the 1989 Tiananmen incident, the 1997 Asian financial crisis, the 2003 Severe Acute Respiratory Syndrome (SARS) epidemic, the 2008 Sichuan earthquakes, and the 2008 global economic meltdown. This does not mean that he has overlooked the many daunting challenges that China faces. On the contrary, over the past two decades, Hu has often been ahead of other Chinese intellectuals in calling attention to these challenges, such as economic disparity, environmental degradation, energy inefficiency, public health crises, official corruption, and the loss of state assets. While many Chinese leaders and scholars have been encouraged by the fact that China is now the world's largest exporter and second-largest economy, Hu has eschewed triumphalism and chosen to remind the public that China has also become the world's largest carbon emitter and second-largest energy consumer.[12]

While noting these serious problems, Hu still holds the optimistic view that China will continue its high-speed economic growth in the next decade and beyond due to a combination of factors. These include the country's solid industrial foundation, newly built world-class infrastructure, high rates of investment savings and foreign investment, large domestic market, human resource advantages, and, last but certainly not least, the country's commitment to transitioning toward an environmentally friendly mode of economic growth that is driven by domestic demand. In *China in 2020*, Hu argues that, by 2020, China will likely not only surpass the United States as the largest economy in the world, but also — because of its accomplishments in education, innovation, and clean energy — emerge as a "mature, responsible, and attractive superpower."

As for the second major theme, Chinese exceptionalism, Hu acknowledges the prevailing wisdom in Western international relations scholarship, which holds that an emerging superpower will destabilize the existing international system due to zero-sum competition with the existing superpower over spheres of influence, natural resources, market access, and military superiority. But Hu believes that China's rise to superpower status will be an exception to the rule. In his words, China will constitute a "new type of superpower." Hu observes that, in an increasingly interdependent world, China has neither the resources nor the incentive "to replace the United States and become the sole leader in the world. Rather, China needs to cooperate with the United States in order to cope with global challenges in economics, politics, energy, and the environment."

Of course, foreign analysts of China will not be so naïve as to take Hu's arguments at face value. Both Chinese optimism and exceptionalism will, and should be, subjected to continual scrutiny as Chinese decision-makers adjust to constantly changing domestic and international circumstances. Many of Hu's propositions reflect an ideal rather than a reality, and they are properly understood to be well-intended aspirations and promises rather than predetermined conditions or inevitable prospects. Even if Hu genuinely believes — and I think he does — that China should neither pursue a strategy of replacing the United States as the sole super-power in the world, nor adopt belligerent and bullying policies towards its neighboring countries, he cannot ensure that this will be the case. The logic and nature of superpower competition, some international relations scholars argue, is likely to encourage the emerging superpower to behave in a more aggressive and hostile way towards the existing superpower.[13]

Foreign critics may also reasonably wonder how representative Hu's views are of China's mainstream intellectual and policy communities. In fact, both Chinese optimism and Chinese exceptionalism have a large number of domestic critics. It is important to note that Chinese assessments of the PRC's quest for superpower status and its implications for peace and prosperity in the world are as diverse and controversial in China as elsewhere. But foreign decision-makers and analysts should not be too quick to discount the significance of Hu's prognostications. In a way, Hu actually proposes a comprehensive strategic framework for Chinese decision-makers to guide the next stage of China's rise, seeking to maximize the country's positive impact on the world and minimize the negative effects of its meteoric development. The stakes in a conflict between superpowers are too high, and policymakers and public intellectuals in the United States, China, and elsewhere should explore all options and scenarios. Therefore, it is essential for foreign analysts to acquire a more nuanced and accurate understanding of this influential Chinese thinker — including his life experiences, professional background, scholarly pursuits, and overall worldview. Meanwhile, Hu's arguments should also be evaluated within the broader context of strategic thinking in the PRC, especially as compared with the way other public intellectuals in the country view Chinese optimism and exceptionalism.

Hu Angang: From "Sent-Down Youth" to High-Profile Economist

Hu Angang was born to a family of intellectuals in Anshan City, Liaoning Province, in 1953. During the 1950s, Anshan City was home to China's largest steel and iron factory and was considered the "capital of the steel industry of the PRC." The term "Anshan steel" (鞍钢, *angang*) became part of Hu's name, reflecting the socioeconomic and political environment in which he was born. That was, of course, an era in which the country was fanatically obsessed with the development of the steel industry. Hu's parents, natives of Zhejiang Province, were both graduates of Shanghai Jiaotong University, one of the top engineering schools in the country, and they worked in this northeastern industrial city after graduation. Hu's parents were once awarded the titles of "National Model Workers" for their devotion and contribution to the country's rapid drive for industrialization during the Mao era.

Hu Angang has three siblings (all brothers), all of whom attended college after the Cultural Revolution, obtained advanced academic degrees, and studied in North America (the United States or Canada). Hu Angang's wife, Zhao Yining, is the chief reporter for China's liberal newspaper *21st Century Business Herald* and a public intellectual in her own right. Her interviews with influential leaders in China and abroad, such as Henry Paulson, former U.S. secretary of the treasury, have often spurred lively intellectual and policy discussions in the country. She is also the author of the best-selling book *Grand Games: When the Chinese Dragon Faces the American Eagle.*[14]

Hu Angang grew up during the Cultural Revolution, the era in which China's educational system — including elementary schools, middle schools, and colleges — was largely paralyzed. Chinese students were generally engaged in political campaigns and ideological indoctrination rather than academic work. Although catastrophic for the entire nation, the Cultural Revolution affected Hu Angang's age cohort the most. They were in elementary and middle school when the revolution began and suffered turbulent changes and extraordinary hardships during their adolescence. In 1969, at the age of 16, without finishing his middle school education in Beijing, Hu was sent to a collective farm in Beidahuang, the desert area of the Nen River Valley of China's northeast Heilongjiang Province (also known as the "Great Northern Wilderness"). Hu worked in this extremely arduous environment as a young farmer, or what the Chinese call a "sent-down youth" (下乡知青, *xiaxiang zhiqing*), for seven years. When the Cultural Revolution ended in 1976, Hu moved to Hebei Province, where he served as a manual laborer on a geological team, continuing to work in a rural environment.

All of these arduous and humbling experiences, as Hu later described, actually helped him cultivate valuable traits, such as diligence, endurance, adaptability, and humility.[15] The hardships in the countryside were so extreme that he not only remembered rural China, but also developed a strong interest in subjects such as economic inequality, the regional and urban-rural gap, resource scarcity, and grain safety — topics he would later focus on in great depth in his academic career. Hu's experiences led him to believe, as he stated provocatively, that "one who has no knowledge of rural China does not know about China; one who does not understand China's poverty-stricken regions does not have a real understanding of China."[16]

As for his undergraduate education, Hu Angang belonged to the "famous class of 1982." This class of students, ranging in age from late teens to early thirties, passed the national entrance exams in late 1977 and early 1978, as a result of Deng Xiaoping's policy initiatives to select students based on their academic credentials rather than political backgrounds. This group entered college in March and October of 1978 in two clusters and graduated in 1982. The ratio of those who took the exam and those who were admitted to this class was 29 to 1, compared with a ratio of 2 to 1 in 2007.[17] This famous "class of 1982" was extraordinary not only for having passed the most competitive college entrance exams in the PRC's history, but also for having yielded a large number of the most talented national leaders in all walks of life.

After receiving a bachelor's degree in metallurgy from the Tangshan Institute of Technology, he earned a master's degree in metal pressure processing at the Beijing Institute of Iron and Steel (now the Institute of

Science and Technology Beijing), where he studied from 1982 to 1985, and received a doctoral degree in engineering from the Institute of Automation of the CAS in 1988. Hu's undergraduate and graduate education seemed to reflect the influence of his native city and his parents' professional careers in the steel industry. During his PhD studies, however, Hu Angang became interested in researching China's socioeconomic development, a relatively new field in the country at that time. He participated in two research projects in 1985, which helped determine his professional career. The first was a feasibility study on the establishment of the National Information Center at the CAS, and the other was a study on the use of a mathematical model to forecast and make strategic assessments of China's socioeconomic conditions in 2000.

According to Hu, two other events also strongly influenced his decision to devote his career to studying economics and demography.[18] One was the publication of a World Bank report in 1985, *China: Long-Term Development, Issues and Options*, which offered comprehensive empirical information and laid out analytical paradigms describing the possible developmental paths and choices for China in 2000.[19] The other was the release of the Brundtland Commission's report, *Our Common Future*, in 1987.[20] This landmark report highlights the importance of sustainable development in the world and much-needed new international thinking and cooperation to meet new global challenges. In his PhD program, Hu also studied under Professor Ma Shijun, who represented China in signing the Brundtland Declaration. Not surprisingly, Hu Angang frequently cites these two documents in *China in 2020*.

In 1988, Hu completed his doctoral dissertation, *Population and Development in China: A Systemic Analysis and Policy Measures*, under the supervision of He Shanyu (automation expert), Ma Bin (economist), Zheng Yingping (game theory expert), and Ma Zhengwu (computer simulation expert). The dissertation focused on the demographic impetus for and constraints on China's economic development. In Hu's view, the characteristics of China's large population constituted the most important factor for forecasting the country's future condition. After finishing his PhD, Hu began work at the Ecological and Environmental Research Center of the CAS. He played an instrumental role in the establishment of the National Economic Database of the Center. Hu also greatly contributed to national comprehensive power index research, a subject he often references in *China in 2020*.

As both a prolific writer in scholarly publications and a frequent commentator in the Chinese media, Hu soon emerged as one of the highest-profile public intellectuals in the country. In 1991, he was awarded the title "PRC-trained PhD with outstanding contributions" jointly by the State Education Commission and the State Council's Academic Degrees Committee. Hu was invited to join the Chinese Economists 50 Forum (中国经济50人论坛, *Zhongguo jingji wushiren luntan*), which includes the country's 50 most prominent economists (e.g., then Peking University professor who later served as senior vice president and chief economist of the World Bank Lin Yifu, and China Europe International Business School professor Wu Jinglian) and government technocrats (e.g., Governor of the People's Bank Zhou Xiaochuan and then director of the State Administration of Taxation Xiao Jie, who is now the minister of finance). In 2000, Hu won a "Sun Yefang Economics Paper Award," one of China's most prestigious awards for scholarly publications in economics. Hu was also named several times by the Chinese media as one of the top 10 economists in the country.

Hu has earned awards and public recognition largely because he is not an "ivory tower" type of academic economist who is interested exclusively in economic theories and mathematical modeling. Instead, he has been actively engaged in important public policy debates. For example, he has made frequent appeals in recent years — in both official briefings and media interviews — for China to promise to curb carbon emissions within a clearly outlined timetable.[21] In his view, this should not only be done to relieve international pressure, but also to meet the internal demands of transforming the country's economic development model. Commenting on Deng Xiaoping's famous motto, "It doesn't matter if a cat is white or black, as long as it catches mice," Hu argues that for China to pursue sustainable development at home and be a responsible stakeholder in the 21st century, it must transform from a "black cat" into a "green cat."[22]

Hu Angang's Experience Abroad and Nationalistic Sentiments

Hu Angang spent much of the 1990s outside mainland China, serving as a post-doctoral fellow at Yale University from 1991 to 1992, a visiting professor at Murray State University in Kentucky in 1993, a research fellow at the School of Arts and Sciences at M.I.T. in 1997, and a guest lecturer for the Department of Economics at the Chinese University of Hong Kong in 1998. He also worked on a short-term basis as a visiting professor at Japan's Keio University in 2000, a visiting professor at Harvard University's Kennedy School of Government in 2001, and a visiting fellow at a China research center in France in 2003. These foreign study and work experiences have not only significantly broadened Hu's perspective, but also have inspired him to promote China studies at home. It has often been said that the field of China studies (中国学, *Zhongguo xue*) exists not *in*, but *outside of*, China. In the 1990s, as Hu Angang observes, Western scholarship, especially American scholarship, on China studies was far more advanced in both theoretical paradigms and data-driven empirical research than its cousin in China.[23]

One of Hu Angang's foremost professional objectives, therefore, is to make China the true center of China studies, and for PRC scholarship to obtain what he calls "the authentic right to speak" (话语权, *huayu quan*) on the subject.[24] In recent years, Hu has often expressed to the Chinese media the nationalistic sentiment that, without PRC scholars' own well-grounded China studies, they simply cannot have a dialogue with their Western counterparts on an equal footing. Without a doubt, Hu is particularly interested in policy issues on the domestic front. Under his leadership, the Center for China Studies has become a leading venue for public policy discourse in the country. The Center's aforementioned series of policy briefs, *Reports on the China Situation*, has become one of the best-known sources of policy analysis for the Chinese government. For example, when China was beset by the SARS epidemic in the spring of 2003, the Center issued 32 reports. The reports provided policy recommendations on various issues related to the health crisis, including media coverage, public opinion, foreign reactions, the state budget for health care, and the impact on the economy and tourism.[25] Hu was also invited to participate in two small roundtable discussions on combating the SARS epidemic, which were held at the State Council and chaired by Premier Wen Jiabao himself.

In 2004, in the aftermath of SARS, Hu Angang wrote a report in which he argued that the "insecurity in health" (健康不安全, *jiankang bu'anquan*) would be the largest challenge to China's security and development in the future. According to Hu, China experienced a paradoxical development over the past decade: while per-capita income increased significantly, the number of people with chronic diseases also increased considerably. Meanwhile, he noted, China had the largest consumption of both tobacco and alcohol in the world. According to an official Chinese study conducted in 2010, China had the world's largest population of smokers (310 million), and every year about one million Chinese people were dying of cancer related to smoking.[26] In addition, approximately 200 million to 300 million people in China lacked access to clean drinking water.[27] Hu's assessment of the health care crisis as China's most daunting challenge received much attention in the official Chinese media in the years to follow.

Hu's foreign studies also broadened his thinking on the role of public intellectuals. Hu drew inspiration from his studies of, and contact with, prominent Western economists. The late Angus Maddison, the prominent British economist, was instrumental in influencing Hu's thinking and research on China's economic development. Hu's role model was the late Paul Samuelson, a U.S. economist and a Nobel laureate, who refused to serve as an advisor to the White House. Although Hu enjoys being frequently consulted by Chinese leaders, he has always identified himself as an independent scholar rather than as an aide to a top leader or advisor to the government. "To speak on behalf of poor people," Hu claims, is the "supreme principle of my professional career."[28] This may also explain why he did not pursue a career working for the Research Office of the State Council or the Central Policy Research Office of the Central Committee of the Chinese Communist Party (CCP) when such opportunities were presented to him in 1993.[29]

Hu's identity as an independent public intellectual has allowed him to criticize official policies. Hu was one of the first scholars to appeal for the reallocation of resources to China's inland region. In 1994, he made the bold suggestion that China should end the special economic zone distinction and abolish preferential treatment for the coastal region.[30] Because of this suggestion, Hu became very popular among officials in inland provinces, while some in special economic zones accused him of opposing Deng Xiaoping's open door policy.[31] As some foreign analysts observed, Hu was among the first group of Chinese scholars to advocate for "green

GDP growth."[32] According to Hu, China should not measure development merely by "black GDP numbers," but also must subtract the immense and variable costs of environmental destruction from impressive GDP numbers in order to measure "green GDP growth," a more accurate gauge of development. While acknowledging the serious demographic challenges that are likely to confront China in the 21st century, Hu has steered clear of sensationalist predictions like those of Lester Brown, who posed the controversial question, "Who will feed China?" Hu was reportedly the first scholar to challenge Brown's excessively pessimistic prognosis.[33]

Hu seems able to achieve a delicate balance between maintaining easy access to policymakers, on the one hand, and retaining his public image as a credible and independent scholar, on the other. The public has sometimes castigated other well-known Chinese economists for their seeming lack of professional integrity, as they serve only the interests of the rich and powerful, especially vested corporate interest groups. Hu Angang has not earned such a negative reputation in the eyes of the public. To the contrary, some of Hu's most populist policy initiatives were later accepted or implemented by the Chinese government. Examples include:

- Initiatives for an ecologically sound energy efficiency policy (1988)
- Policy recommendations (jointly made with Wang Shaoguang) on the tax division between the central and local governments (1994)
- An appeal to ban the business involvement of the Chinese military (1998)
- An appeal for a more balanced regional development strategy, especially for accelerating development in the country's western region (1999)
- Policy recommendations for reducing or abolishing the agricultural tax on farmers (2001)
- A proposal for an employment-centered new mode of economic development (2002)
- Initiatives designed to strengthen China's public health care system (2004)

Hu has also long been a strong advocate for political reforms in China. It is important to note Hu's belief that the priority of political reforms should be the development of technocratic decision-making in social-welfare policy, involving more open discussion and more consultation with think tanks, rather than the adoption of a Western multiparty system, though he does believe in institutional checks and balances.[34] In his view, various provinces in the country — big and small, rich and poor, coastal and inland — should share resources and developmental opportunities. In the mid-1990s, Hu proposed, amid great controversy, a "one province, one vote" system for the formation of the Financial Committee of the National People's Congress (NPC), and hinted at a similar method to determine membership in the Politburo of the CCP. In his judgment, this would not only give every province a voice in party policy but would also encourage more-genuine efforts to ease local dissatisfaction with the central government and ameliorate the disparities between coastal and inland provinces.[35]

Hu Angang has been criticized by his peers in China on various grounds: for example, for his lack of academic disciplinary focus; for sacrificing publication quality for quantity; for a lack of scholarly rigor in data selection, in regard to the documentation and research methodology in some of his publications; and for inappropriately mixing academic objectivity with subjective nationalistic sentiments. In 2008, for instance, Hu published an 800-page book on Mao Zedong and the Cultural Revolution, which received mixed reviews.[36] In the book, Hu offers a more positive view of Mao than is standard, noting his "contributions" to China's rise in the 21st century. In Hu's view, China's pre-1978 social and economic development should not be underestimated. Similar views are also expressed in *China in 2020*, in which Hu argues: "From Mao's ideas, Deng Xiaoping derived many conceptual innovations concerning reform and opening." Critics will certainly challenge this view by pointing out the sharp contrasts between Mao's revolutionary fanaticism and Deng's economic pragmatism.

Hu's more positive evaluation of Mao and the Mao era, his populist approach that privileges socioeconomic egalitarianism, and his favorable views on the consolidation of state-owned enterprises (SOEs) have led some analysts, both in China and abroad, to identify him as a "left" or "new left" intellectual.[37] His most biting critics have called him a "hack writer" of the authoritarian regime, because of his 2010 article (co-authored with

Hu Lianhe) that criticizes the Western separation of powers.[38] In defending himself, Hu does not apologize for his broad and interdisciplinary approach to China studies. He notes that he is not an academic economist in the conventional sense, but instead is one who can combine knowledge in economics, politics, culture, and ecology to give a more holistic analysis of a rising China. Hu refuses to be labeled a "left," "new left," or "liberal" scholar, arguing that none of these labels accurately reflects his values and worldviews.

As for the accusation that excessive nationalistic sentiment shapes his scholarship, Hu is not defensive. He admits that he is first and foremost a patriotic Chinese citizen, not a seemingly value-free "China hand" (中国通, *Zhongguo tong*). As he states clearly, *China in 2020* "represents my efforts to observe China as an insider, to understand China as a researcher, to forecast China's future as a participant in its evolution, and, as a scholar of the era following Deng Xiaoping, to help construct China."[39] In Hu's view, his scholarship should be judged simply by the validity of his arguments and their effectiveness in shaping China's intellectual and policy debates.

Reasons for Chinese Optimism

In general, the Chinese public is now widely conscious that their country is ascendant or, in Hu Angang's words, is en route to the "status of a new superpower." A triumphal mood has begun to take hold in the PRC since the start of the century. A series of historic events — China's accession to the World Trade Organization (WTO), Beijing's successful hosting of the Olympics, Shanghai's reemergence as a cosmopolitan center as evident during the World Expo, the dynamic infrastructure development in both coastal and inland regions, the launch of the country's first manned space program, and the country's ever-growing economic power — have understandably instilled feelings of pride and optimism in the Chinese people.

China's economic strengths in today's world can be felt in numerous ways. Around the time of *China in 2020*'s publication, China had foreign reserves of $2.4 trillion, accounting for 30.7 percent of the world's total and making the PRC the largest foreign reserve country for the fourth consecutive year.[40] In the last quarter of 2010, the PRC (including Hong

Kong) held 24.3 percent of all U.S. Treasury securities.[41] Not surprisingly, as a lead article of the *Economist* magazine observed, "Optimism is on the move."[42] "For the past 400 years," the article notes, "the West has enjoyed a comparative advantage over the rest of the world when it comes to optimism." But in 2010, a large number of public opinion surveys consistently revealed a different trend. According to the Pew Research Center, as cited in the article, some 87 percent of Chinese think their country is going in the right direction, as compared with only 30 percent of Americans.[43]

Some of the main reasons for Hu Angang's optimistic assessment of China's path toward becoming a superpower — its impressive state assets, newly built infrastructure, large domestic market, and advantages in human resources — are empirically well grounded. In *China in 2020*, as well, Hu provides a wealth of information and statistics to support his thesis. While Hu directly speaks to some of China's remarkable accomplishments, others are not discussed by Hu but are often referred to by other PRC scholars. It is worth highlighting four major areas that give reason for optimism about China's future.

The Rise of China's Flagship State-Owned Enterprises

For most of the 1980s and 1990s, and especially on the eve of China's accession to the WTO in 2001, analysts in both China and abroad viewed the prospects of Chinese state-owned enterprises, particularly Chinese commercial banks, very negatively. This cynical view was understandable because in 1998, for example, bad bank loans accounted for 40 percent of the capital of China's state-owned commercial banks. In 2008, however, the percentage of bad loans among these banks had fallen to 2 to 3 percent, as Hu Angang notes. The total wholesale profit of China's state-owned enterprises also increased more than threefold during this period — from 2 percent in 1998 to 7 percent in 2008. Hu was one of the first Chinese economists in the reform era to criticize "market fundamentalism" and favor the consolidation of large SOEs. He argues that the "market is by no means omnipotent and one should not idealize it."[44]

The 2008 global financial crisis would seem to support this thesis proffered by Hu and like-minded colleagues. Interestingly, in early 2009, four of the world's top 10 banks (in terms of market capitalization) were

Chinese. The Industrial and Commercial Bank of China (ICBC), China Construction Bank, and the Bank of China topped the list.[45] A decade ago, U.S. banks dominated the top-10 list and no PRC-based bank was even close to being included. If the economic success of a country is measured by the number of companies that make it on the *Fortune Global 500* list, then the PRC undoubtedly represents one of the greatest triumphs in the contemporary world. The number of PRC companies on the list increased from 3 in 1995 to 46 in 2010.[46] It is important to note that the top 15 Chinese companies on the 2010 *Fortune Global 500* list were all SOEs.

Transportation and Infrastructure

Last decade, China made truly breakneck progress in the transportation and infrastructure sectors, especially in the construction of roads, railways, bridges, and ports. By the end of 2010, the total length of highways in the country had reached 74,000 kilometers, second only to the United States.[47] China did not have a high-speed railway until 1999 when the Qinhuangdao and Shenyang High-Speed Railways were built, and yet by 2010 the country's total length of high-speed railways had reached 7,400 kilometers, the highest in the world. It is expected that by 2020, high-speed railways (on which trains travel upwards of 200 kilometers per hour) in China will total 18,000 kilometers in length, which will represent more than half of the world total.[48] The world's three longest sea bridges are now all located in China: the Qingdao Gulf Bridge (41.6 km), the Hangzhou Bay Bridge (36 km), and the East Sea Grand Bridge (32.5 km), each having been completed in the latter half of the 2000s.

As of 2009, of the world's 10 largest container ports, six were located in the PRC (Shanghai, Hong Kong, Shenzhen, Guangzhou, Ningbo, and Qingdao).[49] Two decades earlier, in 1989, none of the PRC's ports were among the top 20.[50] China's rapidly developed infrastructure projects, especially some of its state-of-the-art transportation facilities, are not only the envy of other developing countries, but have also become a showcase for developed countries such as the United States. This newly built transportation infrastructure will promote commerce, both domestically and internationally, making China more competitive in the world economy in the years and decades to come.

Emerging Middle Class

Hu Angang and other Chinese scholars who are optimistic about China's continuing growth often stress the great significance of the rapid emergence and explosive growth of the Chinese middle class. They credit this expansion with potentially stimulating the country's domestic demand, and thus underwriting high growth rates for the foreseeable future. To a certain extent, China today is already one of the world's major middle-class markets. In 2009, for example, China's auto production output and sales volume reached 13.8 million and 13.6 million, respectively, making the PRC the world's leading automobile producer and consumer for the first time.[51]

In his 2010 book, which was based on a large-scale, nationwide survey, the distinguished sociologist Lu Xueyi noted that the middle class (based on a definition that combines occupation, income, consumption, and self-identification) constituted 23 percent (243 million) of China's total population, up from 15 percent in 2001.[52] Lu predicted that the Chinese middle class would grow at an annual rate of 1 percent over the following decade or so.[53] Lu also held that in about 20 years the Chinese middle class would constitute 40 percent of the PRC population — on par with Western countries — making the PRC a true "middle-class nation."[54] According to a study around the same time by two analysts at the Brookings Institution, China accounted for only 4 percent of global middle-class spending in 2009 (enough to be the seventh-largest middle-class country in the world) but could become the "largest single middle-class market by 2020, surpassing the United States."[55]

Education and Innovation

Hu Angang devotes two chapters of *China in 2020* to the importance of education and innovation, including the role of science and technology, to China's rise as a superpower. According to Hu, as a large country that lacks natural resources, China should prioritize the development of human resources. Hu and his optimistic colleagues believe that the PRC has, in fact, made tremendous progress in all levels of education. Since 2001, for example, English has been offered in almost all elementary and middle schools in all county-level cities across the country. In the United States, by contrast, the percentage of elementary and middle schools that offered foreign language courses decreased from 31 percent and 71 percent, respectively, in 1997 to 25 percent and 58 percent in 2008, mainly due to budgetary constraints. Moreover, as of 2010, only 3 percent of elementary schools and 4 percent of middle schools in the United States presently offered Chinese courses.[56]

As Hu documents, the number of Chinese with access to higher education reached nearly 98 million in 2009 — 543 times that of the 1949 figure (185,000). In 2009, with 21 million registered college students, "China already surpassed the United States (with 18 million in college) to rank first in the world in terms of students in higher education." In post-graduate studies, for every seven PhD degree recipients in the United States, one is a PRC citizen.[57] Science and technology papers published by Chinese citizens in major international journals in 2008 "accounted for 11.5 percent of the world total, second only to the United States' 26.6 percent." In some research areas, such as life sciences and biotechnology, nanotechnology, laser technology, and electric cars, China has become a world leader. In 2010, the Chinese leadership issued the *National Medium- and Long-Term Talent Development Plan (2010–2020)*, a blueprint for creating a highly skilled national workforce by the end of this decade, including ambitious objectives to recruit and cultivate foreign-educated Chinese nationals (known as returnees).[58]

Challenging Chinese Optimism

Public intellectuals in present-day China are by no means unanimous in sharing the optimism exemplified by Hu Angang's work. In fact, prominent scholars in academic fields ranging from economics to sociology, political science, education, and international relations actively debate both sides of this proposition. This discourse is shaped by their academic writings, policy briefings, media commentaries, blog postings, as well as participation in semi-scholarly Chinese websites such as *China Election and Governance* and the Chinese version of the *Financial Times* online. These popular websites have apparently survived official censorship despite bold criticism of the Chinese authorities.[59] In general, critics argue bluntly that Chinese optimism is wrong-headed because China's mode of economic growth is neither desirable nor sustainable.

It should be noted that much of this criticism does not directly challenge Hu Angang's arguments, but rather serves as a response to the new public discourse on the so-called "China model" (中国模式, *Zhongguo moshi*).[60] Nevertheless, these critics tend to believe that optimists' overall prognostications of China's economic and political trajectories (such as Hu's) are highly misleading. They reject the optimists' central argument that China's hybrid system of market economics and authoritarian Leninist statism represents a sound direction for China's continuing rise, let alone a "role model" for other countries' development. These pessimists' criticism is as broad and comprehensive as the assessments of Chinese optimists, covering all of the important economic, social, political, and foreign policy domains.

Critics acknowledge China's impressive economic growth during the reform era, but they believe that it was mainly, if not entirely, achieved through socioeconomic circumstances such as cheap labor, the nature of the early phase of industrialization, technological "free riding" through imitation, and a lack of concern for energy efficiency or environmental protection. According to many distinguished scholars, such as Cai Fang, director of the Institute of Population and Labor Economics of the Chinese Academy of Social Sciences (CASS), China's "demographic dividend," the term that Hu Angang also uses to refer to a rise in the rate of economic growth due to an increasing share of working-age people in a population, was expected to come to an end several years ago.[61] According to Cai, the labor shortage in China's southern and eastern cities at the end of the last decade was a harbinger of far-reaching, important changes to come for the Chinese economy.

Another critic is the well-known economist Yu Yongding, president of the China Society of World Economics and former director of the Institute of World Economics and Politics at CASS, who has also served as a member of the Monetary Policy Committee of the People's Bank of China. He argues that not only has "China's rapid growth been achieved at an extremely high cost," but also the state-led and export-driven growth model "has now almost exhausted its potential."[62] According to Yu, over-investment in real estate development by local governments and large SOEs, expenditures that now account for nearly a quarter of the country's total investment, is particularly worrisome. As Yu describes, the bursting of the real estate bubble will not only be a shock for "those economists and strategists busily extrapolat[ing] its future growth path to predict when it will catch up to the United States," but will also be devastating for China, the country that has just "surpassed the threshold for a middle-income country."[63] Yu also argues that some of China's widely perceived competitive advantages are double-edged swords — such as China's large holdings of foreign reserves, which may cause significant instability in the Chinese economy when foreign currencies, such as the U.S. dollar, fluctuate substantially.[64] Yu cautions that it is not impossible that China may eventually fall back to low-income status rather than attain superpower status.

As for the meteoric rise and ever-growing power of China's large SOEs on the world stage, the critics believe that the oligopoly of SOEs not only jeopardizes the commercial interests of foreign companies, but also hurts the country's own private enterprises, thus detracting from the long-term potential of China's market economy. This explains the new wide use of the Chinese concept, "The state advances and private companies retreat" (国进民退, *guojin mintui*), to criticize the growing trend toward "strong government, weak society." A study conducted by Chinese scholars shows that the total profits made by China's 500 largest private companies in 2009 were less than the total revenues of two SOE companies, China Mobile and Sinopec.[65] Ironically, the private sector's net return on investment was 8.18 percent, compared to the 3.05 percent return of SOEs in the country in 2009.[66] The impressive growth of China Mobile has been attributed, at least partially, to the company's monopoly of telecommunications in the Chinese domestic market. With large SOEs monopolizing the telecommunications sector, there is no incentive for these flagship companies to pursue technological innovation. This explains a paradoxical phenomenon: while China's large SOEs have dramatically increased their profitability and standing among the *Fortune Global 500* since the early 2000s or so, no single Chinese brand has truly distinguished itself in the global market. The focus on Chinese innovation seems to be more rhetoric than substance.

Xu Xiaonian, professor of economics and finance at the China Europe International Business School in Shanghai and former managing director of China International Capital Corporation Limited, a large state-owned financial company, has emerged as a leading critic of SOE development. Xu uses the Chinese term (权贵资本主义, *quangui zibenzhuyi*), which can be translated as "crony capitalism" or "state capitalism," to express his reservations about the growing trend of state monopoly in present-day China.[67] He believes that, with the rapid expansion of SOEs, China has, in fact, begun to reverse Deng Xiaoping's plan for the country's development. In his view, China is drawing the wrong lessons from the global financial crisis and heading in the wrong direction.[68] According to Xu, the main beneficiaries of SOE growth are corrupt officials, not the Chinese public. Xu believes that, in today's China, entrepreneurs only exist in the private sector, not in SOEs, because SOE managers have neither an entrepreneurial spirit nor a sense of responsibility for their companies' losses.[69]

Many critics also believe that business special interest groups have become too powerful. According to Sun Liping, a professor of sociology at Tsinghua University, the real estate interest group accumulated tremendous economic and social capital throughout the 2000s.[70] The power of this corporate interest group explains why it took 13 years for China to pass an anti-monopoly law, why the macroeconomic control policy in the mid-1990s was largely ineffective, and why the widely perceived property bubble in coastal cities continued to grow. In each of these cases, corporate and industrial interest groups have encroached upon the governmental decision-making process, either by creating governmental policy deadlock or manipulating policies in their own favor.

In February 2010, the Chinese government admitted that more than 70 percent of the 121 companies under the State-Owned Assets Supervision and Administration Commission (SASAC), a body overseeing China's largest SOEs, were engaged in the real estate business and property development.[71] These companies also ran about 2,500 hotels throughout the country. The official media also criticized these companies for "not doing their proper business" (不务正业, *buwu zhengye*). According to Xinhua News Agency, the Chinese government ordered 78 SASAC companies to withdraw their investments in the real estate business.[72] Some have speculated that some portion of China's stimulus package (4 trillion yuan, or $586 billion) in the wake of the 2008 global financial crisis was used — inappropriately — for property development. According to a senior researcher in the Ministry of Housing and Urban-Rural Development, about 32 percent of the stimulus package was invested in real estate.[73] Sun also holds that increasing speculation in property development aggravates the country's economic disparities, making the prospect of joining the middle class even more remote, if not downright impossible, for families of the urban lower class. Sun highlights two parallel and politically dangerous trends — oligarchy at the top and fragmentation at the bottom — that are gaining momentum and may eventually cause a devastating "cleavage" (断裂, *duanlie*) in the country.[74]

In contrast to Hu Angang's optimistic view of education and innovation in China, critics point out the various forms of so-called "education corruption" (教育腐败, *jiaoyu fubai*) that have emerged in the past two decades: the rapid expansion of higher education at the expense of quality, favoritism in admissions, excessive drives for donations and numerous fees, academic inbreeding in appointments and the promotion of faculty, political interference in teaching and research, and plagiarism.[75] Some scholars argue that China's international competitiveness is severely damaged by these problems. One study showed that among PRC-born recipients of doctorates related to science and technology from U.S. universities in 2002, only 8 percent returned to China by 2007, the lowest rate among all countries (by comparison, India's return rate was 19 percent, Taiwan's was 57 percent, Mexico's was 68 percent, and Thailand's was 92 percent).[76] This study apparently undermined the Chinese government's claim that it had been successful in recruiting foreign-educated Chinese returnees to work in the PRC.

Most importantly, as many critics argue, innovation-led economic growth can only be achieved in a politically free and open environment, a far cry from the tight political control and media censorship that characterizes present-day China. Liu Junning, a well-known political scientist, is also cynical when it comes to Chinese optimism. He believes that China, when viewed from a historical perspective, is not really on the rise, but is "experiencing a fundamental crisis in faith," resulting largely from the prolonged absence of freedom of belief and genuine political reforms in the country.[77]

Some critics believe that the Chinese optimism associated with the "China model" often leads to an arrogant foreign policy mindset, another departure from Deng Xiaoping's low-profile approach. In a widely circulated article, Zi Zhongyun, a distinguished international relations scholar and former director of the Institute of American Studies at CASS, launched a bold critique of Chinese optimism, especially the Chinese notion of the "magnificent era" (盛世, *shengshi*), which has been popularly used by the political establishment in recent years to characterize today's China.[78] In the article, Zi states bluntly that beneath this superficial "magnificent era," there is a profound sense of crisis in the making and deep concern about the decay of the regime. On the domestic front, as she observes, China's political reform has basically halted, and censorship has almost returned to the horrendous height reached during the era of the Cultural Revolution. On the foreign policy front, what happened in 2010 reminds her of the decade of the 1960s when China had mostly enemies and only two or three "friends," none of which could feed their people.

This line of criticism of the "China model" by intellectuals like Cai Fang, Yu Yongding, Xu Xiaonian, Sun Liping, and Zi Zhongyun is notable because none of them are considered to be anti-government political dissidents. On the contrary, most of them are well-established public intellectuals who may even have close ties with senior leaders in the Chinese government.[79] While some of their views may be a bit sensational, they have forcefully challenged the prevalent feeling of confidence in China today. It is fair to point out that Hu Angang himself does not deserve criticism for some of the problems associated with the China model or Chinese optimism, such as economic determinism, crony capitalism, vested corporate interest group politics, or the neglect of demographic challenges. In terms of forecasting demographic challenges confronting China, Hu Angang offered warnings at least as early as any of these critics. Arguably, Hu has also been more foresighted and more instrumental than these critics in pushing for fundamental changes in China's mode of economic growth and protecting the interests of vulnerable social groups. More importantly, Hu's optimism about China's future is *not* based on the pursuit of an aggressive foreign policy.

Debating Chinese Exceptionalism

In international affairs, every nation may subscribe to some form of exceptionalism because each has its own unique history, idiosyncratic culture, distinct geography, and specific socioeconomic and political circumstances. An extraordinary characteristic or a combination of characteristics in a given country may lead the country to behave in an exceptional way. In particular, great powers' "exceptionalism" may have a greater impact on world affairs. For example, American exceptionalism refers to the view that the United States, for a variety of reasons — its absence of feudalism historically; Puritan roots; endowment of a large continent with abundant natural resources; melting-pot ethnic composition; democratic ideology combining republicanism, egalitarianism, individualism, and populism; and its great sense of confidence and responsibility — differs profoundly from other nations, including Great Britain and other European states.[80] While proponents of American exceptionalism differ in important ways, a common argument of this school of thought is that the United States is a lasting "shining city on a hill," which may be exempt from the cycle of power shifts in world affairs and historical forces that have affected most, or all, other great powers.

Chinese exceptionalism (中国特殊论, *Zhongguo teshulun*) is a relatively new term used in the Chinese discourse of international affairs, although one may reasonably argue that the Chinese are more aware of their long and often glorious history, and rich and generally distinct culture, than any other people in the world. Most of the recent writings on Chinese exceptionalism are related to discussions of the China model, the perceived unique experience of China's economic miracle. In 2004, Kang Xiaoguang, a professor at People's University and a former colleague (and occasional co-author) of Hu Angang at the Ecological and Environmental Research Center of the CAS, wrote a long, scholarly article on this topic and was among the first group of Chinese scholars who used the term.[81] More recently, Chinese scholars have begun to link the concept to the argument of "China's peaceful rise."[82]

The most influential Chinese proponent of the notion of China's peaceful rise or peaceful development is Zheng Bijian, former vice president of the powerful Central Party School and an aide to many top leaders in the PRC. Zheng argues that China's rise to major-power status will not, and should not, follow the conventional pattern of conflict or war between great powers.[83] Zheng argues that China's rise differs profoundly from the conventional pattern of the rise and fall of great powers, and will not result in a hegemonic conflict, for four major reasons. First, while great-power politics in recent world history involved intensified ideological tensions as, for example, in the Cold War between the Soviet Union-led communist bloc and the U.S.-led capitalist camp, a rising China does not intend to pursue ideological warfare with the West. In Zheng's words, China is only interested in exporting computers, not ideology or revolution.[84] Second, in contrast to Western imperialist powers that established many military bases overseas during their expansion, China will not seek a similarly belligerent and militarism-oriented foreign policy. Zheng believes that the notion of a peaceful rise could help prevent China from taking the road to militarism. Third, China must learn lessons from Western industrialization, which consumed vast amounts of unsustainable resources, and thus will likely pursue an industrial development strategy that is more energy efficient. Fourth and finally, China will not engage in large-scale emigration, which may cause anxieties and problems for other countries, especially China's neighbors.

Hu Angang largely shares Zheng Bijian's strategic vision for China's peaceful rise. In *China in 2020,* he goes a step further by more systemically examining the domestic impetus for and constraints on China's benevolent foreign-policy objectives. Based on Hu's analysis, Chinese exceptionalism is attributable to a number of factors specific to China. First, having endured a century of foreign invasions and humiliations, China is guided by the Chinese traditional notion of "not doing to others what you do not want others to do to you." Hu believes that China will neither pursue a hegemonic foreign policy nor impose its own will on others. Second, rather than adopting the industrial development model of the West, with high environmental costs and high energy consumption, Hu believes China must strive to be a "resource-efficient, environmentally friendly superpower focused on green development." Third, the Chinese leadership's emphasis on domestic development will likely continue as the country prioritizes policies that address economic disparities, the lack of public health care, energy inefficiency, and ecological challenges. This domestic and people-centric approach will prevent the country from pursuing a belligerent foreign policy. Fourth, the development of human resources has been the most important impetus of China's rise. For the same reason, China's superpower status ultimately depends on a "transition from a knowledge-closed nation into a knowledge-open nation and from a country lagging in science and technology into a country spear-heading global innovation." A knowledge economy, as Hu characterizes it, should be "defined less by competition than by cooperation." Hu concludes, therefore, that "China's rise represents an opportunity for the rest of the world rather than a threat."

Foreign analysts, of course, are not so naïve as to confuse promises with reality. The true objectives of Chinese foreign policy must ultimately be judged by actions rather than the words of the Chinese leaders and their advisors like Zheng Bijian and Hu Angang. Some Western critics may even argue that these notions of a peaceful rise and Chinese exceptionalism are nothing but diplomatic gestures on the part of Chinese leadership to temper the concerns of the PRC's neighboring countries and other major powers about the emergence of a militarily strong and expansionist China.

It is important to note, however, that there is another school of thought — which also considers the notion of China's peaceful rise to be naïve — that is increasingly gaining momentum in the PRC. Ever since Zheng articulated his concept, Chinese critics have been cynical about its acceptance both domestically and abroad.[85] For example, Yan Xuetong, a well-known political scientist at Tsinghua University, observes that the notion of China's peaceful rise is confusing and ineffective due to three contrasting interpretations of the terms "rise" and "peaceful." The first interpretation considers both "rise" and "peaceful" as goals, and therefore holds that China seeks an exceptional way to rise that differs from the many powers in history that rose to prominence through military means. The second interpretation treats "peaceful" as a means and "rise" as an end, and therefore suggests that China uses "peaceful" in name only in order to achieve its desired end — that is, to rise. The third interpretation regards "peaceful" as an end and "rise" as a means, and therefore understands China to be seeking to contribute to world peace.[86] According to Yan, tensions between these contrasts will immediately emerge in the policymaking process, because no government will be so rigid as to adhere to one promise when international politics is an ever-changing game. Thus, as Yan implies, the concept of a "peaceful rise" is no more than wishful thinking. Other Chinese critics, including those in the military, such as Major General Luo Yuan, criticize "Pacifism" (和平主义, *heping zhuyi*) or the "Pan-Pacifist approach" (泛和

平化, *fan hepinghua*), which are popular among some members of the Chinese foreign policy establishment.[87] Luo explicitly argues that this pacifist thinking will lead China to follow the path of post-World War II Japan — falling into a trap set by the United States that prevents it from becoming a superpower.

The strongest and most explicit critique of Chinese exceptionalism was the 2010 best seller *The China Dream*, written by Senior Colonel Liu Mingfu, director of the Institute of Military Development at the National Defense University (NDU). In the book, Liu explicitly argues that China should pursue a new developmental strategy of "military rise" (军事崛起, *junshi jueqi*) to obtain and secure a global leadership position from which it can compete with the United States.[88] Liu believes that China's rise fits within the pattern of shifts in power in the international system, and he therefore rejects the idea of Chinese exceptionalism. In his analysis, a hegemonic conflict is inevitable. Liu Mingfu's book is not based on serious scholarly research, but rather on snapshots of historical events and random references to views expressed by some Chinese and foreign strategic thinkers. A majority of Chinese leaders and public intellectuals may not agree with Liu's arguments and strategic perspective, but Liu's view does reflect the thinking among a subset of international relations scholars, opinion leaders, and, especially, military strategists in the PRC.

In the book, Liu Mingfu explicitly states that the overall goal of China's modernization is to become "the most powerful country in the world" (头号强国, *touhao qiangguo*).[89] To justify this strategic goal, Liu argues that all of China's paramount leaders over the last century shared this same objective: in the 1911 Revolution, Sun Yat-sen said that his dream was to build China into "the number one richest and strongest country in the world" (世界第一富强之国, *shijie diyi fuqiang zhiguo*); Mao's "Great Leap Forward" was nothing but an attempt to surpass the United States; and Deng Xiaoping's "keeping a low profile" strategy (韬光养晦, *taoguang yanghui*) strived to achieve, in three steps, Chinese national rejuvenation above all others by the middle of the 21st century.[90] According to Liu, China's replacement of the United States as the sole superpower, or what Liu labels the "superpower succession" (冠军国家更替, *guanjun guojia gengti*), is not far off. Liu appeals to Chinese leaders and the public to remember that China should not have any "illusions" about American goodwill regarding "China's rise" or about scenarios that describe peaceful coexistence between the existing superpower and the emerging superpower.

In Liu's view, the United States is determined to contain China economically, politically, ideologically, and, most importantly, militarily. Liu's beliefs are widely shared by other analysts in the Chinese military establishment. Former minister of defense Liang Guanglie made the strong public pronouncement that "peace does not fall from the sky."[91] Liang seemed to echo one of Liu's central arguments: the need to accelerate China's military modernization. The real and ultimate means to facilitate China's rise, according to some Chinese analysts, especially those in the military, is to build strong armed forces to compete with the United States. Liu argues that this is not so much because China wants to defeat the United States as it is because the United States wants to defeat China.[92] Becoming a military superpower, Liu argues, should be the "Chinese dream," without which China will have only all sorts of "nightmares."[93]

These debates over Chinese optimism and Chinese exceptionalism illustrate the importance of Hu Angang's work — its originality, complexity, foresightedness, and comprehensiveness. They also reveal the diversity of views that exists within present-day China's intellectual community, and how widely assessments of the country's future differ.

Each reader, of course, can arrive at his or her own judgment of the author's analyses, the prospects of a rising China, and its implications for peace and prosperity in the 21st century. It is reasonable to assume, however, that the ideas, debates, and visions competing in China matter greatly — not only for China's own future development, but also for its interaction with the outside world. As a leading proponent of Chinese optimism and exceptionalism, Hu Angang can help increase our knowledge and enhance our understanding of the pressing issues and long-term challenges that this rapidly changing country faces. Considered from an even broader perspective, Hu's intriguing and forward-looking views, as articulated in *China in 2020*, may also contribute to growing international recognition that, in the new global environment, we all must find novel ways to think about power and responsibility.

Notes

This chapter is an edited version of the introduction to the Hu Angang volume of the Thornton Center Chinese Thinkers Series, published by the Brookings Institution Press. See Cheng Li, "Introduction: A Champion for Chinese Optimism and Exceptionalism," in Hu Angang, *China in 2020: A New Type of Superpower* (Washington, DC: Brookings Institution Press, 2011), xv-xl. The author thanks Zach Balin, Sally Carman, Eve Cary, Sean Chen, Jordan Lee, Ryan McElveen, and Lucy Xu for their very helpful comments on earlier versions of this chapter.

1 Robert Gilpin, "The Theory of Hegemonic War," *Journal of Interdisciplinary History*, Vol. 18, No. 4 (1988): 591–613; and Robert Gilpin, *The Political Economy of International Relations* (Princeton, NJ: Princeton University Press, 1987).
2 Recent English works that offer different assessments of China's rise include: Susan L. Shirk, *China: Fragile Superpower* (Oxford: Oxford University Press, 2008); James Kynge, *China Shakes the World: A Titan's Rise and Troubled Future — and the Challenge for America* (New York: Mariner Books, 2007); Martin Jacques, *When China Rules the World: The End of the Western World and the Birth of a New Global Order* (New York: Penguin Press, 2009); and Edward S. Steinfeld, *Playing Our Game: Why China's Rise Doesn't Threaten the West* (Oxford: Oxford University Press, 2010).
3 A few noticeable exceptions include Mark Leonard, *What Does China Think?* (New York: Public Affairs, 2008); Yu Keping, *Democracy is a Good Thing: Essays on Politics, Society, and Culture in Contemporary China* (Washington, DC: Brookings Institution Press, 2008); and Wang Hui, *China's New Order: Society, Politics, and Economy in Transition* (Cambridge, MA: Harvard University Press, 2006). For collections of writings by Western and Chinese scholars, see Robert S. Ross and Zhu Feng, eds., *China's Ascent: Power, Security, and the Future of International Politics* (Ithaca, NY: Cornell University Press, 2008); and Richard Rosecrance and Gu Guoliang, eds., *Power and Restraint: A Shared Vision for the U.S.-China Relationship* (New York: Public Affairs, 2009).
4 Hu Angang, *Zhongguo: Zouxiang Ershiyi Shiji* [China: Toward the 21st Century] (Beijing: China Environmental Science Press, 1991), 127.
5 The Center for China Studies, Tsinghua University, *Hu Angang: Guoqing yanjiu yu jiaoshu yuren* [Hu Angang's research on China studies and his teaching and training of the new generation] (Beijing: Tsinghua University, unpublished monograph, 2010), 8.

6 See http://business.sohu.com/85/79/article13737985.shtml, May 16, 2001.
7 For a list of Hu Angang's writings, see Hu, *China in 2020*, 195–199.
8 *Hu Angang: Guoqing yanjiu yu jiaoshu yuren*, 62 and 104.
9 Ibid., 52.
10 For more discussion of the growing role of think tanks and other interest groups in China's policymaking process, see Cheng Li, "China's New Think Tanks: Where Officials, Entrepreneurs, and Scholars Interact," *China Leadership Monitor*, No. 29 (Summer 2009); and Linda Jakobson and Dean Knox, "New Foreign Policy Actors in China," Stockholm International Peace Research Institute Policy Paper, No. 26 (September 2010).
11 Hu Angang, *2020 Zhongguo: Quanmian Jianshe Xiaokang Shehui* [China in 2020: Building a Well-Off Society] (Beijing: Tsinghua University Press, 2007).
12 See Hu's speech at the School of Public Policy and Management, Tsinghua University, http://www.sppm.tsinghua.edu.cn/ggjj/26efe4892607e79901260 d56bcbf0007.html, January 8, 2010.
13 John J. Mearsheimer, *The Tragedy of Great Power Politics* (New York: Norton, 2001).
14 Zhao Yining, *Da Jiaoliang: Dang Zhongguo Long Yudao Meiguo Ying* [Grand Games: When the Chinese Dragon Faces the American Eagle] (Hangzhou: Zhejiang renmin chubanshe, 2010).
15 See http://elite.youth.cn/mj/200903/t20090309_874370.htm.
16 Hu Angang, *Zhongguo fazhan qianjing* [Prospects of China's development] (Hangzhou: Zhejiang renmin chubanshe, 1999), 6.
17 *Shijie ribao* [World Journal], January 7, 2008, A3.
18 Ibid., 5–6.
19 World Bank, *China: Long-Term Development, Issues and Options* (Baltimore: Johns Hopkins University Press, 1985).
20 See http://www.un-documents.net/wced-ocf.htm.
21 *China Daily*, July 4, 2010, and September 16, 2010; and also http://www. chinadaily.com.cn/zgrbjx/2009-09/16/content_9090404.htm.
22 See http://business.sohu.com/20091208/n268772861.shtml.
23 *Hu Angang: Guoqing yanjiu yu jiaoshu yuren*, 72.
24 Ibid., 61.
25 For a list of the special reports, see http://ccs.tsinghua.edu.cn.
26 *Renmin ribao* [People's Daily], September 5, 2010, 11.
27 Hu, *"Zhongguo renlei bu'anquan de zuida tiaozhan"*; and also see http:// business.sohu.com, June 19, 2005.
28 Hu, *Zhongguo fazhan qianjing* [China's Development Prospects] (Hangzhou: Zhejiang People's Press), 8.

29 *Hu Angang: Guoqing yanjiu yu jiaoshu yuren*, 9.
30 Zhang Xiaoxia, *Zhongguo gaoceng zhinang* [China's top think tanks], Vol. 1 (Beijing: Jinghua chubanshe, 2000), 176-79; and also see http://www.pinggu. org/bbs/thread-278591-1-1.html.
31 Zhang, *Zhongguo gaoceng zhinang*, 182–83.
32 Joshua Cooper Ramo, *The Beijing Consensus* (London: The Foreign Policy Centre, 2004), 22–23.
33 *Liaowang dongfang zhoukan* [Oriental Outlook Weekly], April 11, 2005.
34 Hu, *Zhongguo fazhan qianjing*.
35 Quoted from Wu An-chia, "Leadership Changes during the Fourth Plenum," *Issues and Studies*, Vol. 30, No. 10 (October 1994), 134. Hu Angang, *Zhongguo fazhan qianjing*, 312.
36 Hu Angang, *Mao Zedong yu Wenge* [Mao Zedong and the Culture Revolution] (Hong Kong: Strong Wind Press, 2009). Tang Shaojie, "Ping Hu Angang Mao Zedong yu Wenge" [Comments on Hu Angang's Mao Zedong and the Cultural Revolution], *Ershiyi shiji* [Twenty-First Century], No. 116 (Nov. 2009): 113–119.
37 Tsai Wen-Shuen, "Zhonggong zhizheng dianfan de zhuanyi" [The Paradigm Shifts of CCP's Rule] (Taipei, unpublished paper, 2009).
38 Hu Lianhe and Hu Angang, "Zhongguo weihe buneng gao sanquan fenli" [Why China should not adopt the separation of powers], *Renmin ribao* [People's Daily], May 10, 2010. For criticism, see http://www.rfa.org/cantonese/commentaries/weipu-05262010124134.html?encoding=traditional.
39 Hu, *China in 2020*, Chapter 1.
40 *Shijie ribao*, February 21, 2010, A1.
41 See http://www.treasury.gov/resource-center/data-chart-center/tic/Documents/mfh.txt.
42 For the online version of the *Economist* article, see http://www.economist.com/node/17732859.
43 Ibid.
44 Hu, *Zhongguo fazhan qianjing*, 14.
45 See http://finmanac.blogspot.com/2009/02/top-10-banks-in-world-by-market.html.
46 *Caifu* [Fortune], China Edition, October 2010, 125–130.
47 *Shijie ribao*, December 30, 2010, A3.
48 *Shijie ribao*, February 14, 2010, A10.
49 "Trading Places: The World Largest Container Ports," *Economist*, August 24, 2010. Also see http://www.economist.com/node/16881727.

50 Ibid. Hong Kong was on the 1989 list of the top 20 ports, but it did not belong to the PRC until 1997.

51 The annual growth rates of output and sales are 48 percent and 46 percent, respectively. Quoted from Zhang Xue, "Domestic auto sector undergoes structural adjustments," *Economic Daily*, February 9, 2010.

52 Lu Xueyi, *Dangdai Zhongguo shehui jiegou* [Social Structure of Contemporary China] (Beijing: Shehui kexuewenxian chubanshe, 2010), 402–406.

53 *Zhongguo qingnian bao*, February 11, 2010.

54 *Zhongguo xinwen zhoukan* [China Newsweek], January 22, 2010. Euromonitor International, a London-based research and consultant firm, forecast that China's middle class will reach 700 million in 2020, about 48 percent of the country's total population. See http://www.euromonitor.com/Chinas_ middle_class_reaches_80_million.

55 Homi Kharas and Geoffrey Gertz, "The New Global Middle Class: A Crossover from West to East" in Cheng Li, ed., *China's Emerging Middle Class: Beyond Economic Transformation* (Washington, DC: Brookings Institution Press, 2010), 38.

56 *Shijie ribao*, December 22, 2010, A3.

57 *Shijie ribao*, April 9, 2010, A1.

58 For more discussion on this topic, see Wang Huiyao, "China's National Talent Plan: Key Measures and Objectives," http://www.brookings.edu/ papers/2010/1123_china_talent_wang.aspx.

59 See http://www.blockedinchina.net/?siteurl=www.ftchinese.com.

60 For the main arguments of the China model, see Pan Wei, ed., *Zhongguo moshi: Jiedu renmin gongheguo de liushinian* [China Model: A New Developmental Model from the Sixty Years of the People's Republic] (Beijing: Central Compilation and Translation Press, 2009). Hu Angang is a contributor to this edited book.

61 Cai Fang, "A Tale of Two Cities: Chinese Labor Market Performance in 2009 and Reform Priority in 2010," East Asia Forum, December 25, 2009; and also see http://news.xinhuanet.com/fortune/2006-08/03/content_ 4913519.htm.

62 Yu Yongding, "A Different Road Forward," *China Daily*, December 23, 2010. Also see http://www.chinadaily.com.cn/opinion/2010-12/23/content_11742757. htm.

63 Ibid.

64 See http://www.iwep.org.cn/Corporation/infoDetail13.asp?cInfoId=177& dInfoId=200.

65 *Beijing shangbao* [Beijing Business Daily], August 30, 2010. Also see http://news.xinhuanet.com/fortune/2010-08/30/c_12496387.htm

66 See http://xuxiaonian.blog.sohu.com/160724498.html.

67 In his book, *The End of the Free Market: Who Wins the War between States and Corporations?* (2010), Ian Bremmer, the president of Eurasia Group, also expressed concern about the rise of state capitalism in China.

68 For Xu Xiaoning's views, see http://xuxiaonian.blog.sohu.com/158818651. html. Also *Lianhe zaobao* [United Morning News], August 1, 2010; http://finance.ifeng.com/opinion/zjgc/20100830/2567934.shtml.

69 See http://finance.ifeng.com/news/20101205/3005151.shtml.

70 Sun Liping, *"Zhongguo jinru liyi boyi de shidai"* [China is entering the era of a conflict of interests], http://chinesenewsnet.com, February 6, 2006.

71 *Qianjiang wanbao* [Qianjiang Evening News], February 11, 2010. Also see http://www.chinanews.com.cn/estate/estate-1spl/news/2010/02-11/2121577. shtml.

72 See http://bt.xinhuanet.com/2010-03/19/content_19293215.htm.

73 See http://news.xinhuanet.com/fortune/2009-03/17/content_11024848.htm. Zhang Ping, Minister of the National Development and Reform Commission, however, told reporters at the National People's Congress' annual meeting in March 2010 that "no penny in the stimulus package has been invested in real estate." See http://www.sc.xinhuanet.com/content/2010-03/07/content_19178284.htm.

74 Sun Liping, *Duanlie: 20 shiji 90 niandai yilai de Zhongguo shehui* [Cleavage: Chinese Society since the 1990s] (Beijing: Shehui kexue wenxian chubanshe, 2003); and Sun Liping, *Zhuanxing yu duanlie* [Transition and Cleavage] (Beijing: Tsinghua University Press, 2004).

75 For more discussion on this topic, see Ren Jianming, "Woguo jiaoyu fubai de xianzhang qushi" [Status and Trends of China's Educational Corruption], in Yang Dongping, ed., *Zhongguo jiaoyu de zhuanxing yu fazhan 2006* [Transition and Development of China's Education 2006] (Beijing: Shehui kexue wenxian chubanshe, 2007).

76 Michael G. Finn, "Stay Rates of Foreign Doctoral Recipients from U.S. Universities," 2007. This paper was prepared for the Division of Science Resources Statistics of the National Science Foundation by the Oak Ridge Institute for Science and Education, January 2010, 6.

77 Liu Junning, "Jingshen weiji shi zui gengben de weiji" [Crisis in faith is the most fundamental crisis], *Nanfengchuang* [South Wind], October 9, 2010.

78 *Jingji guancha bao* [Economic Observers], December 25, 2010. Also see http://www.chinaelections.org/NewsInfo.asp?NewsID=195247.

79 Cai Fang, for example, gave a presentation at the Politburo meeting.

80 For more discussion on American exceptionalism, see Seymour Martin Lipset, *American Exceptionalism: A Double-Edged Sword* (New York: Norton, 1997); Deborah L. Madsen, *American Exceptionalism* (Jackson, MS: University Press of Mississippi, 1998); and Godfrey Hodgson, *The Myth of American Exceptionalism* (New Haven, CT: Yale University Press, 2010).

81 Kang Xiaoguang, "Zhongguo teshulun: Dui Zhongguo dalu 25 nian gaige jingyan de fansi" [Chinese Exceptionalism: Reflection on China's 25-Year Reform], *Confucius 2000*, June 2004. Also see http://www.confucius2000.com/poetry/zgtsldzgdl25nggjydfs.htm.

82 For an excellent review of the Chinese discussion of Western literature on a rising China, see Liu Yawei, "'Zhongguo teshulun': yiweizhe shenme?" [What does "China Exceptionalism" Mean?], *21 shiji guoji pinglun* (The 21st Century International Review), Vol. 1, No. 1 (2010): 11–15.

83 Zheng Bijian, *China's Peaceful Rise: Speeches of Zheng Bijian, 1997–2005* (Washington, DC: Brookings Institution Press, 2005).

84 Zheng, *China's Peaceful Rise*, 10.

85 Representative works include Wang Jian, Li Xiaoning, Qiao Liang, and Wang Xianghui, *Xin zhanguo shidai* [New Era of Warring States] (Beijing: Xinhua chubanshe, 2004) and Xiong Guangkai, *Guoji zhanlue yu Xin junshi biange* [International Strategy and Revolution in Military Affairs] (Beijing: Tsinghua daxue chubanshe, 2003).

86 Yan Xuetong, "Foreword" in Yan Xuetong, Sun Xuefeng, and others, eds., *Zhongguo jueqi jiqi zhanlue* [The rise of China and its strategy] (Beijing: Peking University Press, 2005), 2.

87 Quoted from http://china.dwnews.com/news/2010-12-16/57200778.html.

88 Liu Mingfu, *Zhongguomeng–hou Meiguo shidai de daguo siwei yu zhanlue dingwei* [The China dream: The great power's mindset and strategic stance in the post-American hegemony era] (Beijing: China Friendship Press, 2010).

89 Ibid., 21.

90 Ibid., 3–16.

91 See http://news.xinhuanet.com/mil/2010-12/28/c_12926497.htm.

92 Ibid., 273.

93 Ibid., 290.

Chapter 3

Yu Keping (Political Scientist): Making Democracy Safe for China

People are more impressed by the power of our example rather than the example of our power.

— Bill Clinton

"American discourse about China," observes Richard Madsen, a distinguished sinologist in the United States, "has long been as much about ourselves as about China."[1] Far too often we American analysts evaluate China according to our own preconceived notions of what the country is like rather than paying attention to the Chinese mentality and reality. Throughout history, American views, values, and interests have shaped our assessments of and debates on China's political trajectory, especially the possibility and desirability of democracy in the world's most populous country. Optimists often envision the promotion of democratic principles in China as the best way to fulfill President Woodrow Wilson's century-old idealistic appeal that "the world must be made safe for democracy."[2] A democratic China, they believe, would not only mollify ideological and political tensions between China and the West but also inspire Chinese policymakers to abide by international norms and standards. In contrast, pessimists are cynical about the prospect of China's political progress toward democracy in the foreseeable future. In their view, China's remarkable economic development makes the one-party system more resilient and thus more capable of resisting any significant political change.[3] According to these pessimists, this resilient Chinese authoritarian regime, with its rapid economic and military modernization, inevitably constitutes a significant threat to the United States.

Largely absent from the conversation in the English-speaking communities of contemporary China studies, however, are knowledge and understanding of the Chinese discourse about the country's political future. In fact, since the late 1990s, and especially in recent years, Chinese public intellectuals have engaged in heated debate over various aspects of China's political reform. Since 2005, Chinese scholars and the official media have fostered a nationwide, public discussion about democracy, which American political scientist David Shambaugh calls the "democracy wave" debates.[4] This Chinese discourse reflects new thinking about democracy, governance, and civil society in the scholarly communities of the PRC. But unfortunately, as noted by a Singapore-based scholar, "[M]ost leading social scientists in China do not write in English and most of their work has not been translated."[5] As a result, these scholars' work goes largely unread by members of the Western academic and policymaking communities.

It is critically important, however, for the outside world to understand the ongoing Chinese intellectual and political discourse. Although foreign pressure or influence may have played an important role from time to time in the political development of China, ultimately only China's leaders and its people can decide the country's political trajectory. The following three interrelated questions are crucial to any analysis of China's political future: First, what incentives do Chinese leaders have for pursuing political reforms? Second, what factors or obstacles will prevent them from doing so? And third, what measures should China adopt to help overcome these obstacles?

Arguably no other person has been more articulate in addressing these three questions than Yu Keping. In fact, the aforementioned "democracy wave" debates in China began with Yu's now well-known article entitled "Democracy is a Good Thing."[6] The article, which was based on Yu's interview with the Hong Kong–based *Ta Kung Pao* in 2005, was reprinted first in the *Beijing Daily* in the fall of 2006 and, since then, has appeared in almost all of the country's major newspapers.[7] In 2007, the *Southern Daily*, a leading liberal newspaper in China, ranked "Democracy is a Good Thing" as one of the year's most influential articles.[8] That same year, Yu himself was named by the Chinese media as one of the most influential public intellectuals in China. In 2008, the Chinese media counted Yu among fifty people deemed to have influenced China's development most significantly over the previous three decades.[9]

In a way, Yu's thesis recalls Winston Churchill's famous witty remark: "Democracy is the worst form of government, except all the others that have been tried." Using clear and simple language, Yu directly addresses the profound suspicion and concern that surround a question deeply rooted in the minds of many Chinese nationals: Why is democracy good for China? The public discourse on the desirability of democracy that Yu's article has stimulated is much needed for the country, currently in the midst of a far-reaching socioeconomic transformation. If democracy will lead to chaos, or even the dissolution of the country, there is no incentive for the Chinese leaders and people to pursue it. In addition, if democracy is perceived by the country's political, economic, and cultural elites as something that will undermine, rather than enhance, their interests, there will be no strong consensus for such a political future in China. Therefore, the greatest intellectual challenge for Yu and other like-minded scholars is to make democracy safe for China, both conceptually and procedurally.

Objective, Organization, and Outlook

In *Democracy is a Good Thing*, Yu Keping aims to help those in the English-speaking communities of China studies better understand some of the dynamic new thinking occurring in the PRC around Chinese political reforms and democracy. It features translations of some of Yu Keping's most important essays on politics, society, and culture in contemporary China. These essays, selected by Yu himself, were all originally published in Chinese; most of them appeared in prominent academic journals and magazines in China between 2006 and 2008.

Democracy is a Good Thing is organized into four thematic parts. Part one highlights political changes in post-Mao China, especially in the wake of the agenda for political reforms announced at the recent 17th National Congress of the Chinese Communist Party (CCP). It also includes an overview of the groundbreaking developments in the academic disciplines of political science and public administration in reform-era China, illustrating how these developments contribute to the diffusion of international norms throughout the country. Part two focuses on China's emerging civil society. In that section, Yu provides comprehensive information about, and a thorough analysis of, the types, status, and characteristics of China's civil society organizations, as well as the government's administrative regulations that both guide and restrict those organizations. Part three examines various challenging dichotomies that the country faces. Among them are culture and modernity, economic growth and sustainability, and human society and environmental protection. The final part places China's ongoing socioeconomic and political transformation within the broader context of global governance. The author argues for a delicate balance between the need to preserve the Chinese cultural and sociopolitical identity in the era of globalization and the imperative for the country to participate more actively in the construction of a harmonious world.

The four sections of *Democracy is a Good Thing* present multidimensional political changes occurring within the Chinese state and across Chinese society while reinforcing a central thesis about the feasibility of democracy in China. While acknowledging many of the potential problems that democracy may cause, Yu argues that there is a way by which China can make a transition to democracy with "minimum political and social costs."[10] Yu calls this approach "incremental democracy" and suggests that China's political reforms should be incremental over time and manageable in scale. These political reforms include intraparty democracy, grassroots elections, and legal reforms. Yu believes that these reforms will ultimately result in a "democratic breakthrough" when various existing political forces are ready for such a drastic change. This approach, in Yu's view, is the best way to achieve a political "soft landing" in China.[11]

Universal Values of Democracy

One frequently raised question about Yu Keping's conception of democracy is whether or not it is similar to most of the rest of the world's, especially the West's. Conceptual clarity is essential in the political and intellectual dialogue between the Chinese and the outside world. At the same time, foreign analysts need to understand the political context in which Chinese leaders and their advisors, such as Yu Keping, address this question. Like Chinese leaders, Yu Keping does not argue that China should experiment with multiparty democratic competition, nor does he believe that the country should move toward an American-style system based on a tripartite division between the executive, legislative, and judicial branches of government. In fact, while stating unambiguously that China should draw some positive elements from the Western political culture and system, Yu maintains that "Westernization of the Chinese political system" should not be a political objective for China.

Yu's position is understandable. Even those who are most optimistic about the potential democratization of China do not expect the country to develop a multiparty system in the near future. Chinese thinkers such as Yu have every reason to argue that the PRC's version of democracy will, and should, have its own unique features. After all, British democracy, Australian democracy, Japanese democracy, Mexican democracy, and American democracy all differ from each other in important ways. They all, however, feature institutional checks and balances, political choice, constitutionalism, an independent media, and certain civil liberties. China's political system can have its own unique characteristics, but it must include these same elements to be considered democratic in nature.

Throughout his writings, Yu Keping clearly and consistently advocates "universal values of democracy" (民主的普世价值, *minzhu de pushijiazhi*). When Yu states that "democracy is a good thing," he means that it is good for all of human society, not just for the Americans or the Chinese. In his discussion of cultural developments in the era of globalization, Yu observes, "[G]lobalization not only makes people realize that they share a common fate but also helps them identify with such basic values as freedom, equality, justice, security, welfare, and dignity. Pursuit of such basic values is the core principle, as well as the ultimate destination, of cultural globalization."[12]

It is interesting to note that China's recent leaders have also spoken about the universal value of democracy. In a meeting with a delegation from the Brookings Institution in Beijing in October 2006, Premier Wen Jiabao spent a substantial amount of time explaining China's objectives for political democracy.[13] He defined democracy in largely the same way as many in the West would explain it. "When we talk about democracy,"

Premier Wen said, "we usually refer to the three most important components: elections, judicial independence, and supervision based on checks and balances."[14] In addition to expressing such sentiments in private forums, Wen and President Hu Jintao made repeated public announcements about the importance of democracy in building an ever-stronger Chinese state. Indeed, the word democracy became a mainstay in the political speeches of many among the Chinese leadership during the Hu-Wen administration.

Both Yu's thesis about democracy and Wen's remarks about China's roadmap for political development reflect new thinking in the liberal wing of the Chinese political establishment. For a long time, the party doctrine has portrayed Western democracy as a system that represents only the interests of a small number of the rich and powerful. To Chinese critics, politics in the West has particular problems that result from the way in which campaigns are financed. At the same time, Chinese leaders and scholars have tended to overemphasize the uniqueness of China's conditions and the Chinese characteristics of their economic and political systems. Make no mistake: not all Chinese leaders or public intellectuals agree with the enthusiastic views toward democracy articulated by Premier Wen and Professor Yu. One may even reasonably assume that Wen and Yu represent a minority view in both the Chinese leadership and scholarly communities.

As some Chinese scholars have observed, the fact that Yu argues that "democracy is a good thing" implies that many in the country hold the opposite view — that "democracy is a bad thing."[15] According to Shi Tianjian, a political scientist at Duke University, Yu's thesis does not necessarily reflect an ideological breakthrough in the CCP establishment, but it does reflect a new trend or a new school of thought emerging from the Chinese leadership. "It is a major change as one previously considered a thing as bad, but now views the same thing as good," observes Shi.[16] All these observations highlight the originality and importance of Yu's thesis in the Chinese political discourse. The following pages provide a more detailed description of Yu's professional career, his main scholarly contributions, and how his views differ from those of other prominent Chinese thinkers on the issue of democracy.

Yu Keping: A Thinker from a New Generation

The Chinese media often identify Yu Keping as a "rising star of the new generation of CCP theoreticians" (中共理论新秀, *Zhonggong lilun xinxiu*).[17] His scholarly accomplishments have earned him a positive reputation in the field of political science in China. This is evidenced by the fact that he concurrently serves as a guest professor at roughly a dozen of the country's most prestigious universities, including Peking, Tsinghua, Renmin, Beijing Normal, Nankai, Fudan, Shanghai Jiaotong, Zhejiang, Xiamen, Sichuan, Jilin, the Harbin Institute of Technology, and China National School of Administration. Very few political scientists, Chinese or foreign, have received the academic honor of teaching at so many top schools in the PRC.

In addition to being actively engaged in academic research and theoretical thinking, Yu is also an insider in the Chinese political establishment. From 2001 to 2015, he served as deputy director of the Central Compilation and Translation Bureau (CCTB) under the Central Committee of the CCP. This is a ministry-level official position. Therefore, Yu has a dual identity as a scholar-official (学者型官员, *xuezhexing guanyuan*). The CCTB is a major research institution responsible for four important tasks: translating the classic foreign language works of Marxist theoreticians into Chinese; translating the works of the top Chinese leaders into foreign languages; conducting research on Chinese socialism in both theory and practice; and conducting research on new theoretical developments in the social sciences and philosophy around the world.[18] Although much smaller than the Central Party School (CPS), the CCTB also serves as a major think tank for the Chinese leadership, especially in the area of theoretical research. Yu currently also serves as director of both the China Center for Comparative Politics and Economics and the Center for Chinese Government Innovations at Peking University. These two university-based think tanks have kept abreast of both the global trends in social science research and China's domestic political changes.

Throughout the reform era, a number of CCP establishment theoreticians have played important roles in attaining ideological breakthroughs. For example, in 1978, Hu Fuming, then an instructor of philosophy at Nanjing University, published an article entitled "Practice Is the Sole

Criterion for Testing Truth" in the *Guangming Daily*, challenging the orthodox view of the CCP leadership, which abided by the tenets of Maoism. Not long thereafter, the party jettisoned Maoism in favor of the policies of reforming and opening the country to the outside world. In 1991, when party conservatives criticized Deng Xiaoping's bold market reforms, Zhou Ruijin, then deputy editor in chief of the *Liberation Daily*, wrote an article that was highly controversial at the time, rejecting the simplistic and dichotomist way of thinking about socialism and capitalism. Both theoretically and practically, the article justified the acceleration of market liberalization in the country, especially in the pacesetter city of Shanghai. In 2003, Zheng Bijian, then vice president of the Central Party School, delivered a keynote speech at the Boao Forum in Hainan, outlining the reasons why China's rise would not threaten the rest of the world.[19] Zheng's work was used extensively by Hu Jintao in his formulation of the "theory of China's peaceful rise." It should be noted that Hu Fuming, Zhou Ruijin, and Zheng Bijian were all born in the 1930s and belong to a generation of CCP theoreticians who had their formative experiences in the Communist Revolution and the first decade of the PRC. Yu's generation of CCP theoreticians, on the other hand, came of age during the Cultural Revolution and became actively engaged in intellectual discourse in the reform era. Thus, in many ways, their views differ profoundly from those of the preceding generation.

Yu Keping was born to a family of humble means in Zhuji County, Zhejiang Province, in 1959. He grew up during the Cultural Revolution. In 1976, at the age of seventeen, he began to work as a farmer in Huashan Village in his home county, where he later became a village cadre. Yu's background resembles those of many prominent leaders of the so-called fifth generation, including PRC President Xi Jinping, Premier Li Keqiang, and PRC Vice President Li Yuanchao, as well as the experiences of distinguished public intellectuals and artists such as economist Hu Angang, sociologist Li Yinhe, historian Qin Hui, movie director Zhang Yimou, and artist Chen Danqing. The hardships many people from this generation sustained in the countryside fostered valuable traits, such as endurance, critical thinking abilities, and humility, as well as an intimate knowledge of rural China.[20]

As a result of Deng Xiaoping's policy initiatives, China resumed the use of college entrance exams in 1978. Yu was among the first group of students to enter college after passing the most competitive entrance exams in the history of the PRC. He enrolled in a three-year program in the Department of Political Science and History at Shaoxing Normal College in his native province. Following graduation, Yu spent the next ten years in Chinese educational institutions, first as a graduate student and then as an instructor. He received a master's degree in philosophy from Xiamen University in 1985 and then became one of the PRC's first two doctoral recipients in political science when he was awarded a PhD in 1988 by Peking University.[21] Yu's doctoral advisor was Professor Zhao Baoxu, who is often regarded, in both China and abroad, as a founder of the academic field of political science in the PRC.

Throughout Yu's time in school, China was undergoing a series of phenomenal social and economic changes. Indeed, the decade between 1978 and 1988 was an exciting period marked by an enthusiasm among Chinese youths for drawing lessons from the Cultural Revolution and absorbing all sorts of new knowledge, including Western liberal ideas. According to Li Jingpeng, a political science professor at Peking University who taught Yu in the late 1980s, as a student Yu not only showed enormous interest in Western intellectual history and recent trends but also paid particular attention to the selective application of Western theories to China's political development.[22] Yu's doctoral thesis was entitled "An Analytical Framework for Contemporary Chinese Politics."

Like many prominent social scientists in his generation, Yu has spent significant time overseas. In the mid-1990s, he taught as a visiting professor at schools such as Duke University in the United States and the Free University of Berlin in Germany. Over the years, through a voracious reading of Western social science writings, Yu has developed wide-ranging intellectual interest in Western thought. He was particularly influenced by the work of prominent Western thinkers such as Jurgen Habermas, Harold Laski, and Lester M. Salamon. Yu has also collaborated with distinguished American and European scholars, including Arif Dirlik, Anthony Saich, and Thomas Heberer. He served as consultant for a government innovation project organized by the United Nations Development Programme and currently is a board member for several international journals, such as Global Studies in Great Britain and New Political Science in the United States.[23] In 2008, Yu was awarded an honorary doctorate degree by the

University of Duisburg-Essen in the German federal state of North Rhine-Westphalia; he was the tenth Chinese national in German history to be awarded such a degree.

Since the beginning of his academic career, Yu has been known for unconventional thinking and bold ideas. In 1990, for example, Yu argued in a scholarly article that human rights should be considered fundamental values of human society.[24] At the time, the Chinese media and mainstream scholarly communities rejected the concept of human rights and often characterized it as a hypocritical Western idea or a term used in anti-China rhetoric. To a great extent, Yu's view of human rights challenged the ideological status quo of the time.

Yu was also among the first group of Chinese scholars in the PRC to study civil society and non-governmental organizations (NGOs). According to Yu, civil society and NGOs are not the "patents of the West." As he articulates in a section of *Democracy is a Good Thing* on China's social transformation and civil society, NGOs, with their diverse and dynamic roles, could share the burden of governance and contribute to a harmonious society. In Yu's view, the rapid rise of Chinese NGOs has profoundly changed state-society relations in the country. Yu believes that, under the current conditions, the objective for the Chinese government and the public should be "good governance" (善治, *shanzhi*) instead of the traditional goal of "good government" (善政, *shanzheng*). Probably earlier than anyone else in China, Yu applied these Western concepts to contemporary Chinese political values.

For Yu, the basis of good governance is cooperation between the public and the government, with the aim of maximizing public interest in the process of societal management. This does not mean that conflict should be prohibited, but rather that both sides should be willing to negotiate and compromise. Changes in state-society relations will naturally put greater pressure on the government, which needs to constantly adjust its policies to meet the demands of an ever-changing society. Yu lists ten basic components of good governance: legitimacy, transparency, efficiency, stability, responsibility, responsiveness, rule of law, justice, participation, and honesty.

Yu's research has also contributed a great deal to effecting good governance in central-local relations. To help local officials improve their leadership skills and search for local government reforms and innovations, Yu initiated the program of China Local Government Innovation Awards, which is jointly administered by the Central Compilation and Translation Bureau, the Central Party School, and Peking University. Through the first three rounds of competition, more than 1,100 local governments submitted applications, and forty awards were bestowed. In this regard, Yu is not only a thinker but also a doer.

It should be noted that several leading public intellectuals in Yu's generation who once had the dual identity of scholar-official have become full-time officials. Examples include Wang Huning, Cao Jianming, and Xia Yong. All were in their late forties or early fifties at the time of appointment, all were well-accomplished scholars in the fields of political science and law, and all had spent several years as visiting scholars at leading universities in the United States and Europe. Wang served as dean of the law school at Fudan; Cao was president of the East China University of Political Science and Law; and Xia worked as director of the Institute of Law at the Chinese Academy of Social Sciences. Until the 18th Party Congress, Wang was a member of the secretariat and director of the Central Policy Research Office of the CCP Central Committee, serving as one of the top aides to then general secretary Hu Jintao; Cao is procurator general of the Supreme People's Procuratorate; and Xia held the position of director of the Central Bureau of Secrecy of the CCP Central Committee and was later purged.[25] Their high-ranking official positions did not allow them to participate in intellectual discourse or to publish their scholarly work.

In contrast, Yu Keping has actively engaged in academic research and debate. His remarkably long list of scholarly publications from the past decade, which can be found at the end of *Democracy is a Good Thing*, shows his diverse professional interests and ardent commitment to his field of expertise. Yu is a prolific writer. His most famous works include *Liberation of Thoughts and Political Progress* (2008), *Democracy is a Good Thing* (2006), *The Institutional Environment of Chinese Civil Society* (2006), *Globalization and Sovereignty* (2004), and *Incremental Democracy and Good Governance* (2003). These widely circulated and well respected publications are transforming the Chinese view of political reforms, civil society, governance, and cultural modernization in the era of globalization.

Yu's most important contribution, however, is his endeavor to offer a roadmap for China's democratic future.

Mapping a Chinese Path to Democracy

For many political and cultural elites in present-day China, the idea of democracy probably generates more fear than hope. Fear over a democratic transition is deeply rooted in the mindset of the Chinese, who believe it could lead to one of several disastrous futures. Among the possibilities are prolonged domestic chaos (乱, *luan*), another 1989 Tiananmen-like tragedy, the loss of privilege or power on the part of the establishment, vicious political conflicts among leaders, the rise of demagogues, an anti-China conspiracy by foreign powers, the breakdown of the multiethnic nation, and the uprising of a large number of poor and resentful social groups, such as migrant laborers. From the perspective of the political establishment, China cannot afford the tensions and possible frictions generated by that fear.

In an interview with the Chinese media, Yu Keping identified three major obstacles to governmental reforms and democratic experiments in the country. First, there is no strong incentive for government officials to experiment with democratic reforms. Second, government reforms involve significant political risk, and officials worry that the current political environment has a low degree of tolerance for any mistakes. Consequently, officials are not willing to take such a risk. Third, "institutional inertia" does not encourage bold political experiments. To a large extent, political reforms involve the readjustment of interests and redistribution of power. Understandably, no institution or interest group is eager to experience heavy losses in power and privilege as a result of political reforms.[26]

In 2005, of 200 Chinese officials and scholars who were surveyed, 50 percent believed that China's economic and political reforms had been constrained by "elite groups with vested economic interests" (既得利益集团, *jide liyi jituan*).[27] A good example of how government officials and business interest groups have formed a "wicked coalition" can be found in the realm of real estate development.[28] Some Chinese observers believe that the various players associated with property development have emerged as one of the most powerful special interest groups in the present-day PRC.[29] According to Sun Liping, a sociology professor at Tsinghua University, the real estate interest group has accumulated tremendous economic and social capital since the mid-1990s.[30] The group includes not only property developers, real estate agents, bankers, and housing market speculators, but also some government officials and public intellectuals (i.e., economists and journalists) who promote and protect the interests of property developers and investors.[31] Not surprisingly, another recent survey of Chinese local officials conducted by the Central Party School showed that 90 percent of the officials were unwilling to pursue large-scale political reforms.[32]

Despite, or perhaps because of, these obstacles to political reform, Yu believes that democracy should be seen as a solution for China rather than a problem. He argues that democracy provides answers to some of the daunting challenges that China now faces. Although democracy could possibly undermine legal institutions, cause political divisions within the country, and is generally less efficient than a dictatorship because of the time required for negotiation and compromise in the policymaking process, Yu believes that it provides more political legitimacy and long-term stability than an authoritarian regime. In his view, the social and cultural changes fostered by successful economic development since 1978 have also generated political pressure to increase the autonomy of civil society. In addition, public concern about elite groups with vested economic interests, and especially public grievances over official corruption, should be seriously addressed rather than suppressed. In Yu's words, "[A]ll power must be effectively balanced; otherwise, it inevitably leads to arbitrary rule and corruption."[33]

Recognizing these obstacles has led Yu Keping to pay close attention to charting a roadmap for China's democratic development. According to Yu, a premature rush to democracy or "the unconditional promotion of democracy will bring disastrous consequences to the nation and its people."[34] Based on this line of thinking, Yu has developed three important concepts. First is the "price of democracy" (民主的代价, *minzhu de daijia*) that the country has to pay. This price is sometimes so high as to be unacceptable. "It requires the wisdom of the politicians and the people," Yu argues, "to determine how to pay the minimum political and social price in order to attain the maximum democratic effects."[35] Reducing "political and administrative costs" in China's democratic pursuits, therefore, should be the central concern. Whether or not the Chinese public will achieve strong public consensus about democracy largely depends on its calculation of these perceived costs.

The second concept that Yu has developed is "incremental democracy" (渐进民主, *jianjin minzhu*). Under the current sociopolitical circumstances, in Yu's view, China's transition to democracy should not, and will not, be achieved through radical means. Instead, it should be carried out in multiple dimensions and through an incremental process. These dimensions include: intra-party democracy, grassroots elections, administrative reforms, and the growth of civil society. Yu has particularly emphasized intraparty democracy. In his view, absent "intraparty democracy," it will be "difficult to attain democracy in China."[36] According to Yu, "if grassroots democracy means pushing forward democracy from the bottom up, intraparty democracy entails doing so from the inside out." As he describes, the focus of improving intraparty democracy "lies in the reform of intraparty election, decision-making and policymaking systems, and the system of oversight."[37]

Yu goes into great detail on why incremental democracy is the optimal strategy for Chinese political reform. He believes that gradual changes are conducive to China's own historical experiences. Democracy requires sufficient political, economic, social, and legal capital. Attaining positive improvement in all of these areas not only will quantitatively increase democratic feasibility but will also eventually result in a fundamental qualitative "breakthrough." Meanwhile, incremental political development will gain momentum when an increasingly large portion of the public benefits from socioeconomic reforms. Yu, however, does not offer a timetable for when "the democratic breakthrough" will occur.

Third, Yu has developed the notion of "dynamic stability" (动态稳定, *dongtai wending*) to characterize the CCP's new approach to dealing with sociopolitical tensions in the country. While Chinese political and cultural elites may have valid reasons for being concerned about the need for social stability, their obsession over stability may be counterproductive in the new demographic and political environment.[38] Yu refers to the Chinese authorities' traditional approach to attaining stability as a strategy for "static stability" (静态稳定, *jingtai wending*) based on "holding everything in place" (以堵为主, *yidu weizhu*).[39] Instead, Yu advocates dynamic stability based on "channeling everything into its proper place" (以疏为主, *yishu weizhu*). New mechanisms such as public hearings, opinion surveys, letter petitions, and group protests are good examples. In his words, "'dynamic stability' aims to maintain order through negotiation instead of repression."[40]

According to Yu, the Chinese authorities should negotiate with social forces and should constantly adjust policies to meet the needs of the general public in order to maintain dynamic stability. In present-day China, the CCP holds power, but power does not necessarily mean legitimate authority or good governance. With regard to dynamic stability, legitimate authority is more important than power because good governance can lead to stability, order, trust, and efficiency.[41] Yu believes that the best way to prevent social unrest or revolution is to promote good governance rather than rely on strict control.

As a whole, these three concepts — the price of democracy, incremental democracy, and dynamic stability — aim to draw a roadmap for a new phase of China's sociopolitical development. Of course, Yu Keping has not been alone in advocating for democracy in today's China. Distinguished scholars such as Jiang Ping (former president of China University of Political Science and Law), Xie Tao (former vice president of Renmin University), Zhou Ruijin (former deputy editor in chief of *People's Daily*), Li Rui (former personal secretary to Mao), Cao Siyuan (a prominent scholar in the field of bankruptcy law), He Weifang (a law professor at Zhejiang University and a leading scholar on constitutionalism in China), Liu Junning (a long-time leading advocate for political reforms), and Mao Shoulong (a professor of public administration at Renmin University) have all actively participated in the political and intellectual discourse about democracy in China.

Xie Tao, for example, has argued that the assessment of a political system should not just be a theoretical question but also a practical one, as it affects the lives of millions of Chinese people. In an article widely circulated in the Chinese media, Xie asks pointedly, "How is it possible that China's political system is a good one, when it could not prevent the national madness of the Great Leap Forward and the Cultural Revolution, and could not protect basic human rights?"[42] Some scholars, such as He Weifang and Cao Siyuan, even argue that China should make the transition from a Leninist party-state political system to a constitutional state. In that regard, their proposed democratic transition for China seems far more radical than Yu's.

Some overseas Chinese dissidents argue that Yu's democratic roadmap for China is nothing more than an empty promise to the Chinese people and the outside world. For example, Hu Ping, the author of "On Freedom of Speech," one of the first and most comprehensive papers on the democratic movement in the PRC and one that shaped intellectual discourse during the Democracy Wall Movement in Beijing in 1979, criticizes Yu for creating a "false notion" in the outside world that the CCP is interested in democracy.[43] Hu believes that any discussion of democracy that does not seriously consider a multi-party system will lead nowhere. In addition, Hu argues that Yu's proposed mechanisms for dynamic stability fundamentally differ from democratic principles such as freedom of speech and freedom of assembly.

Criticism of Yu's thesis emanates not only from those "New Right" thinkers who advocate a more radical path for China's democratic future but also from those "New Left" public intellectuals who challenge the desirability and feasibility of democracy for the country. They believe that any serious effort to move toward political democracy in China may unleash long-restrained social tensions and quickly undermine the CCP's capacity to allocate social and economic resources. Pan Wei, a Berkeley-educated political science professor at Peking University, favors legalistic political reforms instead of democratic elections and is more interested in a Singaporean-style rule of law than Western-style democracy. He bluntly criticizes what he calls "democracy worship and election obsession" among his Chinese colleagues. Pan is cynical about Yu's concept of incremental democracy. In his view, both intraparty elections and grassroots democracy are primarily "political shows."[44] Pan argues that, in a country such as China, without the rule of law, it would be a disaster to move toward democratic elections. In his words, "[T]he CCP will split if the party adopts elections; and the PRC will disintegrate if the country adopts elections."[45]

The new wave of intellectual and political discourse about China's future democracy initiated by Yu Keping and other Chinese thinkers will likely continue in the years to come. This wave can probably best be characterized as an attempt to make democracy safe for China. Each reader can make his or her own judgment about the significance and implications of this Chinese intellectual discourse about democracy. It is reasonable to assume, however, that ideas matter in China, as well as elsewhere in the world. As an emerging economic power, China is searching for its new international image and core political values. The information and insights that Yu presents in *Democracy is a Good Thing* may not only reveal Chinese perspectives, anxieties, and dilemmas but could also be indicative of the future political trajectory of the country.

Notes

This chapter is an edited version of the introduction to the Yu Keping volume of the Thornton Center Chinese Thinkers Series, published by the Brookings Institution Press. See Cheng Li, "Introduction: Making Democracy Safe for China," in Yu Keping, *Democracy is a Good Thing: Essays on Politics, Society, and Culture in Contemporary China* (Washington, DC: Brookings Institution Press, 2009), xvii–xxxi. The author thanks Zach Balin, Elizabeth Brooks, Sally Carman, Ryan McElveen, Robert O'Brien, and Lucy Xu for their very helpful comments on earlier versions of this chapter.

1 Richard Madsen, "China in the American Imagination," *Dissent* (Winter 1998): 54.
2 President Woodrow Wilson used these words in his appeal to the U.S. Congress on February 3, 1917, to ratify his call for a declaration of war on Germany.
3 For a representative work in this school of thought, see James Mann, *The China Fantasy: Why Capitalism Will Not Bring Democracy to China* (New York: Penguin, 2008). An earlier, hardcover version is entitled *The China Fantasy: How Our Leaders Explain Away Chinese Repression* (New York: Viking, 2007).
4 David Shambaugh, "Let a Thousand Democracies Bloom," *International Herald Tribune*, July 6, 2007.
5 Tang Shiping, "Coming Intellectual Power," *China Security*, Vol. 4, No. 2 (Spring 2008): 14–15.

6   Yu, *Democracy is a Good Thing*, Chapter 1.

7   Yu Keping, "Minzhu shige haodongxi" [Democracy Is a Good Thing], in *Minzhu shige haodongxi,* edited by Yan Jian (Beijing: Shehui kexue wenxian chubanshe, 2006).

8   See www.chinanews.com.cn/gn/news/2008/01-01/1120420.shtml (August 20, 2008).

9   *Nanfang Zhoumo* [Southern Weekend], December 12, 2007, 1; and *Nanfang Dushi Bao* [Southern Metropolis Daily], July 7, 2008, 7.

10 For a more comprehensive discussion of Yu's ideas about the democratic transition in China, see Yu Keping, *Zengliang minzhu yu shanzhi* [Incremental Democracy and Good Governance] (Beijing: Shehui kexue wenxian chuban- she, 2003); and Yu Keping, *Zhongguo gongmin shehui de xingqi yu zhili de bianqian* [The Emergence of Civil Society and Its Significance for Governance in Reform China] (Beijing: Shehui kexue wenxian chubanshe, 2002).

11 See www.hi.chinanews.com.cn/hnnew/2005-10-20/29705.html (August 20, 2008).

12 Yu, *Democracy is a Good Thing*, Chapter 8.

13 This discussion of Wen's meeting with the Brookings Institution delegation is based on John L. Thornton, "Assessing the Next Phase of a Rising China," memo, December 2006, en.chinaelections.org/newsinfo.asp?newsid=14914; and "Riding the Dragon: Brookings Launches New Center with a Journey Across China," November 2007; as well as this author's notes.

14 For Wen's detailed remarks and more discussion of the definition of democ- racy, see Cheng Li, "Introduction: Assessing China's Political Development," in *China's Changing Political Landscape: Prospects for Democracy*, edited by Cheng Li (Washington, DC: Brookings Institution Press, 2008), 1–21.

15 Xie Maoshi, "Minzhu bushige huaidongxi" [Democracy Is Not a Bad Thing], *Zhongguo jingji shibao* [China Economic Times], January 15, 2007, 4.

16 For Shi Tianjian's comments on Yu's argument about democracy, see www. westca.com/Forums/viewtopic/t=105658/lang=schinese.html (August 20, 2008).

17 See, for example, the popular China Elections and Governance website, www.chinaelections.org/NewsInfo.asp?NewsID=100984 (August 20, 2008).

18 For more discussion of the role of the CCTB, see www.cctb.net/wjjj/2003103 00001.htm (August 20, 2008).

19 In Zheng Bijian's view, the theory of China's peaceful rise not only means that the country will become a major economic and cultural player in the world, but also requires a list of "won'ts" — China won't launch war to plunder the resources of other countries, won't export ideology, won't export economic development models to other countries, won't pursue an industrial

development strategy that consumes a large amount of unsustainable resources, won't challenge the existing order of the international system, won't engage in large-scale emigration, and won't establish colonies overseas. For a more detailed discussion, see Zheng Bijian, *China's Peaceful Rise: Speeches of Zheng Bijian, 1997–2005* (Washington, DC: Brookings Institution Press, 2005).

20 For a more detailed discussion of the collective characteristics, see John Pomfret, *Chinese Lessons: Five Classmates and the Story of the New China* (New York: Henry Holt and Company, 2006); and Cheng Li, "China's Fifth Generation: Is Diversity a Source of Strength or Weakness?" *Asia Policy,* No. 6 (July 2008): 53–93.

21 The other is Wang Puqu, presently vice president of the Macao Polytechnic Institute.

22 *Nanfang zhoumo,* December 27, 2007, 8.

23 This discussion is based on the laudation that was delivered by Professor Thomas Heberer at the honorary degree ceremony at the University of Duisburg-Essen on May 20, 2008, www.uni-duisburg-essen.de/oapol/Aktuelles_mit_en.shtml.

24 *Nanfang zhoumo,* December 27, 2007, 8.

25 Xia Yong was purged in July 2016 for a "serious violation of party regulations."

26 Shu Taifeng, "Yu Keping: Zhengfu chuangxin xuyao gengduo de kuanrong" [Yu Keping: Government Innovations Require Greater Tolerance], *Dongfang liaowang zhoukan* [Oriental Outlook Weekly], April 8, 2008.

27 China's Reform Institute (Hainan) conducted this survey. See chinanews.com, January 19, 2006.

28 *Zhongguo xinwen zhoukan* [China Newsweek], January 13, 2006; *Liaowang* [Outlook], December 5, 2005; and www.chinesenewsnet.com, December 12, 2005.

29 The other powerful interest groups include monopoly industries such as telecommunications, oil, electricity, and automotive, all of which have a huge stake in government policies. See Sun Liping, "Zhongguo jinru liyi boyi de shidai" [China Is Entering the Era of a Conflict of Interests], February 6, 2006, www.chinesenewsnet.com.

30 Sun, "Zhongguo jinru liyi boyi de shidai."

31 Jin Sanyong, "Zhongyang difang cunzai mingxian boyi" [The Open Game that the Central and Local Governments Play], February 10, 2006, www.zisi.net.

32 *Shijie Ribao* [World Journal], December 25, 2006, A3. Originally in *Beijing Ribao* [Beijing Daily], December 18, 2006.

33 Yu, *Democracy is a Good Thing*, Chapter 3.

34 Yu, *Democracy is a Good Thing*, Chapter 1.

35 Ibid.

36 Yu, *Democracy is a Good Thing*, Chapter 3.

37 Ibid.

38 Yu, *Democracy is a Good Thing*, Chapter 6.

39 This is based on Yu Keping, "Ideological Change and Incremental Democracy in Reform-Era China," in *China's Changing Political Landscape*, edited by Cheng Li, 54–55.

40 Ibid.

41 For a more detailed discussion of Yu's argument about dynamic stability, see "Dongtai wending yu hexie shehui" [Dynamic Stability and Harmonious Society], *Zhongguo tese shehuizhuyi yanjiu* [Studies on Socialism with Chinese Characteristics], No. 3 (2006): 25–28.

42 Xie Tao, "Zhiyou minzhu shehuizhuyi caineng jiu Zhongguo" [Only Democratic Socialism Can Save China], August 20, 2008, www.chinaelections.org/NewsInfo.asp?NewsID=100318; also see Xie Tao, "Minzhu shehuizhuyi moshi yu Zhongguo de qiantu" [The Model of Democratic Socialism and the Prospects of China], *Yanhuang chunqiu* [Chinese History], No. 2 (2007).

43 Hu Ping, "Yu Keping fangmei jianghua xiaoyi" [Comments on Yu Keping's Speeches in the United States]. See hk.epochtimes.com/7/4/20/43430.htm, April 20, 2007.

44 See pkunews.pku.edu.cn/zdlm/2008-03/27/content_120756.htm, March 27, 2008.

45 The quote is from www.chinesenewsnet.com, April 25, 2006. For more discussion of Pan Wei's criticism of democratic worship and election obsession, see Pan Wei, "Toward a Consultative Rule of Law Regime in China," *Journal of Contemporary China*, Vol. 12, No. 34 (February 2003): 3–43; and also *Debating Political Reform in China: Rule of Law vs. Democratization*, edited by Suisheng Zhao (New York: M. E. Sharpe, 2006). It should be noted that criticism of Yu's thesis also comes from the "Old Left" scholars, in addition to the "New Right" and "New Left." According to the Old Left scholars, Yu's view on democracy not only advocates Western liberal theory but also attempts to overthrow the Chinese Communist Party. See, for example, Cheng Mengyun, "Bo Minzhu shige haodongxi" [Refuting Yu's "Democracy Is a Good Thing"], January 6, 2007, www.zaobao.com/special/forum.pages5/forum_1x070106.html.

Chapter 4

He Weifang (Legal Scholar): Fighting for a Constitutional China through Public Enlightenment and Legal Professionalism

We are here not because we are law-breakers; we are here in our efforts to become law-makers.

— Emmeline Pankhurst, leader of the British suffragette movement

The right rulings make a country great because the event is seen by all.

— Stephen Breyer, Associate Justice, U.S. Supreme Court

One evening in the fall of 2011, almost five months before the dramatic downfall of heavyweight political leader Bo Xilai, I sat in an auditorium at the Law School of Peking University listening to a panel discussion on China's judicial reforms.[1] The Beida Law Society, a student organization on campus, sponsored this public forum featuring He Weifang and Xu Xin, two distinguished law professors in Beijing.[2] The auditorium was crowded with several hundred people (mainly students and young faculty members but also some Chinese journalists). As I listened to this engaging and enlightening discussion, it occurred to me that I was witnessing a profound political movement for constitutionalism unfolding in the PRC.

What struck me — and shocked me as a foreign visitor — was not only that the entire discussion was explicitly critical of the CCP for its resistance to any meaningful judicial reform but also that the atmosphere was calm, reasonable, and marked by a sense of humor and sophistication in the expression of ideas. Both professors criticized the CCP's omnipresent role in the country's legal system, especially in regard to the infinite power of the Central Commission of Politics and Law (CCPL) of the CCP.[3] In the words of He Weifang, many recent well-known cases of injustice were largely due to the "invisible hand" of the CCPL. Both speakers called for a fundamental change in the role and presence of the CCPL, including the abolition of the politics and law commissions at all subnational levels.

As part of China's overall political reforms, He and Xu proposed prioritizing judicial reforms, with a focus on judicial independence. They argued that judicial reforms align with the need for social stability and thus should be considered the least disruptive way to ease China's much-needed political transformation. They outlined several important systematic changes for China's legal system:

- transferring the leadership of judicial reforms from the CCPL to the NPC in the form of a yet-to-be-established judicial reform committee, one in which legal scholars, lawyers, and representatives of non-governmental organizations would constitute more than half of the members;
- adjusting the role of the CCP from appointing presidents of courts and chief prosecutors to only nominating them (an independent selection committee, rather than the party organization department, would make these appointments);
- prohibiting interference by the CCP in any legal cases, especially by prohibiting judges from being CCP members and banning party organizations within law firms;
- reducing the power of both presidents of courts and chief prosecutors in order to enhance procedural justice; and
- establishing a constitutional review system, including a new constitutional committee and constitutional court.

In addition, Professor Xu presented a comprehensive plan for establishing a protection and guarantee system. He specifically addressed important issues such as how to ensure budget security for an independent judicial system; how to provide job security for legal professionals; how to prevent corruption and other power abuses in law enforcement; how the rule of law can ensure citizens' democratic rights, including through the development of the jury system; and how to protect the legal rights of vulnerable social groups.

The panel discussion was also politically and intellectually stimulating thanks to an interactive session with the audience that covered a broad range of questions from students. One attendee asked, "If judicial reform is the lowest-risk approach for China's political transformation, where does the strongest resistance come from?" Professor Xu responded bluntly, "The strongest resistance comes from the CCP leadership, and this is most evident in senior leader Wu Bangguo's recent statement widely proclaiming the 'five no's' for China."[4]

Another audience member opined, "Wasn't it a wise decision on the part of the former Libyan justice minister Mustafa Abdul Jalil to denounce the Libyan leader Muammar Gaddafi before the collapse of the regime?" Professor He did not directly answer this intriguing question but instead shared the story of Qing dynasty minister (ambassador) to the United States Wu Tingfang, a British- and U.S.-educated lawyer who decided to support Sun Yat-sen's 1911 Revolution because, as He said somewhat jokingly, "Wu wisely stated that 'the Qing dynasty cannot be saved (清朝没救了, *Qingchao meijiule*).'"

Still another attendee wanted to know, "What's the incentive for the CCP and powerful special interest groups to pursue judicial reform that may very well undermine their own power and interests?" Professor He replied, "It's the result of a domino effect — a natural and inevitable consequence of the fundamental change of state-society relations in China. From the perspective of CCP leaders, some may want to be remembered in history as having been on the right side."

This episode of openness and pluralism in intellectual and political discourse, though eye-opening and surprising for foreign observers like me, is by no means unique in present-day China. In recent years an increasing number of well-known professors and opinion leaders have shown that they are not afraid of publicly expressing their controversial views, including sharp criticism of CCP authorities. Such remarks would have been considered politically taboo or even "unlawful" just a few years ago. Never before in the six-decade history of the PRC has the Chinese general public, and especially the rapidly growing legal community, expressed such serious concerns about the need to restrain the power of the CCP and to create a much more independent judicial system.

Like He Weifang and Xu Xin, many other prominent legal scholars in the country frequently give public lectures and panel discussions on similar topics, with many of these events being webcast on the Chinese Internet.[5] In November 2010, for example, the death of the distinguished constitutional scholar Cai Dingjian led to year-long nationwide memorial activities honoring his advocacy for the rule of law in China.[6] Cai's last words, "Constitutional democracy is the mission of our generation," were widely cited in both the country's official media and social media.[7]

These examples do not necessarily mean that Chinese authorities have loosened their control of the legal profession. On the contrary, liberal legal scholars and human rights lawyers are often among the main targets for harsh treatment, including imprisonment. Yet the movement for rule of law in the country seems to have already reached a moral and political high ground. It gained further momentum in the wake of crises such as the defection of former Chongqing police chief Wang Lijun to the U.S. consulate in Chengdu, the downfall of Politburo member Bo Xilai and the subsequent murder charge against his wife, and graphic tales told by blind human rights activist Chen Guangcheng of torture and other abuses of power by Chinese law enforcement. Both the frequent manifestations of social unrest and the growing transparency of factional infighting in the CCP leadership in recent years further underscore the urgency of developing a credible legal system.

He Weifang and China's Legal Development: Objectives of *In the Name of Justice*

In the Name of Justice is a collection of the English translations of He Weifang's representative work from 2001 to 2011. He Weifang has been at the forefront of the country's bumpy path toward justice and judicial independence for well over a decade. A proponent of reform over revolution, He's political and professional endeavors have largely paralleled the painstaking quest for rule of law in China during this crucial period of sociopolitical transformation. *In the Name of Justice* examines some of the most important topics in China's legal development, including judicial independence, judicial review, legal education, the professionalization of lawyers and the selection of judges, capital punishment, and the legal protection of free speech, religious freedom, and human rights. In the volume, He also offers a historical review of Chinese traditional legal thought, enhanced by cross-country comparisons.

Though maintaining his characteristically optimistic personality, He is also keenly aware of the political, institutional, and cultural barriers to genuine constitutional development in China. To promote constitutional governance in a culture that lacks a strong legal tradition — and in a political system that is largely lawless — is an overwhelming task. It requires the country's legal scholars and other professionals, as a group, to be fully engaged in educating and enlightening the public (and elites, as well) rather than merely pursuing academic and judicial research. Not surprisingly, Professor He is highly regarded in the Chinese legal world for his dual roles as a practitioner and a thinker, as an advocate and a scholar. In addition to presenting a selection of He's important academic writings, *In the Name of Justice* also includes some of his public speeches, media interviews, and open letters, providing comprehensive and accurate accounts of his distinctively broader role as a public intellectual, as opposed to a more narrowly focused, "ivory tower" scholar of legal studies.

In 2011 the U.S.-based *Foreign Policy* magazine appropriately recognized He Weifang as one of the top 100 global thinkers.[8] The English-speaking world, including the China studies community in the West, however, remains mostly unfamiliar with He's scholarly writings and personal efforts to guide China's legal development, reflecting a serious discrepancy in our understanding of the intellectual and policy discourse in this rapidly changing country.

This chapter presents the personal and professional background of He Weifang, the intellectual and political contexts essential to understanding his pursuits, and the legal and policy debates that his work has stimulated. This discussion can help readers grasp He Weifang's extraordinary contributions in the domains of public enlightenment and legal professionalism.

Understanding He Weifang and his remarkable endeavors is critical because, of all the issues sparked by China's ongoing economic and sociopolitical transformation, the development of the Chinese legal system is arguably the most consequential. The paradoxical trends of growing public demand for rule of law, on the one hand, and continued party interference in legal affairs, on the other, present an intriguing political phenomenon. How this battle unfolds carries strong implications for the country's social stability, economic development, and political trajectory; and its ramifications extend far beyond China's national borders. He's political and intellectual journey is a fascinating story of one man's courageous fight to promote justice within the world's largest authoritarian regime. His story enriches our more general understanding of the pluralistic and dynamic nature of present-day China. Moreover, He's ideas, as collected in *In the Name of Justice*, provide invaluable insights and well-grounded assessments of the prospects for constitutionalism in China.

Public Enlightenment: Views, Values, and Courage

To better understand He Weifang's views, values, and courage, one needs to know something about the broader intellectual enlightenment movement in China. Public enlightenment (启蒙, *qimeng*) has been an enduring aspiration of Chinese intellectuals in contemporary China. Over the past century, major sociopolitical crises at home, which were usually accompanied by strong ideological influences from abroad, often led forward-looking Chinese intellectuals to develop new ideas, views, and values in order to "wake up" the public and the nation. The May Fourth Movement in 1919, occurring in the wake of the collapse of the Qing dynasty, was a turning point in China's modern history and marked the first enlightenment movement in the Middle Kingdom. Hu Shih, one of the most prominent intellectual participants in the movement, characterized it as the "Chinese Renaissance" for the embrace of foreign ideas regarding science and experimentation.[9]

The Chinese intellectual ferment in the post-Mao era from the late 1970s to the late 1980s, especially the critical reflection on the decade-long political fanaticism and human suffering of the Cultural Revolution and the subsequent call for humanism, was often seen as the second enlightenment movement. In a sense, the post-Mao enlightenment was a strong wave of intellectual and public awakening that fulfilled the unaccomplished tasks of the May Fourth Movement.[10] Unfortunately, this second enlightenment ended tragically with the 1989 Tiananmen Square incident.

Toward a Third Enlightenment Movement in Contemporary China?

In recent years, a third wave of public enlightenment has arguably been emerging — even despite the tight control that the Chinese authorities have maintained, particularly over the media. A third enlightenment is the subject of a recent volume, *The Enlightenment and Transformation of Chinese Society*, edited by Zi Zhongyun, a distinguished scholar and former director of the Institute of American Studies at the CASS. In the book Zi pointedly asks, "Why do we need a 'new enlightenment' now?"[11] The answer lies, as she and other contributors describe, in the growing tension between rapid socioeconomic transformation and the stagnation of political reforms, between China's economic rise on the world stage and the party's ideological stance that resists universal values, and between revolutionary changes in telecommunication and the government's strict media censorship.[12]

In Zi's view, China needs a new enlightenment because of what she calls "obscurantism" (蒙昧主义, *mengmei zhuyi*), which refers to the efforts of officials opposed to democratic change.[13] These officials and some conservative public intellectuals, as Zi describes, have spread the false notion that democracy is not suitable for the Chinese people and that universal values are nothing but a Western conspiracy against China. She particularly warns against the danger of nationalism, which inspires a tendency to perpetuate social injustices in the name of state interests.[14]

According to PRC liberal intellectuals, enlightenment means that people are liberated from obscurantism and ignorance, from having blind faith in myths or in a dictator. One important aspect of the post-Cultural Revolution enlightenment movement was its strong critique of — and break from — the shadow of Mao worship.[15] What has been highly disturbing in recent years, in the view of Chinese liberal critics, is the fact that Mao worship and myths about the "glorious" Cultural Revolution have resurged in the country — most noticeably in Chongqing under Bo Xilai, who himself, many liberal critics believe, was very much a Mao-like figure in terms of the personality cult that surrounded him.[16]

Under these political and ideological circumstances, Chinese liberal intellectuals have begun mobilizing for a new wave of enlightenment. The overarching theme of this latest and ongoing intellectual ferment, some prominent Chinese scholars observe, is rule of law and constitutionalism. According to Xu Youyu, a distinguished scholar at the Institute of Philosophy at the CASS, the enlightenment movement in the post-Mao era was heavily engaged in the philosophical discussion of humanism. By contrast, in this latest enlightenment movement Chinese public intellectuals are more interested in discussing law-related issues, including "rule of law, the protection of individual rights, and limiting the scope of authority and restraining the power of the government."[17] In Xu's words, Chinese liberal intellectuals seem to have highlighted "constitutional democracy" as their overall programmatic concept.[18] Along the same line of thinking, Wei Sen, a professor of economics at Fudan University, believes that enhancing the awareness of the constitutionally granted rights of taxpayers is "a top priority for the 'new enlightenment.'"[19]

He Weifang's views are similar to those of Zi Zhongyun, Xu Youyu, and Wei Sen. As He argues forcefully in *In the Name of Justice*, "[C]onstitutionalism and the rule of law are the best safeguards of liberty and the foundation of good governance in China."[20] He believes that "a rigorous system of auditing tax revenues, fiscal budgets, and government spending ... is a very important manifestation of constitutional government" in democracies.[21] Early in his career, He recognized the daunting challenges confronting China's legal scholars. His LL.M. thesis in 1985 examines religious influences in the development of law in the West.[22] As He observes, the religious sentiment in the Western tradition that "everyone is equal before God" is what laid the cultural foundation for the legal consciousness — namely, that "everyone is equal before the law."[23] China has apparently lacked such a cultural foundation for the profoundly important notion of rule of law.

In his 1994 article on the comparative study of legal cultures, He Weifang describes the enormous difficulty of, and outlines various effective approaches to, transplanting the Western legal system in different cultural environments such as China:

No legal system can be transplanted to another cultural circumstance without itself undergoing change, and that system cannot play the same role as it did in its original circumstance. Legal transplantation might be considered a two-way development. On one hand, foreign legal systems and ideas transform the native culture; on the other hand, they are themselves altered by the influence of that culture. During this process, some systems or ideas will be rejected because of sharp conflicts with native traditions; some will partly revise the native culture, establishing a new system different from both the system in its original place and the culture before transplantation; and lastly some systems and ideas may be absorbed by the native tradition completely. This can lead to the curious position where a transplant can even be believed to be an essential part of the native culture and defended as such by nationalists.[24]

He firmly believes that a "successful mixture of different legal cultures requires profound study of the foreign and native cultures."[25] In practice, He has long been committed to disseminating scholarly research to a much broader audience and to fully participating in the latest wave of the public enlightenment movement, especially the spreading of Western views of constitutionalism and what he believes to be the universal value of rule of law. Tellingly, He's life experience and intellectual journey personify the nation's arduous struggle to make the rule of law more than just official lip service and more than just documents in libraries; He wants them to be legally binding and publicly recognized norms and practices. For He, the implementation of rule of law and the coordination of judicial reforms through public discourse can be as important as the making of laws itself.

The He Weifang Phenomenon: A Legal Scholar's Public Outreach

A native of Shandong Province's Muping County (located between Yantai City and Weihai City), He Weifang was born on July 17, 1960. He's father, a doctor in the People's Liberation Army (PLA), was demobilized to work in a civilian hospital when He was three years old. In the midst of the Cultural Revolution, his mother brought ten-year-old He and two of his siblings back to their native village of Jianggezhuang (comprising about 800 households) in Muping County.[26] He obtained most of his elementary and middle school education at schools in that village. When the PRC resumed its higher education entrance examinations in 1977, He took the exams but failed to be accepted as he scored only 4 out of 100 points on the mathematics test. He took the exams again the following year and was accepted. Although he chose the Department of Chinese Literature at Shandong Normal College as his preferred program, he was instead admitted to the newly reestablished law program at the Southwest College of Political Science and Law in Chongqing, a school he "had never heard of before."[27]

During his college years, from 1978 to 1982, He was primarily interested in two broad subjects. The first was the "national madness of the decade-long Cultural Revolution," which was most notable for its political persecution, torture, and human suffering. To legally and judicially prevent such a tragedy from recurring was a main concern for this young law school student.[28] This concern naturally led him to develop, especially in his junior year, a strong interest in a second broad subject: the "ideas of the European Age of Enlightenment." He became absorbed in reading the classic works of Rousseau, Voltaire, Locke, Montesquieu, and Milton. At a time when books on law and the Western legal system were extremely rare in China, the writings of these great Western philosophers were enormously helpful to He's educational development.

As a law student, He conducted intensive research on church-state relations in medieval Europe. He wrote his undergraduate thesis on Catholic canon law and the role of religion in legal and judicial development in European states — a subject that he continued to focus on in his graduate studies under the supervision of Professor Pan Huafang at China University of Political Science and Law (CUPSL) from 1982 to 1985.[29] After receiving a master's degree, He remained at CUPSL as an instructor and research fellow at the Institute of Comparative Law. He was promoted to associate professor of law in 1992. He helped establish *Comparative Law* (比较法研究, *bijiaofa yanjiu*), the PRC's first scholarly journal on comparative law, and served as deputy editor of this quarterly Chinese publication. For almost a decade, He also served as editor-in-chief of *Peking University Law Journal*, a prominent journal in China that covers both foreign and Chinese legal issues.

In the early 1990s, in collaboration with several other young legal scholars, He engaged in a number of major translations of textbooks on Western legal thought and systems.[30] He also served as editor of *Constitutionalism Studies* (宪政译丛, *xianzheng yicong*), a translation series published by SDX Joint Publishing Company. He's instrumental role in translating important English language legal books into Chinese and his editorship of the journal *Comparative Law* greatly contributed to the dissemination of Western legal thought among Chinese law school students and the newly emerging community of legal professionals in the country. As He described, the Western legal system and intellectual evolution can serve as a mirror, reflecting some of the characteristics of Chinese legal development.[31]

In 1995, after working at CUPSL for a decade, He moved to Peking University, where he served as an associate professor of law. His main faculty responsibility thus changed from research to teaching. Four years later, he was promoted to full professor. He has always been a popular professor on campus, even being named one of the "Top Ten Teachers" of Peking University Law School for three consecutive years (1998–2000) and designated the best teacher in the entire university in 2000.

Like many of his law school colleagues of the same generation, He had the opportunity to study in Western countries as a visiting scholar. In 1993 he participated in a two-month program on research techniques in social sciences at the University of Michigan in Ann Arbor. He was a visiting scholar at the East Asian Legal Studies program at Harvard University from July 1996 to January 1997. In addition, over the last two decades, He has frequently visited the United States, Japan, and European countries, giving lectures, participating in academic conferences, and attending court hearings. An admirer of American democracy, He has explicitly expressed reservations about the notion of "moneyocracy," the term that many critics in China and elsewhere use to characterize the U.S. political system. He observes, for example, "If a [Chinese] company can spend RMB 400 million to advertise a liquor product, it is really not so big a deal for Americans to spend $240 million to elect a president who will hold the position for four years or even eight years."[32]

Firsthand experience overseas, especially extensive professional exchanges with foreign legal scholars, have not only enriched He's thinking on legal issues but also broadened his perspective in his efforts to promote the rule of law in China. He believes that China is in the midst of a crucial historical transition that needs many "Chinese Madisons" and "Chinese Hamiltons" to guide the country along the right track to constitutional development. He was profoundly inspired by his role model, Hu Shih, the aforementioned leading figure in the May Fourth Movement, a legendary figure in contemporary China. He's reference to these intellectual and political giants in both the West and China reflects his outlook on China's future political transformation rather than his own personal ambition. As He expressed in a number of interviews, "I will never be able to approximate the same level of Hu Shih's academic excellence, dedication to China's embrace of the modern world, and sense of how to maintain appropriate scholarly distance from political events."[33]

Fang Zhouzi, a well-known critic in the Chinese media, has criticized He Weifang for his lack of productivity in academic work and for his "trivial role" in legal scholarship. For Fang, He's contribution has not extended beyond a mere promotion of "legal literacy" (法律普及, *falü puji*) in China. In Fang's judgment, He is not qualified to be a law professor at Peking University. Fang's criticisms of He, however, have elicited a strong backlash on Chinese online message boards.[34] Tong Zongjin, an associate professor at CUPSL, has used the fact that He's scholarly publications have frequently been cited by distinguished law professors in the United States to reject Fang's critique. Yuan Weishi, a well-respected Chinese historian, has also vigorously defended He's contributions from a broader perspective. According to Yuan, He has helped shape legal development in China through his instrumental role in public enlightenment *vis-à-vis* the concepts of civil society and judicial independence. In Yuan's words, "The impact of one powerful open letter or one profound public speech can be far more valuable than that of one hundred academic essays combined."[35]

He has the ability to write so powerfully and speak so profoundly because he can draw from his scholarly work on comparative law and longstanding stance on the importance of legal professionalism. Having remained in close contact with China's rapidly changing society, He has, on a number of important occasions, played a distinct role in either voicing vigorous dissent or winning a landmark battle in the name of justice. Thus the Chinese phrase "He Weifang phenomenon" first came into popularity several years ago, as a way to reference the keen desire of public intellectuals to participate in political and policy discourse, as well as the strong impact liberal legal scholars can have on public thinking and social norms.[36]

He Weifang himself has stated that he aims to serve as "a public speaker promoting basic judicial concepts."[37] In every year since 1998, he has delivered or participated in about thirty to fifty public lectures or panel discussions on college campuses (not including the institutions where he has taught) and with local governments, non-governmental organizations, and legal institutions (such as courts) throughout the country.[38] In some of his public speeches at colleges, students have waited outside lecture halls for three to four hours in order to get a seat, with many having to sit on the floor.[39]

In addition to public lectures, He has been known for his public outreach through social media. Between 2006 and 2008, for example, He's blogs had a total of 3.7 million hits.[40] By the summer of 2012, his blog on sina.com had a total of 16 million hits.[41] Unlike most of his colleagues in China's law schools who usually devote their time to academic research and writing, He has frequently written for popular magazines and has been interviewed by a variety of media outlets. Altogether, He has tendered several hundred nonacademic articles and media interviews over the last dozen or so years.

In 2001 He was selected by *China Youth*, a popular magazine in the PRC, as one of the top 100 young people likely to shape China in the 21st century.[42] Within two years he had already begun to leave important marks on China's legal development. In 2003, for instance, in the wake of the tragic death of twenty-seven-year-old migrant worker Sun Zhigang, He and five other legal scholars in Beijing submitted a request to the Standing Committee of the NPC, asking that the "Regulation for Internment and Deportation of Urban Vagrants," adopted by the Chinese government in 1982, be deemed unconstitutional. The news of the request circulated widely throughout the country. Within a month, Premier Wen Jiabao announced the abolition of the regulation, bringing to an end two decades of legal discrimination against migrants.[43]

He's provocative remarks at the famous New Western Hills Symposium in 2006, including his assertion that China's party-state structure is "a serious violation of the constitution and law" because it exempts itself from constitutional controls and proper registration as a legal entity, are considered the strongest critique of the CCP party-state in PRC history.[44] He argued that the CCP should be registered as a "corporate legal person" (社团法人, *shetuan faren*), as otherwise the existence of the CCP itself is unconstitutional. He believes that the party should have its own bank account and the party and state should have separate coffers. The salaries of CCP leaders also should not come from state coffers, which is based on the incomes of vast number of taxpayers in the country, but instead should come from party membership dues. In the symposium, He also proposed that the PRC make a political transition on two fronts. The first would be to make a constitutional move to strip the CCP of its control of the PLA, thus transforming the party army into the state army. The second would be to divide the CCP into two rival factions with a new mechanism of checks and balances within the party, eventually leading to a multi-party political system similar to that in democratic Taiwan.

In the later days of President Hu Jintao's rule, He took a critical view of Hu's concept of a "harmonious society." In He's view, lawyers by profession are the products of a legal culture that respects dissent and conflict. He argued that "lawyers inherently conflict with prosecutors, with judges, and even with public opinion. Lawyers will lose their practical utility and professional purpose if a culture does not respect conflict. Genuine harmony in a given society should be based on the respect for conflict through legal process."[45]

He's voice of reason drew mainstream attention during major political events, such as the CCP's decision to close the weekly liberal media outlet *Freezing Point* in 2006;[46] the Tibetan protest for religious freedom on the eve of the Beijing Olympics in 2008;[47] the controversy over Bo Xilai's Cultural Revolution-style campaign, especially its disregard for the rule of law, in Chongqing in 2009 to 2011;[48] the call for launching a judicial review process, which He characterized as the never-woken "sleeping beauty," following the bullet train crash in Wenzhou in 2011; and Chinese public outrage over the death penalty verdict in the financial fraud case of private entrepreneur Wu Ying in 2012.[49]

A Liberal Scholar on All Fronts: Consistency and Constraints

He Weifang has been known as a vocal opponent of the death penalty for over a decade. According to PRC criminal law, a total of fifty-five crimes are punishable by death, including tax evasion, embezzlement, bribery, and drug trafficking.[50] To abolish capital punishment — and to end the long history of cruelty in China's criminal system, especially public executions — has been a recurring topic in He's public lectures.[51] As a result of the indefatigable campaign by He Weifang and other liberal-minded public figures, in 2007 the Chinese authorities decided to instruct the Supreme People's Court to review all capital punishment cases. The number of executions dropped sharply, from as many as 15,000 people annually in the 1990s to about 1,700 people in the year 2008, according to estimates by Amnesty International.[52]

In his public speeches, He constantly expresses the notion that the purpose of criminal law is not just retribution — though he certainly does not in any way advocate for cruelty and violence — but rather rehabilitation.[53] The irony, as He has pointed out, is that "while the state does not allow anyone to kill people, the state in fact executes people."[54] This manner of state behavior has an effect on the public psychology in any given country. In He's view, to the degree that the government is cruel, so is the public. He further argues that human beings cannot be without compassion and sympathy for each other. One's sympathy should extend even to criminals.[55]

He's liberal views are also evident in his comments on the sensitive issue of Taiwan and other controversial foreign policy matters. Regarding Taiwan, He believes that the mainland should respect the reality of the over sixty years of separation and existence of the Republic of China. In light of international law, the cross-strait relationship cannot be framed simply as a central government-province relationship. Taiwan has its own government, judicial system, passports, and territory. He believes that the mainland government should allow more international space for Taiwan. A truly close relationship between the mainland and Taiwan, in his view, depends upon the mainland's improvement in rule of law, human rights, democracy, and freedom.[56]

He is critical of the Chinese government's policy of supporting totalitarian regimes such as North Korea. He believes a foreign policy that supports the dictators of North Korea is akin to suppressing the democratic demands of the Korean people. He challenges the notion that China's strategic interest in the Korean Peninsula should be driven by the need for a "buffer zone." He considers this professed "need" to be the external extension of the internal policy of "stability overrides everything" (稳定压倒一切, *wending yadaoyiqie*), which means in this case that so-called stability comes at the expense of the freedom and human rights of the Korean people. He argues that today's narrow-minded "national interest" may be tomorrow's national liability or national scourge.

Following the visit of blind human rights activist Chen Guangcheng to the U.S. embassy in Beijing in the spring of 2012, He Weifang commented on his microblog that such a visit was "consensual" and that CCP authorities should not make a big deal of it by punishing Chen or condemning the U.S. government.[57] Not surprisingly, some conservative public intellectuals, such as Peking University professor Kong Qingdong, labeled He a traitor and a "running dog" of Western anti-China forces.[58] In fact, from time to time, He Weifang has expressed reservations about certain aspects of Western countries' policies toward China. He argues that Western governments and politicians should deal with China in a more responsible manner, rather than solely expressing radical views so as to cater to domestic political audiences. According to He, such domestically determined foreign policy pronouncements only "fuel nationalism in China."[59]

Largely due to He Weifang's good reputation, especially among the country's youth, the Chinese authorities have been hesitant to persecute him. But this does not necessarily mean that He is exempt from punishment or threats by CCP hardliners for his liberal views and public outreach. In a number of instances over the past decade or so, He has been subjected to tremendous political pressure and faced with the possible loss of his teaching job.

At the end of 2007, the Guanghua Law School of Zhejiang University in Hangzhou invited He Weifang to join the faculty. In July 2008, He accepted the offer and resigned from Peking University. However, as He was about to move to Hangzhou for the 2009 spring semester, the Zhejiang University administration withdrew its offer. It was widely believed that He's signing of Charter 08, a manifesto that adopted the name and style of the anti-Soviet Charter 77 issued by dissidents in

Czechoslovakia, offended the Chinese authorities.[60] Eventually, Peking University reinstated him. For the following two years, however, He was assigned to teach in Shihezi, a small city in remote Xinjiang, as part of an exchange program.

He looks back on his two years in "exile" in Xinjiang from 2009 to 2011 with resigned humor. He stated that for those two years he was following in the "footsteps of several renowned Chinese intellectuals, such as the writer Wang Meng and poet Ai Qing, who were exiled to Xinjiang during the Mao era."[61] In fact, these two years allowed him to reach out to a broader audience, both geographically and ethnically.[62] Yet when He finished his teaching assignment in Xinjiang and returned to Beijing in early 2011, he found himself in the midst of another political storm.

The Courage to Challenge Bo Xilai and Wang Lijun

Enlightenment movements — in China and elsewhere — often require political courage from those who attempt to challenge authority and power.[63] In his famous 1784 essay "What Is Enlightenment?" Immanuel Kant asserts that "hav[ing] the courage to use your own intelligence is the motto of the enlightenment."[64] Quoting the German jurist Rudolf von Jhering, He Weifang considers his professional pursuits in an authoritarian political system as a "struggle for the law."[65] The tremendous personal danger He faced in his own struggle for the law was most evident in his courageous legal and political fight against Bo Xilai and Wang Lijun before their dramatic downfalls.

Soon after Bo Xilai moved from Beijing to Chongqing, where he served as party chief starting in late 2007, this ambitious politician launched two idiosyncratic initiatives: "singing red songs" and "striking the black mafia" (唱红打黑, *changhong dahei*). For the first initiative, Bo requested that both officials and ordinary Chongqing residents sing revolutionary songs to lift their spirits. This was a way for Bo to highlight his background as a communist princeling, or member of the "red nobility," making him an ideal successor to the red regime that his father's generation established. This initiative also reflected Bo's Cultural Revolution-like mentality and behavior, with which he intended to mobilize the masses to achieve his ideological and political objectives.[66]

The second initiative was a police campaign that Bo launched in Chongqing in 2009 to arrest what he called the "gangsters of the underground mafia," who were often supported by corrupt law enforcement officials in the city. In June 2008, prior to launching this campaign, Bo transferred his protégé Wang Lijun — then police chief of Jinzhou City, Liaoning Province — to Chongqing, where Wang served as executive deputy police chief. Then, in July 2009, Wang was promoted to police chief, and in the same month Bo and Wang mobilized a total of 30,000 police officers in the city to participate in the "striking the black mafia" campaign, which led to the arrests of 5,789 people.[67] According to the *Chongqing Evening News*, Bo ordered the city's police to arrest approximately 9,000 criminals.[68] A handful of those arrested were quickly tried and executed, including Wen Qiang, the former executive deputy police chief and head of the municipal government's justice department. The execution was highly publicized across the country.

Before Bo's dramatic downfall, his ideological and political campaigns had gained considerable momentum. Five of the nine members of the Politburo Standing Committee of the CCP, China's supreme leadership body, visited Chongqing, fueling speculation that these most powerful party leaders had endorsed Bo's campaign. Meanwhile, many distinguished PRC public intellectuals made pilgrimages to Chongqing. Some left-wing intellectuals called Bo's Chongqing development model the "Thousand Days' Reform," a nod to the famous "Hundred Days' Reform" of the late Qing dynasty.[69] According to Kong Qingdong, Bo's "Chongqing model" — which was known for its tough measures in dealing with "underground mafia" on the political front, "singing red songs" on the cultural front, and the promotion of "common prosperity" on the economic front — paved the way for China's future development.[70] Wang Shaoguang, a professor of public administration at the University of Hong Kong, praised the Chongqing model of socioeconomic development as "Chinese-style socialism 3.0."[71] With his loud bravado popular not just among the Chongqing public, Bo earned the title "man of the year" in a 2009 online poll conducted by the national paper *People's Daily*.[72]

A large number of law professors and legal professionals in the country, however, expressed serious reservations about Bo's campaign from its outset.[73] He Bing, the associate dean of the law school at the China University of Political Science and Law, was among the most outspoken of the liberal intellectuals who challenged the resurgence of Mao fever and the remnants of the Cultural Revolution exemplified in Bo's campaign.[74] He Bing sarcastically questioned what the nostalgia for the Mao era espoused by Bo and other like-minded people was trying to glorify: Was it the political persecution of the Anti-Rightist campaign? The economic catastrophe that resulted from the Great Leap Forward? Or perhaps the sociopolitical chaos of the Cultural Revolution?

He Weifang, too, was deeply troubled by the Cultural Revolution-era nostalgia held by some in the country. Strongly believing that the Chinese nation should deeply reflect on the tragedy of the Cultural Revolution, He once poignantly reminded his countrymen that the famous writer Ba Jin's appeal for the establishment of a Cultural Revolution museum was sadly ignored. For the education of future generations, He went on to argue, "The Chinese should do as the Germans have done: establish something like a monument for Jews who died in the Nazi era."[75]

Equally important, He pointed out, was the troubling way in which Bo Xilai and Wang Lijun dealt with crimes and the underground mafia in Chongqing. He referenced the Nazis when making critical remarks about the ideological and police campaigns to the Chinese media in May 2011:

> I believe that the attempt to purify society through draconian methods was the idea of the Nazis. The mafia was a century-long problem for Italy. But under the rule of Benito Mussolini, it was effectively controlled, and the public was very happy. Many dictators in fact began their iron-fisted rule in the name of social justice, doing things that pleased the public. But consequently, liberty and independent intellectuals were soon in jeopardy.[76]

The Li Zhuang Case: Defending Lawyers' Rights

The direct confrontation between law enforcement in Chongqing, led by Bo Xilai and Wang Lijun, and liberal legal scholars, represented by people like He Weifang and He Bing, came to a head in the Li Zhuang case — arguably the most important trial of the PRC in the past three decades.[77]

This was a case that He Weifang warned could set "China's legal reform back thirty years."[78]

The case, however, turned into a big victory for the Chinese legal professional community. With its twists and turns and its far-reaching impact, the case constitutes a telling story about the effects of the enlightenment movement. For He, although the episode reveals the sad reality of political interference in legal affairs in the country, it also shows "the glimmer of the rule of law in China."[79]

Li Zhuang was a lawyer at the Beijing-based Kangda law firm. In November 2009, Li was commissioned by the relatives of a suspect named Gong Gangmo in Chongqing to be his defense lawyer. Gong, a rich entrepreneur, was arrested during Bo's "striking the black mafia" campaign and was charged as "heading a mafia" of thirty-four people that was allegedly involved in homicide, bribery, illegal gambling, drug and gun trafficking, and other criminal activities. When Gong and other "mafia members" were arrested in June 2009, the Chongqing and national media called this prosecution "the first case of Chongqing's 'striking the black mafia' campaign."[80]

As a defense lawyer, Li Zhuang found that most of the charges lacked evidence. In addition, he found that the Chongqing police had horrifically tortured Gong and other suspects in this case. On December 10, however, a few weeks after Li took the case, his client Gong Gangmo reported to prosecutors that Li had encouraged him to fabricate his statement about police torture. The following day, Li was recalled to Beijing by his law firm and was suspended. One day later, the Chongqing police arrested Li in Beijing and took him back to Chongqing on charges of fabricating evidence.[81]

In January 2010, the court sentenced Li to a jail term of two years and six months. Li filed an appeal with the First Intermediate Court of the Chongqing Municipality. Surprisingly, during the appeal trial, Li pleaded guilty despite the fact that his defense lawyers stated that he was not guilty. When the Chongqing Intermediate Court sustained the first trial conviction and handed down a sentence of eighteen months of imprisonment, Li screamed at the court, claiming that it had not kept its promise to exempt him from a jail term. Li revealed that his guilty plea had been the result of threats and pressure from the Chongqing authorities.

The Li Zhuang imbroglio took a further twist in April 2011 when Chongqing prosecutors attempted to level new charges against Li for falsi-fying evidence in a case three years earlier. The objective of the Chongqing police, many observers believed, was to send Li back to jail again when his first prison term ended in June 2011. The Chongqing authorities' eagerness to give Li a longer jail term was widely interpreted as an effort to deny Li the opportunity to criticize Bo and Wang's campaign, which likely would have undermined Bo's chances for promotion at the 18th Party Congress in the fall of 2012. Zhu Mingyong, a defense lawyer for the "mafia," bluntly stated at the court trial that the whole case against the "Gong Gangmo mafia was false," arguing that in order to justify the campaign, "the Chongqing police used illegal methods to convert a simple homicide case and a few common criminal cases into a complicated plot of organized crime by a mafia."[82] Zhu concluded by stating explicitly, "The director of this drama is the Chongqing Public Security Bureau."[83]

The new charges the Chongqing police leveled against Li Zhuang outraged the entire Chinese legal community. It demonstrated great unity and solidarity in condemning the Chongqing authorities for undermining the rights of defense lawyers and for disregarding the legal process. In hundreds of blog posts, lawyers and law firms throughout the country expressed their support for Li, proclaiming that the case against him was "an insult and threat to China's rapidly expanding community of law-yers."[84] Chinese liberal media outlets reported extensively on develop-ments in the Li case. *Caixin* magazine, for example, criticized the fact that Li's lawyers were not allowed to "exercise their legal right to read case documents, meet their client, or investigate the case."[85] To support Li's defense, a group of prominent Chinese legal scholars formed a consulting team, which included Jiang Ping, the former president of China University of Political Science and Law; Zhang Sizhi, the founder of *Chinese Lawyers* magazine and lead defense lawyer for the "Gang of Four" trial; Professor He Weifang; Professor He Bing; and a number of well-known lawyers, such as Chen Youxi. Wei Rujiu, a member of the team, described their effort this way: "Defending Li Zhuang is defending the right to work as a lawyer in China and the ideal of justice."[86]

He Weifang's instrumental role in the Li Zhuang case cannot be over-stated.[87] Immediately after Li's arrest, He was alerted to the political motivation of the Chongqing authorities. When the official media in Chongqing and elsewhere launched a campaign of character assassination against Li before the trial, including accusations of involvement in prostitution, He expressed his dissent. He argued that questions of Li's guilt or innocence aside, the original prosecution process lacked integrity. The flaws in the legal process were abundant; for example, defense requests for the case to be transferred to a court in a city other than Chongqing were rejected, witnesses in police custody were not allowed to appear at Li's first trial, and defense lawyers were denied access to witnesses whose statements contradicted Li's. He vigorously criticized the Chongqing court for severely depriving defense lawyers of certain basic rights granted to them in criminal proceedings.

He Weifang's most important dissent was an "Open Letter to Legal Professionals in Chongqing," which he published on April 12, 2011. This letter, which serves as the prologue to *In the Name of Justice*, is a milestone in China's long journey toward judicial independence and rule of law. By July 2012, the web link to the letter had received about a quarter of a million hits, and there were over 14,000 comments on the author's blog. Additionally, hundreds of media outlets and websites also published or posted the open letter. In this letter, He highlights the destructive and unlawful nature of Bo Xilai's "striking the black mafia" campaign, including its unambiguous rejection of "independent exercise of adjudicative and prosecutorial powers" — as was specifically evident in the Li Zhuang case.[88]

Given subsequent events, He's letter has become even more important. In the letter, He directly admonishes then police chief Wang Lijun, writing that "respect for judicial independence is equally important for major power holders." He warned Wang that what happened to his predecessor Wen Qiang (who was purged and then executed) could also happen to him, because "without judicial independence no one is safe." Perhaps He's words influenced Wang's decision, ten months later, to break his patron-client ties with Bo Xilai and seek refuge in the U.S. consulate in Chengdu. This letter of remarkable foresight undoubtedly conveyed a much-needed warning to the nation about radicalism, violence, abuse of power, the rise of a demagogic dictator, and the complete retreat of justice and law.

On April 22, 2011, Chongqing prosecutors suddenly dropped the new charges against Li Zhuang, and about two months later Li was released from prison. It seems that He Weifang and China's emerging legal community won a public opinion battle on the importance of the rule of law.

Legal Professionalism: Dimensions, Priorities, and Prospects

Public enlightenment about the rule of law, though important, cannot by itself lead to constitutional governance in a given country. Ultimately, the development of an independent judicial system requires legal professionalism—another domain in which He Weifang has made great contributions. The Chinese legal community's collective efforts to defend lawyers' rights in the Li Zhuang case is testimony to the remarkable advances in legal professionalism that have occurred in post-Mao China, especially during the preceding two decades. Yet the urgency with which legal professionalism should be developed as well as the larger prospects for China's constitutional change remain topics of heated debate in the country. He Weifang's views on these issues represent the liberal perspective among PRC legal scholars. A brief review of the development of the judicial system and the coming-of-age of Chinese lawyers and judges reveals how much China's legal professional community has accomplished over the past two decades, but also how many daunting problems it still has to overcome.

Overcoming Cultural and Political Barriers: Building a Legal System from Scratch

The Chinese legal tradition is weak primarily due to what He Weifang calls the tight "integration of moral and political authority." As He observes, "Moral authority, intellectual authority, political authority, and religious authority were combined to form an insurmountable challenge to any attempt to limit the power of the sovereign in ancient China."[89] For example, He notes that Mencius, the most prominent philosopher in the Confucian school of thought who also wrote substantially on law, "consistently emphasizes filial piety and assigns it a higher value than law."[90] He believes that this explains why in China's long history the norm of "rule by virtue" (德治, *dezhi*) has consistently prevailed over other forms of governance such as rule of law (法治, *fazhi*).

During the first three decades of the PRC, legal nihilism and legal instrumentalism dominated the public view of law in the country. A good example of legal nihilism is embodied in remarks Mao made at an important CCP Politburo meeting in August 1958: "Every one of our party resolutions is law, and every meeting itself is law, and we can therefore maintain social order through resolutions and meetings."[91] The neglect of even a basic legal consciousness accounted for the fact that, from 1949 to 1978, the PRC promulgated only two laws, one being the constitution itself and the other the marriage law.

In Mao's China, law was largely seen as a tool of the ruling class to maintain its power and exercise its dictatorship. In the late 1950s and early 1960s, it was quite common for officials at various levels of the leadership to serve concurrently as public security chief, principal prosecutor, or court president.[92] Not surprisingly, prior to the late 1990s, when discussing the role of law in the country, Chinese authorities often used the phrase "to use law to rule the country" rather than "to govern the country according to the law."[93] These two phrases are fundamentally different in connotation. The former emphasizes the utility of law from the party perspective, and the latter emphasizes that no individual, group, or party should be above the law.[94] In 1996 the Institute of Law at the CASS convened a conference discussing these two Chinese phrases and concluded by adopting the second notion.[95]

Since economic reforms began in 1978, many top leaders who suffered from the lawlessness of the Cultural Revolution, such as Deng Xiaoping and Peng Zhen, former chairman of the Law Committee of the NPC, have made systematic efforts to issue important laws. Over the years, many laws have been established in China, including the criminal law and the code of criminal procedure in 1979, the general principles of civil law in 1987, the administrative procedure law in 1989, the administrative punishment law in 1996, and the property law in 2007. The promulgations of these laws, in the words of He Weifang, constitute "landmark events in China's legal development."[96]

The main motivation for the Chinese leadership to issue these laws has not been liberal legal thinking but rather self-interest, as the late Cai

Dingjian — one of the prominent drafters of some of these laws — stated, specifically referring to the CCP leadership's desire to vindicate property rights.[97] China's transition to a market economy requires more laws and regulations, without which the economy would fall into anarchy. In July 1981, the State Council established the Research Center of Economic Laws, which was responsible for drafting large-scale economic legislation. From 1979 to 1993, among the 130 laws approved by the NPC, more than half were in the areas of economic and administrative law.[98]

According to the Chinese authorities, China's legal framework was largely established by the end of 2010. This legal system includes seven main functional areas: the constitution, civil and commercial law, administrative law, economic law, social law, criminal law, and litigation and non-litigation procedural law. According to the official account, China has promulgated 239 laws in the reform era. The State Council has issued an additional 690 administrative rules and regulations, and local governments have issued about 8,600 local laws and regulations. Taken together, these developments are a substantial improvement over the legal vacuum of Mao's China.[99] Admittedly, many of these laws either have not been implemented or are insufficiently enforced, but they nonetheless represent an important foundation on which a more effective system can be built over time.

He Weifang on Lawyers and Judges: Specialized Training and Professional Standards

Nearly keeping pace with this rapid emergence of a Chinese body of law has been a burgeoning legal profession.[100] In the early years of the PRC, the country had only four colleges that specialized in politics and law.[101] Only a few universities had law departments. Moreover, these were all closed during the Cultural Revolution. In 1977, Peking University, Jilin University, and the Hubei Institute of Finance and Economics admitted law students for the first time since the Cultural Revolution, with the entire country registering only 200 law students that year.[102] Even then, the legal specialization remained only part of the broad academic major called "politics and law" (政法, *zhengfa*). By 1980 fourteen colleges and law departments in the country had admitted an underwhelming total of 2,800 undergraduate law students.[103] It is also interesting to note that in the early 1980s, there were only about 3,000 lawyers in the PRC, a country of approximately one billion people.[104]

By the end of 2010, however, this group had expanded by a factor of sixty-eight to include 204,000 licensed lawyers.[105] That year alone, about 40,000 PRC nationals received licenses to become registered lawyers in the country. And in 2011 China's 640 law schools and law departments produced roughly 100,000 law graduates.[106] These numbers should continue to swell in coming years. Meanwhile, the programs in legal studies — such as jurisprudence, constitutional law, administrative law, criminal law, civil law, procedural law, and environmental law — have become well-established professional subfields over the past two decades. As He Weifang described in a public talk, there were hardly any textbooks on law when he began his undergraduate studies in 1978; now, law-related books usually constitute one-fourth of the books in an academic bookstore.[107] In 2007 about 400 books and 70,000 scholarly articles on law, including translated works, were published in the country. In 2009 China had over 200 professional journals that focused on law.[108]

In addition, legal aid institutions and programs have begun to establish a presence in China. In 1992 the Socially Vulnerable Group Protection Center at Wuhan University became China's first non-governmental legal aid institution. Other legal aid institutions have since arisen, including Peking University's Women's Rights Legal Research and Service Center, Tsinghua University's Constitution and Citizens' Rights Protection Center, and the Oriental Public Interest Lawyers' Legal Aid Firm. These organizations have pursued many public interest litigation cases.[109] By the end of 2009, there were 3,274 registered legal aid institutions with 13,081 staff members in the country.[110] In 2010 a total of 8,189 Chinese volunteer lawyers worked on issues related to minors' rights, with the Beijing Children's Legal Aid and Research Center and the Beijing Legal Aid Office for Migrant Workers winning some important legal cases in this area.[111] The phrase "rights protection lawyers" (维权律师, *weiquan lüshi*), emerged in roughly the past decade, reflecting the great strides made by a small but influential coterie of rights protection lawyers that have devoted their careers to human rights issues.

One of the most important contributions that He Weifang has made in promoting China's legal professionalism was his famous 1998 article on "Ex-Servicemen of the PLA Now Serving at Court."[112] The article boldly criticizes the trend of ex-servicemen of the PLA — the majority of whom have not had any formal legal training — becoming a main source of judges in the country. He criticizes this practice as being akin to appointing demobilized servicemen to be medical doctors, arguing that, because a judge is as responsible as a medical doctor for the life and death of people, the position requires specialized knowledge and thus professional training.

For He Weifang, judiciary specialization (司法专业化, *sifa zhuanyehua*) should consist of many specific components, including professional training of lawyers and judges, separation between judicial and administrative functional areas in legal and law enforcement institutions, and, ultimately, an increase of judicial power and authority. By the very nature of their profession, lawyers are responsible for containing state power. Yet lawyers are also professionally interested in developing legal norms to reshape state power. Lawyers can enable the expression of public resentment and grievances against the government through legal channels rather than street protests. On many occasions over the past decade or more, He proposed that China should jettison undergraduate legal education in favor of the Western model of providing specialized legal training via postgraduate law schools.[113]

As for the professional specialization of judges, He argues that a judge must have received formal legal education and should possess both a capacity for superb legal thinking and an analytical mind. The relationship between the public security sector, prosecutors, and the courts should be well defined. Judicial power should be independent not only from external interference but also from internal restriction. According to He, both communist ideology and the traditional Chinese conception of law were the cause and consequence of "a judicial process dominated by laymen."[114] He argues that a sound legal system "is highly dependent on different legal practitioners having the same educational background."[115]

He's foresight and outspoken stance on the promotion of legal professionalism in China have yielded some very positive results. For example, the PRC established the judicial examination system in 2001. Not only are lawyers and legal scholars no longer considered state officials (as they were in China's recent past), but they also now boast an unprecedented degree of political autonomy and a steadily increasing level of professionalism. At least partly because of He Weifang's initial advocacy, judges and judicial staff members now wear robes and use gavels in court.[116] Despite these advances, He is quick to point out that Chinese judges remain a long way from being able to maintain professional standards for judicial independence or even the spirit of judicial professionalism.

Judicial Independence as the Top Priority

Legal development in China, like elsewhere in the world, is certainly not a linear process. The rapid expansion of and growing demand for professionalism in the Chinese legal community have paradoxically led the Chinese authorities, especially conservative leaders, to more aggressively strengthen the CCP's monopoly over the legal system. As He Weifang observes in *In the Name of Justice*, the party's supremacy over the judicial system has remained the defining feature of the Chinese legal system. The legal community and the general public "simply do not have a means to restrict the power of the top leader."[117]

In an article published in 2007, He criticized the trend, widespread at various levels of leadership, in which the head of the public security bureau is simultaneously a member of the standing committee of the party committee or the secretary of the politics and law commission — an arrangement that effectively places police power above judicial power. He believes that this led the police to become an important force in the maintenance of the CCP's monopoly on state power and in the suppression of any resistance to this system.[118]

What particularly troubles He Weifang and many like-minded people are the "three chiefs conferences" at various levels of government, which constitute a re-convergence of power among the police chief, the attorney general, and the chief judge. These "three chiefs" of vastly different functional areas often "work in a coordinated fashion so that the cases are decided before they even go to trial."[119] This practice is most evident in the fact that the president of the Supreme Court is now supposed to report the court's work to the chairman of the Central Commission of Politics and Law or even to the police chief (minister of public security), rather than to the NPC as China's constitution specifies. This has led He to pointedly ask: "How can a judiciary like this exercise effective supervision and constraint over police power?"[120]

Since a top priority of the CCP leadership is the maintenance of its own rule, it is no surprise that the police have become more powerful, not only in terms of their influence on socioeconomic policies but also in terms of their budget allocation. For example, the total amount of money used for "maintaining social stability" in 2009 was 514 billion yuan — almost identical to China's total national defense budget (532 billion yuan) that year. The Chinese government budget for national defense in 2012 was 670.3 billion yuan, while the budget for the police and other public security expenditures was 701.8 billion yuan (an 11.5-percent increase).[121]

Three factors have contributed to the growing power of the police force. First, the Arab Spring led CCP leaders to fear that they could face an outcome similar to that of, say, the Mubarak regime. Second, business elites — especially those who work in state-monopolized industries such as banking, oil, electricity, coal, telecommunications, aviation, railways, tobacco, and shipping — have often bribed government officials and formed a "wicked coalition." This coalition constantly talks about the need for stability in the country but in fact is more concerned about maintaining its own interests.[122] Finally, the quantity and scale of group protests have increased in recent years, with some becoming increasingly violent. In response, the authorities have often used administrative or political methods to fire local officials, crack down on protests, or apply what sociology professor Sun Liping and his colleagues at Tsinghua University have called "campaign-method governance" (运动式治理, *yundongshi zhili*).[123] These methods are largely arbitrary, being executed at the personal direction of individual leaders and often disregarding the law and the legal process.

The growing power of the Central Commission of Politics and Law — and the police force that implements its decisions — not only has generated much criticism from Chinese public intellectuals, especially legal scholars, but has also created a vicious cycle by which the more fiercely the police suppress social protests, the more violent and widespread the protests become. As some PRC scholars have put it, "The more you are obsessed with social stability, the less you will have of it."[124] A popular sentiment in the country is particularly revealing: "Big protests lead to big settlements; small protests, small settlements; no protests, no settlements."[125] As He Weifang has insightfully pointed out, the rapidly growing power of the Internet and social media may not necessarily be conducive to the promotion of rule of law and legal procedures; sometimes Internet discourse is a distorting mirror, representing extreme views.[126]

In addition to the growing number of social protests, the rapid increase of petition letters also reflects the failure of the judicial system. Every year, the various levels of the government receive a combined total of over 10 million petition letters. Three fairly recent remarkable events — Wang Lijun's defection to the U.S. consulate, the downfall of Bo Xilai, and Chen Guangcheng's visit to the U.S. embassy — have further revealed major flaws in the Chinese political system in general and the police and law enforcement apparatus in particular.

He Weifang believes that all of these developments, resulting from the CCP authorities' heavy reliance on the use of police, reflect an urgent need for an independent judicial system. He argues bluntly that China is in the midst of a race between a bottom-up revolution and judicial reform. This race will not require eighty — or even twenty — years to complete; it will likely conclude much sooner. In He's words, the CCP has no other way to go (无路可走, *wulu kezou*).[127] For He and many like-minded legal scholars, the judicial reform outlined in the beginning of this chapter is the approach entailing the lowest political cost and risk for what will be China's inevitable political transformation. He told the Hong Kong media that the tension between liberal leaders, such as then premier Wen Jiabao, and conservative leaders reflected the tension between, on the one hand, the party's desire to surrender some of its power and privilege in order to promote rule of law and on the other, the party's desire to retain its monopoly on power at all costs.[128] The discussion within the CCP leadership regarding the need to reduce the power and influence of the Central Commission of Politics and Law, as indeed took place at the 18th Party Congress, is an encouraging development.[129] Speaking more broadly, China's judicial reforms and bold move toward constitutionalism should become top priorities if the leadership wants to avoid a bottom-up revolution.

Prospects for Constitutionalism in China: Three Contending Views

China has a constitution, but its government does not adhere to constitutionalism. Since the founding of the PRC in 1949, China has had four separate constitutions, promulgated in 1954, 1975, 1978, and 1982, with the 1982 constitution having undergone four amendments, adopted in 1988, 1993, 1999, and 2004.[130] He Weifang believes that China's current constitution has two major defects. The first is "intrinsic, something that cannot be solved by minor amendments, because it was formulated at a time (1982) when constitutionalism was still seen in an ideologically tinged light....The second major defect is that even this unsatisfactory constitution is not well implemented."[131]

According to Xia Yong, a well-known legal scholar who previously served as director of the State Secrecy Bureau under the State Council, the world has seen three types of constitutions: the revolutionary constitution, the reform constitution, and the constitution based on constitutionalism (宪政宪法, *xianzheng xianfa*).[132] Xia believes that China is in the midst of transitioning from the reform constitution to constitutionalism. Only this latter type can provide political legitimacy and enduring social stability, because it embodies the basic principle that "there is no other law above the constitution."[133]

Students of the Chinese legal system, however, hold vastly different views on the future prospects of constitutionalism in the PRC. The three contending perspectives — pessimistic, optimistic, and pragmatic — stem from contrasting assessments of China's political and legal development at present.

Pessimists believe that the Chinese legal system is incompatible with constitutionalism. They believe that virtually all of the key elements of the current PRC constitution reflect the influence of both a Leninist approach to constitutionalism and the supreme authority of the party-state structure. The PRC constitution does not contain any provisions for constitutional adjudication or judicial review, which are often regarded as the foundation of constitutionalism. As some Western scholars argue, constitutionalism should entail creation of a state organ with the authority to legitimately interpret the meaning of the constitution and "determine whether any action by the state apparatus (or others) exceeds their authority to act under that framework."[134] There is no such independent state organ in China. Chinese courts are not given the ability to exercise such review power; they merely apply the law, with no power to interpret it when adjudicating cases.[135]

Pessimists often emphasize that, in the absence of the supreme authority of the constitution, the rule of law loses any real significance. For the courts, police, and prosecutors in the PRC, the primary concern is political accountability rather than legal accountability. Under these circumstances, any efforts on the part of legal professionals and the public to use the law against the party-state's autocratic rule and to demand constitutionally granted rights are akin to what some critics call "asking the tiger for his skin" (与虎谋皮, *yuhu moupi*).[136] As M. Ulric Killion argues, in the absence of a separation of powers, popular sovereignty, or independent judicial review, "neither liberty nor social rights will be protected."[137]

As both political structure and values are at the heart of constitutionalism, some pessimists point out that, partly due to the Confucian cultural tradition and partly due to socioeconomic circumstances, the Chinese public does seem to enjoy economic liberties, rising living standards (for most), and newly obtained civil and political rights. Therefore, the concerns of the Chinese public may profoundly differ from those of liberal legal professionals like He Weifang. The public is not especially interested in gaining legal rights that relate to political issues or establishing institutional mechanisms that impinge on the control of the regime. According to this view, the Chinese public places greater value on the "competent leader" than it does on "competent law."[138]

In contrast, optimists believe that critics of the Chinese legal system, especially those in the West, are too quick to reject the party-state political organization on the grounds that such a system is inherently despotic and thus incompatible with constitutionalism. As Larry Backer argues, the prevailing pessimistic view in the West about the prospect of Chinese constitutionalism is "both anachronistic and too simple-minded for the emerging possibilities in states like China."[139] For Backer, China presents "an interesting variant on constitutionalism."[140] He argues that, in the case of China, one needs to "focus on party rather than state, grounded in separation of powers principles in which the administrative function is vested in the state while political authority overall is vested in the party under law."[141] Institutionalizing the role of the party leadership within the Chinese constitutional framework may therefore represent "the most appropriate way of further legitimating constitutionalism within the Chinese legal order."[142]

Other scholars challenge the conventional view that the Chinese constitution is static and unchanging. Instead, they believe that judges, lawyers, and Chinese citizens can use the courts as a mechanism for constitutional litigation — a process that Chinese legal scholars call the "judicialization of the constitution" (宪法司法化, *xianfa sifahua*). Thomas Kellogg argues that efforts by actors inside and outside the government can make the Chinese constitution into a legally operative principal document.[143] Along this same line of thinking, Xia Yong argues that, although China has neither a Western-style separation of powers nor federalism, in reality the PRC's constitution recognizes three powers (legislative, executive, and judicial) and a functional division between central and local powers.[144]

Many optimists believe that the NPC can play a crucial role in constitutional adjudication and judicial review. Some argue that the foundation of constitutional review in the Chinese constitution already exists in the form of the Division of Check and Filing under the Standing Committee of the NPC. This pronounced mechanism, created by an amendment to the Working Procedure in 2005, can be regarded as the first stage of the activation process, according to the optimists.[145] Some foreign scholars also point out that it took a long time for many Western constitutional democracies to practice constitutional review. As Michael Dowdle observes:

France's constitution, for example, did not articulate a practice of constitutional review until 1958, some eighty years after the initial establishment of her constitutional foundation, and that practice did not begin protecting the political and civil rights enumerated in that constitution until the 1970s. Britain developed a practice resembling judicial review only in the 1990s. The Dutch constitution, now entering its second century, forbids judicial review. Sweden's constitution articulates a judicial review practice, but as of 1987 Sweden had not yet resorted to this practice in its two-hundred-year history.[146]

Dowdle also argues that many of today's successful constitutional systems actually emerged out of environments in which neither democracy nor the rule of law initially enjoyed significant normative support from the public. Constitutional values are often the product, rather than the cause, of successful constitutional experience.[147]

It should be noted that optimists are divided into two broad and profoundly different camps: those who believe that the CCP can be a force for the promotion and implementation of Chinese constitutionalism, and those who believe a constitutional China can be achieved only after the end of one-party rule.

Yu Keping's call for fundamental political reforms places him in the first camp. For Yu, constitutionalism means the constitution is the ultimate basis for the operation of state power. As Yu observes, the CCP constitution dictates that the "CCP should operate within the sphere allowed by the constitution and law," although in practice this principle has often been violated in the PRC.[148] Like other liberal scholars in the Chinese political establishment, Yu believes that "the CCP leadership cannot claim it governs the country by law unless the party is subject to the rule of law."[149] This does not mean that China should establish a law on political parties or move to a multiparty system but rather that the party should strictly comply with both the PRC constitution and the CCP constitution to regulate party affairs and member behavior. Specifically, Yu calls for political reforms in the three major relationships the CCP has with other institutions in accordance with the PRC constitution: the relationships with the NPC, with the government or the state council, and with judicial institutions.[150]

In the wake of the Bo Xilai crisis, an increasing number of liberal leaders and scholars in the CCP recognize the need to surrender some of the party's power and privilege. It is interesting to note that Wang Huning, a top aide to three Chinese presidents and the former dean of the Law School at Fudan University, republished his 1986 article in which he argues that "public security, prosecutors, and the court merging into one" was one of the main reasons for the prevalent human rights violations, such as torture and vandalism, during the Cultural Revolution. He states unambiguously that the "Cultural Revolution could happen only in a country without an independent judicial system."[151]

According to the second camp of optimists, China's constitutional future is not based on the scenario that the CCP may transform itself. Rather, these scholars hold that a bottom-up revolution can take place at any time, as the party has lost its legitimacy in the wake of many recent scandals, especially with regard to rampant official corruption. He Pin, a seasoned New York–based analyst of Chinese elite politics, believes that China's current political and socioeconomic problems — and its painful experiences during the decade-long democratic transition — have not been caused by the public enlightenment movement for constitutionalism and democracy but are the consequences of a long-standing authoritarian and lawless political system.[152]

Zhang Lifan, a well-known scholar in Beijing, has argued that "China is not in danger, but the CCP is."[153] He states that many CCP elites do not care whether or not the CCP collapses but instead are only concerned about the well-being of their own families. The large-scale outflow of capital in recent years, presumably by corrupt officials, further illustrates the lack of confidence party elites place in the country's sociopolitical stability. According to a 2011 report released by the Washington-based organization Global Financial Integrity, from 2000 to 2009 China's illegal capital outflow totaled $2.74 trillion, five times more than the total amount from second-ranked Mexico.[154]

Optimists in both camps believe that an increasingly vibrant legal community in the country will likely contribute to the establishment of an independent judicial system. But neither camp of optimists can provide a convincing roadmap or model for a constitutional China. Understandably, many scholars take a pragmatic view. Randall Peerenboom, for example, argues that "legal reforms are path dependent and in that sense inherently local. Thus, no single model is likely to work everywhere given the diversity of initial starting conditions and the complexity of the reform process."[155] In a sense, the constitutionalism and democratization of a given country arise not by design but out of necessity — the necessity to deal with contextual problems such as the abuse of police power and official corruption.[156]

Pragmatists reject the pessimists' cultural incompatibility thesis, citing the World Bank's recent rule of law index: five East and Southeast Asian countries or jurisdictions — Singapore, Japan, Hong Kong, Taiwan, and South Korea — rank in the top quartile.[157] As pragmatists observe, these entities usually place priority on economic growth over civil liberty. Over time, however, "as the legal system becomes more efficient, professionalized, and autonomous, it comes to play a greater role in the economy and society more generally."[158]

Pragmatists recognize the long road constitutional development faces in countries such as China. They also believe, however, that one should not "dismiss the importance of transformative processes simply because at the present time they seem too subtle or glacial for our tastes."[159] Quite often, the evolution of the legal profession and pressures from lawyers and civil society that "seem glacial today could suddenly revolutionize the system tomorrow."[160]

While pragmatists have serious reservations about both the possibility of the CCP subjecting its power to constitutional supremacy and the role of the NPC in exerting legal constraints on the party in the short term, they do believe it is worthwhile to make an effort on these fronts. As Ji Weidong, dean of KoGuan Law School at Shanghai Jiaotong University, stated, it may take decades or longer to make the rule of law a way of life. However, judges and lawyers as a group need to start moving right away. "Step by step, they will lead institutional change."[161]

As for He Weifang, it is difficult to characterize him as either an optimist or a pessimist, an idealist or a pragmatist. On the one hand, he is optimistic in that he has devoted his entire career to fighting for justice and constitutionalism in China. It is in part due to his tireless efforts that the country has witnessed remarkable growth in the legal profession. The victory of the landmark case of Li Zhuang and He's bold and effective challenge of some of the most formidable and ruthless politicians also may have enhanced his sense of optimism. On the other hand, however, he is soberly aware that party leaders wield unrestrained power, that there is unprecedented official corruption, that many high-profile lawsuits result in unfair verdicts, and that civil rights activists are treated in an unlawful manner. What is truly remarkable about He Weifang is the fact that he seems to have combined, in a marvelously engaging and balanced way, both idealism and pragmatism in his search for a constitutional China.

While He Weifang's works and personal history reveal one truly extraordinary Chinese legal scholar's intellectual and political odyssey, these are situated in the broader experience of China's journey into the

21st century — the country's painful search for a sound, safe, and sustainable political and legal system. Based on He Weifang's insights and foresight, the struggle for justice and rule of law will most likely become the prevailing issue in the next phase of China's political transformation.

The two epigraphs that open this chapter remind us of equally arduous undertakings in Western democracies. Emmeline Pankhurst's courage and determination underpinned the victory of the British suffragette movement.[162] Justice Stephen Breyer's remarks in China in 2012 highlight the lessons learned and strengths derived from the growth of American constitutional democracy and its uncompromising adherence to justice.[163] These quotes remind us that He Weifang's words and endeavors, frustration and inspiration, courage and vision are by no means alien to Western readership. Perhaps more than anything else, his work highlights the common aspirations, transnational values, and enduring strength of the human spirit observable in our rapidly changing world.

Notes

This chapter is an edited version of the introduction to the He Weifang volume of the Thornton Center Chinese Thinkers Series, published by the Brookings Institution Press. See Cheng Li, "Introduction: Bringing Ethics Back into Chinese Discourse," in He Weifang, *In the Name of Justice: Striving for the Rule of Law in China* (Washington, DC: Brookings Institution Press, 2012), xvii–xlix. The author thanks Zach Balin, Eve Cary, John Langdon, Jordan Lee, Andrew Marble, Ryan McElveen, and Lucy Xu for their very helpful comments on earlier versions of this chapter.

1 The panel was entitled "The Top-Level Design of China's Judicial Reforms." This term (改革的顶层设计) was first used in the party documents of the fifth plenum of the 17th Central Committee of the Chinese Communist Party in October 2010. The notion emphasizes the overall vision and structural coherence of political reform on the part of the party leadership. It highlights the importance of the direction, path, and possible breakthrough of reforms. He Weifang and Xu Xin apparently borrowed this concept to argue for the necessity of fundamental reform in China's judicial system.

2 Xu Xin (徐昕, 1970–), a native of Fengcheng, Jiangxi Province, is a professor of law and director of the Research Center of the Judicial System at the Beijing Institute of Technology. He received a PhD in law from Tsinghua

University and taught at the Southwest University of Political Science and Law before joining the Beijing Institute of Technology in 2010. More details on this panel can be found on He Weifang's blog; see Xu Xin and He Weifang, "Guanyu sifa gaige dingceng sheji de duihua" [The dialogue about the top-level design of China's judicial reform], December 12, 2011, http://blog.qq.com/qzone/622009820/1323671026.htm.

3 The Central Commission of Politics and Law of the CCP, known as *zheng-fawei* (政法委), oversees all legal enforcement authorities, including the Supreme People's Court, Supreme People's Procuratorate, Ministry of Justice, Ministry of Public Security, and Ministry of State Security, making it a very powerful organ. All the provincial, municipal, and county party committees have their own politics and law commissions.

4 Wu Bangguo was the second-highest ranking leader in the Politburo Standing Committee of the CCP and was chairman of the NPC. His famous "five no's" refer to no multiple party system, no pluralism in ideology, no checks and balances or bicameral parliament, no federal system, and no privatization. He made this statement at the fourth plenary session of the 11th National People's Congress, held in Beijing on March 11, 2011. See *Zhongguo xinwenwang* [China Newsnet], March 11, 2011, www.china.com.cn/2011/2011-03/11/content_22114099.htm.

5 For examples of He Weifang's public speeches, see online videos at http://v.youku.com/v_show/id_XNDU2ODU3OTI=.html (October 5, 2008) and www.youtube.com/watch?v=8VJE2CFkTqE (December 3, 2011).

6 Cai Dingjian (蔡定剑, 1955–2010), a native of Xinjian County, Jiangxi Province, was a leading scholar of constitutional studies in China. He served as a staff member and deputy bureau chief of the Bureau of Staff of the Standing Committee of the NPC from 1986 to 2003. Prior to his premature death from cancer in 2010, he served as a professor of law and the director of the Institute of Constitutional Research at China University of Political Science and Law. His main publications include *Xianzheng jiangtan* [Constitutional forum] (Beijing: Law Press, 2010).

7 For example, see Guo Guangdong, "Weishenme zheme duoren jinian Cai Dingjian?" [Why do so many people commemorate Cai Dingjian?], *Nanfang zhoumo* [Southern Weekend], November 26, 2010. Also see www.infzm.com/content/52858.

8 "The FP Top 100 Global Thinkers," June 27, 2012, www.foreignpolicy.com/articles/2011/11/28/the_fp_top_100_global_thinkers?page=0,18.

9 Hu Shih, *The Chinese Renaissance* (Chicago: University of Chicago Press, 1933). For an excellent study of the intellectual discourse about the May Fourth Movement, see Chow Tse-Tsung, *The May Fourth Movement: Intellectual Revolution in Modern China* (Cambridge, MA: Harvard University Press, 1960).

10 Han Yongmei, "Jin Guantao jiaoshou: Wusi shi weiwangcheng de qimeng yundong" [Interview with Professor Jin Guantao: The May Fourth Movement was an unfulfilled enlightenment movement], *Lianhe zaobao* [United Morning News], April 19, 2009, www.zaobao.com/special/face2face/pages1/face2face090419.shtml.

11 Zi Zhongyun, ed., *Qimeng yu Zhongguo shehui zhuanxing* [The enlightenment and transformation of Chinese society] (Beijing: Shehui kexue wenxian chubanshe, 2011), 164.

12 Xu Youyu, for example, asserted that when China is in the midst of a rapid economic rise but has lost its political direction, public enlightenment is particularly essential. Xu Youyu, "Qimeng zai Zhongguo" [Public enlightenment in China], in Zi, *Qimeng yu Zhongguo*, 101.

13 Zi, *Qimeng yu Zhongguo*, 171.

14 Ibid., 173.

15 Ibid., 158–59.

16 Ibid. In the months preceding the Bo Xilai crisis, Su Wei, a scholar close to Bo at the Chongqing Party School, compared Bo and Chongqing mayor Huang Qifan to former leaders Mao Zedong and Zhou Enlai in comments circulated in both the Chongqing and national media. See Sina Global Newsnet, September 20, 2011, http://dailynews.sina.com/bg/chn/chnnews/ausdaily/20110920/18402783790.html.

17 Xu, "Qimeng zai Zhongguo," 102.

18 Ibid.

19 Wei Sen, "Xin qimeng yu Zhongguo shehui zhuanxing de yixie genbenxing wenti" [New public enlightenment and some fundamental issues in the transition of Chinese society], in Zi, *Qimeng yu Zhongguo*, 124.

20 He, *In the Name of Justice,* Chapter 2.

21 He, *In the Name of Justice,* Chapter 3.

22 He Weifang, *Jiaohuifa de lishi fazhan, hunyin zhidu ji dui shisufa de yingxiang* [A study of canon law: Its development, matrimonial institutions, and influence on secular law], LL.M. thesis (Beijing: China University of Political Science and Law, 1985).

23 He Weifang also made this point in many of his public talks in China in recent years. For example, see He Weifang, He Qinhua, and Tian Tao, eds., *Falü wenhua sanrentan* [A tripartite discussion of legal culture] (Beijing: Peking University Press, 2010), 102.

24 He Weifang, "The Methodology of Comparative Study of Legal Cultures," *Asia Pacific Law Review* 37 (July 1994): 39.

25 Ibid., 40.

26 This discussion is based on He Weifang, "Cong xixue fanhui bentu" [Return to academic indigenization from Western learning], March 1, 2010, www.aisixiang.com/data/detail.php?id=31928.

27 Ibid. The Southwest College of Political Science and Law was later renamed the Southwest University of Political Science and Law.

28 Ibid.

29 Before 1983, China University of Political Science and Law was named Beijing College of Political Science and Law.

30 For the full citations of these translated books, see "Further Reading: The Writings of He Weifang" at the end of: He Weifang, *In the Name of Justice: Striving for the Rule of Law in China* (Washington, DC: Brookings Institution Press, 2012).

31 See He Weifang's interview on the Renmin website, October 8, 2007, http://edu.people.com.cn/GB/8216/85218/104692/6349432.html.

32 He, *In the Name of Justice,* Chapter 3.

33 He Weifang, "Wo weishenme likai Beida?" [Why did I leave Peking University?], July 18, 2008, http://news.ifeng.com/opinion/200807/0718_23_660688.shtml.

34 For the views of both sides, see "Fang Zhouzi paohong He Weifang" [Fang Zhouzi bombards He Weifang], Duowei News, August 13, 2011, http://china.dwnews.com/news/2011-08-13/58008432.html.

35 Wu Zuolai, "Wo weishenme zhichi He Weifang?" [Why do I support He Weifang?], *Dongfang zaobao* [Oriental Morning News], August 16, 2011.

36 Wang Zhaoxiang, "Xingyin falü de langman qishi" [The romantic knight who chants rule of law], *Dongfang fayan* [Oriental Legal Guardian], May 9, 2004.

37 He, *In the Name of Justice,* Chapter 3.

38 Pan Congxia, "He Weifang: 'Shoumen laohe' de budao famen" [He Weifang: A Famennian gatekeeper], *Nandu zhoukan* [Southern Metropolis Weekly], December 5, 2008.

39 Jiang Hao, "Afterword" in He, He, and Tian, *Falü wenhua sanrentan*, 254.

40 Pan, "He Weifang: 'Shoumen laohe' de budao famen."

41 See http://blog.sina.com.cn/heweifang (accessed July 22, 2012). He Weifang has several other blogs; see www.bullogger.com/blogs/heweifang; http://blog.caijing.com.cn/heweifang; and http://heweifang2009.blog.163.com.

42 Peng Bo and Wang Lin, eds., *Keneng yingxiang ershiyi shiji Zhongguo de yibai ge qingnian renwu* [The 100 young people who may shape China in the 21st century] (Beijing: Zhongguo renmin chubanshe, 2001).

43 For a more detailed discussion of the Sun Zhigang case, see Yu Xiang, "Sun Zhigang's Death and Reform of Detention System," *Magazine* (China Society for Human Rights Studies), June 27, 2012, www.humanrights.cn/zt/magazine/20040200482694708.htm.

44 He, *In the Name of Justice,* Chapter 5.

45 Chen Youxi, "Falüren shalong" [Legal professionals' salon], April 28, 2012, http://wq.zfwlxt.com/newLawyerSite/BlogShow.aspx?itemTypeID=b3572aed-0599-4632-8969-9c2200730162&itemID=430fd40c-b0f8-40d8-9242-a04f0088aa35&user=10420.

46 He, *In the Name of Justice,* Chapter 9.

47 He, *In the Name of Justice,* Chapter 11.

48 He, *In the Name of Justice,* prologue.

49 For more on the Wu Ying case in 2012, see Chuin-Wei Yap, "China Court Spares Life of Millionaire," *Wall Street Journal,* April 21–22, A7; and "Wu Ying an nizhuan" [The reversal of the Wu Ying case], *Shijie ribao* [World Journal], April 21, 2012, A12. For He Weifang's views and input in this case, see Kuang Ping, "He Weifang tan Wu Ying an" [He Weifang comments on the Wu Ying case], *Sanxiang dushibao* [Hunan Metropolis Daily], April 29, 2012.

50 Andrew Jacobs, "China Limits the Crimes Punishable by Death," *New York Times,* July 30, 2009, 12. In 2011, the Chinese government reduced the number of crimes punishable by death from sixty-eight to fifty-five. See "Zhongguo feichu shisanxiang sixing" [China abolishes 13 items of crimes punishable by death] Duowei News, May 2, 2011, http://china.dwnews.com/news/2011-05-02/57676561.html.

51 He, *In the Name of Justice,* Chapter 10.

52 Quoted from Jacobs, "China Limits the Crimes Punishable by Death."

53 He Weifang, "Yizhi baoyuan: He Weifang zaitan feichu sixing" [Using justice rather than revenge: The death penalty revisited], *Jingji guancha bao* [Economic Observer], May 28, 2011.

54 Ibid.

55 He, *In the Name of Justice,* Chapter 10.

56 See "Ying zhengshi Zhonghua Minguo" [To be realistic about "the Republic of China"], *Lianhe zaobao* [United Morning News], October 13, 2011.

57 Zhou Xi, "Zhendui Chen Guangcheng shijian meiguo mingque jujue xiang zhongfang daoqian" [The United States firmly rejects China's request for an apology regarding the case of Chen Guangcheng], May 2, 2012, http://boxun.com/news/gb/china/2012/05/201205062112.shtml.

58 Du Junli, "Kong Qingdong shidai de Beida" [Peking University in the era of Kong Qingdong], November 16, 2011, http://cul.cn.yahoo.com/ypen/20111116/702822.html.

59 He, *In the Name of Justice,* Chapter 11.

60 He Weifang, "Bo Xilai liyong shehui bingtai peizhi geren chongbai" [Bo Xilai uses social ills to cultivate his cult of personality], *Xianggang Jingji ribao* [Hong Kong Economic Daily], April 17, 2012.

61 Peter Foster, "Leading Chinese dissident claims freedom of speech worse than before Olympics," *The Telegraph*, April 27, 2009, www.telegraph.co.uk/news/world-news/asia/china/5230707/Leading-Chinese-dissident-claims-freedom-of-speech-worse-than-before-Olympics.html.

62 Chen Fang, "He Weifang: Bianjiang guilai" [He Weifang: Return from the borderland], October 21, 2011, http://cul.cn.yahoo.com/ypen/20111021/652595.html.

63 Zi Zhongyun observed that courage is always part of enlightenment movements. Zi, *Qimeng yu Zhongguo*, 8.

64 Immanuel Kant, "*Beantwortung der Frage: Was ist Aufklärung?*" [Answering the question: What is enlightenment?], *Berlinische Monatsschrift* [Berlin Monthly] (1784).

65 He, *In the Name of Justice*, prologue.

66 For more discussion of Bo's campaigns in Chongqing, see Yawei Liu, "Bo Xilai's Campaign for the Standing Committee and the Future of Chinese Politicking," *China Brief* 11, No. 21, November 11, 2011, www.jamestown.org/single/?no_cache=1&tx_ttnews%5Btt_news%5D=38660.

67 "Chongqing dahei yingxiong Wang Lijun 'qiwucongwen' yinfa weibo reyi" [Chongqing hero Wang Lijun's change of leadership posts triggers heated discussion in microblogs], *Xinwen wanbao* [Evening News], February 3, 2012.

68 *Chongqing wanbao* [Chongqing Evening News], January 16, 2010.

69 For an excellent review of left-wing intellectuals' support for Bo Xilai and his Chongqing model, see Rong Jian, "Benxiang Chongqing de xuezhemen" [The scholars who adored the Chongqing model], April 28, 2012, www.21ccom.net/articles/zgyj/gqmq/article_2012042858663.html.

70 "Beida jiaoshou Kong Qingdong liting Bo Xilai" [Peking University professor Kong Qingdong supports Bo Xilai], *Chongqing ribao* [Chongqing Daily], August 23, 2011; also see "Beida jiaoshou Kong Qingdong liting Bo Xilai" [Peking University Professor Kong Qingdong supports Bo Xilai], www.wenxuecity.com/news/2011/08/23/1451756.html. Some critics of Bo Xilai's campaign methods reject Kong's assertions. Qian Liqun, also a professor of literature at Peking University, argues that Bo adopted two radical and potentially destructive economic policy initiatives. The first was radical land reform to seize farmers' land in the name of urbanization, and the second was promoting socialist public ownership to consolidate state control over economic affairs, undermining the private sector. See Qian Liqun, "Lao hongweibing dangzheng de danyou" [Worries about the rule by the old Red Guards], *Wenzhai* [Digest], February 19, 2012.

71 Wang Shaoguang, "Chongqing jingyan shi Zhongguo shi shehuizhuyi 3.0" [The Chongqing experiment is Chinese-style socialism 3.0], June 9, 2010, www.sociologyol.org/shehuibankuai/shehuipinglunliebiao/2010-06-09/10387. html.

72 *Shijie ribao* [World Journal], January 3, 2010, A2.

73 It was widely known among legal professionals and lawyers in the country that Wang Lijun, with the support of Bo Xilai, adopted an "innovative unlawful procedure" along with the generous use of torture in his campaign in Chongqing. "Chongqing dahei juzhang beiba" [Chongqing police chief purged], *Shijie ribao* [World Journal], February 3, 2012, A11.

74 He Bing, "Cong 'xuemaoxuan' dao 'changhongge'" [From "studying Mao's work" to "singing red songs"], April 24, 2011, http://hebing1.blog.sohu. com/171382733.html.

75 He Weifang, "Gaige benshen jiushi gaibian guoqing" [China's reform is to change national conditions], *Huashang bao* [Chinese Merchants Daily], May 19, 2012.

76 He, "Yizhi baoyuan."

77 For example, Sida Liu, an assistant professor of sociology and law at the University of Wisconsin at Madison, called this case "the most important trial since the Gang of Four trial in 1980." See Sida Liu, "The Most Important China Legal Case since the Gang of Four Trial?" July 22, 2012, http://practicesource.com/australian-asian-legal-eye/the-most-important-china-legal-case-since-the-gang-of-four-trial.

78 Ian Johnson, "Trial in China Tests Limits of Legal System Reform," *New York Times*, April 19, 2011, www.nytimes.com/2011/04/20/world/asia/20china. html?_r=2&ref=world.

79 Xu and He, "Guanyu sifa gaige dingceng sheji de duihua."

80 See "Chongqing dahei diyian" [The first case of Chongqing's "striking the black mafia" campaign], Xinhua Newsnet, January 5, 2010, http://news. xinhuanet.com/legal/2010-01/05/content_12759416.htm.

81 For more discussion of the details, see Xu Xunlei, "Lüshi Li Zhuang an shoupian baodao pouxi" [An analysis of the first media coverage of the lawyer Li Zhuang case], Renmin Net, February 23, 2010, http://media.people.com.cn/GB/40628/11011197.html.

82 See Zhu Mingyong's court statement, March 11, 2010, http://blog.sina.com.cn/s/blog_4b5857fb0100hauo.html.

83 Ibid.

84 Su Renyan, "Zhongguo shiliuwan lüshi duijue Bo Xilai" [China's 160,000 lawyers versus Bo Xilai], *Kaifang* [Open], May 2011, 16.

85 "Judicial Process and One Lawyer's Bold Stand," *Caixin Online*, April 22, 2011, http://english.caixin.com/2011-04-22/100251590.html.

86 Quoted in Johnson, "Trial in China Tests Limits of Legal System Reform."

87 Many international journalists praised He Weifang's crucial role in defending Li Zhuang. See, for example, Jeremy Page, "China Leaders Laud 'Red' Campaign," *Wall Street Journal*, June 20, 2011.

88 He, *In the Name of Justice,* prologue.

89 He, *In the Name of Justice*, Chapter 2.

90 Ibid.

91 Quoted from Chen Su, *Dangdai Zhongguo faxue yanjiu, 1949–2009* [Research on law in contemporary China, 1949–2009] (Beijing: Zhongguo shehui kexue wenxian chubanshe, 2009), 27.

92 Ibid., 26.

93 These two terms have exactly the same pronunciation in Chinese but quite different Chinese characters and thus meanings: "to use law to rule the country" (以法制国) and "to govern the country according to the law" (依法治国). Zhou Tianwei [Cedric T. Chou], *Fazhi lixiang guo: Sugeladi yu Mengzi de xu'ni duihua* [An ideal state of law: A virtual dialogue between Socrates and Mencius] (Taipei: Commonwealth Press, 1998).

94 Yu Keping, *Yifa zhiguo yu yifa zhidang* [Governing the country and the party by law] (Beijing: Zhongyang bianyi chubanshe, 2007), 2.

95 Chen, *Dangdai Zhongguo faxue yanjiu*, 239.

96 He, "Gaige benshen jiushi gaibian guoqing."

97 Cai Dingjian, "The Development of Constitutionalism in the Transition of Chinese Society," *Columbia Journal of Asian Law* 19, No. 1 (Spring–Fall 2005): 27.

98 Cai Dingjian, "Yifa zhili" [Rule of Law], in Yu Keping, ed., *Zhongguo zhili bianqian sanshi nian: 1978–2008* [China's political reform toward good governance: 1978–2008] (Beijing: Shehui kexue wenxian chubanshe, 2008), 142.

99 Ren Miao, "Falü wenben chengxing, fazhi rentong shangyuan" [The texts of laws are all available, but the rule of law is still far off], *Duowei Times,* March 18, 2011, 17.

100 For discussion of a more optimistic view of China's legal development in terms of professional expansion, see Cheng Li and Jordan Lee, "China's Legal System," *China Review*, No. 48 (Autumn 2009): 1–3.

101 Chen, *Dangdai Zhongguo faxue yanjiu*, 13.

102 He, He, and Tian, *Falü wenhua sanrentan*, 87.

103 Chen, *Dangdai Zhongguo faxue yanjiu*, 114.

104 Gu Xin, "Revitalizing Chinese Society: Institutional Transformation and Social Change," in Wang Gungwu and John Wong, eds., *China: Two Decades of Reform and Change* (Singapore: Singapore University Press and World Scientific Press, 1999), 80.

105 See "Woguo lüshi renshu yi chao ershiwan" [The number of China's lawyers surpasses 200,000], China Lawyers' Network, January 10, 2011, www. zgdls.com/2011/lvjieneican_0110/114973.html.

106 Ren, "Falü wenben chengxing, fazhi rentong shangyuan," 17.

107 He, He, and Tian, *Falü wenhua sanrentan*, 87.

108 Chen, *Dangdai Zhongguo faxue yanjiu*, 238.

109 Liu Donghua and Yang Xiaolei, *Gongyi falü yanjiu, diyijuan* [Public interest research], Vol. 1 (Beijing: Falü chubanshe, 2010), 22.

110 Ibid., 19.

111 Ibid., 119, 128.

112 He Weifang, "Fuzhuan junren jin fayuan" [Ex-servicemen of the PLA now serving at the court], *Nanfang zhoumo* [Southern Weekend], January 2, 1998.

113 He, *In the Name of Justice*, Chapter 7.

114 He, *In the Name of Justice*, Chapter 1.

115 He, *In the Name of Justice*, Chapter 7.

116 He, "Gaige benshen jiushi gaibian guoqing."

117 He, *In the Name of Justice*, Chapter 2.

118 He Weifang, "The Police and the Rule of Law: Commentary on 'Principals and Secret Agents,'" *China Quarterly*, No. 191 (September 2007): 671.

119 He, *In the Name of Justice,* prologue.

120 He, "The Police and the Rule of Law," 672.

121 "Kanshou Chen Guangcheng" [Watching Chen Guangcheng], *Shijie ribao* [World Journal], May 3, 2012, A4.

122 He Weifang made a similar point on the convergence of money and power and the vested interest groups' claim to maintain social stability at all costs. See *Mingbao* [Hong Kong], March 23, 2012.

123 Sun Liping and others, *Yi liyi biaoda zhiduhua shixian shehui de changzhijiu'an* [Institutionalization of interest expression mechanisms and the realization of long-term stability], report delivered at the Tsinghua University Social Development Forum, April 19, 2010.

124 "越维越不稳怪圈" in Chinese. Ibid. Ma Jian, a Chinese writer who resides in the United Kingdom, made a similar point referring to China's problems in maintaining social stability: "The more policemen in a country, the less security in that country." Ma Jian, "Zhongguo weiyi de anquan zhidi: Meiguo dashiguan" [China's only secure place: The U.S. Embassy], BBC, May 9, 2012, www.bbc.co.uk/zhongwen/simp/chinese_analysis/2012/04/120430_us_embassy_chengguangcheng.shtml.

125 "大闹大解决,小闹小解决,不闹不解决" in Chinese.

126 He, "Yizhi baoyuan."

127 Xu and He, "Guanyu sifa gaige dingceng sheji de duihua."

128 He Weifang, "Wenzong zhencheng tui zhenggai" [Premier Wen sincerely promotes political reforms], *Mingbao* [Hong Kong], March 23, 2012.

129 Following leadership reshufflings in Guangdong, the heads of the politics and law committees at the municipal and prefecture levels no longer consecutively serve as heads of the Public Security Bureau, undermining the power of the police. See *Shijie ribao* [World Journal], June 6, 2012, A12.

130 For more discussion of the evolutionary changes of the PRC constitution, see Thomas E. Kellogg, "Constitutionalism with Chinese Characteristics? Constitutional Development and Civil Litigation in China," Indiana University Research Center for Chinese Politics and Business Working Paper 1, February 2008, 1–41; and M. Ulric Killion, "Building Up China's Constitution: Culture, Marxism, and the WTO Rules," *Loyola of Los Angeles Law Review* 41, Nos. 2–4 (2008): 563–602.

131 He, *In the Name of Justice*, Chapter 3.

132 Xia Yong, "Zhongguo xianfa gaige de jige jiben lilun wenti" [Several basic theoretical issues in China's constitutional reform], in Yu Keping, ed., *Zhongguo xuezhe lun minzhu yu fazhi* [Chinese scholars on democracy and rule of law] (Chongqing: Chongqing chubanshe, 2008), 185.

133 Ibid., 186.

134 Quoted in Larry Cata Backer, "A Constitutional Court for China within the Chinese Communist Party: Scientific Development and a Reconsideration of the Institutional Role of the CCP," *Suffolk University Law Review* 43, No. 3 (June 22, 2010): 593. Backer, an optimist about Chinese constitutional development, rejected this notion.

135 Guobin Zhu, "Constitutional review in China: An unaccomplished project or a mirage?" *Suffolk University Law Review* 43, no. 3 (June 2010): 625.

136 Eva Pils, "Asking the Tiger for His Skin: Rights Activism in China," *Fordham International Law Journal* 30, no. 4 (2006): 1286.

137 M. Ulric Killion, "China's Amended Constitution: Quest for Liberty and Independent Judicial Review," *Washington University Global Studies Law Review* 4 (February 2005): 78.

138 Zhou, *Fazhi lixiang guo: Sugeladi yu Mengzi de xuni duihua*, 174, 200.

139 Backer, "The Party as Polity, the Communist Party, and the Chinese Constitutional State: A Theory of State-Party Constitutionalism," *Journal of Chinese and Comparative Law* 16, No. 1 (October 2009): 155.

140 Ibid., 157.

141 Ibid., 101.

142 Backer, "A Constitutional Court for China within the Chinese Communist Party," 597.

143 Kellogg, "Constitutionalism with Chinese Characteristics?" 4.

144 Xia, "Zhongguo xianfa gaige de jige jiben lilun wenti," 201.

145 Zhu, "Constitutional review in China: an unaccomplished project or a mirage?" 625.

146 Michael William Dowdle, "Of Parliaments, Pragmatism, and the Dynamics of Constitutional Development: The Curious Case of China," *Journal of International Law and Politics* 35, No. 1 (2002–03): 24–25.

147 Ibid., 30.

148 Yu, *Yifa zhiguo yu yifa zhidang*, 6.

149 Ibid., 3.

150 Ibid., 13–14.

151 Wang Huning, "Wenge fansi yu zhengzhi gaige" [Reflections on the Cultural Revolution and the reform of China's political system], *Wenzhai* [Digest], February 23, 2012; originally appeared in *Shijie jingji daobao* [World Economic Herald], May 1986.

152 He Pin, *Keyi queding de Zhongguo weilai* [China's future can be determined] (New York: Mirror Books, 2012), 178, 419.

153 Zhang Lifan's blog, February 1, 2012, http://blog.sina.com.cn/s/blog_4b86a 2630100zhuv.html.

154 "Xiang haiwai banqian" [Money flows overseas], April 20, 2012, A4.

155 Randall Peerenboom, "Law and Development of Constitutional Democracy: Is China a Problem Case?" *Annals of the American Academy of Political and Social Science, Law, Society, and Democracy: Comparative Perspectives* 603 (January 2006): 196.

156 Wei, "Xin qimeng yu Zhongguo shehui zhuanxing de yixie genbenxing wenti," 111.

157 Peerenboom, "Law and Development of Constitutional Democracy," 196.

158 Ibid., 194.

159 Dowdle, "Of Parliaments, Pragmatism, and the Dynamics of Constitutional Development," 195.

160 Ibid.

161 Ji Weidong, "The Mission and Authority of the Supreme Court," July 10, 2012, http://english.caixin.com.

162 The epigraph is from Paula Bartley, *Emmeline Pankhurst* (London: Routledge, 2002), 100.

163 The epigraph is from Hu Shuli, Duan Hongqing, and Fang Xuyan, "Kanbujian de quanli" [Invisible power], *Caixin New Era*, June 5, 2012, http://china.caixin.com/2012-06-05/100397117.html.

Chapter 5

He Huaihong (Philosopher and Ethicist): Bringing Ethics Back into Chinese Discourse

Civilization is a stream with banks. The stream is sometimes filled with blood from people killing, stealing, shouting and doing the things historians usually record, while on the banks, unnoticed, people build homes, make love, raise children, sing songs, write poetry and even whittle statues. The story of civilization is the story of what happened on the banks. Historians are pessimists because they ignore the banks for the river.

— Will Durant, The Story of Civilization

I first met Professor He Huaihong at a small café near the Law School of Peking University on an autumn afternoon in 2011. Actually, I came not to meet with him, but with his wife, Shao Binhong, executive editor of the journal *International Economic Review* and a researcher at the Chinese Academy of Social Sciences (CASS). Shao is a former CCTV anchorwoman, best known for her primetime feature program, "Oriental Portraits."[1] We wanted to discuss Sino-American economic relations on the tenth anniversary of China's accession to the WTO. Shao brought along her husband He Huaihong to the meeting.

Although fully engaged in the conversation, Professor He only occasionally made comments. He struck me as a soft-spoken, humble, gracious, and knowledgeable gentleman. At the end of the meeting, he gave me his two recently published volumes, *The Hereditary Society* and *The Selection Society*. These two books served as the expanded version of his famous "dual study" of elite selection in ancient China and the ethical foundation of the governing structure of pre-1905 China.

I came to more fully appreciate He Huaihong's scholarship and his intellectual contributions, especially in the field of ethics, almost a year later. In the autumn of 2012, I began to solicit recommendations from scholars in China for a volume on ethics for the Thornton Center Chinese Thinkers series, which is published by the Brookings Institution Press. To my surprise, the three distinguished Chinese public intellectuals I contacted — political scientist Yu Keping, legal scholar He Weifang, and philosopher Xu Youyu — all singled out He Huaihong as the most influential ethicist in China today.[2] I spent the following months immersed in He's writings, enthralled by his philosophical and historical narratives on ethical perplexity in present-day China. Fascinated by the depth and breadth of his intellectual inquiry, I frequently met with Professor He when I visited Beijing. He and I had numerous substantial discussions and e-mail exchanges over the ensuing three years.

It was hardly a coincidence that the three aforementioned prominent Chinese scholars, though strikingly different in terms of academic field, political status, and worldview, all regard He Huaihong as the country's leading ethicist. Combining masterful expertise on Chinese philosophical tradition with a deep knowledge of Western ethical theories, He Huaihong has produced a steady stream of widely respected scholarly publications on ethics and morality for almost three decades. He Huaihong is not an academic who isolates himself in an ivory tower and produces research that can only be understood by a handful of peers. On the contrary, He is known for his role as a public intellectual who is keenly interested in linking past with present, bridging East and West, and blurring academic boundaries.

By 1989, He Huaihong had already translated *Meditations,* the reflections of Marcus Aurelius, who was emperor of ancient Rome (161–180 CE) and one of the most important Stoic philosophers. *Meditations* is a monumental work in ethics that focuses on nature as a source of guidance, peace, and inspiration at a time of tremendous physical tension and moral pressure. In November 2007, during his visit to Singapore, then premier Wen Jiabao told journalists that *Meditations* was his "bedside book," and that he had read it more than 100 times.[3] The first Chinese version of this

Marcus Aurelius masterpiece, translated by He Huaihong and published by the China Social Science Press in 1989, has sold more than half a million copies.[4]

Over the past three decades, through scholarly publications of both original works and translations, frequent lectures at academic conferences and in public forums, commentaries, and featured interviews in print, on television, and on social media, He Huaihong has emerged as one of the most influential thinkers in the country. These endeavors have transformed the Chinese public's understanding of the moral predicament underlying many news headlines and controversial issues in this rapidly changing country. Perhaps more effectively and constructively than anyone else, He Huaihong is bringing ethics back into Chinese discourse.

During the past half-century, the PRC has experienced several incredible human-made dramas: Red Guard fanaticism, a loss of education for a whole generation during the Cultural Revolution, the Tiananmen tragedy, an economic miracle and the subsequent rise of money worship, rampant official corruption and the resulting legitimacy crisis of the Chinese Communist Party, and the ongoing and painstaking search for modern virtues in an ancient civilization. He Huaihong was not only a first-hand witness to all of these extraordinary events; he also played a key role as a philosopher, historian, and social critic, exploring the deeper intellectual and sociological origins of these events and their profound impact on society's moral codes.

What, then, is the current status of ethics and morality in China? What are the causes of the widely perceived moral decay (道德滑坡, *daode huapo*) and crisis of trust (信任危机, *xinren weiji*) in Chinese society? Why is ethical discourse critically important to assessing China's reemergence in the 21st century? Is analyzing ethical issues sufficient to reveal the sociopolitical challenges and the ideological vacuum that China now confronts as a nation? In a given country, what is the relationship between individual moral standards and social ethical norms, or between moral principles and the political system? How can China build a forward-looking and globally oriented moral order from the shards of the broken traditional ethical code? How should the Chinese reconstruct their ethical norms? What kind of contemporary values and beliefs should the Chinese embrace? How should they tread the fine line between preserving Chinese ethical norms and promoting universal values at a time of unprecedented, multidimensional, fast-paced globalization?

Social Ethics in a Changing China, published by the Brookings Institution Press in 2015, includes some of He Huaihong's most important and representative works and sheds valuable light on all of these important questions. In a broader sense, *Social Ethics in a Changing China* not only highlights the imperative for ethical discourse in a country that is increasingly seen by many as both a materialistic giant and a spiritual dwarf, but also represents an innovative effort to rebuild the Chinese collective consciousness and social norms necessary for an ethical awakening. The ramifications of reestablishing systems of beliefs and ethics will be felt beyond China's national borders, especially now that the country is reemerging as a global power.

Chinese Concerns and Debates about Moral Decay

It seems a paradox — an irony — that Chinese concerns about moral decay are mounting in a period when China is perceived by many people both at home and abroad to be rising, or reemerging, on the world stage. Top Chinese leaders — from Jiang Zemin and Hu Jintao to Xi Jinping — have often linked China's remarkable economic development in the reform era with what they have called "cultural advancement" (文化振兴, *wenhua zhenxing*) and "spiritual civilization" (精神文明, *jingshen wenming*). At the turn of the century, Jiang Zemin claimed that the CCP in the new environment of the 21st century should represent the "progressive course of China's advanced culture," "advanced productive forces," and "fundamental interests of the overwhelming majority of the Chinese people."[5] This so-called Theory of the Three Represents constituted a guiding ideological framework for China's development.

In the Hu Jintao era, the CCP even claimed that China had reentered its "magnificent era," similar to that of the Tang and Song dynasties.[6] For many years, the political establishment and official media used that phrase to characterize the achievements under Hu's leadership, especially in reference to landmark events like the 2008 Beijing Olympics and the 2010 Shanghai Expo. This complacent notion was met with steep criticism in the country, however, not only from liberal public intellectuals but also from some senior officials.[7]

Ever since he became the top CCP leader in 2012, Xi Jinping has promoted the "Chinese dream" and "the great rejuvenation of the Chinese nation."[8] In a widely reported speech delivered in the fall of 2014 at an international conference in Beijing — celebrating the 2,665th anniversary of the birth of Confucius — Xi claimed that the CCP does not advocate cultural nihilism but instead venerates Confucianism and other important aspects of Chinese tradition.[9] For Xi, China's rise to prominence on the world stage should not stem solely from its economic accomplishments but also from public confidence in its cultural values and social ethics.[10]

Despite top Chinese leaders' emphasis on cultural and ethical advancement, they have not completely denied the moral predicament in reform-era China. On a number of occasions in the late 1980s, for example, Deng Xiaoping acknowledged that the greatest mistake committed during the first decade of post-Mao reforms lay in the domain of education, referring not only to young students in schools, but also to the general public and the inadequacy of its ideological and ethical development.[11] Probably the Chinese leadership's most candid recognition of its failure to reestablish a belief system and reconstruct social ethics came from Wen Jiabao. In 2011, following several horrifying food and drug safety scandals, then premier Wen made an astonishingly forceful statement about the poor state of ethics in the country: "These scandals are strong enough to show that the moral decay and loss of trust have reached an extremely serious point."[12] Wen further argued: "A country that fails to embody the high moral standards of its citizens can never become a truly powerful country or a respected nation."[13] Xi Jinping, with a similar sense of foreboding at the Politburo's first meeting under his leadership in 2012, referred pointedly to the rampant corruption among officials and its terrible impact on public confidence in the CCP: "Many facts tell us that corruption has become so widespread that it will ultimately destroy the party and the nation."[14]

Chinese public sentiment offers a more comprehensive explanation of the aforementioned concerns of the CCP leadership. The crises of trust and morality, which are commonplace in Chinese daily life, are reflected today in general empirical facts, as observed by Gao Zhaoming, professor of ethics at Nanjing Normal University.[15] In a large survey conducted in 2014, "loss of trust" was ranked as the top "social disease" in China. Of those surveyed, 88 percent believed (60.2 percent fully agreed and 27.8 percent agreed somewhat) that China has been beset by a "social disease of moral decay and the loss of trust."[16] The extent of the country's ethical and moral problems is made all too clear by the long list of widely occurring dishonest practices and dangerous goods, such as commercial fraud, tax fraud, financial deception, shoddy and dangerous engineering projects, fake products, tainted milk, poisonous bread, toxic pills, and the decline in professional ethics among teachers, doctors, lawyers, Buddhist monks, and especially government officials.

These seemingly anecdotal social phenomena are actually symptomatic of what He Huaihong calls two "worrying aspects of our moral miasma": the "level of severity" and "the scale of the moral disruption." The first concern is that corruption is widespread across all levels of government. It has infected not only senior National leaders such as former minister of railways Liu Zhijun, former head of the National Energy Administration Liu Tienan, former police chief and Politburo Standing Committee member Zhou Yongkang, and former vice chairman of the Central Military Commission Xu Caihou, each of whom was charged with stealing an exorbitant amount from state coffers. But even at lower levels, civil servants such as village heads, town heads, and local bank managers "are able to accumulate tens or even hundreds of millions of *yuan* in bribes. A district bureau chief may own dozens of houses."[17]

As for the second worrying aspect, He Huaihong believes that corruption is not just a problem of governmental officials; it is a "failure of society" and signifies the collapse of ethical codes in the nation. Fearing legal liability or blackmail, bystanders offer no help when a little girl is hit by a car or an elderly person falls in the street: the Chinese media have reported countless tragic stories like these over the past decade.[18] As He Huaihong discusses in a chapter of *Social Ethics in a Changing China*, behavior on the streets can even turn savage.[19] People who behave like this share one common characteristic: "They attempt to relieve their anger through violence. They try to use violence to solve their problems." When a female driver was severely beaten by a male driver in a recent road-rage incident in Chengdu and a video of the episode was posted online, a large number of social media commentators blamed the female driver for her poor driving habits. As He Huaihong argues, all of these troubling phenomena indicate "fundamental trust and fundamental kindness are being lost in our society."[20]

The breakdown in society's value system is captured in a nationwide survey on the spiritual life of contemporary Chinese people conducted in 2014 by the Modern Chinese Thought and Culture Research Institute at East China Normal University. Nearly 60 percent of respondents agreed that "people's values differ and therefore there should be no good or bad, right or wrong regarding moral issues." As Xu Jilin, a prominent historian of Chinese thought who helped design this research tool, observed, this staggeringly high figure reflects the crisis of moral standards in today's China.[21]

Similarly, a large number of Chinese scholars from diverse fields — law, sociology, politics, economics, philosophy, and history — have expressed serious concerns about moral decay and the loss of trust in contemporary China. According to Zhang Weiying, a prominent economist and former dean of the Guanghua School of Management at Peking University, "What China needs most is not law, but heavenly principles (天理, *tianli*). There can be no genuine rule of law if such law neither complies with heavenly principles, nor speaks to conscience."[22]

In place of heavenly principles and law, some observers find present-day China filled with regrettable "hidden rules" (潜规则, *qian guize*), a term coined by Wu Si, a prominent historian and former chief executive editor of the popular magazine *China through the Ages* (炎黄春秋, *Yanhuang chunqiu*).[23] According to Wu Si, at a time of moral decline and loss of trust, "hidden rules" based on connections, favoritism, and unethical deal-making tend to replace ethical codes and social norms. For example, as can happen in other countries, a young aspiring actor might follow such rules to obtain a role in a film, on television, or in a play by granting sexual favors to a casting director. "Hidden rules" have now infiltrated virtually all aspects of Chinese public life.

Even the field of education has been infected by corruption, according to Zi Zhongyun, who is former director of the Institute of American Studies at CASS and who served as an interpreter for both Mao Zedong and Zhou Enlai. In a widely viewed 2014 media interview in China, she recounted an extraordinary story about a middle school student who was caught cheating but whose father accused the school of being unfair to his son. In a bizarre (but also revealing) twist of logic, the father reasoned: for a kid from a nonofficial family who had no privileges or special access, cheating was the only "fair game." The father claimed the school's crackdown on cheating meant "there would be no fairness at all for kids who come from humble families."[24] According to Zi, the moral decay of the Chinese nation, which has already seeped into the critically important domain of education, is "very sad and enormously frightening."[25]

For Sun Liping, a distinguished professor of sociology at Tsinghua University, the predicament that confronts the country is rooted in "social decay" (社会溃败, *shehui kuibai*).[26] In his view, the greatest threat to China is not social unrest, but social decay. Whereas most analysts of China (both domestic and foreign) are concerned about mass protests and serious tensions between interest groups, Sun is more worried about social decay, which, at its core, indicates the abuse of power. In China today, argues Sun, power is neither constrained by external forces in society nor controlled by any internal mechanism. As a result, corruption has not only reached an unprecedentedly large scale among officials but has also spawned a wide assortment of social phenomena, such as unrestrained interest groups, serious erosion of social equity and justice, convergence of money and power, loss of professional ethics, and a decline in basic moral standards. All of these problems, says Sun, reflect the fundamental flaw in China's market reform: the failure to reestablish values for a renewed civilization.

Two main factors — or historical circumstances — have contributed to moral decay in present-day China. First, Mao's philosophy of violent class struggle, especially the violent Red Guard movement during the Cultural Revolution, had a detrimental effect on the country's ethical foundation. By way of illustration, in his discussion of Red Guard violence, He Huaihong recalls an incident that might be incomprehensible to those unfamiliar with the details of the Cultural Revolution: "Another Red Guard group had caught someone that they claimed was an 'old conservative boss.' They shot him in the head in front of a hotel and then went to eat inside, leaving the body in the street. All evening, going in and out of the hotel, they just pretended not to see it."[27] It is astonishing that this sort of humiliation, torture, and murder occurred in public, before the eyes of so many people. The Cultural Revolution was an extraordinary period, during which children condemned parents, husbands betrayed wives, and students tortured teachers — all for political and ideological reasons. In the aftermath of such a dark episode of recent Chinese history, many Chinese asked themselves how they could ever again believe or trust anyone in a position of authority.

The intellectual ferment of the post-Mao era from the late 1970s to the late 1980s, particularly the critical reflection on the decade-long political fanaticism and human suffering of the Cultural Revolution, resulted in a subsequent call for humanism.[28] In a sense, the Chinese discussion of humanism represented a search for an ethical and moral awakening. Unfortunately, this movement toward enlightenment did not last long, partly because of the government's crackdown on large-scale public discourse on the political and ethical sources of the turmoil. The famous writer Ba Jin's appeal for the establishment of a Cultural Revolution museum, for example, was sadly rejected. Most of all, the search for ethical awakening ground to a halt because the nation was caught up in another overwhelmingly rapid socioeconomic transformation — market reform, which heralded what became recognized as the era of money worship.[29]

Money worship, He Huaihong believes, is another factor contributing to the crisis of faith and moral decay.[30] Today, four decades after Mao's death, China is very different, not only in its national character but also in the concerns of its citizens. As a nation, China is set to become one of the world's economic giants — or, by some accounts, already is one.[31] But the country fails to show the world its true values and beliefs. As individuals, "Chinese now have drummed up their purses, but their spirit tends to be empty," says Zi Zhongyun.[32] Conducting extensive interviews with Chinese people in all walks of life has led Evan Osnos, former foreign correspondent in Beijing for *The New Yorker*, to a similar observation: "The Cultural Revolution dismantled China's ancient belief systems, and the economic revolution that followed could not rebuild them. Prosperity had yet to define the ultimate purpose of the nation and the individual. There was a hole in Chinese life that people called the 精神空虚, *jingshen kongxu* — 'the spiritual void.'"[33]

A well-known Chinese saying vividly casts present-day China's spiritual and moral decay in a historical narrative of loss: "China lost its Middle Kingdom with the end of the Ming; its Han ethnicity with its conquest by the Qing; its faith with the Cultural Revolution; and its morality with economic reform."[34]

Not all Chinese ethicists and public intellectuals agree with this negative assessment of the current state of ethics. As some point out, moral decay was lamented even in the ancient days of the Middle Kingdom. As early as the Spring and Autumn Period (770–476 BCE), when etiquette and a code of ethics were carefully observed, the "disintegration of propriety" (礼崩乐坏, *libeng yuehuai*) represented a growing concern. And throughout the entire 20th century, if not earlier, writers in both China and abroad described the "deep-rooted bad habits" of the Chinese people (国民劣根性, *guomin liegenxing*).[35] These traits are most evident in some of writer Lu Xun's well-known fictional characters. The provocative writings of the Taiwanese author Bo Yang, especially his famous book *The Ugly Chinaman*, reaffirmed this long-standing criticism of China's ethical and cultural norms.[36] According to some PRC critics, the influential works of Lu Xun, Bo Yang, and others have helped concoct a value-laden and false dichotomy between Confucian ethical rubbish and Western ethical essence. This, they say, has given rise to "a die-hard lie" both about Chinese culture and about the status of ethics in China today, for the Chinese are neither better nor more abhorrent than any other nationals in terms of their propensity for barbarism, ignorance, tyranny, and cruelty. As an anonymous Chinese scholar concludes, "The crimes conducted by the Chinese during the past century could not be worse than the crimes and atrocities inflicted on various groups of indigenous populations by colonial racists in world history."[37]

Other Chinese scholars have attempted to downplay the extreme depth of moral decay in today's China by pointing out that major socioeconomic transformation and political change are bound to have an impact on a country. As world history makes clear, a nation in the throes of rapid socioeconomic transformation is likely to experience some form of spiritual and ethical crisis.[38] As one Chinese scholar has observed, the former Soviet Union and other post-Communist Eastern European countries all experienced such crises, witnessing money worship take hold during their socioeconomic and political transitions.[39] The same could be said of many European countries between the 15th and 17th centuries, and the United States from 1865 to 1914, when the country went through Reconstruction, the Gilded Age, and the Progressive Era, periods that were marked by rapid industrialization and a surge in immigration.[40]

Tu Weiming, former director of the Harvard–Yenching Institute at Harvard University and currently a professor of philosophy at Peking University, believes that the ongoing Chinese discourse on morality could not only bring ethics back into critical focus but also encourage the Chinese to reconsider their traditions, especially Confucianism, in a more positive light.[41] According to Tu, of the five spiritual leaders who shaped civilizations around the world — Confucius, Socrates, Buddha, Jesus, and Mohammed — only Confucius has suffered constant maligning in contemporary China. Among extant civilizations, according to Tu, only the Chinese civilization has persisted for five thousand years without interruption.[42] In Tu's view, this remarkable continuity stems from the Confucian tradition, and Confucian ethical codes for individual behavior will likely become part of the common language of citizens of the world in the 21st century.[43]

Some Chinese scholars find that the ongoing intellectual discourse on morality in China is itself a very encouraging development. While the field of philosophy has been largely marginalized around the world in recent decades, the subfield of ethics seems to have attracted an increasing number of Chinese scholars and students.[44] Li Zehou, Chen Jiaying, and Li Meng, for example, represent three different generations of distinguished Chinese philosophers whose important works on ethics have enriched this subfield.[45] For He Huaihong, critical views of ethics, culture, politics, and history (as exemplified in the above discussion) have significantly broadened his thinking.

This review of Chinese concerns and debates about the country's ethical status provides a broad context in which to assess He Huaihong's scholarly work. He's intellectual journey has understandably been very challenging. He has needed to address tough questions, both politically and intellectually, on individual moral standards versus social ethics, morality versus legality, personal responsibility versus institutional accountability, and cultural pluralism versus universal values. More importantly, He

Huaihong has strived to construct a new intellectual framework for Chinese social ethics. The personal and professional experiences of this leading Chinese ethicist provide deeper insight into what he hopes to accomplish in China's search for a new ethical order.

He Huaihong and His Search for a Philosophy of Life

He Huaihong was born in a rural area of Qingjiang County (now Zhangshu City), Jiangxi Province, in December 1954. The Cultural Revolution began just as he was entering middle school. As a teenager, he worked as a porter in Nanchang County, Jiangxi Province, for a year. He belongs to the so-called lost generation, born in the 1950s, as his formative years coincided with the "decade of political turmoil" (1966–76). In his pre-college education, which included classical Chinese and history, He Huaihong was largely self-taught. In 1972, at eighteen, He was recruited to the PLA and was stationed in an economically disadvantaged region of Inner Mongolia for six years.[46]

In 1979 he was transferred from Inner Mongolia to Shanghai, where he later attended an eighteen-month program at the Political Institute of the Air Force. There he spent most of his time studying English and reading scholarly works by both Chinese and Western authors. Like most of his generation, He Huaihong never had formal training in any foreign language, but he was very fond of languages. Reading foreign language materials, especially literature and intellectual history, served, in He's words, as "a magnificent door" into to an entirely new world.[47] As a young man who had just escaped "long imprisonment in an intellectual desert filled with dogmatic worship," He Huaihong was thirsty for knowledge and extremely receptive to anything foreign and fresh.[48] As he later recalled, at that time he could recite many passages in English from Ernest Hemingway's novel *The Old Man and the Sea*. In the late 1980s, He taught himself Latin, French, and German.

After graduating from the Political Institute of the Air Force, He Huaihong began teaching at the Air Force Academy in Beijing in the fall of 1980. After he was demobilized in the early 1980s, he briefly worked as a researcher at the Academy of Social Sciences of Jiangxi Province in Nanchang. In 1984 he took the entrance examination for graduate school and enrolled in the ethics program (first for a master's degree and then for a doctoral degree) at Renmin University in Beijing. The university had very strong programs in the social sciences and the humanities, including philosophy and ethics.

The post-Cultural Revolution years were an exciting period in which young Chinese were extremely enthusiastic about absorbing Western liberal ideas. This was a time in which the old faith and attitudes had collapsed and new ones had yet to be established. Unlike their counterparts in today's China, who seem unbothered by the lack of ideological beliefs, college students and young professionals at that time often sensed something important missing from their lives. During that period, He Huaihong became profoundly interested in the works of Western philosophers, including Socrates, Plato, Immanuel Kant, and John Rawls. He was curious about many longstanding issues: how the interaction between human beings and the environment shapes human relationships, the differences in moralities across cultures, the true meaning of Chinese national character, how to evaluate ethics through cross-cultural comparisons, and the circumstances under which a new set of ethical codes in a given country can be established.[49]

During this time, He Huaihong began to think he would devote his career to the study of ethics. What attracted him to the field was its concern with the "philosophy of life" (人生哲学, *rensheng zhexue*) and focus on people.[50] His first book, *Contemplating Life: Comments on Pascal*, was published in 1988 and is about the 17th-century French mathematician, physicist, and philosopher Blaise Pascal. This legendary intellectual giant not only made great contributions to science but also laid the foundation for important philosophical theories that emerged in the following centuries, such as existentialism, pragmatism, and voluntarism. He Huaihong was particularly intrigued by the way in which Pascal dealt with philosophical paradoxes such as those between infinity and limits, faith and reason, and death and life. The following remarks make clear the impact of Pascal's work on He Huaihong's own philosophical view: "Human beings are finite space-time existences, but they seek to reach beyond their own limitations to become infinite. It is when people feel limited in the face of [the] infinite, that they sense their trivialness, and feel a mysterious fear and trembling. Yet, people will never give up and relax their efforts."[51]

Pascal's concept of the three hierarchical levels of greatness in human beings — from lowest to highest, the greatness of an emperor or a head of state, the greatness of spirit and thought, and the greatness of benevolence and kindness — has deeply influenced He Huaihong's philosophy.[52]

Throughout He Huaihong's career — whether in his academic writings or wider public outreach, in his painstaking efforts to reestablish a new ethical order for China or in his call for a Chinese ethical dialogue with the West and the world — the philosophy of life, or the principle of life, has always been a central theme.[53] He believes that "whether Chinese or foreign, ancient or modern, life should always be the first and foremost concern."[54] He Huaihong delineates three reasons for this belief. First, "life is the primary and most fundamental value of humanity; it is the precondition for all other human values." Second, "life is precious in itself — that is, it is precious as an end in itself, not just as a means." And third, "the life of every person is equally valuable."[55]

In the summer of 1982, He Huaihong read the English translation of Jean-Paul Sartre's *Being and Nothingness* and became fascinated with existentialism, particularly Sartre's two types of being: "being-in-itself" and "being-for-itself." While human beings can only approximate "being-in-itself," "being-for-itself" is the being of consciousness. This concept has greatly influenced He Huaihong's work, especially his theory of conscience and the notion of "minimum moral standards." Over the ensuing years, He delved more deeply into the works of other important proponents of existentialism, such as Gabriel Marcel, Karl Jaspers, Martin Heidegger, Albert Camus, and, especially, 19th-century pioneers Friedrich Nietzsche and Søren Kierkegaard. Their works helped He Huaihong eventually depart from Sartre's more extremist views of self-being in the realization that Sartre's philosophy is "too far away from reality, and too far from the lives of real people."[56]

In his early professional career, He Huaihong made an exceptional contribution to the dissemination of Western ideas and values in China through translation. He translated into Chinese nine important classic books on ethics, totaling approximately 1.6 million words.[57] In addition to the aforementioned *The Meditations* by Marcus Aurelius (1989), he translated or co-translated *Introduction to Ethics* by Frank Thilly (1987), *Moral Maxims* by François de La Rochefoucauld (1987), *A System of*

Ethics by Friedrich Paulsen (1988), *Anarchy, State, and Utopia* by Robert Nozick (1991), and *On Tyranny* by Leo Strauss (2006). Among Chinese scholars and students of ethics and philosophy, He Huaihong is widely credited as the translator who introduced John Rawls's masterpiece *A Theory of Justice* (1989, 2001, 2009) to Chinese readers. Besides his scholarly contributions and translations in the field of philosophy and ethics, He Huaihong has also published many commentaries for a general Chinese readership on a wide range of subjects, such as Fyodor Dostoevsky's novels, Jean-Paul Sartre's plays, and José Ortega y Gasset's essays.

Despite his extensive research and publications on Western philosophy and foreign cultures as a young scholar in the 1980s, He Huaihong did not forsake his study of Chinese philosophy and traditional culture. He remained keenly aware of the need to make up for the years of his educational development that were lost due to the Cultural Revolution. He referred to his age cohort as "the generation growing up with a deep fracture in Chinese tradition and culture."[58] He dedicated himself to a strictly and extensively planned study of important Chinese classics, and read all major works on traditional ethics, ranging from the main classics in the pre-Qin, pre-Wei and Jin, and pre-Sui and Tang eras, as well as those from the Song, Yuan, Ming, and Qing dynasties. As He Huaihong recalls, this decade-long "educational make-up" gave him a "more comprehensive understanding of the main elements of Chinese history and culture as well as its origins and ramifications."[59]

In his doctoral dissertation, "Contract Ethics and Social Justice" (1990), He Huaihong explored the philosophical logic behind various existing propositions relating to life preservation, promotion of law, property rights, and equal distribution of profits, all from the standpoint of justice. He also analyzed the ideals of equality and liberty, including their contrasting priorities, in light of the debate between John Rawls and Robert Nozick. This discussion bore strong relevance for China in the late 1980s and early 1990s, when the private sector reemerged. One year before receiving his PhD, He began teaching philosophy and ethics at the China Youth University for Political Sciences in Beijing. He served as a visiting scholar at Harvard University from 1993 to 1994, which he calls the "most pleasant and productive year of learning and reading in my career."[60] During this period of foreign study, he recognized the importance of cultural pluralism and the need for diversity and mutual respect in a globalized world.[61] After returning to China, He taught at the Institute of Chinese Studies of the Chinese Academy of Arts in Beijing from 1995 to 1998.

In 1994 He Huaihong wrote *A Theory of Conscience: The Transformation of Traditional Morality in the New Society*, which, in his preface to the 2009 edition, he described as his most important book on Chinese ethics.[62] This book has been widely considered "a groundbreaking work in the study of the Chinese traditional philosophy."[63] Partly because of the book's significant contribution to the field of philosophy and ethics, Peking University's Department of Philosophy recruited He Huaihong to its faculty in 1998. He has been a full professor in the department ever since, serving also as the director of the department's Ethics Program for many years. As He Huaihong points out, Peking University was the cradle of the contemporary Chinese study of ethics.[64] Established in 1912, the Department of Philosophy has had many leading scholars serving on its faculty over the century, including Cai Yuanpei, Hu Shih, Jiang Menglin, Xiong Shili, Liang Shuming, Feng Youlan, Zhu Guangqian, Zhang Dainian, and Tang Yijie. The founders of the CCP, Chen Duxiu and Li Dazhao, taught in the department early in their careers. The first contemporary Chinese textbook on ethics was written by Liu Shipei, the first book on the history of Chinese ethics was written by Cai Yuanpei, and the first Chinese book on comparative ethics was written by Huang Jianzhong — and each of these three authors served as a professor of philosophy at Peking University at the respective times of publication.[65]

Over the past two decades, the department has recruited a number of internationally renowned scholars, including Rainer Schäfer, who previously taught at the University of Heidelberg and the University of Bonn, and the aforementioned Tu Weiming. Inspired by both the great tradition of philosophical study at Peking University and extensive exposure to Western schools of thought through professional exchanges, He Huaihong has been remarkably prolific in his intellectual pursuits over the past two decades.

He Huaihong is also one of very few Chinese scholars who combines a grasp of Chinese ethical theories with broad expertise in the culture, history, religion, literature, and politics of the country. His study of the circulation of Chinese elites over time, or what he calls the dynamics between "the hereditary society" and "the selection society" (Chinese meritocracy), provides a novel perspective on China's three-thousand-year history, pointing to the development of a unique sociopolitical structure — a system that holds cultural and intellectual elites in high esteem and has therefore promoted social mobility and equality of opportunity.[66] While the system was certainly never free from abuses of power, nepotism, factionalism, and corruption, traditional China did establish a "true selection society in which learning was for the purpose of advancement and the ruling elite was selected from the best scholars."[67] As He Huaihong has documented, throughout China's long history the door to membership in the ruling class has often been open to those of humble origins. In the Ming dynasty, for example, over 50 percent of officials (进士, *jinshi*) were born into third-generation nonofficial families.[68] This historical fact, He Huaihong argues, shows that China was, in Tocquevillian terms, part of the global march toward modernity, as it reflects a shift toward equality.[69]

Over the past decade, He Huaihong has become more conscious of his role as an ethicist in a country searching for cultural and ethical rejuvenation. Hence, he has written several nonacademic books for a general readership, emphasizing the centrality of life in ethical discourse, and he has been an active participant, through the news media, in the public discourse on ethics.[70] In the early 2000s, for example, he wrote several dozen essays as part of his column "Bottom-Line Ethics" in the popular newspaper *New Beijing Daily*, commenting on a wide range of ethical and moral issues, such as animal rights, the death penalty, and respect for minority groups.[71] His most important objectives, He asserts, are "to tell stories about our own history, to resolve the problems confronting our nation, and to build our own research framework."[72]

Minimum Moral Standards and Maximum Ethical Concerns

Arguably the most important contribution that He Huaihong has made to the field of ethics is twofold: his theoretical concept of minimum moral standards, and his broad and multidisciplinary approach to promoting maximum ethical concerns.

Minimum Moral Standards: Universal Ethics

For the past half-century, if not longer, Chinese society has repeatedly and continually failed to observe minimum moral standards. In He Huaihong's words, that failure "threatens the very foundation of our society."[73] In He's view, it is imperative that the Chinese nation maintain a bottom line in ethical codes and social norms. Over the past two decades, the phrase most frequently used in his scholarly writing and public outreach is "minimum moral standards" (底线伦理, *dixian lunli*). There are a number of English translations of He Huaihong's concept of minimum moral standards, including "bottom-line ethics," "minimalist ethics," and "moral minimalism."[74] The concept can be traced back to the writings of Western philosophers such as Immanuel Kant, William David Ross, and John Rawls, all of whom sought a consensus on basic moral norms or a primary moral obligation.[75] After World War II, philosopher Theodor W. Adorno, a German exile living in the United States, returned to his homeland and wrote *Minima Moralia: Reflections from Damaged Life*, which further developed the concept of minimum moral standards in the wake of the horrible tragedies spurred by fascism in the first half of the 20th century.[76]

He Huaihong has substantially advanced the theory of minimum moral standards, especially by combining it with Chinese traditional philosophy. He divides minimum moral standards into three categories: first, basic natural and social responsibilities that every person must meet; second, standards associated with laws and social institutions; and third, professional ethics and morality in specific areas of human activity, such as in the government and on the Internet.[77]

He Huaihong argues that society and individuals should all fulfill their own responsibilities. For society, these fall in the realm of social justice; for individuals, they pertain to basic obligations, the foremost being "respect for human life and liberty."[78] Furthermore, minimum moral standards should be (1) *perpetual* (in the sense of "continuity between traditional society and modern"), or honored at all times; (2) *objective*, so that they are not subject to changes in different circumstances; and (3) *universal*, in the sense of being beyond cultural and ethnic boundaries.

The first of these traits, He Huaihong believes, links to the Chinese traditional concept of conscience (良心, *liangxin* or 良知, *liangzhi*), which was thought to guide individuals in the development of basic moral and ethical codes. In *A Theory of Conscience*, He systematically explores traditional culture's close attention to these basic moral standards and the view that conscience is a natural and inherent gift.[79] This is reflected in the remarks of early Chinese philosopher Mencius, for example, who noted that "humans all have the feeling of compassion."[80]

Traditional Chinese ethics also provides a rational basis for why obtaining consensus on minimum moral standards is both feasible and desirable. Confucius's motto, "Do not do unto others what you would not have done to yourself," succinctly articulates the rationality of such a consensus.[81] He Huaihong agrees that a human being's fundamental sense of compassion, sympathy, and responsibility is real, "but it is often weakened by a range of influences to the point that it no longer disciplines us and drives our conduct."[82] Therefore, he claims that "we need to work on every level of our consciousness: beliefs, emotions, rationality, experience, intuition. We must not reject any idea on any level that could help us in our fight to improve the environment. And we must hope that no matter how minimal it may be, we can find some broad-based consensus and broad-based will to act."[83]

As for the second trait, objectivity, He Huaihong argues that because minimum moral standards are based on objective criteria, they should not be subject to change and can never be lowered. Otherwise, these standards would be more like "springboards" (弹簧, *tanhuang*) than "bottom lines" (底线, *dixian*).[84] That is to say, they are basic global norms that aim to ban murder, theft, fraud, and rape, and they call for a compassionate and humane approach to dealing with other people.[85] Because this ethical code is so basic and minimal, it is able to draw maximum consensus.

This emphasis on objectivity leads to the notion of universal ethics (普遍伦理, *pubian lunli*), the third trait of He Huaihong's theory of minimum moral standards. In He's view, such standards should apply equally to all individuals, all groups, all classes, and all nations without exception.[86] This does not mean that human values around the world are or should be the same. In He's words, "People's values and ultimate concerns are varied; they may contradict and even clash with each other."[87] He Huaihong reasons that an ethical system consists of two main components, normative principles and value-based beliefs, so that "when we consider universal ethics, we must give priority to the norms of moral behavior rather than value systems."[88]

At the same time, He Huaihong adamantly believes in universal values (普世价值, *pushi jiazhi*) and argues that universal ethics are achievable for the same reason that some values are shared universally. For He Huaihong, "human nature does not vary much in this world" and "traditional Chinese moral habits bear creditable comparison with those of any culture in the world."[89] He also believes that values, like ideas, can be disseminated across national borders. In a recent article on American democracy and constitutionalism, He Huaihong explains that the May Fourth Movement introduced many Western ideas into China — not only Marxism, but also so-called Mr. Democracy, Mr. Science, Mr. Law, and Mr. Morality.[90] Some of these concepts notably stirred intellectual discourse in 20th-century China. In He's words, "without reference to Western ideas, a modern and contemporary Chinese history would not know where to start. These ideas and values have been deeply assimilated into our daily lives and various institutions."[91]

In a sense, while minimum moral standards are not subject to change, ideological values, cultural norms, and social ethics in a given country do transform, sometimes quite profoundly. Cong Riyun, a well-known public intellectual and professor at the China University of Political Science and Law, recently posed an intriguing question: Which "cultural gap" is bigger, the one between present-day China and the present-day United States, or the one between China today and the China of 200 years ago? Cong's answer was undoubtedly the latter, as he facetiously estimated that more than half of the women in the country today would probably commit suicide if they suddenly found themselves living in 19th-century China. This point illustrates the impact of the dissemination of Western values in China over the past couple of centuries.[92]

He Huaihong's concept of minimum moral standards not only provides a realistic paradigm to deal with moral decay in Chinese society, but also aims to reaffirm universal ethics and universal values — notions that have unfortunately been rejected by most Chinese leaders and conservative intellectuals.[93]

Maximum Ethical Concerns: Political and Cultural Transformation

Some critics argue that He Huaihong's emphasis on ethics may divert public attention from the problems of China's political system. For example, Hou Shuyi, a professor of law at the Shandong Institute of Technology, refers to He's "moral self-discipline" (道德自律, *daode zilü*) as wishful thinking.[94] Hou states that one should not overlook the fact that Confucian ethics were the ideological basis of autocratic imperial rule and were invoked to maintain the legitimacy and order of the feudal system. Moreover, unless institutional restraint and legal mechanisms are given priority, any discussion of ethics can be highly misleading and certainly will not prevent moral decay. In Hou's view, good governance in a given country is not based on moral self-discipline, but instead relies on sound and sustainable political institutions.[95]

He Huaihong does recognize both the flaws of traditional Chinese ethics and the political and institutional factors underlying moral decay in present-day China. As he observes, "In traditional morality, the most important elements are not attitudes and behaviors among individuals or between an individual and society, but self-knowledge, self-development, and moral self-perfection."[96] He Huaihong considers morality "to be mainly the morality of society and social norms." Ethics refers not to individual ethics (个人道德, *geren daode*) but, first and foremost, to institutional ethics (制度伦理, *zhidu lunli*), meaning the justice of the institutional system — how it constrains the behaviors of individuals, especially those in power.[97] He Huaihong states explicitly that "in today's world, if we wish to protect our safety and our dignity, rule of law is the only option."[98] As for individuals, He believes that ethical awakening is actually the "people's awakening" or "individual liberalization," which should involve a transformation in the relationship between the state, society, communities, and individuals.

He Huaihong has been openly critical of excessive interference in societal autonomy and individual liberty by the PRC's political powers.[99] In his view, such interference has destroyed part of the country's traditional ethical foundation and has caused the remaining parts to lose their constraining power.[100] He finds that even the Chinese leadership's recent efforts to promote ethical reconstruction usually have not taken into consideration the need for autonomy in ethical discourse. Just as morality should not operate in place of institutions and law, it should also have its own function — for example, to achieve consensus in society on the basis of the aforementioned minimum moral standards.[101] In He's view, the mixing of political propaganda and ideological doctrines with ethical discussion does not resonate well with the Chinese public.[102]

In 2005, eight years before President Xi Jinping launched his bold political campaign against official corruption, He Huaihong outlined six integrated measures to deal with this rampant problem: (1) make it harder (不能, *buneng*), (2) make it riskier (不敢, *bugan*), (3) make it unnecessary (不必, *bubi*), (4) make it contemptible (不屑, *buxie*), (5) make it shameful (不忍, *buren*), and (6) make it undesirable (不欲, *buyu*). Ultimately, He has called for broad-scoped, system-wide efforts to curtail corruption, including "a constitutional set of checks and balances."[103]

Along with this much-needed political transformation, He Huaihong proposes the establishment of new moral principles (新纲常, *xin gangchang*), including the following three: "the people set guidelines for the government" (民为政纲, *minwei zhenggang*), "rightness sets guidelines for human beings" (义为人纲, *yiwei rengang*), and "the living set guidelines for all things" (生为物纲, *shengwei wugang*). Next, he proposes five new constants, borrowed from "virtues identified in the classics — benevolence (仁, *ren*), rightness (义, *yi*), ritual (礼, *li*), wisdom (智, *zhi*), and faithfulness (信, *xin*) — as well as five redefined relationships."[104] He calls for a new cultural transformation amid the rapidly changing sociopolitical environment of 21st-century China and the challenging ecological conditions that the world faces.[105] He Huaihong identifies many important distinctions between the old and new moral principles. The new ethics represents a move toward equality between people and requires that those of high status fulfill their duties toward those of low status. That is to say, those who govern should be accountable to citizens. The new ethics also emphasizes the importance of environmental protection. As some commentators observe, He Huaihong's new principles reflect his deep concern about ethical governance in modern society.[106]

Although these new principles are directed primarily at the Chinese people, they reflect He Huaihong's profound desire to place Chinese ethical discourse in a global context and to have "an academic dialogue on an equal footing with the West and the world."[107] Portions of *Social Ethics in a Changing China* are concerned with ethical duties in the realm of international relations, especially as so many issues now constitute serious threats to the survival of humanity: weapons of mass destruction, environmental and ecological degradation, ethnic cleansing, widespread violence and terrorism, and cyber-security, to name a few.[108] As He points out, "Our material and military power is at an extraordinary peak, but the spiritual and cultural bonds that keep us connected to one another have never been weaker."[109]

He Huaihong's global perspective and his keen interest in having China engage in an ethical dialogue with the West spring not only from his familiarity with Western ethics, but also from the Chinese sentiment that Western ethical theories promote exclusivity. In the eyes of many non-Westerners, Western modernity reflects military and economic conquest, colonial rule, and Western centrism in the cultural domain.[110] In a way, the international dialogue on ethical issues that He Huaihong and like-minded Chinese scholars seek can promote cross-cultural understanding.

While He Huaihong's thinking, as captured in *Social Ethics in a Changing China*, grows out of the intellectual odyssey of one truly extraordinary Chinese ethicist, it also reflects the broader experience of China's journey into the 21st century — namely, the country's painful attempt to recover from the severe moral decay caused by the destruction of Chinese ethical principles over the last century. The ongoing Chinese ethical discourse is among the most important factors that will determine the trajectory and impact of China's rise on the world stage. The general English-speaking readership — and analysts of China, in particular — will benefit tremendously from becoming well informed about this Chinese ethical discourse — and the philosophical and political insights that flow out of it.

Notes

This chapter is an edited version of the introduction to the He Huaihong volume of the Thornton Center Chinese Thinkers Series, published by the Brookings Institution Press. See Cheng Li, "Introduction: Bringing Ethics Back into Chinese Discourse," in He Huaihong, *Social Ethics in a Changing China: Moral Decay or Ethical Awakening?* (Washington, DC: Brookings Institution Press, 2015), xv-xl. Thanks go to Ming Ching Chai, Yinsheng Li, Yuxin Zhang, and Tony Zhao for their research assistance; and Meara Androphy, Zach Balin, Ryan McElveen, Lucy Xu, and Jing Jing Zhang for their very helpful comments on early versions of this chapter. I am also grateful to Daniel B. Wright for arranging my first meeting with He Huaihong and his wife, Shao Binhong, in Beijing in October 2011.

1 Shao Binhong produced about 300 episodes of the CCTV feature program "Oriental Portraits" (东方之子, *dongfang zhizi*) in the 1990s and became a household name in the country.

2 Yu Keping and He Weifang are the authors of the two earlier volumes of this series: Yu Keping, *Democracy is a Good Thing: Essays on Politics, Society, and Culture in Contemporary China* (Washington, DC: Brookings Institution Press, 2009), and He Weifang, *In the Name of Justice: Striving for the Rule of Law in China* (Washington, DC: Brookings Institution Press, 2012). Both were named by U.S.-based *Foreign Policy* magazine as among the world's 100 most influential thinkers in 2011. *Foreign Policy* website, November 28, 2011, http://foreignpolicy.com/2011/11/28/the-fp-top-100-global-thinkers-4. Xu Youyu offered me the recommendation through his wife, Professor Yang Gonghua, China's leading epidemiologist.

3 Gui Yang, "Pandian lingdaoren jianshu" [Review the books recommended by leaders], Xinhua Newsnet, December 17, 2013, http://news.xinhuanet. com/book/2013-12/17/c_125870261_4.htm. There are over two dozen Chinese translations of *Meditations,* most of them from English versions. Probably the earliest one was translated by Liang Shiqiu. See Liang Shiqiu, *Chensi lu* [Meditations] (Taipei: Hsieh-chih Industrial Library, 1958). Liang's volume was a Chinese translation from the English translation by C. R. Haines, *Communings with Himself of Marcus Aurelius Antoninus, Emperor of Rome* (London: William Heinemann, 1916).

4 This number was provided by He Huaihong. See also Wang Jingjing, "He Huaihong: Rang wenhe chengwei zhuliu taidu" [He Huaihong: Let the moderate attitude be the mainstream one], *Huanqiu renwu* [Global Characters], No. 24 (2013).

5 "Sange daibiao zhongyao sixiang" [Important thoughts on the Three Represents], Xinhua Newsnet, January 21, 2003, http://news.xinhuanet. com/ziliao/2003-01/21/con-tent_699933.htm.

6 "Shengshi dayuebing" [Parade in the booming and golden age], People's Net, October 1, 2009, http://022net.com/2009/10-1/502335113149597. html.

7 For example, Zi Zhongyun stated bluntly that underneath this superficial "booming and golden age," there is a profound sense of crisis in the making and deep concern about the moral decay of the regime. Hao Yu, "Zi Zhongyun: Chongjian Zhishifenzi dui 'daotong' de dandang" [Resuming the role of intellectuals in ethics], *Jingji guancha bao* [Economic Observers], December 25, 2010. See also http://chinaelections.com/article/101/180995.html.

8 Xi Jinping, *Guanyu shixian zhonghua minzu weida fuxing de Zhongguo meng lunshu zhaibian* [Excerpts on the realization of the great rejuvenation of the Chinese dream] (Beijing: Central Literature Publishing House, 2013).

9 *Shijie ribao* [World Journal], September 25, 2014, A5.

10 For more discussion of Xi Jinping's effort to promote Confucian values, see Evan Osnos, "Confucius Comes Home," *The New Yorker*, January 13, 2014.

11 Xinhua Newsnet, February 23, 2015, http://news.xinhuanet.com/ziliao/2005-02/23/content_2608913.htm.

12 Wen Jiabao, "Jiangzhenhua, chashiqing" [Examine the facts, and tell the truth], China Newsnet, April 14, 2011, http://china.com.cn/policy/txt/2011-04/18/content_22381581_2.htm. It should be noted that some Chinese officials publicly rejected Wen's notion about the moral landslide. Fang Ming, "Wen Jiabao nuchi Zhongguo chengxin queshi yinqi renmin buman" [Premier Wen Jiabao angrily stated that the loss of trust causes resentment among the people], Sina Global News, October 22, 2011, http://dailynews.sina.com/gb/chn/chnnews/ausdaily/20111022/20172861650.html.

13 Ibid.

14 Xinhua Newsnet, November 19, 2012, http://news.cntv.cn/18da/20121119/103379.shtml.

15 Gao Zhaoming, *Daode wenhua: cong chuantong dao xiandai* [Moral culture: From tradition to modernity] (Beijing: Renmin chubanshe, 2015), 53.

16 Xu Yanhong, Yuan Qing, and Tan Feng, "Dangqian shehui bingtai diaocha fenxi baogao" [Survey report on the social diseases of present-day China], *Renmin luntan* [People's Forum], September 1, 2014, http://paper.people.com.cn/rmlt/html/2014-09/01/content_1476497.htm.

17 He, *Social Ethics in a Changing China*, Chapter 8.

18 He, *Social Ethics in a Changing China*, Chapter 1. Also see Xu Jilin, "Ruhe chongjian Zhongguo de lunli yu xinyang" [How to rebuild China's ethics and faith], *Jinrongjia* [Financier], August 10, 2014, http://chuansong.me/n/593505.

19 He, *Social Ethics in a Changing China*, Chapter 9.

20 He, *Social Ethics in a Changing China*, Chapter 8.

21 Xu, "Ruhe chongjian Zhongguo de lunli yu xinyang."

22 Zhang Weiying, "Dangjin Zhongguo zui que tianli" [What present-day China needs the most is heavenly principles or ethics], *Wenzhai* [Digest], October 6, 2013. See also Duowei News, http://opinion.dwnews.com/news/2013-10-06/59335074-all.html.

23 Wu Si, *Qian guize: Zhongguo lishi zhong de zhenshi youxi* [The hidden rules: Real games of Chinese history] (Shanghai: Fudan daxue chubanshe, 2009).

24 Zi Zhongyun, *Xiansheng cengjing zheyang shangxue: Zi Zhongyun he tade xiaoyuan* [When I was attending school: Zi Zhongyun and her experience on campus] (Beijing: CITIC Publishing House, 2014).

25 Ibid.

26 Sun Liping, "Zuida weixie fei shehui dongdang ershi shehui kuibai" [The greatest threat to China is not social unrest, but the social decay of the country], *Nanfang ribao* [Southern Daily], February 28, 2009. See also 21CN Net, http://news.21cn.com/today/zhuanlan/2009/02/28/5930537.shtml. For more discussion of Sun Liping's notion of social decay, see Sun Liping, *Shouwei dixian: Zhuanxing shehui shenghuo de jichu zhixu* [Minimal responsibility: The basic order of social life in a transformational Chinese society] (Beijing: Shehuikexue wenxian chubanshe, 2007).

27 He, *Social Ethics in a Changing China*, Chapter 6.

28 The call for humanism in the post-Mao era was most evident in literature of the time. Representative works include Dai Houying "Ren a ren" [Stones in the wall], *Huacheng* [City of Flowers], No. 11 (November 1980); Dai Houying, *Shiren zhisi* [Death of a poet] (Shanghai: Taibai wenyi chubanshe, 1994); and Lu Xinhua, "Shanghen" [Scar], *Wenhui Daily*, August 11, 1978.

29 He, *Social Ethics in a Changing China*, Chapter 7.

30 Gao, *Daode wenhua*, 538.

31 He, *Social Ethics in a Changing China*, Chapter 4.

32 Zi Zhongyun, "Renxing, wenhua zhidu" [Humanity, culture, and institution], Consensus Net, August 2, 2012, http://21ccom.net/articles/zgyj/gmht/article_2012080164907.html.

33 Osnos, "Confucius Comes Home." For his work that won the 2014 National Book Award, see Evan Osnos, *Age of Ambition: Chasing Fortune, Truth, and Faith in the New China* (New York: Farrar, Straus and Giroux, 2014).

34 "Mingwang zhihou wu huaxia, manqing zhihou wu hanren, wenge zhihou wu xinyang, gaige zhihou wu daode" (明亡之后无华夏, 满清之后无汉人, 文革之后无信仰, 改革之后无道德).

35 "Guomin liegenxing: yige wenhua de huangyan" ["Deep-rooted bad habits" of the Chinese people: A lie about the Chinese culture], *Tushuguan* [Library], March 1, 2012, http://360doc.com/content/12/0301/16/904434_190857084.shtml.

36 Lu Xun, *The True Story of Ah-Q* (Beijing: Foreign Languages Press, 1960); and Bo Yang, *Choulou de zhongguoren* [The Ugly Chinaman] (Taipei: Yuanliu chuban, 2009).

37 "Guomin liegenxing."

38 Gao, *Daode wenhua*, 99.

39 Li Xiaohong, *Zhongguo zhuanxingqi shehui xinyong huanjing yanjiu* [Study of social credit and trust in China's transitional period] (Beijing: Economic Publishing House, 2008), 1.

40 Ibid.

41 Tu Weiming, "Rujia renwen jingshen de pushi jiazhi" [Universal values of the Confucian human spirit], *Renmin luntan* [People's Forum], August 11, 2014. See also People's Net, http://theory.people.com.cn/n/2014/0806/c112848-25414997.html.

42 Tu, "Rujia renwen jingshen de pushi jiazhi."

43 Ibid.

44 Gan Shaoping, *Lunlixue de dangdai jiangou* [Modern construction of ethics] (Beijing: China Development Press, 2015), 22.

45 For their representative works, see Li Zehou, *Lunlixue gangyao* [Outline of ethics] (Beijing: Renmin ribao chubanshe, 2010); Chen Jiaying, *Hewei lianghao shenghuo* [What is the good life?] (Shanghai: Shanghai wenyi chubanshe, 2015); and Li Meng, *Ziran shehui* [Nature society] (Shanghai: SDX Joint Publishing Company, 2015).

46 Part of this discussion about the personal and professional life of He Huaihong is based on He Huaihong, *Zixuan ji* [Selected works] (Guilin: Guangxi Normal University Press, 2000).

47 He, *Zixuan ji*, 338.

48 Ibid.

49 Ibid., 349.

50 Ibid.

51 He Huaihong, "Kewang wuxian" [In search of the unlimited], Xilu Net, October 23, 2002, http://club.xilu.com/hnzqz3/msgview-135899-24174.html.

52 He Huaihong, *Bi tiankong geng guangkuo* [Wider than the sky] (Shanghai: SDX Joint Publishing Company, 2003), 3.

53 He, *Social Ethics in a Changing China*, Chapter 11.

54 He Huaihong, "Cong 'zunzun qinqin xianxian' dao 'ziyou pingdeng boai'" [From "respect, love, and virtue" to "freedom, equality, and fraternity"], Chinese Studies Net, November 16, 2014, http://bbs.gxsd.com.cn/forum. php?mod=viewthread&tid=962524.

55 He, *Social Ethics in a Changing China*, Chapter 18.

56 He, *Zixuan ji*, 343–44.

57 Ibid., 346.

58 Ibid., 353.

59 Ibid., 356.

60 Ibid., 348.

61 Ibid., 349.

62 He Huaihong, *Liangxin lun* [A theory of conscience], revised ed. (Beijing: Peking University Press, 2009), 1.

63 Shao Zijie, "Zhou Zhixing duihua He Huaihong: Fenlie shidai de zuidi xiandu gongshi" [Zhou Zhixing's dialogue with He Huaihong: minimum consensus at a time of split], Consensus Net, August 13, 2011, http://21ccom. net/articles/sxwh/shsc/article_2011081343175.html.

64 He Huaihong, *Shengsheng dade* [The great virtue of life-giving] (Beijing: Peking University Press, 2011), 134.

65 Ibid.

66 He, *Zixuan ji*, 358.

67 He, *Social Ethics in a Changing China*, Chapter 3.

68 He Huaihong, *Xuanju shehui* [The selection society], revised ed. (Beijing: Peking University Press, 2011), 100.

69 He, *Social Ethics in a Changing China*, Chapter 3.

70 He Huaihong, *Zunzhong shengming* [Respect life] (Guangzhou: Guangdong Jiaoyu Publishing House, 1998).

71 He, *Social Ethics in a Changing China*, Chapter 13. Also see He Huaihong, *Zhongguo de youshang* [The sorrow of China] (Beijing: Law Press, 2011), 258.

72 He, *Zixuan ji*, 341.

73 He, *Social Ethics in a Changing China*, Chapter 10.

74 For a more detailed discussion of the conceptual development of minimum moral standards, see He, *Shengsheng dade*, 193.

75 Ibid., 192.

76 Theodor Adorno, *Minima Moralia: Reflections from Damaged Life*, translated by E. F. N. Jephcott (New York: Verso, 2006).

77 He, *Social Ethics in a Changing China*, Chapter 10.

78 He, *Liangxin lun*, 337, 241; Dao Erdeng, "Du He Huaihong Xin 'Gangchang'" [On He Huaihong's *New Principles*], *Nanfang Zhoumo* [Southern Weekly], August 6, 2013. See also http://infzm.com/content/93455; and Yin Zhenqiu, "He Huaihong 'dixian lunli' sixiang chouyi" [Discussion of He Huaihong's "minimum moral standards"], *Daode yu wenming* [Morality and Civilization], No. 2 (2010).

79 He, *Liangzin lun*, 7.

80 "Ceyin zhixin, renjieyouzhi" [恻隐之心, 人皆有之].

81 "Jisuo buyu, wushi yuren" [己所不欲, 勿施于人].

82 He, *Social Ethics in a Changing China*, Chapter 1.

83 He, *Social Ethics in a Changing China*, Chapter 15.

84 Liu Lu, "Zhengzhi meiyou namenan" [Honesty should not be difficult], *Jiefang ribao* [Liberation Daily], May 9, 2014. See also Chinese Writers Net, http://www.chinawriter.com.cn/2014/2014-05-09/203192.html.

85 Shao, "Zhou Zhixing duihua He Huaihong."

86 Ibid.

87 He, *Social Ethics in a Changing China*, Chapter 2.

88 Ibid.

89 He, *Social Ethics in a Changing China*, Chapter 8.

90 He Huaihong, "Meiguo shi you yige guannian chansheng de guojia, zhege guannian jiushi 'Duli Xuanyan'" [The United States is a country that was born with a concept, and that concept is called the *Declaration of Independence*], *Fenghuang dushu* [Phoenix Reading], November 26, 2013, http://chuansong.me/n/240070.

91 Ibid.

92 Cong Riyun, "Pushi jiazhi yu Zhongguo daolu" [Universal values and China's path], Consensus Net, June 14, 2013, http://congriyun.blog.21ccom.net/?p=10.

93 One exception in the Chinese leadership is Wen Jiabao, who wrote an important article on the challenges confronting Chinese foreign policy. In it, he argued that things such as democracy, rule of law, freedom, and human rights are not particular to Western countries. Rather, they are common values pursued by mankind and therefore should be seen as universal values, to which China should also adhere. See Wen Jiabao, "Our Historical Tasks at the Primary Stage of Socialism and Several Issues Concerning China's Foreign Policy," Ministry of Foreign Affairs of the People's Republic of China website, February 26, 2007, http://www.fmprc.gov.cn/mfa_chn/ziliao_611306/tytj_611312/zcwj_611316/t300993.shtml.

94 Hou Shuyi, "Beida jiaoshou He Huaihong tan daode cai zui budaode" [Peking University Professor Huaihong's view of morality as the most immoral], Hexun Net, October 10, 2007, http://opinion.hexun.com/2007-10-10/100865161.html.

95 Ibid.

96 He, *Social Ethics in a Changing China*, Chapter 2.

97 Xu Linling, "He Huaihong: Xunqiu jiduan zhijian de zhongdao he houdao" [He Huaihong: Seeking kindness and the middle path between extremes], *Nanfang renwu zhoukan* [Southern People Weekly], November 10, 2013, and also http://www.nfpeople.com/story_view.php?id=4958.

98 He, *Social Ethics in a Changing China*, Chapter 9.

99 He, *Social Ethics in a Changing China*, Chapter 14.

100 Dao, "Du He Huaihong 'Xin Gangchang'."

101 Wang, "He Huaihong."

102 Xu, "He Huaihong."

103 He, *Social Ethics in a Changing China*, Chapter 12.

104 He, *Social Ethics in a Changing China*, Chapter 5.

105 He, *Social Ethics in a Changing China*, Chapter 1.

106 Dao, "Du He Huaihong 'Xin Gangchang'."

107 He, *Zixuan ji*, 359.

108 He, *Social Ethics in a Changing China*, Chapters 16, 17, and 18.

109 He, *Social Ethics in a Changing China*, Chapter 19.

110 Xu Jia, *Zhongguo jinxiandai lunli qimeng* [Modern Chinese ethical enlightenment] (Beijing: Zhongguo shehui kexue chubanshe, 2014), 343.

III

The Dynamics and Constraints of Chinese Think Tank Development

Chapter 6

China's New Think Tanks: Where Officials, Entrepreneurs, and Scholars Interact

> *Coming together is a beginning. Keeping together*
> *is progress. Working together is success.*
>
> — Henry Ford

> *If you look everywhere in the world where there is a genuine commitment*
> *to shared decision-making, good things are happening.*
>
> — Bill Clinton[1]

Never in the sixty-year history of the People's Republic of China have Chinese political, economic, and cultural elites paid as close attention to think tanks as they have in recent years. In March 2009, the State Council approved the establishment of a new think tank in Beijing, the China Center for International Economic Exchanges (CCIEE), which immediately was bestowed the moniker "super think tank" (超级智库, *chaoji zhiku*).[2] Former vice premier Zeng Peiyan, a political heavyweight, took up the role of chairman, and several current or former ministerial level officials, prominent business leaders, and internationally renowned scholars were appointed vice chairmen.

Four months later, the CCIEE organized an international conference on the global financial crisis and the role of think tanks in promoting international cooperation on issues of global importance. This so-called "Global Think Tank Summit" drew approximately 900 attendees. Among them were 150 former or current government leaders (Chinese and foreign), officials from international organizations such as the World Bank and the United Nations Conference on Trade and Development (UNCTAD), about 450 scholars and think tank representatives from around the world, roughly 200 businesspeople, and 150 journalists.[3] China's top leaders made their presence known at the conference, with then premier Wen Jiabao on hand to meet with distinguished guests and then executive vice premier Li Keqiang delivering a keynote address. For almost a week, Chinese media outlets covered this event as headline news.[4]

The CCIEE is not the only think tank in China that has engaged in high-profile policy discussions or facilitated broad international exchanges in recent years. The academic association known as the Chinese Economists 50 Forum, which includes the country's 50 most prominent economists and government technocrats, conducted an intensive dialogue in late August 2009 with leading American economists. They discussed the measures necessary to promote economic recovery on a global scale. Similarly, the China Institute of Strategy and Management (CISM), headed by one of China's leading strategic thinkers, Zheng Bijian, hosted a conference called the "Strategic Forum for a U.S.-China Clean Energy Partnership" in the fall of 2009. Both events were co-sponsored by a top American think tank, the Brookings Institution, and were held at the Diaoyutai State Guesthouse in Beijing. As was the case at the CCIEE summit, top Chinese leaders such as then executive vice premier Li Keqiang attended and spoke at these engagements.

In contrast to many of their counterparts in the West, where independence from the government is usually considered a mark of credibility, Chinese think tanks often strive for strong ties to the government, and they especially value close connections with the upper stratum of the Chinese leadership. According to its charter, the CCIEE operates "under the guidance and supervision of the National Development and Reform Commission (NDRC) in terms of its business scope."[5] In 2016, Zhang Xiaoqiang, who was former vice minister of the NDRC, served as the executive director of the CCIEE and ran the operations of this super think tank. The NDRC, whose purview is the macroeconomic management of the Chinese economy, is widely considered to be the most important ministry in the Chinese government. Another indicator of the CCIEE's close ties to the Chinese leadership is its physical proximity to the levers of power: its current office is located only a few hundred meters from Zhongnanhai, the headquarters of both the Chinese Communist Party and the State Council.[6]

The growing importance of think tanks in China and the frequency with which they are able to facilitate international exchanges is understandable given China's rising stature on the world stage. Many Chinese people are now cognizant of the fact that their country is not only in the midst of profound socioeconomic transformations, but is also rapidly emerging as a major player in global affairs. They seek to understand the complex and intertwined international challenges that China faces in order to take intelligent positions on the issues involved.

As Chinese think tanks begin to develop the "revolving door" quality that has long described their peer institutions in other countries, business leaders from major state-owned companies and domestic (or Hong Kong–based) private companies now play crucial roles in the management of think tanks. In reaction to government policies that strongly affect their business interests, these business leaders have made financial contributions to think tanks as a way to gain managerial influence over them. Meanwhile, an increasing number of foreign-educated "returnees" find think tanks to be ideal institutional springboards for reintegrating themselves into the Chinese political establishment and playing a role in shaping the public discourse. This chapter takes a close look at the formation of three prominent think tanks in the country — the China Center for International Economic Exchanges, the Chinese Economists 50 Forum, and the China Center for Economic Research at Peking University. This discussion adds a new analytical wrinkle to the long-standing and complicated relationship between power, wealth, and knowledge.

Tripartite Elites in Think Tanks

A detailed analysis of the composition of Chinese think tanks, with a special focus on the newly established CCIEE, reveals several important developments. The most notable is that three distinct groups of elites — current and retired government officials, business leaders, and public intellectuals — have become increasingly active in promoting their personal influence, institutional interests, and policy initiatives through these semi-governmental organizations. In present-day China, think tanks have become not only important venues for retired government officials to pursue new phases in their careers, but also crucial institutional meeting grounds where officials, entrepreneurs, and scholars can interact.

This new phenomenon suggests that the relationship between these three elite groups, and their relative importance *vis-à-vis* policy planning, may start to change. Three trends deserve our attention. First, a growing number of government and party leaders now seek positions in prominent think tanks and universities both during and after their tenures in office. Second, business leaders from major state-owned companies and domestic private companies now play crucial roles in China's think tanks. These leaders seek to gain influence through their financial contributions in order to push back against government policies that negatively affect their businesses. Third, public intellectuals, especially well-known economists who received PhD degrees overseas, have now become almost equal partners in this tripartite group of think tank elites. Indeed, to a certain extent, the once-clear distinction between officials and scholars is blurring as an increasing number of foreign-educated returnees now become government leaders. Examining a new think tank, such as the CCIEE, will help to illustrate these three trends, and thus provide greater insight into the important dynamics in the Chinese political system and policymaking process.

The Evolution of Think Tanks in China: A Review

Think tanks (智库, *zhiku* or 思想库, *sixiangku*) are by no means new to China. In fact, one could argue that they played important roles in the country as early as the time of Confucius. However, since the establishment of the PRC, and especially during its first three decades, the role and influence of think tanks have been largely dependent on the preferences and characteristics of the country's top leader. Mao Zedong disregarded modern science and technology, dismissed rationality in government policy, and held intellectuals in rather low esteem. Major decisions during the Mao era, such as the launch of the Cultural Revolution, the movement of China's national defense industry to the so-called interior "third front" (三线, *sanxian*), and reconciliation with the United States in the early 1970s, were largely made by Mao and by Mao alone.[7]

While Deng Xiaoping greatly elevated the economic and sociopolitical status of intellectuals during his tenure, he felt no need to consult think tanks when making decisions. Indeed, Deng's most significant decisions — for example, establishing special economic zones first in south China and then in Shanghai's Pudong District — have been attributed in large part to his own visionary thinking and political courage. It was widely known that in his final years, Deng preferred to listen to his daughters' gossip rather than read expert reports.

When Hu Yaobang and Zhao Ziyang led political and economic affairs in the 1980s, they were the "patron saints" of a group of liberal intellectuals in the government and in the Central Committee of the Chinese Communist Party who were usually affiliated with think tanks. Some of these scholars later lent support to the 1987 liberal movement and the 1989 Tiananmen uprising. Following these two events, which brought about the fall of both Hu Yaobang and Zhao Ziyang, many of these intellectuals sought amnesty in the West.

Although some think tanks were closed as a result of the Tiananmen incident, the think tank system survived and even became more institutionalized over the ensuing two decades. This has largely been due to the fact that China's growing integration with the world economy has required more scholars with professional expertise, especially in the areas of international economics and finance. Without a doubt, Jiang Zemin, Zhu Rongji, and their generation of technocratic leaders paid more attention to the role of think tanks than did their predecessors.

It has been widely noted that in the early 1990s Jiang Zemin often received advice from scholars at Shanghai-based institutions such as Fudan University, East China University of Political Science and Law, the Shanghai Academy of Social Sciences, and the Shanghai Institute for International Studies. Indeed, over the course of that decade, several prominent young scholars with experience in the field of foreign studies moved from Shanghai to Beijing, where they worked closely with Jiang in areas such as policy planning, propaganda, Taiwan affairs, and foreign relations. For example, Wang Huning, former dean of the law school at Fudan, later served as a personal assistant to Jiang and is now director of the Central Policy Research Office of the CCP's Central Committee. In the same vein, Li Junru, a scholar who spent much of his career at the

Shanghai Academy of Social Sciences, later served as vice president of the Central Party School (CPS). Both men, Wang and Li, are believed to have been principal players in the development of Jiang's so-called "theory of the three represents" (三个代表理论, *sange daibiao lilun*).[8]

Former premier Zhu Rongji also relied heavily on the advice of several scholars in the 1980s and early 1990s. These included Wu Jinglian, who has been a research fellow at the Development Research Center of the State Council, and Lou Jiwei, who served for a time as Zhu's personal assistant, later served as executive vice minister of finance and chairman of the China Investment Corporation (CIC), and was until recently minister of finance. Li Wei, another of Zhu's personal assistants and a largely self-taught financial technocrat, currently serves as president of the Development Research Center of the State Council.

Following in Jiang's footsteps, Hu Jintao turned the CPS into a prominent think tank in the late 1990s when he served as president of the school. For two decades now, the CPS has functioned as a leading research center for the study of China's domestic political reform and international relations. China's two most distinguished strategic thinkers — Zheng Bijian (former vice president of the CPS) and Wang Jisi (former director of the Institute of International Strategic Studies of the CPS and former dean of the School of International Studies at Peking University) — both played decisive roles in the development of Hu's theory of "China's peaceful rise."[9]

Wang Huning, Li Junru, Zheng Bijian, and Wang Jisi have dual identities as officials and scholars. In fact, they are in many ways more like government officials than members of the scholarly community. Yet, their close contact with top leaders and their considerable influence over China's decision-making process also enhances the role of think tanks in present-day China. Of course, most members of think tanks are not as close to the center of power as these intellectual celebrities. Many think tank members choose to exert influence over China's decision-making process by adopting a more independent stance and by offering more-critical views of current policies.

In their 1999 book *Voices* (呼喊, *huhan*), Ling Zhijun and Ma Licheng, two senior reporters for the official newspaper *People's Daily*, observed that five distinct voices existed in post-Deng China: (1) the voice of mainstream society that follows Deng's reform policies; (2) the voice of dogmatism that advocates a return to a planned, socialist economy; (3) the voice of nationalism; (4) the voice of feudalism influenced by neo-Confucianism and Asian values; and (5) the voice of democracy. The authors unambiguously argued for a pluralistic outlook and portrayed the "voice of democracy" in a remarkably positive light.[10]

Although members of think tanks are more often interested in pursuing "reform from within" rather than "revolution from without" (Chapter 15 will focus on this topic), they often differ in their particular views, values, and visions. Some may be "at once within the system and at odds with it," as a *Washington Post* correspondent in Beijing observes.[11] Others, especially those in universities or in the private sector, may be interested both in working cooperatively with policymakers and in exposing flaws in China's political system and socioeconomic policies. These intellectuals do not consider these endeavors to be contradictory or inappropriate, but instead see this approach as an effective way to exert influence over China's decision-making process.

While the intellectual pluralism that Ling Zhijun and Ma Licheng promoted over a decade ago has only increased in recent years, today's Chinese think tanks tend to concentrate on several key issues: China's economic rise and rebalancing, structural changes in the domestic economy, political stability, social justice, energy security, the new world order, and the country's international image.[12] Mainstream, official think tanks have utilized their abundant human and financial resources to dominate the policy discourse. A group of emerging, privately owned, and privately operated think tanks, including the Unirule Institute of Economics (天则经济研究所, *tianze jingji yanjiusuo*), the Friends of Nature (自然之友, *ziran zhiyou*), and the Boyuan Foundation (博源基金会, *Boyuan jijin-hui*), have remained marginal players in the broader landscape of policy-making and public opinion formation.[13] In 2006, at the "First Forum on China's Think Tanks" in Beijing, the Chinese authorities, for the first time in the PRC's history, designated the top 10 think tanks in the country, further enhancing the status and influence of the older, more established institutions (see Table 6.1).

These "top 10" think tanks are all considered state-sponsored institutions. They were established during different periods throughout PRC history, though none of China's newest think tanks made the list. Among

Table 6-1: Top 10 Think Tanks in China, as Designated by Chinese Authorities at the "First Forum on China's Think Tanks" in 2006.

Rank	Name	Head	Year Founded	Location
1	Chinese Academy of Social Sciences (中国社会科学院)	Chen Kuiyuan	1977	Beijing
2	Development Research Center of the State Council (国务院发展研究中心)	Zhang Yutai	1981	Beijing
3	Chinese Academy of Sciences (中国科学院)	Lu Yongxiang	1949	Beijing
4	Academy of Military Sciences (中国军事科学院)	Liu Chengjun	1958	Beijing
5	China Institute of International Studies (中国国际问题研究所)	Ma Zhengang	1956	Beijing
6	China Institute of Contemporary International Relations (中国现代国际关系研究院)	Cui Liru	1980	Beijing
7	China National Committee for Pacific Economic Cooperation (中国太平洋经济合作全国委员会)	Mei Ping	1986	Beijing
8	China Association for Science and Technology (中国科学技术协会)	Han Qide	1958	Beijing
9	China International Institute for Strategic Society (中国国际战略学会)	Xiong Guangkai	1979	Beijing
10	Shanghai Institute for International Studies (上海国际问题研究所)	Yang Jiemian	1960	Shanghai

Source: Yang Qinglin, "Keyingxiang gaoceng juece Zhongguo shida zhiku shouci gongkai liangxiang" [The first public appearance of China's top ten think tanks that can affect high-level decision-making], *Renminwang* [People's Daily Web], November 9, 2006, http://finance.people.com.cn/GB/1037/5019209.html.

the top 10, the youngest is the China National Committee for Pacific Economic Cooperation (CNCPEC), which was founded in 1986. Some of these think tanks are gigantic government institutions with many employees. For example, in 2009 the Chinese Academy of Social Sciences (CASS) consisted of 31 research institutions, 45 research centers, and

4,200 employees, of which 3,200 were members of the research staff (and these numbers do not even include provincial branches).[14] The China Institute of Contemporary International Relations (CICIR), which is operated by the Ministry of State Security, is much smaller. Yet even it has 380 employees, including 150 senior researchers.[15] At least half of these top 10 think tanks concentrate on China's foreign relations and international affairs. In 2006, none of them was headed by an economist or a leader with a strong background in economic affairs, despite the fact that some, including the Development Research Center of the State Council and the China National Committee for Pacific Economic Cooperation, focus primarily on economic issues.

To a certain extent, these "established" think tanks and their recent descendants, such as the CCIEE, are similar in terms of their close ties to the Chinese government. Nevertheless, the former find it increasingly difficult to keep abreast of changes in the domestic and international policy environments and to ensure that their research agendas, personnel, financial resources, and international exchanges keep apace. At least three factors have augmented the need to establish new kinds of think tanks that are more progressive and innovative in thinking about China's future. First, the end of strongman politics and the emergence of a collective system of leadership in post-Deng China have pushed officials to seek the support of think tanks as a way to increase legitimacy for their policy positions. Second, China's growing integration with the world economy requires input from scholars with professional expertise, especially those who specialize in international investment and finance. Third, the rapid development of China's market economy has not only made China's economic and sociopolitical structures more pluralistic, but has also given rise to a broad array of interest groups. These interest groups, especially those in the business sector, work carefully to influence government policy and shape public opinion (see Chapter 13). All three of these factors are evident in the initial formation and subsequent composition of the CCIEE. A close look at the dynamic interactions that take place, on the one hand, between the Chinese leadership and the country's prominent think tanks, and, on the other hand, among the tripartite players in the Chinese think tank communities themselves helps to elucidate important trends in the governance of this rapidly changing country.

The "Revolving Door" for Officials

An important indicator of China's political institutionalization over the past two decades has been the degree to which government and party officials have been subject to retirement age rules.[16] Remarkably, at the 17th National Congress of the CCP, held in 2007, all leaders who were born before 1940 were, without exception, forced to retire from the Central Committee. Similarly, at the 18th National Congress of the CCP, held in 2012, none of the leaders born before 1945 were appointed to the 18th Central Committee. This retirement age requirement has created an increased sense of regularity and fairness in the circulation of elites and has contributed to ending the possibility of life tenure for Chinese political leaders.[17] In 2007, for example, several senior leaders who had previously served on the Politburo, including then vice president Zeng Qinghong (born in 1939), then vice premier Wu Yi (born in 1938), and then vice premier Zeng Peiyan (born in 1938), all retired. Wu Yi, former minister of commerce and one of the most respected female leaders in the country, told the media that she was determined to "retire completely from all leadership positions" (裸退, *luotui*).[18] She was not alone. In fact, most other top leaders — Jiang Zemin, Li Peng, Zhu Rongji, Zeng Qinghong, Li Ruihuan, and Qiao Shi in the pre-2002 Politburo Standing Committee (PSC), and Hu Jintao, Wu Bangguo, and Wen Jiabao in the pre-2007 PSC — have largely disappeared from public view since their retirement. None of them now holds any important leadership position in the country.

This political norm seems to have begun to change with the recent appointment of former vice premier Zeng Peiyan as chairman of the CCIEE. Zeng is the highest-ranking former leader to now hold a non-honorary chairmanship at a major institution. Previously, Vice President of the CPS Zheng Bijian and Deputy Chief-of-Staff of the People's Liberation Army Xiong Guangkai also left their state leadership positions to head think tanks (the China Reform Forum and the China International Institute for Strategic Society, respectively), but they had been only ministerial level leaders. Qian Qichen, another former vice premier, holds the only honorary deanship of the School of International Studies at Peking University, and he has hardly spent any time at the school since his appointment a few years ago.

The appointments of former high-ranking officials as leaders of the CCIEE, and the subsequent media coverage of these leaders, may pave the way for other retired high-ranking Chinese officials to pursue careers in the leadership of think tanks, universities, and other important institutions. Dai Bingguo, a state councilor who was a chief advisor for President Hu Jintao on foreign affairs, has served as chairman of the board of Jinan University in Guangzhou and honorary dean of the Institute of International and Strategic Studies at Peking University since retiring from the government in March 2012. Similar to their counterparts in other countries, Chinese think tanks have increasingly become a "revolving door" for past and future government officials.

Table 6.2 shows the leadership composition of the CCIEE, including the chairman, senior advisors, and vice chairmen in 2009. While those with government or party backgrounds constitute a majority of the leadership, a number of prominent scholars and business leaders are also included. In addition to Zeng Peiyan, a number of former high-ranking leaders (ministers or provincial governors) serve on the leadership of the CCIEE, including Tang Jiaxuan (former minister of foreign affairs), Wang Chuncheng (former director of the Office of the Economic and Financial Leading Group of the CCP Central Committee), Liu Huaqiu (former director of the Foreign Affairs Office of the CCP Central Committee), Teng Wensheng (former director of the Central Policy Research Office of the CCP Central Committee), Lu Ruihua (former governor of Guangdong), and Xu Rongkai (former governor of Yunnan). All of these retired leaders were in their late sixties or early seventies when they joined the leadership of the CCIEE.[19]

The state-run Xinhua News Agency reported that the formation and composition of the CCIEE leadership reflect an important effort to extend the "sustainable utility" (余热, *yure*) of retired high-ranking officials.[20] Over the past two decades or so, Chinese authorities have usually transferred high-ranking party or government leaders who reached retirement age to less important leadership bodies such as the NPC or the Chinese People's Political Consultative Conference (CPPCC) at the national, provincial, or municipal levels before their full retirement. It now seems likely that some of these retired or semi-retired leaders will begin to find their way into the leadership of major think tanks and educational institutions that focus on policy research and world affairs.[21]

Table 6-2: The Leadership of the China Center for International Economic Exchanges (CCIEE), 2009.

Position at CCIEE	Name	Other Current/Former Position	Year Born	Professional Identity	Educational Background	Educational Level
Chair	Zeng Peiyan	Former Vice Premier	1938	Official	Tsinghua Univ.,	Undergraduate
Senior Advisor	Tung Chee Hwa	Vice Chair, CPPCC & Former Chief Executive of Hong Kong	1937	Entrepreneur and Official	Univ. of Liverpool	Undergraduate
Senior Advisor	Jiang Zhenghua	Former Vice Chair of the NPC	1937	Scholar and Official	Xi'an Jiaotong Univ., & Int'l Institute for Population Studies, India	Master's
Senior Advisor	Tang Jiaxuan	Former Minister of Foreign Affairs	1938	Official	Peking Univ. & Fudan Univ.	Undergraduate
Senior Advisor	Xu Kuangdi	President of Academy of Sciences & Former Shanghai Mayor	1937	Official	Beijing Institute of Iron and Steel	Undergraduate
Exec. Vice Chair	Wang Chunzheng	Former Director of the Office of the Economic and Financial Leading Group of the CCP Central Com.	1938	Official	Renmin Univ.	Master's
Exec. Vice Chair	Li Yining	Professor at Peking University	1930	Scholar	Peking Univ.	Undergraduate
Exec. Vice Chair	Liu Zunyi	President of the Chinese University of Hong Kong	1944	Scholar	Stanford Univ., & U.C. Berkeley	PhD
Exec. Vice Chair	Zhang Xiaoqiang	Vice Chair of NDRC	1952	Official	Peking Univ.,	Undergraduate
Exec. Vice Chair	Chen Yuan	Chair of China Development Bank	1945	Entrepreneur and Official	Tsinghua Univ., & CASS	Master's

Title	Name	Position	Birth Year	Career Type	University	Education
Exec. Vice Chair	Qian Yingyi	Dean of School of Economics and Management, Tsinghua University	1961	Scholar	Tsinghua Univ., Columbia Univ., Yale Univ., & Harvard Univ.	PhD
Exec. Vice Chair	Jiang Jiemin	General Manager of China National Petroleum Corporation	1956	Entrepreneur and Official	Shandong Univ.,	Undergraduate
Exec. Vice Chair	Wei Liqun	Executive Vice-President of China National School of Administration	1944	Official	Beijing Normal Univ.	Undergraduate
Permanent Vice Chair	Zheng Xinli	Former Deputy Director of the Central Policy Research Office of the CCP Central Com.	1945	Official	Beijing Institute of Iron and Steel & CASS	Master's
Vice Chair	Feng Guojing (Victor Fung)	Chairman of International Chamber of Commerce	1945	Entrepreneur	MIT & Harvard Univ.	PhD
Vice Chair	Lu Ruihua	Former Governor of Guangdong	1938	Official	Sun Yat-sen Univ.	Master's
Vice Chair	Liu Huaqiu	Former Director of the Foreign Affairs Office	1939	Official	Foreign Affairs College	Undergraduate
Vice Chair	Zhang Yutai	Director of the Development Research Center of the State Council	1945	Official	Beijing Aviation Institute	Undergraduate
Vice Chair	Zhang Guobao	Vice Chair of NDRC	1944	Official	Xi'an Jiaotong Univ.	Master's
Vice Chair	Li Rongrong	Former Minister of the SASAC	1944	Official	Tianjin Univ.	Undergraduate
Vice Chair	Xu Rongkai	Former Governor of Yunnan	1942	Official	Tsinghua Univ.	Undergraduate

(Continued)

Table 6-2: *(Continued)*

Position at CCIEE	Name	Other Current/Former Position	Year Born	Professional Identity	Educational Background	Educational Level
Vice Chair	Lou Jiwei	Chair of China Investment Corporation	1950	Entrepreneur and Official	Tsinghua Univ. & CASS	Master's
Vice Chair	Teng Wensheng	Former Director of the Policy Research Office	1940	Official	Renmin Univ.	Undergraduate
Vice Chair	Dai Xianglong	Chair of National Council for Social Security Fund	1944	Official	Central Institute of Finance and Economics	Undergraduate
Secretary General	Wei Jianguo	Former Vice Minister of Commerce	1947	Official	Shanghai Institute of Foreign Languages	Undergraduate

Notes: CASS = Chinese Academy of Social Sciences; CCP = Chinese Communist Party; Com. = Committee; CPPCC = Chinese People's Political Consultative Conference; Exec. = Executive; Int'l = International; NDRC = National Development and Reform Commission; NPC = National People's Congress; SASAC = State-Owned Assets Supervision and Administration Commission; U.C. = University of California; Univ.=University.

Table 6.3 catalogues high-ranking government officials (both incumbents and retirees) who served, in 2009, as deans or honorary deans of colleges that concentrate on international affairs, journalism, and economic management. Former minister of foreign affairs Li Zhaoxing served as dean of both the Zhou Enlai School of Government at Nankai University in Tianjin and the School of Diplomacy and International Relations at the Foreign Affairs College in Beijing. Former vice minister of foreign trade and China's chief negotiator during the World Trade Organization accession talks Long Yongtu served as dean of the School of International Relations and Public Affairs at Fudan University. The deanships of the schools of journalism and communication at Beijing's top three universities — Peking, Tsinghua, and Renmin — were all held by retired senior government and party leaders who were formerly in charge of propaganda. As Table 6.3 also shows, two current ministers who are in charge of financial and economic affairs in the country, Governor of the People's Bank of China (PBOC) Zhou Xiaochuan and former minister of the State-Owned Assets Supervision and Administration Commission (SASAC) Li Rongrong, served as the honorary deans of the School of Management at University of Science and Technology of China and the School of Management at Tianjin University, respectively.

Li Rongrong also served as vice chairman of the CCIEE, along with several other current ministerial level leaders, including then director of the Development Research Center of the State Council Zhang Yutai and then vice ministers of the NDRC Zhang Xiaoqiang and Zhang Guobao. In addition, then executive vice president of the Chinese Academy of Governance Wei Liqun and then chairman of the National Council for Social Security Fund Dai Xianglong served concurrently as full minister-rank leaders in the State Council. The significant presence of incumbent government officials in the leadership of the CCIEE seems to suggest that think tanks are not necessarily the "final stops" for politicians in their careers. On the contrary, the "revolving door" of China's top think tanks may help current affiliates advance to higher posts in the years to come.

The "revolving door" function of Chinese think tanks, especially in relation to elite upward mobility, is perhaps most evident in the case of the Chinese Economists 50 Forum. The forum was founded in 1998 and claims to include the most-accomplished academic economists in Beijing. The mission of the forum is to provide policy recommendations to the

210　*The Power of Ideas*

Table 6-3:　Current or Former Government Officials Who Serve as Deans/Honorary Deans of Schools, 2009.

Field	Name	Official Position	Position in Educational Institution
International Relations	Qian Qichen	Former Vice Premier	Honorary Dean of School of Int'l Studies, Peking Univ.
	Li Zhaoxing	Former Minister of Foreign Affairs	Dean of Zhou Enlai School of Government, Nankai Univ.; Dean of School of Diplomacy and Int'l Relations, Foreign Affairs College
	Long Yongtu	Former Vice Minister of Foreign Trade	Dean of School of Int'l Relations and Public Affairs, Fudan Univ.
	Chen Jian	Former Deputy Secretary General of the United Nations	Dean of School of International Relations, Renmin Univ.
	Xiong Guangkai	Former Deputy Chief of Staff of the PLA	Honorary Dean of School of Int'l and Public Affairs, Shanghai Jiaotong Univ.
Journalism	Zhao Qizheng	Former Director of the Information Office of the State Council	Dean of School of Journalism and Communication, Renmin Univ.
	Shao Huaze	Former President of the *People's Daily*	Dean of School of Journalism and Communication, Peking Univ.
	Fan Jingyi	Former Editor-in-Chief of the *People's Daily*	Dean of School of Journalism and Communication, Tsinghua Univ.
	Gong Xueping	Former Deputy Party Secretary of Shanghai	Honorary Dean of School of Journalism and Comm., Fudan Univ.
	Song Zhao	Vice Minister of the Propaganda Department of Shanghai	Dean of School of Journalism and Communication, Fudan Univ.

(Continued)

Table 6-3: *(Continued)*

Field	Name	Official Position	Position in Educational Institution
Management	Zhou Xiaochuan	Governor of People's Bank	Honorary Dean of School of Management, China Univ. of Science and Technology
	Li Rongrong	Minister of State-Owned Assets Supervision and Administration Commission	Honorary Dean of School of Management, Tianjin Univ.
	Lu Ruihua	Former Governor of Guangdong	Honorary Dean of School of Management, Zhongshan Univ.
	Jiang Yiren	Former Vice Mayor of Shanghai	Honorary Dean of Antai School of Economic Management, Shanghai Jiaotong Univ.
	Liu Ji	Former Vice President of Chinese Academy of Social Sciences	Honorary Dean of China Europe Int'l Business School
	Li Jinhua	Former General Director of Audit	Honorary Dean of School of Management, Central China Univ. of Science and Technology
	Cheng Siwei*	Former Chair of the National People's Congress	Dean of Graduate School of Management, Chinese Academy of Sciences

Notes: Comm. = Communication; Int'l = International; and Univ. = University.
*Cheng passed away in 2015.

government on major economic issues. Over the past decade or so, the forum has organized annual conferences, economic policy lecture series, internal roundtable discussions, academic seminars, foreign exchanges, and policy briefings for the national leadership.[22]

The forum is led by a seven-member academic committee, including the country's most influential economists and government technocrats: Liu He (director of the Office of the Economic and Financial Leading Group of the CCP Central Committee), Wu Jinglian (fellow at the Development Research Center of the State Council), Fan Gang (former member of the Monetary Policy Committee of the People's Bank of China and current president of the China Development Institute), Justin Lin (former senior vice president and chief economist of the World Bank), Yi Gang (vice governor of the People's Bank and deputy director of the Office of the Economic and Financial Leading Group of the CCP Central Committee), Xu Shanda (former deputy director of the State Administration of Taxation), and Wu Xiaoling (former vice governor of the People's Bank and current vice chairman of the NPC's Financial Committee). As has been widely noted, Liu He now serves as chief economic advisor to President Xi Jinping, and Wu Jinglian once served as a key advisor to Premier Zhu Rongji. The forum has a permanent staff that handles daily operations and the above-mentioned activities. The forum also retains a council of entrepreneurs, which is headed by two famous business leaders: Chairman of the Stone Group Corporation Duan Yongji and Chairman of Legend Holdings Liu Chuanzhi.

Table 6.4 presents all 50 members of the forum as they were in 2009. Most of the members have dual identities as scholars and officials. Based on their main professional work at the time, 25 of these members (or 50 percent) could be classified as government officials. Many held ministerial level positions, including some of the most important positions in China's economic and financial leadership. In 1998, when the forum was founded, 14 of these 25 officials worked as research fellows in think tanks, as university professors, or both. Justin Lin, for example, was a professor at Peking University at the time. Ten years later, he and many others became substantively involved in China's economic decision-making process.

The group's most prominent leaders are Governor of the People's Bank Zhou Xiaochuan, then deputy director of the Office of the Leading Group for Financial and Economic Affairs Liu He (now director of the office), then chairman of CIC Lou Jiwei (former minister of finance), then director of the State Taxation Bureau Xiao Jie (now minister of finance), then director of the Research Office of the State Council Xie Fuzhan (now governor of Henan), then director of the State Statistics Bureau Ma Jiantang (now executive vice president of the Chinese Academy of Governance), former director of the Office of the Leading Group on Agriculture Chen Xiwen, Vice Governor of the People's Bank Yi Gang,

Table 6-4: Members of the Chinese Economists 50 Forum, 2009.

Name	Year Born	Current Academic Position	Current Official Position	Main Identity	Degree
Cai Fang	1956	Director, Institute of Population & Labor, CASS	Advisor to Minister, Ministry of Human Resources & Social Welfare	Scholar	PhD
Cao Yuanzheng	1954	Guest Professor, Fudan Univ.	Deputy CEO, Bank of China International Holdings Limited	Entrepreneur	PhD
Chen Dongqi	1956	Researcher, CASS	Vice President, Institute of Macroeconomics, NDRC	Official	PhD
Chen Xiwen	1950	Professor, Renmin Univ.	Deputy Director, Office of the Leading Group on Agriculture	Official	BA
Fan Gang	1953	Director, National Institute of Economics	Member, Currency Policy Committee of the People's Bank	Scholar	PhD
Fan Hengshan	1957	Guest Professor, Wuhan Univ. and Renmin Univ.	Director, Regional Economy Department, NDRC	Official	PhD
Guo Shuqing	1956	Guest Professor, Wuhan Univ., Renmin Univ., and CASS	Chairman, China Construction Bank	Entrepreneur	PhD
Hai Wen	1958	Vice President, Peking Univ.	Director, China International Trade Promotion Committee	Scholar	PhD
He Liping	1958	Chair, Department of Finance, Beijing Normal Univ.	Advisor, China Economic Reform Fund	Scholar	PhD

(Continued)

Table 6-4: *(Continued)*

Name	Year Born	Current Academic Position	Current Official Position	Main Identity	Degree
Hu Angang	1953	Director, China Studies Center of CAS; Professor, Tsinghua Univ.	Member, China's Land Resources Committee	Scholar	PhD
Jiang Xiaojuan (f)	1957	Professor, CASS	Deputy Director, Research Office of the State Council	Official	PhD
Li Jiange	1949	Professor, CASS and Shanghai Univ. of Economics and Finance	Chair, China International Capital Cooperation Limited	Entrepreneur	MA
Li Xiaoxi	1949	Director, Institute of Economics & Resources, Beijing Normal Univ.	Advisor, Shanxi, Shaanxi, and Qinghai Governments	Scholar	PhD
Li Yang	1951	Professor, CASS	Vice President, CASS	Official	PhD
Liang Youcai	1943	Chief Economist, China National Information Commission		Scholar	BS
Lin Yifu	1952	Professor, Peking Univ.	Senior Vice President and Chief Economist, World Bank	Official	PhD
Liu He	1952	Guest Professor, Peking Univ. and Renmin Univ.	Deputy Director, Office of the Leading Group for Financial and Economic Affairs	Official	MPA
Liu Shijin	1955	Guest Professor, CASS	Deputy Director, Development Research Center, State Council	Official	PhD

Name	Year	Position	Position	Type	Degree
Liu Wei	1957	Dean, School of Economics, Peking Univ.	Advisor, Beijing Government	Scholar	PhD
Lou Jiwei	1950	Guest Professor, CASS	Chair, China Investment Corporation	Entrepreneur	MA
Long Yongtu	1943	Dean, School of International Affairs, Fudan Univ.	Secretary General, Boao Forum for Asia	Official	BA
Ma Jiantang	1958	Guest Professor, Beijing Normal Univ. and Renmin Univ.	Director, National Bureau of Statistics	Official	PhD
Mao Yushi	1929	Chair, Unirule Institute of Economics		Scholar	BS
Qian Yingyi	1961	Dean, School of Economics and Management, Tsinghua Univ.		Scholar	PhD
Sheng Hong	1954	Professor, Shandong Univ.		Scholar	PhD
Shi Xiaomin	1950		Deputy Head, China Economic Reform Association	Official	BA
Song Guoqing	1954	Director of Population and Economics, CASS	Chief Economist, China's Stock Exchange Commission	Scholar	PhD
Song Xiaowu	1947	Guest Professor, Renmin Univ. and CASS	Deputy Director of Northeastern Dev't Office, State Council	Official	MA
Tang Min	1953		Deputy Secretary General, China Development Fund	Official	PhD

(Continued)

Table 6-4: *(Continued)*

Name	Year Born	Current Academic Position	Current Official Position	Main Identity	Degree
Wang Tongshan	1948	Director, Institute of Quantitative and Technical Economics, CASS		Scholar	PhD
Wang Jian	1954	Professor, CASS	Deputy Secretary General, China Macroeconomic Association	Official	BA
Wei Jie	1952	Deputy Director, Economic Research Center, Tsinghua Univ.		Scholar	PhD
Wen Tiejun	1951	Dean, School of Rural Development, Renmin Univ.	Deputy Secretary General, China Macroeconomic Research Fund	Scholar	PhD
Wu Jinglian	1930	Fellow, Development Research Center, State Council		Scholar	BS
Wu Xiaoling (f)	1947	Guest Professor, Tsinghua Univ.	Deputy Chair, Financial Committee, NPC	Official	MA
Xia Bin	1951	Guest Professor, Renmin Univ.	Director, Inst. of Finance, Dev't Research Center, State Council	Official	MA
Xiao Jie	1957	Guest Professor, CASS	Minister of Finance	Official	PhD
Xie Duo	1960	Guest Professor, CASS	CEO, China Foreign Exchange Center	Official	MA
Xie Fuzhan	1954	Professor, Central China Univ. of S & T	Party Secretary, Henan Province	Official	Master's
Xie Ping	1955	Guest Professor, Renmin Univ., Nankai Univ., and CASS	Central Huijin Investment Company Limited	Entrepreneur	PhD

Name	Birth Year	Academic Affiliation	Government/Other Position	Type	Degree
Xu Shanda	1947	Guest Professor, Tsinghua Univ. and Peking Univ.	Deputy Director, State Taxation Administration Bureau	Official	Master's
Yang Weimin	1956	Guest Professor, Tsinghua Univ.	Director, Development Planning Department, NDRC	Official	PhD
Yi Gang	1958	Professor, Peking Univ.	Vice Governor, People's Bank	Official	PhD
Yu Yongding	1948	Director, Institute of World Economics and Politics, CASS		Scholar	PhD
Zhang Shuguang	1939	Director, Unirule Institute of Economics		Scholar	Master's
Zhang Weiying	1959	Dean, School of Economic Management, Peking Univ.	Member, Economic Reform Fund	Scholar	PhD
Zhang Xiang	1941	Dean, School of Management, Shanghai Jiaotong Univ.	Secretary General, Boao Forum for Asia	Official	PhD
Zheng Xinli	1945	Guest Professor, Renmin Univ. and CASS	Deputy Director, Office of Policy Planning	Official	Master's
Zhou Qiren	1950	Director, China Economic Research Center, Peking Univ.		Scholar	PhD
Zhou Xiaochuan	1948	Guest Professor, Tsinghua Univ. and China Univ. of S & T	Governor, People's Bank	Official	PhD

Source and Notes: http://www.50forum.org.cn/index_expert.asp. CAS = Chinese Academy of Sciences; CASS = Chinese Academy of Social Sciences; Dev't = Development; CEO = Chief Executive Officer; Inst. = Institute; NDRC = National Development and Reform Commission; NPC = National People's Congress; S & T = Science and Technology; Univ. = University. (f) denotes female.

then chairman of the China Construction Bank Guo Shuqing (now governor of Shandong), and then deputy director of the Research Office of the State Council Jiang Xiaojuan (now deputy secretary general of the State Council). Several members of the forum currently serve on the 18th Central Committee of the CCP, including Liu He, Lou Jiwei, Xiao Jie, Guo Shuqing, Xie Fuzhan, and Ma Jiantang as full members, and Jiang Xiaojuan as an alternate member.

Several scholars have recently also assumed important official positions as administrators. Examples include Cai Fang, who currently serves as vice president of CASS, and Liu Wei, who currently serves as president of Renmin University. A few economists have recently been promoted to very important positions. For example, Yang Weiming, who was director of the Development Planning Department of NDRC in 2009, was appointed deputy director of the Office of the Leading Group for Financial and Economic Affairs in 2011. Fifteen members of the Chinese Economists 50 Forum (Wu Jinglian, Zhou Xiaochuan, Yi Gang, Ma Jiantang, Li Yang, Yu Yongding, Qian Yingyi, Guo Shuqing, Wu Xiaoling, Xie Fuzhan, Xiao Jie, Song Guoqing, Zhou Qiren, Xia Bin, and Fan Gang) previously served or currently serve on the influential Monetary Policy Committee of the People's Bank. Both the large number of retired officials taking positions in the leadership of the CCIEE and the many cases of scholars in the Chinese Economists 50 Forum becoming officials suggest that the doors of China's prominent think tanks are already revolving.

A New Kind of Boss and New Sources of Funding

For most of the PRC's history, think tanks have been fully funded by the Chinese government. The only "bosses" of Chinese think tanks have been political officials. Recently, however, economic globalization and China's market reforms have each profoundly changed the way Chinese think tanks operate. As with their counterparts in other countries, the tasks of paying salaries and securing funding for research have become central concerns for Chinese think tanks. Not surprisingly, a new kind of boss — the entrepreneur — now plays an important role in the leadership of China's new think tanks. This trend is particularly noticeable in the case of the CCIEE.

According to reports in the Chinese media, the CCIEE aims to raise a total of 500 million yuan, of which only 1 percent (5 million yuan) will come from the Chinese government.[23] According to Wei Jianguo, secretary-general of the CCIEE, research expenses and salaries for a proposed total of 96 research staffers will largely depend on the success of the institution's fundraising campaign.[24] This explains why several business leaders currently serve as either advisors or vice chairmen in the leadership of the CCIEE. C.H. Tung, the former chief executive of the Hong Kong Special Administrative Region, is currently a vice chairman of the National Committee of the Chinese People's Political Consultative Conference. He also serves as chairman of the Hong Kong–based China-United States Exchange Foundation. The governing board of the foundation in 2009 included several business tycoons, such as Chairman of the Hang Lung Group Ronnie Chan, Chairman of Wheelock and Company Peter Woo, and Chairman of Hopewell Holdings Gordon Wu. The foundation aims to support research in areas that are important to U.S.-China relations, including the environment and climate change, energy security, anti-terrorism, nuclear non-proliferation, food security, multilateral trade, the international financial order, controlling the spread of pandemics, drug trafficking, and financial crimes.[25]

Feng Guojing (Victor Kwok-king Fung), chairman of the Li & Fung group of companies, not only serves as vice chairman of C.H. Tung's China-United States Exchange Foundation, but also serves as vice chairman of the CCIEE. Feng is also chairman of the International Chamber of Commerce, a prestigious international business organization. Feng's company is generally regarded as one of the world's most influential trading companies. A U.S. citizen, Feng was ranked by *Forbes* magazine as one of the 400 richest people in the United States in 2005.[26] Presumably, both C.H. Tung's foundation and Feng's company have provided substantial financial support to the CCIEE.

Several CEOs of China's major banks and state-owned enterprises (SOEs) also serve on the leadership of the CCIEE. In China, these leaders of state-owned businesses often have dual identities. They are government officials whose appointments are usually made by the CCP Organization Department rather than their own companies, but they are also widely identified as entrepreneurs because they take business risks domestically and internationally. If their companies are listed on the stock exchange, these firms are responsible to stockholders. In the Chinese context, the term "entrepreneur" (企业家, *qiyejia*) refers both to an owner of private property and a manager of state-owned or joint ventures. Thus, an entrepreneur is defined as a person who possesses property either through the capitalization of personal income or through the operation of a collective, public, or joint-venture enterprise.[27] This definition of entrepreneur differs substantially from the definition that prevails in the West, where entrepreneurs are seen as businesspeople who assume the "risks of bringing together the means of production, including capital, labor, and materials, and receive reward in profit from the market value of the product."[28]

China's heads of state banks and large firms were minimally involved in the activities of Chinese think tanks for most of the PRC's history, but this appears to have changed in recent years. Now Chinese entrepreneurs have become one of the three major players in this new era of Chinese think tank activity.

Founding board members of the CCIEE include Jiang Jiemin, former general manager of the China National Petroleum Corporation, who was later purged on corruption charges related to former PSC member Zhou Yongkang; Chen Yuan, then president of China Development Bank; and Lou Jiwei, former chairman of the China Investment Corporation (see Table 6.2). Most importantly, Li Rongrong, former minister of the SASAC, also served as vice chairman of the CCIEE. The SASAC supervises the 140 largest SOEs in the country, including the gigantic companies that monopolize such key industries as electricity, telecommunications, railways, aviation, shipping, and oil. In 2009 the 122-member council of the CCIEE included numerous CEOs of China's largest banks and companies, such as then president of the Sinosteel Corporation Huang Tianwen, then CEO of the China Shipping Group Company Li Shaode, and then CEO of the State Development & Investment Corporation Wang Huisheng.[29] Without a doubt, these high-powered and well-endowed companies provided much-needed funding for the CCIEE.

The Growing Importance of the "Sea Turtles"

One of the most important new contingents in reform-era life is the elite group of foreign-educated Chinese returnees known as the "sea turtles"

(海归, *haigui*). This term derives from the fact that, in Chinese, the words for "returnee" and "sea turtle" have the same pronunciation. The official Chinese definition of a returnee (留学回国人员, *liuxue huiguo renyuan*) is someone who was born in the PRC, studied overseas as a student or visiting scholar for at least one year, and then returned to China to work on either a temporary or permanent basis.[30] According to this definition, returnees do not include foreign-born ethnic Chinese or Chinese immigrants to foreign countries who return without having studied abroad.

Between 1978, when Deng made the landmark decision to send a large number of students and scholars to study abroad, and 2014, approximately 3,518,400 Chinese nationals studied in foreign countries.[31] According to Chinese official statistics, by the end of 2014, altogether 1,708,800 Chinese students and scholars remained abroad (among them 1,088,900 were still attending educational and research programs), and 1,809,600 had returned to work in China.[32] Based on Chinese data, in 2005 and 2010, Chinese students and scholars who studied in the United States accounted for the largest portion (approximately 37 percent) of PRC citizens studying abroad.[33] In 2015, there were 304,000 Chinese students studying in the United States, a significant increase from the rough estimate of 100,000 in 2010.[34]

The area most strongly influenced by returnees is, not surprisingly, higher education, especially research institutions.[35] In 2004, according to official Chinese data, roughly 81 percent of the Chinese Academy of Sciences, 54 percent of the Chinese Academy of Engineering, and 72 percent of team leaders for national technological research projects were returnees.[36]

Returnees have also dominated top administrative posts at Chinese universities, especially at top schools. In 2005, China's Ministry of Education reported that about 60 percent of all top leaders (presidents, party secretaries, and their deputies) at Chinese universities and research institutions had studied abroad.[37] .According to a study conducted in 2003 by Chinese scholar Chen Xuefei on the faculty profiles, out of 132 top administrators at colleges, departments, research institutes, research centers, and key state labs at Tsinghua University, 102 (77 percent) were returnees.[38] As early as 1999, 75 percent of university-level administrators and 74 percent of college- and department-level administrators at Peking

University were returnees. Among the 100 colleges surveyed by Chen, 51 percent of university-level administrators and 35 percent of college- and department-level administrators were returnees.[39]

Returnees have also assumed the leadership of prominent research centers in the field of China studies. This trend is most strikingly on display at the China Center for Economic Research (CCER) at Peking University, as demonstrated in Table 6.5, which lists the educational backgrounds of the center's entire 24 faculty members in 2005. All of them studied abroad and all received doctoral degrees, mainly from universities in the United States. These U.S.-educated economists have largely redesigned the curricula and research methods in the fields of economics and management at Peking University to be more in line with the American model, particularly the "Chicago model."[40] The CCER has been a key resource for China's economic decision-makers over the last decade. In addition to publishing academic journals, the CCER is also known for its regular internal reports and policy briefs submitted to various agencies in the Chinese government.[41] Five faculty members — Justin Lin, Yi Gang, Hai Wen, Zhou Qiren, and Song Guoqing — are also members of the prestigious Chinese Economists 50 Forum. The CCER seems to have assembled "dream teams" both in the field of Chinese economic studies and in the management of the financial sector of the PRC.

Many research centers, including CCER, have received funding from American and other foreign foundations. For example, the Center of China Studies at Peking University has received grants from the Ford Foundation, the Henry Luce Foundation, the U.S. National Science Foundation (NSF), and the Asia Foundation, among others. Most of these foundations began providing support to social science and legal research in China in the mid-1980s. A three-decade-long effort to promote China's social science research and the diffusion of international norms now seems to have paid off. In 2008, building on the solid foundation of the CCER, Peking University established the National School of Development (NSD), one of the top 25 think tanks in China.

Justin Lin, founder and former director of the CCER, is himself a legendary figure. Born in Taiwan in 1952, he attended both National Taiwan University and National Chengchi University. In 1979, during his military service in Jinmen, Lin decided to defect to the mainland. It was reported that Lin swam to Xiamen using two basketballs for flotation.[42]

China's New Think Tanks

Table 6-5: Educational Backgrounds of the Faculty of the China Center for Economic Research at Peking University, 2005.

Name	Professional Title	Degree	Field	Graduate School	Year of PhD
Chen Ping	Professor	PhD	Physics	U. of Texas at Austin	1987
Gong Qiang	Assistant Professor	PhD	Economics	Northwestern U.	2004
Hai Wen	Deputy Director & Prof.	PhD	Economics	U.C. Davis	1991
He Yin	Assistant Professor	PhD	Economics	U. of Colorado at Boulder	2004
Hu Dayuan	Associate Professor	PhD	Economics	U. of Kentucky	1995
Li Ling	Professor	PhD	Economics	U. of Pittsburgh	1994
Liang Neng	Dean & Professor	PhD	Economics	Indiana U. & U. of Penn.	1990
Lin Yifu (Justin)	Director & Professor	PhD	Economics	U. of Chicago	1986
Lu Feng	Associate Professor	PhD	Economics	U. of Leeds, U.K.	1994
Ma Hao	Professor	PhD	Economics	U. of Texas at Austin	1994
Ping Xinqiao	Associate Professor	PhD	Economics	Cornell U.	1998
Shen Minggao	Associate Professor	PhD	Economics	Stanford U.	2001
Song Guoqing	Professor	PhD	Economics	U. of Chicago	1995
Shi Jianhuai	Associate Professor	PhD	Economics	Osaka U.	1999
Wang Dingding	Associate Professor	PhD	Economics	U. of Hawaii	1990
Wang Hao	Assistant Professor	PhD	Economics	Ohio State U.	2002
Yao Yang	Assoc. Prof., Dep. Dir.	PhD	Economics	U. of Wisconsin at Madison	1996
Yi Gang	Professor	PhD	Economics	U. of Illinois	1986
Zeng Yi	Professor	PhD	Economics	Brussels Free University	1986
Zhang Fan	Associate Professor	PhD	Economics	Wayne State U., Michigan	1994
Zhang Lee	Associate Professor	PhD	Economics	Ohio State U.	1999
Zhao Yaohui	Professor	PhD	Economics	U. of Chicago	1995
Zhao Zhong	Assistant Professor	PhD	Economics	Johns Hopkins U.	2001
Zhou Qiren	Professor	PhD	Economics	U.C. Los Angeles	1995

Source and *Notes*: Cheng Li, "Foreign-Educated Returnees in the PRC: Increasing Political Influence with Limited Official Power," *Journal of International Migration and Integration*, Vol. 7, No. 4 (Fall 2006): 500. For the original data, see http://www.ccer.edu.cn/en/faculty.asp?BigClassName=EN& SecondClassName=Faculty. June 1, 2005. Assoc. = Associate, Dep. = Deputy, Dir. = Director, Penn. = Pennsylvania, Prof. = Professor, U. = University, U.C. = University of California.

From 1979 to 1982, he studied political economy at Peking University, graduating with an MA in economics. He then pursued doctoral studies in economics at the University of Chicago. Lin returned to the PRC in 1987 and worked at the State Council's Research Institute of Rural Development for seven years. As a deputy director of the institute, Lin led several important research projects, and his scholarly work contributed significantly to China's market liberalization process. In 1994 Lin founded the CCER with five other instructors at Peking University and served as director of the center until he was appointed senior vice president and chief economist of the World Bank in 2008. Lin currently serves as honorary president of the NSD and vice chairman of the Economic Affairs Committee of the CPPCC.

Another original member of the CCER who later became an influential figure in China's economic leadership is Yi Gang. He began his studies in the United States in 1980 as an MBA student at Hamline University and then pursued his PhD in economics at the University of Illinois. After graduating in 1986, he began teaching at Indiana University, where he earned a tenured position as an associate professor in 1992. In 1994, after studying and teaching in the United States for 14 years, he returned to China to teach at the CCER. Just three years later he was appointed deputy secretary general of the Monetary Policy Committee of the People's Bank of China, and, after serving as division head of currency policy, he was promoted to assistant governor in 2004 and then vice governor in 2007.[43] In 2009, Yi was appointed to what is arguably the most important position in the PBOC: director of the State Administration of Foreign Exchanges (SAFE). He currently serves as vice governor of the PBOC and deputy director of the Office of the Economic and Financial Leading Group of the CCP Central Committee.

The Increasing Influence of Economists in Public Policy

The career experiences of Justin Lin and Yi Gang, particularly their prominent roles in the economic and financial leadership, suggest the growing power and influence of returnees in present-day China. It is interesting to note that four other distinguished returnee scholars — Jiang Zhenghua, Li Yining, Liu Zunyi (Lawrence J. Lau), and Qian Yingyi — have made it to top leadership posts in the CCIEE (see Table 6.2). Jiang Zhenghua is a scholar turned political leader and recently served as vice chairman of the National People's Congress. He studied at the International Institute for Population Studies in India in the early 1980s and served as a visiting professor at both the University of Paris and Stanford University. As one of the most accomplished experts on demographic issues in China, he has played an important role in China's population policy for the past three decades.

Professor Li Yining, who has taught at Peking University for six decades, was the chief architect of China's adoption of stock markets in the 1980s, one of the most far-reaching economic reforms in the country. The author of 50 books and over 100 academic articles, he has challenged several theoretical propositions in Western economic literature and is an expert on the nature and dynamics of China's reform-era transitional economy. Also of note, Li was the academic mentor of two top leaders of the fifth generation, Premier Li Keqiang and Vice President Li Yuanchao. In fact, Professor Li Yining co-authored a book in 1991 on strategies for China's economic prosperity with three of his graduate students, including Li Keqiang and Li Yuanchao.[44]

Professor Lawrence Lau is a former president of the Chinese University of Hong Kong. He received his undergraduate degree in physics and economics from Stanford University and his PhD in economics from the University of California at Berkeley. He taught at Stanford for four decades, before taking his position in Hong Kong. In addition, he is a personal friend of C.H. Tung and Victor Fung, as well as many senior Chinese leaders.

Professor Qian Yingyi also boasts remarkable professional credentials. Born in 1961 in Zhejiang Province, Qian passed the first national college entrance examination after the Cultural Revolution at the age of 16 and enrolled at Tsinghua University. He moved to the United States for graduate studies in 1982 and spent the next 20 years there. He received a master's degree in statistics from Columbia University, an MBA from Yale University, and a PhD in economics from Harvard University. He has taught at Stanford, the University of Maryland, and the University of California at Berkeley. Qian's presence in the leadership of the CCIEE is highly meaningful, demonstrating that a scholar and a foreign-educated returnee can be on equal footing with ministers of the State Council and CEOs of China's flagship companies.

The increasingly strong representation of "sea turtles" at new think tanks, such as the Chinese Economists 50 Forum, the CCER, and the CCIEE, is an important development that merits further attention. Returnees now regularly help shape the research agendas and research methods in the fields of economics, management, sociology, international relations, demography, and other subjects at their institutions, and they are leaders in China's intellectual and policy discourses. Many of these think tank members simultaneously hold academic positions at research institutions in China and abroad, thereby closely linking these Chinese institutions with their peers overseas. International academic exchanges and collaborative projects can greatly improve the quality of think tank work in China and broaden Chinese perspectives on issues of global significance.

Concluding Thoughts

China is still in the early stages of developing a network of think tanks that can engage in systematic, rigorous research and provide balanced and independent policy analysis to policymakers and the Chinese public. As illustrated by the newly established CCIEE, the growing presence of tripartite elites in think tanks — retired or current government officials, entrepreneurs representing major businesses, and distinguished scholars who are often foreign educated — suggests that these semi-governmental institutions will play an increasingly important role in policymaking in the years to come.

The establishment of the CCIEE has raised some concerns — especially among other think tanks — about the possibility of "super think tanks" monopolizing financial and human resources. Members of more-independent think tanks, such as the Unirule Institute of Economics, fear that they will be further marginalized. Indeed, some Chinese critics argue that the CCIEE is primarily for show — little more than an "image project" (面子工程, *mianzi gongcheng*) that aims to enhance China's international image.[45] These detractors highlight the fact that the number of vice chairmen on the CCIEE's board exceeds the institution's total number of researchers. Others believe that the real function of the CCIEE is to serve as a club for retired officials (养老院, *yanglaoyuan*), an argument that evokes the Imperial Academy (翰林院, *Hanlinyuan*) of traditional China.[46] According to these critics, one should not expect this "old men's club" to generate many innovative ideas or bold policy recommendations.

Perhaps the most important reservation expressed about the CCIEE is that such a close association of prominent officials, business leaders, and well-known scholars might cohere into a "wicked coalition" that represents only China's most powerful interest groups.[47] Consider the property development industry, for example, which some Chinese critics point to as one of contemporary China's most powerful special-interest groups.[48] According to Sun Liping, a sociology professor at Tsinghua University, the real estate interest group has accumulated tremendous economic and social capital throughout the last decade.[49] Ever since the 1990s real estate bubble in Hainan, this interest group has consistently sought to influence government policy and public opinion.[50] The group includes not only property developers, real estate agents, bankers, and housing market speculators, but also a significant number of local and national leaders and public intellectuals (i.e., economists and journalists) who promote the interests of that group (see Chapter 13).[51]

It is encouraging that these criticisms — valid or not — have been allowed to surface in the Chinese media. In the grand scheme of things, this development further complicates the already-complex, dynamic relationship between power, wealth, and knowledge. Only time will tell whether these fascinating changes in the composition of Chinese think tanks will contribute to profound and positive developments in decision-making and elite politics — or whether this new confluence of political, economic, and academic elites will spell trouble for China's future.

Notes

This chapter is an edited version of the author's article that appeared first in Stanford University's online journal, *China Leadership Monitor*. See Cheng Li, "China's New Think Tanks: Where Officials, Entrepreneurs, and Scholars Interact," *China Leadership Monitor*, No. 29 (Summer 2009). The author is indebted to Yinsheng Li for research assistance. The author thanks Zach Balin, Sally Carman, Jordan Lee, Ryan McElveen, Robert O'Brien, and Lucy Xu for their very helpful comments on earlier versions of this chapter.

1 Bill Clinton's speech at the Brookings Institution, May 15, 2014.

2 http://business.sohu.com/20090403/n263180355.shtml, April 3, 2009.

3 For the website of the CCIEE and the "Global Think Tanks Summit," see http://english.cciee.org.cn.

4 China's leading news magazines carried the conference as their cover story. See, for example, *Huanqiu* [Globe], No. 13, July 1, 2009.

5 See http://english.cciee.org.cn.

6 See http://news.backchina.com/2009/6/29/46808.html, June 29, 2009.

7 Hu Angang uses these three examples to characterize the Mao era as the era of individual decision-making. See http://www.people.com.cn, January 9, 2003.

8 In contrast to the Marxist notion that the Communist Party should be the "vanguard of the working class," Jiang's theory claims that the CCP should represent the "developmental needs of advanced forces of production," the "forward direction of advanced culture," and the "fundamental interests of the majority of the Chinese people."

9 For a detailed discussion of the theory of the peaceful rise of China, see Zheng Bijian, *China's Peaceful Rise: Speeches of Zheng Bijian, 1997–2004* (Washington, DC: Brookings Institution Press, 2005).

10 Ling Zhijun and Ma Licheng, *Huhan: Dangjin Zhongguo de wuzhong shengyin* [Voices: Five voices in present China] (Guangzhou: Guangzhou chubanshe, 1999).

11 Steven Mufson, "The Next Generation," *Washington Post*, June 18, 1998, A1.

12 For more discussion on Chinese think tanks in the past decade, see Murray Scot Tanner, "Changing Windows on a Changing China: The Evolving 'Think Tank' System and the Case of the Public Security Sector," *China Quarterly*, No. 171 (September 2002): 559–74. This issue also includes other excellent articles on a variety of issues relating to Chinese think tanks written by Bates Gill, Bonnie Glaser, James Mulvenon, Barry Naughton, Phillip Saunders, and David Shambaugh, among others. For studies conducted by PRC scholars, see Zhu Xufeng, "The Influence of Think Tanks in the Chinese Policy Process: Different Ways and Mechanisms," *Asian Survey*, Vol. 49, No. 2 (March/April 2009): 333–357; and Xufeng Zhu and Lan Xue, "Think Tanks in Transitional China," *Public Administration and Development* Vol. 27, No. 5 (December 2007): 452–464.

13 For more information about the Unirule Institute of Economics and the Boyuan Foundation, see their websites, http://www.unirule.org.cn/Secondweb/TianZeJianJie.asp and http://www.boyuan.hk.

14 http://www.cass.net.cn/about/wygk.htm. Among the 3,200 research staff, 1,676 are senior researchers.

15 http://www.cicir.ac.cn/tbscms/html/byjj.asp.

16 For more discussion of this topic, see Melanie Manion, *Retirement of Revolutionaries in China: Public Policies, Social Norms, Private Interests* (Princeton, NJ: Princeton University Press, 1993).

17 For more detailed discussion of political institutionalization in post-Deng China, see Cheng Li, *Chinese Politics in the Xi Jinping Era: Reassessing Collective Leadership* (Washington, DC: Brookings Institution Press, 2016).

18 *Guangzhou ribao* [Guangzhou Daily], March 18, 2008, 1. Also see http://news.dayoo.com/china/news/2008-03/18/content_3335387.htm.

19 In 2016, the composition of the leadership of the CCIEE remained the same. For the long list of the CCIEE's current leadership, which includes 6 senior advisors, 26 vice chairmen, 105 executive members of the board, and 219 board members, see http://www.cciee.org.cn/list.aspx?clmId=17, accessed January 24, 2016.

20 See Xinhua News Agency, April 16, 2009, http://news.dayoo.com/china/200904/16/53868_5726098.htm.

21 Ibid.

22 For details on the work of the forum, see its website, http://www.50forum.org.cn/home/english/jiangtan.html.

23 *Renmin ribao* [People's Daily], June 19, 2009. Also see http://news.sina.com.cn/c/2009-06-19/012218047932.shtml.

24 *Dongfang zaobao* [Oriental Morning News], June 3, 2009. Also see http://finance.qq.com/a/20090603/004913.htm.

25 For more information about the foundation, see http://www.cusef.org.hk/about-us.

26 See http://www.cnceo.com/webcontent/cnceo/person/fangtan/20051114/044320051114121358.shtml.

27 Zhang Houyi, "The Position of the Private Entrepreneur Stratum in China's Social Structure," *Social Sciences in China*, Vol. 16, No. 4 (1995): 33.

28 *Encyclopedia Americana*, International ed. (Danbury, Connecticut: Grolier Inc., 1992), Vol. 10, 477.

29 See http://cq.takungpao.com/content.asp?id=17060.

30 *Renmin ribao* [People's Daily], January 7, 2003, 10.

31 Wang Yucheng and Shi Rui, "2014 Zhongguo chuguo liuxuerenyuan zaizeng" [Continuing increases in Chinese students and scholars studying abroad], Caixin Newsnet, March 6, 2015, http://china.caixin.com/2015-03-06/100788923.html;

and also "2014 nian chuguo liuxue qushi baogao" [Report on the Status and Trends of Study Abroad in 2014], *Zhongguo jiaoyu zaixian* [China Education Online], October 12, 2014, www.eol.cn/html/lx/2014baogao/content.html.

32 Wang and Shi, "2014 Zhongguo chuguo liuxuerenyuan zaizeng."

33 See "2009 nian Zhongguo chuguo liuxuerenyuan zongshu dadao 22.93 wan" [The Total Number of Chinese Students and Scholars Who Studied Abroad in 2009 Reached 229,300], China News, March 29, 2010, www.chinanews.com.cn/lxsh/news/2010/03-12/2166360.shtml. The total number of Chinese students and scholars who have studied in the United States is based on a speech delivered by China's ambassador to the United States, Zhou Wenzhong, in Seattle on June 1, 2005. See Chinese News Net, June 6, 2005, www.chinesenewsnet.com.

34 China News Net, January 28, 2014, www.chinanews.com/lxsh/2014/01-28/5794212.shtml; and for the data representing 2010, see "2010 nian zhongguo fumei liuxue zongshu jiangda shi wan" [The Total Number of Chinese Students Who Study in the United States is Expected to Reach 100,000 in the Year 2010 Alone], http://edu.qiaogu.com/info_21391. The total number of students who came to study in the United States in 2009 was approximately 98,000. See "Jinnian mei liuxue renshu jiang chuang xingao" [This Year's Total Number of Chinese Students Who Study in the United States is Expected to Break Records], http://news.sina.com.cn/o/2010-03-03/031117154305s.shtml. For the data representing 2015, see *Shijie ribao* [World Journal], November 16, 2015, A6.

35 For further discussion of this topic, see Cheng Li, ed., *Bridging Minds across the Pacific: U.S.-China Educational Exchanges, 1978–2003* (Lanham, MD: Lexington Books, 2005).

36 See http://www.xinhuanet.com, February 16, 2004; and *Renmin ribao* [People's Daily], March 2, 2004, 11.

37 See http://www.chinesenewsnet.com. April 16, 2005.

38 Chen Xuefei, "*Rencai liudong yu liuxue zhi pingshuo*" [Mobility of human resources and an assessment of the effects of study abroad], *Shenzhou xueren* [China's Scholars Abroad], July 2003.

39 My study in 2003 of 936 senior administrators (presidents, party secretaries, vice presidents, and deputy party secretaries) at 134 universities shows that 313 (33.4 percent) of them were returnees. Cheng Li, "Coming Home to Teach: Status and Mobility of Returnees in China's Higher Education," in Li, ed., *Bridging Minds across the Pacific*, 84.

40 Cheng Li, "Foreign-Educated Returnees in the PRC: Increasing Political Influence with Limited Official Power," *Journal of International Migration and Integration*, Vol. 7, No. 4 (Fall 2006): 493–516.

41 For more information about the center, see http://www.ccer.edu.cn/cn/ ReadNews.asp?NewsID=4276.

42 *Shijie ribao* [World Journal], May 28, 2005, A4.

43 Cheng Li, "The Status and Characteristics of Foreign-Educated Returnees in the Chinese Leadership," *China Leadership Monitor*, No. 16 (Fall 2005).

44 The third student was Meng Xiaosu, then personal secretary to Vice Premier Wan Li and currently chairman of the China State Housing & Real Estate Development Group Corporation. Li Yining, Meng Xiaosu, Li Yuanchao, and Li Keqiang, *Zouxiang fanrong de zhanlue xuanze* [Strategic Choices on the Path to Prosperity] (Beijing: Jingji ribao chubanshe, 1991).

45 See, for example, http://www.ckxxw.com/html/c3/2009-07/4732.htm.

46 Xiao Feng, "*Zhongguo xuyao zhiku, buxuyao yulinyuan*" [China needs think tanks, but not the Imperial Academy], *Xinzhoukan* [New Weekly], July 17, 2009.

47 *Zhongguo xinwen zhoukan* [China Newsweek], January 13, 2006; *Liaowang* [Outlook], December 5, 2005; and also see http://www.chinesenewsnet.com, December 12, 2005.

48 The other powerful interest groups include the monopoly industries such as telecommunications, oil, electricity, and automotive. They have a huge stake in government policies. See Sun Liping, "*Zhongguo jinru liyi boyi de shidai*" [China is entering the conflict of interests era], http://chinesenewsnet.com, February 6, 2006.

49 Sun Liping, "*Zhongguo jinru liyi boyi de shidai*" [China is entering the conflict of interests era], http://chinesenewsnet.com, February 6, 2006. Also see Sun Liping, *Duanlie: 20 shiji 90 niandai yilai de Zhongguo shehui* [Cleavage: Chinese society since the 1990s] (Beijing: Shehui kexuewenxian chubanshe, 2003).

50 China's Reform Institute (Hainan) conducted this survey. See http://chinanews.com, January 19, 2006.

51 Jin Sanyong, "*Zhongyang difang cunzai mingxian boyi*" [The open game that the central and local governments play], http://www.zisi.net, February 10, 2006.

Chapter 7

An Imperative for China's New Think Tanks: Seeking Uniqueness and Diversity

Diversity: the art of thinking independently together.

— Malcolm Forbes

In recent years, China's think tanks have sprung up like mushrooms. Their rapid growth comes in response to the new Chinese Communist Party (CCP) leadership's urgent call. On a number of occasions soon after taking office, President Xi Jinping gave instructions to develop think tanks with Chinese characteristics.[1] In November 2013, at the Third Plenum of the 18th Central Committee of the Chinese Communist Party, a CCP Central Committee resolution officially endorsed the concept of "think tanks" for the first time in PRC history.[2] In November of 2014, the Central Leading Group for Comprehensively Deepening Reforms deliberated on the "Opinions on Strengthening the Construction of New Types of Think Tanks with Chinese Characteristics."[3] China's mainstream media have increasingly promoted the importance of think tank development and reported on comparable experiences from the West.

However, China's think tanks are still at an embryonic stage. They lack distinct characteristics (难有特色, *nanyoutese*), and tend to be alike (趋于雷同, *quyuleitong*). It is likely that in the near future, a considerable number of think tanks unable to distinguish themselves from the crowd will be eliminated. Unless some timely adjustments are made, the CCP central leadership's call will hardly be answered and its original goal will not be achieved.

China's Think Tanks Tend to Be Alike

In contrast to the past, current Chinese leaders are more motivated to develop think tanks. Following its economic boom, China is in need of quality professional policy research and expertise to better manage and distribute its resources at home. Socioeconomically, the country's average level of education has been increasing and the middle class has been expanding. College education is now common. With this greater awareness, the Chinese public is increasingly concerned about public policy, and more involved with and critical about the policymaking process.

Abroad, China's rapidly rising international status has led to frequent exchanges with the world on issues related to the economy, trade, security, energy, cyberspace, public health, climate, the environment, and more. In formulating policies to better integrate itself into the international framework and influence world order, China needs to avoid making foreign policy mistakes or taking a roundabout course. In addition, China's think tanks are weak on the international stage when it comes to intellectual and policy discourse, as well as global influence. This is not commensurate with the country's current economic might.

The current environment in which China's think tanks are being established resembles that of the United States in the 1950s and 1960s. During those years, American think tanks also underwent rapid development and transformation. Yet, China and the United States have different political systems, social development paths, and cultural environments. China's think tank development must conform to the state of the country. As for now, the concept of "New Types of Think Tanks with Chinese Characteristics" is still quite ambiguous. My personal understanding is that, compared to traditional think tanks, "New Types of Think Tanks" intend to be more forward-looking in policy discussions; stronger in international discourse; and more diverse in orientation, research agendas, organizational structures, funding sources, and patterns of development.

Like their fast-growing U.S. counterparts half a century ago, current Chinese think tanks are in an early stage of development. Despite the increasing quality of think tanks, one shared characteristic is their uniformity in terms of research subjects, methodologies, and operating models. There is a lack of specialization and distinctiveness. "New Types of

Think Tanks" suggests an alternative to establishing giant, all-inclusive think tanks, such as the Chinese Academy of Social Sciences. They will be replaced by think tanks with specialties and research objectives that demonstrate a commitment to policy discussion and assessment. The "New Types of Think Tanks" will also tolerate different voices. They will not only be more global, but also more capable of providing scientific appraisals and constructive policy recommendations.

Do Not Develop Think Tanks as an Industry

The early stage of think tank development relies on the quality and talent of researchers. In the United States, the "revolving door" mechanism that introduces government officials to think tanks, and *vice versa*, serves as a channel for training and promoting personnel. Due to the presidential elections, about 4,000 positions in the U.S. federal government are vacated or renewed every four years. Many of these officials are political appointees who worked on presidential and congressional campaigns, but many are also scholars from think tanks and universities who may or may not have participated in those campaigns. This phenomenon is not common in China, but changes are underway. The current Chinese government is testing out the "revolving door" mechanism. Traditionally, the Organization Department of the CCP Central Committee oversees personnel turnover, or else officials are promoted to higher positions through local governments. However, Politburo member Wang Huning and Vice Minister of the NDRC Liu He, who both currently serve as chief advisors to President Xi, are among a few who largely advanced their careers within think tanks.

The research staff in think tanks may find it difficult to exert direct influence on the policymaking process. This is no different in the United States. It is hard to measure the degree to which think tanks impact policymaking. Whether or not the U.S. president reads a think tank's published research findings is not publicly available information. And even if the president has read one particular think tank's report, it does not necessarily mean that he or she has embraced the policy recommendation. In general, presidents may have vastly different opinions on the utility of think tanks.

The quality of a think tank's research determines its level of impact. Besides employing talented researchers, having long-term financial support is crucial to a think tank's development. To ensure the quality and relative objectivity of research findings, think tanks must have rules that prevent funding from eroding academic independence. To take the Brookings Institution as an example, very little funding comes from governments — be it the U.S. government or foreign ones. Most financial support comes from individual donations. Furthermore, Brookings does not allow stakeholders to directly fund individual research projects. For instance, scholars do not study financial reform with funding from a bank or a financial institution, nor do they study public health policy with funding from a pharmaceutical company. Despite these restrictions, financing a think tank in the United States is still possible because of a culture of philanthropy, government tax incentives for donations to non-profits, and donors' appreciation for research independence. Most importantly, the public recognizes the importance of public policy. Only when think tanks provide objective, reliable, and independent public policy research can they assist the government in designing policies that benefit the general public, as opposed to a certain interest group or class.

My point here is that one should not encourage the development of think tanks as an industry; this contradicts the fundamental role of think tanks. Think tanks are the brains behind public policy and, unlike McKinsey & Company and the Boston Consulting Group, they are not meant for profit. Think tanks distinguish themselves by their management and operating models. It would be a mistake to develop think tanks as an industry.

Pluralistic Forms of Think Tanks Balance Making of Public Policy

Improving research quality requires an open research atmosphere. In both China and the United States, ideas and initiatives proposed by think tanks can derive from a certain ideology. These ideological differences are not taboo in the United States. However, if a country places ideological restraints on research, it weakens the motivations for conducting thorough research, undermines a think tank's image and reputation, and reduces the quality of its findings. More Chinese scholars and officials are aware that research bears little substantive meaning if it does nothing but explain and cater to the government's slogans and policies. Think tanks must be forward-looking; their job is to evaluate and critique government policies and society's development. They need to improve policies and help policy-makers avoid mistakes. Think tanks whose research blindly serves the demands of policymakers contravene the purpose of these organizations. Doing so is also dangerous because it could ostensibly rationalize a flawed policy and promote its continued development under faulty logic.

Though China and the United States have ideological differences, this should not prevent China from developing pluralistic forms of think tanks to benefit policymaking. It is expected that decision-makers will differ in their views and policy orientations; therefore, an external balancing mechanism is needed. President Xi Jinping referred to the pluralism of think tanks while discussing the "New Types of Think Tank."[4] The diversity of perspectives and voices would provide options for the leadership. Exchanges between China's think tanks and their foreign counterparts would not only help China learn from the West's experience in think tank development, but also help facilitate communication between militaries, businesses, and stakeholders in other areas. They would help mitigate mutual misunderstandings, and shed light on policymaking when confronting challenges like economic rebalancing, financial order, climate change, cyber security, anti-terrorism, and nuclear nonproliferation.

Since China implemented its policy of reform and opening up, the country's think tanks have greatly expanded communication and cooperation with their U.S. counterparts. The Brookings Institution and Tsinghua University's School of Public Policy and Management co-established a research center in Beijing in 2006. Both sides have conducted valuable research on China's economic reform, financial globalization, urban development, energy security, climate change, environmental protection, public health, and, in particular, the development of constructive U.S.-China relations. Some of China's think tanks are planning to establish centers in the United States. These would serve as platforms for policy exchange. This effort also shows that think tanks in China are becoming global.

It is encouraging to see more of China's think tanks coming to the United States to establish overseas branches. This will help them enhance their international impact and reach. However, this cannot be achieved by imposing Chinese ideology and propaganda. China's think tanks will need to earn recognition by demonstrating a sound scientific method and academic credibility. The exchange of thoughts and ideas between think tanks will benefit each one's understanding of the world and, in turn, improve the governing ability of countries.

Notes

This chapter is an edited version of the English translation of the author's Chinese media commentary. See Cheng Li, "Dalu xinxing zhiku jixu dute he duoyuan" [Mainland China's new think tanks urgently need uniqueness and diversity], *Fenghuang zhoukan* [Phoenix Weekly], January 25, 2015, 36–37. The author thanks Yan Wang for the original Chinese interview and editing, Yuxin Zhang for the English translation, and Zach Balin and Lucy Xu for their very helpful comments on early versions of this chapter.

1 Zhang Guozuo, "Zuoqiang xinxing zhiku tisheng guojia ruanshili" [Building New Types of Think Tanks to Enhance China's Soft Power]. Also see *Renmin ribao* [People's Daily], October 14, 2014, www.chinanews.com/sh/2014/10-14/6675278.shtml.
2 Zhu Shuyuan, "Xi Jinping weihe tebie qiangdiao 'xinxing zhiku jianshe'" [Why Xi Jinping particularly emphasized the construction of 'the new type of think tank'], Renmin Net, October 29, 2014, http://theory.people.com.cn/n/2014/1029/c148980-25928251.html.
3 Ibid.
4 Ibid.

Chapter 8

The Prospects for China's
Private Think Tanks

*Building a new type of think tank with Chinese characteristics
is an important and pressing mission. It should be targeted
at promoting scientific and democratic decision-making,
promoting modernization of the country's governing system
and ability, as well as strengthening China's soft power.*

— Xi Jinping

Think tanks have been an essential part of domestic governance and foreign policymaking in the United States. To China, however, this seems to be a new concept. In recent years, think tanks have captured the nation's attention and become a popular area of policy research. President Xi Jinping recently included think tank development in the nation's soft power strategy.[1] Meanwhile, the abundant financial resources of China's state-owned enterprises (SOEs) and private enterprises, government institutions, and civil society organizations could fund the development of think tanks. Even so, recruiting talented researchers, implementing solid research methodologies, and establishing scholarly specializations and positive institutional reputations will take time.

As policy research institutes, think tanks focus mainly on current affairs, but they also need to be forward-looking. Scholars are required to demonstrate academic excellence and a global perspective. They need to avoid writing solely for experts, and instead accommodate a broader audience of non-specialists. Successful think tanks value effective communication: they bear their audience in mind, and adopt different approaches to communicating with the government and with academia. Since China

239

still lacks systematic experience in building global think tanks, China's private think tanks need to explore different approaches to internationalization. China may benefit from analyzing the development experiences of the world's top-tier think tanks and adopting their operating models. However, under the current circumstances, developing private think tanks will not be an easy task. The lack of capital, talent, and policy support presents a long-term predicament, albeit an inevitable one in this early phase of development.

The Brookings Institution was founded by a wholesale businessman, Robert S. Brookings, who used his personal fortune to do so in 1916. At present, China is in a good position to fund think tanks, as many Chinese entrepreneurs possess substantial capital and are looking for ways to contribute to society. These entrepreneurs are passionate about public policy and policy discourse. It is quite possible that China's own "Brookings" will emerge in the next few decades.

However, the crux of developing think tanks lies in attracting quality talent and devising useful policies, rather than receiving financial support. A think tank must assemble a group of renowned or promising scholars who are able to draw the attention of the media, academia, and the general public at home and abroad. In particular, the emergence of social media could facilitate scholars' contributions to a think tank's development. Mastery over media and public discourse can turn a think tank into a prestigious institution.

China's current development strategy favors the growth of think tanks. At a more fundamental level, think tank scholars need a supportive working environment. Scholars should be allowed to choose their own areas of research according to their interests. They also need a team of support staff that prevents them from feeling overwhelmed by financial constraints and personnel shortages. For example, Brookings houses over 100 research fellows and over 300 staffers. These staffers are responsible for research, public relations, media, fundraising, administration, and more. By contrast, China's think tanks have more senior than junior staff, making effective management difficult, as there are too many "generals" and not enough "soldiers." Therefore, think tanks must follow a reasonably balanced organizational structure. Even if a think tank is able to hire quality talent, lacking a developed operating model can be crippling. At the same time, senior fellows and experts in China's think tanks need to make meaningful contributions instead of only holding titular positions, as a think tank's relevance grows out of its ability to generate ideas and provide new perspectives, methods, and ways of thinking.

In China, the employment of retired officials by think tanks in recent years has helped to facilitate institutional development. However, it has also created an unbalanced "revolving door" where retired officials are taken in by think tanks but few think tank scholars are sent into the government. Encouragingly, the recent recruitment of senior fellows from the Chinese Economists 50 Forum and Peking University's China Center for Economic Research into the government counters this phenomenon.[2] I am optimistic that this asymmetrical "revolving door" will adjust with China's growing emphasis on think tank professionalization and the recruitment of returnee scholars.

In terms of their ability to establish solid and systematic research methods that enable balanced and independent policy analysis, China's think tanks are still at an early stage. However, as China's private think tanks pursue and confront the challenges of global development, we have begun to see the fruits of their labor. There have been debates about how "New Types of Think Tanks" (新型智库, *xinxing zhiku*) should position themselves as China emerges as a great power, as well as what the implications of President Xi's pronouncement are for the development of China's existing think tanks. China's rising international status and its rapid domestic development have led to growing calls for developing think tanks that can contribute substantially to China's historical rise. Therefore, it is crucial for emerging Chinese think tanks to learn from the experiences of their counterparts in the West, and to engage in broad and frequent dialogue with the outside world.

Chinese scholars studying China enjoy a unique advantage: they are able to conduct empirical fieldwork on a large scale. In addition to research, it is essential that think tanks learn how to utilize their research findings to promote more-scientific and more-democratic policymaking in the interest of the public, and to deepen the world's understanding of China. These are central issues that China's think tanks need to consider.

"Quality, independence, impact" (高质量、独立性、影响力, *gao zhiliang, dulixing, yingxiangli*) is Brookings's century-old motto (座右铭,

zuoyouming) and the key to its success. I would like to encourage the development of these qualities in China's emerging think tanks, even as I expect China to develop think tanks that are in line with its own cultural and social context. I hope that, after a period of initial growth, Chinese think tanks will emerge as distinctive, pluralistic leaders with strong international influence, and the ability to cultivate their own talented top thinkers.

Notes

This chapter is an edited version of the English translation of the author's Chinese media commentary. See Cheng Li, "Zhongguo minjian zhiku fazhan zhilu" [The development path of China's private think tanks], *Zhongguo xinwen zhoukan* [China Newsweek], No. 689 (December 18, 2014), 43. The author thanks An Ran for the original Chinese interview and editing, Yuxin Zhang for the English translation, and Zach Balin and Lucy Xu for their very helpful comments on early versions of this chapter.

1 "Xi Calls for New Type of Think Tanks," *China Daily*, October 27, 2014; also *China Daily* website, http://www.chinadaily.com.cn/china/2014-10/27/content_18810882.htm.
2 See Chapters 1 and 12 of this volume.

Chapter 9

Dissemination of Ideas and Credibility of Think Tank Research

[Interview with *Wenhui Daily*]

If you have an apple and I have an apple and we exchange these apples then you and I will still each have one apple. But if you have an idea and I have an idea and we exchange these ideas, then each of us will have two ideas.

— George Bernard Shaw

Reputation is crucial to the development of a think tank, no matter in what country. From the experience and perspective of the Brookings Institution, a top think tank in the United States, its reputation is attributed to the institution's lasting emphasis on "quality, independence, impact." This has been the motto of the Brookings Institution for a century.[1]

The Strength of a Think Tank Is Its Scholars, Not Its Funding

Wenhui Daily: In the United States, independent think tanks are mainstream. But in China, independent think tanks still have a long way to go. In your opinion, what is the main reason for this difference?

Li: The main differences between Chinese and American think tanks stem from the different sociopolitical environments and historical backgrounds in which the think tanks have developed. In the United States, independent think tanks are perhaps the most common. Although governmental think

243

tanks exist, they are relatively few in number, and their research findings are usually not available to the public. But the majority of U.S. think tanks are non-governmental and maintain certain degrees of independence.

Yet, independent think tanks in the United States are weaker in some aspects. According to James McGann, the director of the Think Tanks and Civil Societies Program at the University of Pennsylvania, among the 1,800-plus think tanks in the United States, only a couple dozen are truly influential.[2] Many have a very hard time operating because of financial difficulties. A great number of think tanks, especially smaller ones, failed to survive the 2008 economic recession. Understandably, in any given country some think tanks will be more powerful than others. In China, the most influential think tanks, including the Chinese Academy of Social Sciences and the China Center for International Economic Exchanges, have strong historical ties to the government. The Development Research Center (DRC) of the State Council, a government agency, similarly enjoys solid funding and robust human resources.

Another type of think tank that has rapidly developed in China in recent years is those housed in universities. In the United States, these are called "research centers" because they usually focus on teaching, research, and outreach rather than on providing public administration or public policy advice.

Wenhui Daily: How can we facilitate the growth and development of independent think tanks? In China, many independent think tanks have a tough time operating due to brain drain and lack of funding. From your perspective, which of these factors is more important for a think tank's development?

Li: I think the most important determinant of a think tank's success is the quality of its scholars, not funding. The research fellows that a think tank hires need to be well-known or show promise. They need to be voices of authority in their fields so that they draw attention from the media and from academia, both domestically and internationally. As new media develops, human capital will become more and more important to a think tank's development. When a think tank's scholars become leaders in their fields and attract media and scholarly attention, the think tank will naturally gain prominence.

Funding and human capital feed upon each other in a think tank's development. At present, China's environment is conducive to the development of think tanks. Among China's private business owners, there is an abundance of capital, and many wish to exercise influence over policymaking. In the foreseeable future, China will have its own top think tank — its own Brookings.

The Brookings Institution is itself named after a businessman, Robert Brookings. He founded two institutions: the Washington University in St. Louis, a top university in the United States, and the Brookings Institution. Established in 1916, the Brookings Institution is currently raising funds for its centennial celebrations. I believe that in a couple of years, Chinese businesspeople who share the same vision as Robert Brookings will likely engage in the development of think tanks. Sooner or later, China will have its own influential think tanks that are named after individuals, just like the Brookings Institution and the Carnegie Endowment for International Peace.

Wenhui Daily: Since human capital is key to the development of think tanks, how should Chinese independent think tanks prevent brain drain (人才流失, *rencai liushi*)?

Li: This is in fact a two-sided problem. For example, some scholars and former officials who work in the private sector may be interested in using think tanks as a revolving door to reintegrate into the public sector. Many factors are crucial to retaining talented researchers, including political and economic considerations, as well as the need for a positive working environment. Which factor matters most depends on individual context.

Academic freedom is the most important component of a positive working environment. Scholars in a think tank should have the freedom to set their own research agenda and evaluate the academic or political significance of their work, and the institution should provide a team to support them and shield them from financial and professional pressures. The Brookings Institution employs around 120 full-time research fellows and more than 300 support staff, including research assistants, administrative personnel, office managers, and other professionals who work in communications, public outreach, and development (i.e., fundraising). By contrast, most of today's Chinese think tanks lack sufficient support staff, which undermines their research capacities. A successful think tank requires strong operational mechanisms and an appropriate ratio of researchers to support staff.

Having talented researchers is critical, but without complementary operational mechanisms, these assets could become liabilities. The priority for Chinese think tanks, in my view, should be to provide an environment that is conducive to fellows focusing on their research, as opposed to merely listing their names and titles on the institution's webpage. After all, a think tank's aim is to generate new concepts and ideas, influence decision-making, and explore novel research approaches and methodologies.

Wenhui Daily: As you mentioned above, China's think tanks are also "revolving doors." In many cases, we see retired officials joining think tanks, but far less often do we see think tank scholars joining the government. In your opinion, what should China do to change this situation?

Li: China's revolving door phenomenon is deeply rooted in its politics. In the United States and Europe, government officials are most productive and competitive in their fifties and sixties. In China, many leaders at that age would retire due to age limits or term limits on leadership posts (see Chapter 6).[3] Thus, if they want to continue to make use of their experience and talent, a think tank would be the ideal choice.

In the United States, many young talents from think tanks move on to work in the government. This is a result of the two-party political system. The four-year presidential term results in high turnover of personnel every four years. A new administration brings about 4,000 openings in the federal government, and generally at least a quarter of these are filled by staff from think tanks and universities, or by other professionals with solid academic and research backgrounds. This provides an excellent career development opportunity for young think tank scholars. By contrast, China's elite recruitment and promotion works quite differently, because China places more value on local administration experience. Senior party and governmental officials are usually promoted from positions in the local government.[4]

Nonetheless, recently a few prominent think tank scholars have been appointed to important positions in the Chinese government. The problem of China's unidirectional revolving door will resolve itself as the country puts greater emphasis on recruiting financial and socioeconomic policy experts — especially foreign-educated returnees — to its leadership. As think tanks develop and the interaction between media and think tank scholars increases, we will likely see more think tank scholars recruited into the leadership. However, China's political system is fundamentally different from the multi-party systems of Western democracies, so even if an increasing number of young talents from think tanks enter the government, this will not become a main source of elite recruitment in China.

The Independence of a Think Tank Enhances Its Reputation

Wenhui Daily: Although there is a shortage of high-quality independent think tanks in China, we have recently seen an increasing number of consulting and public relations firms flourish. Do you think high-quality independent think tanks may grow out of these firms?

Li: First of all, in the West, think tanks — regardless of whether or not they have a connection to government — are distinct from consulting and public relations firms. There is a fundamental conceptual difference here: think tanks are, by definition, non-profit public policy research institutes, whereas consulting and public relations firms are profit-driven, with their interests often lying beyond public policy research. Most consulting and public relations firms are not as research-oriented as think tanks. They work for particular clients and provide consulting services solely for profit. But sometimes the line is blurred. For example, RAND Corporation, a well-known think tank, also pursues profit, so its research projects are often contracted.

In the case of the Brookings Institution, all research findings are made public and none are tailored to any particular company or individual. The ideal type of funding that we seek is unrestricted, meaning that a donor commits to not interfering at all with our research. Even if funding is tied to a specific area of study or a particular project, a donor cannot place limits on our research methodology or influence the results of a study. As a result of this wall between funding and research, the Brookings Institution has built its reputation for impartiality over time and gained the influence it has today.

Wenhui Daily: Independence is crucial for a think tank, but most think tanks in East Asia are supported financially by governments. Many Japanese think tanks are funded by conglomerates. How do we eliminate the possibility that such think tanks publish findings as directed by their funders?

Li: The Brookings Institution has set up a variety of regulations to ensure independence. We make it very clear when accepting funding that a donor cannot in any way exert influence over our research. Brookings has turned away grants in cases where donors refused to comply with this principle. As such, Brookings has earned and preserved its distinguished reputation for institutional independence.

In American politics, the Brookings Institution has always kept a neutral stance of non-partisanship. Although some believe that Brookings favors the Democratic Party, in fact Republicans have recently led the institute as well. Examples include former president of Brookings (1995–2002) Michael Armacost, who previously served as U.S. ambassador to Japan, and former director of the Foreign Policy Program and vice president of the institution Richard Haass, who is now president of the Council on Foreign Relations. In addition, many members of our Board of Trustees are Republicans.

Wenhui Daily: Although Chinese think tanks are large in number, few have the international influence of high-quality think tanks like the Brookings Institution and RAND Corporation. What do you think is the reason for such a gap?

Li: Multiple factors contribute to a think tank's success: in addition to funding, a think tank's governing philosophy, personnel, and research agendas are all very important. Cultivating these requires time, patience, and persistence. Think tanks in the United States possess a century of experience, so they have developed rapidly in recent decades. In China, though, independent think tanks have only begun to be established in the last ten years, so the current lag is understandable.

Following President Xi Jinping's proposal that think tanks be a crucial element of China's soft power strategy, the development of Chinese think tanks will accelerate in the years to come. Meanwhile, as the economy continues to grow, funding will come from a greater array of sources, including state-owned enterprises, the government, and private firms. These different channels will serve as a much-needed catalyst for the rapid growth of think tanks. But improving the quality of employees, developing sound research methodologies, cultivating distinctiveness, and gaining a reputation all require time.

At the outset, think tanks may experience financial shortages. However, even during this early period, think tanks need to be prudent about their sources of funding, as problematic donations can affect a think tank's reputation and, in turn, growth. Let me remind you of the importance of a good reputation for a think tank's development. Even for millions of dollars in funding, Brookings would never compromise or risk the reputation that it has built up over the last hundred years. A think tank with a good reputation will have many opportunities for funding its development. But if, at an early stage, a think tank compromises its reputation in order to receive funding, the liability that comes with that funding will jeopardize future development.

Wenhui Daily: Some Chinese think tanks have demonstrated a commitment to growing internationally. What changes and innovations do you think are necessary for Chinese think tanks to take on more international projects and operate in a global context?

Li: First of all, Chinese think tanks need to possess a basic understanding of the international research environment, including cross-cultural rules and norms in academia and in policymaking. Due to cultural and sociopolitical differences, Chinese think tanks may not need to unconditionally observe these rules and norms, but they have to understand them. Secondly, Chinese think tanks need to conduct serious academic research. The Brookings Institution is one of the oldest think tanks in the United States, and it has influence at both the national and global levels. This is attributable to the historical value of our previous research projects, including analyses on the establishment of the United Nations and Roosevelt's New Deal, as well as in-depth studies on social welfare, taxation, foreign policy, energy, technology, health policy, immigration, and more. For the Brookings Institution, high-quality research is the foundation of our influence. A think tank's research should not be purely theoretical; it should be the product of a meticulous academic study of contemporary politics or economics, and it must attract international attention. In the field of China studies, PRC scholars have unique cultural and geographical advantages that allow them to access local information and conduct large-scale quantitative studies. But besides the studies themselves, think tanks need to introduce and disseminate credible research findings to the outside world. As to this key aspect, Chinese think tanks still have much to learn.

As a policy research institute, a think tank should keep its research agenda abreast of the latest developments and take a farsighted view of the future. At the same time, researchers must demonstrate academic excellence and global insight. They also need to be able to engage and educate a non-expert audience. A successful think tank places a special emphasis on effective public outreach and information dissemination. For the effective delivery of information, there must be a clear target audience. There is a marked difference, for instance, between addressing the government and engaging academia.

Research Findings Need to Be Communicated through the Best Methods and Channels

Wenhui Daily: The director of the University of Pennsylvania's Think Tanks and Civil Societies Program, Dr. James McGann, notes that think tanks of the future will need to employ new forms of communication. With the development of the Internet and new media, most research papers are no longer read in print. How should think tanks disseminate their research findings under these new circumstances?

Li: "Short, straightforward, and fast" (短平快, *duan ping kuai*) characterize new media, but most of the time new media can only serve as a supplement to primary research papers, as it is difficult to summarize findings from a comprehensive study in just a dozen words. Of course, we are in a time of transformation, and books might only be published online in the future. It is important to note that in the Internet era, not all websites are created equal — some are far more influential than others. Similarly, not all think tank websites receive an equal share of attention. Think tank websites should aim to attract a large number of online visitors and target the right audiences.

A think tank's advantage lies not in the pursuit of "short, straightforward, and fast," but in conducting serious research and producing comprehensive reports. A communication strategy is necessary if a think tank intends to use various types of media to publish research findings simultaneously. This is why the Brookings Institution has a large and experienced communications team. To maintain its leading role in the think tank world, Brookings dedicates significant time and energy to building and updating its website. Within the institution, many staff members are responsible for monitoring the website and updating specific details weekly, if not daily. At the same time, the Brookings Institution interacts frequently with major U.S. and global media. It is a rare day that Brookings scholars do not appear in major newspapers or on prominent television networks around the world. The media is an essential channel for think tank scholars to disseminate their ideas, sway public debate, and indirectly influence public policymaking. Therefore, many think tank scholars place a special emphasis on interacting with journalists and voicing their ideas through media.

Wenhui Daily: During the Arab Spring and the 2011 England riots, "opinion leaders" became very important. They spread ideas rapidly through new media such as Twitter and Facebook, which carried serious consequences for their respective societies. In fact, think tanks are also a type of opinion leader. How can think tanks provide positive guidance and minimize negative outcomes when facing emergency situations?

Li: Based on the motto of the Brookings Institution, we can say that "quality" is a prerequisite. Recruiting accomplished research fellows is therefore utterly crucial. Candidates should be standouts in their fields: some may have extensive government work experience, and others may have a record of significant achievements or an impressive reputation in the public policy domain. Our regulations forbid research assistants from conducting media interviews or publishing articles in their capacities as Brookings employees. These are all key contributors to the consistently high quality of Brookings's research. Although the Brookings Institution makes use of new media, we do so with great care and attention. We do our utmost to avoid publishing inaccurate data, thoughtless opinions, or sensationalist content. This approach is grounded in the culture of Brookings itself.

We understand well the serious social responsibility that accompanies Brookings's reputation and influence, and therefore, in terms of management, we hold ourselves to stricter standards than even academic institutions. For example, we invite internal and external experts to review books and major reports multiple times before publication. This is one way to ensure quality. During media interviews, fellows sometimes need to react quickly, and sometimes they are asked questions about areas in which they are not experts. To maintain our high standards even in these situations, experts all participate in a long training process to improve their ability to identify and make correct judgments in fast-paced settings.

Wenhui Daily: Aside from the government and the media, think tanks also play a role as public intellectuals. In the future, how can think tanks work with the media and the government to enhance their communication power?

Li: Different thinks tanks have different objectives. Some think tanks function primarily as critics of government policy, which is a reasonable approach to take; some keep aloof from the government; and others maintain independence but earn respect from government agencies through high-quality research (the employees of these think tanks frequently appear in government hearings and briefings). The Brookings Institution belongs to the third category. Upon invitation, most government officials are willing to visit the Brookings Institution and deliver a speech, and our researchers give briefings almost weekly to officials in the White House, Congress, and various federal government departments. But, at the same time, the Brookings Institution always retains its independence, and often criticizes government policies, including those related to the Middle East, Asia, health insurance, and immigration. Offering such criticism is our responsibility as public intellectuals. This is a difficult yet necessary balance: on the one hand, as a policy research institution, we need to maintain a close relationship with the government in order to influence policy; on the other hand, we must remain independent so as not to become a mouthpiece of the government. It is our social responsibility to follow and analyze the effects of policies, including forecasting potential side effects.

In the process of assessing and analyzing policies, many think tanks have established a mechanism through which they interact with the government. Sometimes, before advocating a new policy, the government will communicate with and seek feedback from the experts of major think tanks — an extremely positive interaction.

The Brookings Institution strives to contribute to American democracy, particularly through improving social welfare and ensuring equal opportunity for every citizen, as well as assuming responsibility for peace and understanding in the world. In recent years in particular, we have emphasized that researchers need to take global perspectives, so that the Brookings Institution delivers its benefits not only to the United States, but also to the world.

Notes

This chapter is an edited version of the English translation of the author's Chinese media interview. See Cheng Li, "Chenggong de zhiku youqi yao zhongshi youxiao de chuanbo" [Successful think tanks place an emphasis on effective communication], *Wenhui bao* [Wenhui Daily], June 3, 2014, 9. The author thanks Liu Liyuan for the original Chinese interview and editing, Lu Jiaqi for the English translation, and Zach Balin and Lucy Xu for their very helpful comments on early versions of this chapter.

1 See the Brookings Institution homepage: http://www.brookings.edu/about#research-programs.
2 See Think Tanks and Civil Societies Program (TTCSP), University of Pennsylvania, TTCSP Global Go To Think Tank Index Reports (in various years from 2008 to 2015), http://repository.upenn.edu/think_tanks.
3 Cheng Li, "Leadership Transition in the CPC: Promising Progress and Potential Problems," *China: An International Journal*, Vol. 10, No. 2 (August 2012): 23–33.
4 Three quarters of the Politburo members advanced their careers primarily through local administration, especially from the positions of provincial chiefs (party secretaries and/or governors). Cheng Li, "A Biographical and Factional Analysis of the Post-2012 Politburo," *China Leadership Monitor*, No. 41 (Summer 2013): 5–7.

Chapter 10

The Role of Think Tanks in Reconstructing Values in Present-Day China

[Interview with *Phoenix Weekly*]

Nowadays people know the price of everything and the value of nothing.

— Oscar Wilde

"The Central Committee of the Chinese Communist Party (CCP) has decided to expel Xu Caihou, Jiang Jiemin, Li Dongsheng, and Wang Yongchun from the party for violating party disciplines."[1] With this announcement of the expulsion of four high-ranking officials from the party by the Central Commission for Discipline Inspection (CCDI) and the Ministry of Supervision on the last day of June 2014, the party's anti-corruption campaign for the first half of the year came to an end. In addition to two state-level deputy officials (副国级官员, *fuguoji guanyuan*), Xu Caihou and Su Rong, twenty-one "big tigers" — officials at the vice-ministerial level and higher — were charged by the CCDI in the first half of 2014. The party's public effort to combat corruption has captured the attention of overseas observers who study China's internal affairs.

As a Chinese-American scholar who was born in Shanghai in the late 1950s, Cheng Li has been studying China's political system and changes in Chinese society since the 1980s. As the first-ever Chinese-American director of the Brookings Institution's John L. Thornton China Center, a premier think tank in the United States, his opinions and recommendations are

255

valued by the U.S. academic community and today's decision-makers. On the eve of the China-U.S. Strategic and Economic Dialogue, Cheng Li agreed to participate in an exclusive interview with *Phoenix Weekly*. While our last issue focused on the China-U.S. Strategic and Economic Dialogue, this issue will start off with the "crackdown on tigers."[2]

Fighting Corruption Requires Support Systems

Phoenix Weekly: China's anti-corruption campaign is in full swing. Many "big tigers" have been ousted, one after the next. What role do you think the anti-corruption campaign is playing in China's current political ecosystem?

Li: Anti-corruption is playing a very positive role. China is currently faced with serious corruption issues due to the pervasiveness of corruption and the staggering amount of wealth amassed by corrupt officials. The emergence of new media in China has brought the corruption scandals of officials into public view. Especially after the Bo Xilai incident, information about corruption cases can be accessed and obtained through the Internet and various other channels.

What merits our attention is the fact that this anti-corruption crackdown is the largest and most severe since the establishment of the new CCP government in 1949. In 2013 alone, the steps taken to combat corruption were unprecedented with respect to the quantity and rank of corrupt officials who were investigated, arrested, or dismissed. This timely anti-corruption campaign has, to some extent, saved the Chinese Communist Party and the state from a revolution, so it has been a very successful endeavor.

Of course, anti-corruption is, to a large extent, associated with issues of legitimacy and stability. To win the support of the public, the CCP needs to cement its leadership position through a new, institutionalized anti-corruption mechanism. Otherwise, enduring peace and stability will be hard to achieve.

I do not agree with the view, held by some people, that the current anti-corruption campaign is being mounted in vain because it is not being carried out under the rule of law. While current anti-corruption measures are indeed not being implemented through legal mechanisms, can you envision a country establishing the rule of law in just one or two years? That would be impossible. In the current political environment, the anti-corruption campaign is both appropriate and timely. We have already seen officials at all levels change their actions and behaviors. That means the anti-corruption campaign has been a successful source of deterrence.

Phoenix Weekly: Some people say that the key to cracking down on corruption is to establish a property disclosure system for officials. What do you think? Do you think that solving problems on the surface can ultimately address root causes?

Li: Wang Qishan has also said this; he believes that the campaign addresses symptoms (治标, *zhibiao*) but does not deal with root causes (治本, *zhiben*).³ That being said, at the current stage, addressing symptoms has bought time for the government to address root causes. However, in the next few years, the Chinese government must start to introduce and implement institutional, law-based anti-corruption mechanisms, including a property disclosure system, a real estate property ownership certificate registration system, and a conflict of interest verification system for officials. Likewise, the country needs to proceed towards gradual judicial independence and improve relevant legal procedures. Although it is unlikely that China will achieve these goals immediately, the country must stay on track. If it fails to do so, another wave of corruption may strike. This would undo all the progress made in the current ambitious and vigorous anti-corruption campaign, and carry grave consequences for the leadership of the CCP.

China's top leaders, or at least Xi Jinping and Wang Qishan, are aware of this hazard. As a result, the Third Plenary Session of the 18th Central Committee of the CCP laid greater emphasis on judicial reform and establishing the rule of law. I do not think initial judicial reform will take 10 or 20 years — it should only require a few years. Throughout this time, the most urgent task will be to develop and implement relevant support systems. While establishing the rule of law in a country is usually a lengthy process, the public's expectations for law-based anti-corruption measures can no longer be delayed. The general public is eager to see breakthrough progress in establishing the rule of law.

Maintaining Stability Is the Top Priority of the NSC

Phoenix Weekly: The CCP just established the National Security Committee (NSC). What are the implications of its establishment? What role do you think it will play in China's political system?

Li: It is still too early to say. From its conception to its establishment, the NSC has been seen as a coordination mechanism. In my opinion, it will improve and perfect itself with the maturation of China's political system and the refinement of the country's mechanisms for decision-making in the realms of national security and foreign policy. The establishment and operation of a new mechanism requires continuous progress; the NSC may change substantially over the next 10 or 20 years. Surprisingly, the NSC's current emphasis seems to center on maintaining China's stability, as signaled by the staffing of key personnel, including Meng Jianzhu and Zhang Chunxian. However, this posture is not set in stone; the NSC is currently in a trial stage. I think greater adjustments will be made to this mechanism as China's political system matures.

Phoenix Weekly: Do you think this is a step in the reform of China's political system?

Li: I do not think so. If the NSC were part of the government, it would signify an overall structural change. However, the NSC is currently part of the party system, so we have yet to depart from the old framework.

Looking at it from the standpoint of "national security," if the NSC were a part of the government, then the army would be under the government's control rather than the party's. As it stands, the NSC is not pertinent to discussions about a constitutional government.

Phoenix Weekly: What is the biggest difference between the NSC of the CCP and the National Security Council of the United States?

Li: From the very beginning, Chinese leaders have adopted the National Security Council of the United States as a model to guide their preparations for establishing the NSC. In terms of function, from its creation in the 1940s until 9/11, the National Security Council was most often relied on for managing national security diplomacy. After 9/11, the Council's function shifted to the fight against terrorism. When it comes to the NSC of the CCP, its main function — at least for now — lies in maintaining internal stability.

In terms of political structure, the United States follows a multi-party system and hence the National Security Council reports directly to the President. The NSC of the CCP, on the other hand, reports directly to the General Secretary of the party.

As for international status and global ambitions, the United States is a great power with greater interest in and broader influence over international affairs than China. China is a large country and a rising power, but concerns about its own internal affairs outweigh its interest in engaging in international affairs.

Phoenix Weekly: Your research on social issues encompasses the middle class, the tobacco industry, religion, youth, and other areas. From a social standpoint, what, in your opinion, is the biggest challenge currently faced by China?

Li: I think it is very important to rebuild people's values in the country.

China's economic rise has been a very interesting phenomenon. China's economic miracle could not have been achieved without Chinese people's hard work. What lies behind China's success? A simple explanation is that the Chinese people really want to make money. To put it more eloquently, it is the will of the Chinese people to become wealthy through hard work. This cultural attribute was suppressed throughout the Cultural Revolution, but, once it was set loose, it became a forceful driver of the market-oriented economy.

The side effect of unleashing this force has been the rise of money worship, which has caused people to shed more-positive, traditional Chinese attributes and distorted their views on social ethics and interpersonal relationships. The fixation on wealth accumulation has also precipitated widespread corruption and moral decay. Under these circumstances, an emerging great power like China must reassess its priorities and undergo a process of moral reconstruction. This is, in itself, a paradox. On the one hand, we have witnessed moral decay; on the other, this is a new period of rediscovering social morals.

Sometimes we talk too much about China's core interests. In fact, China can recover from a financial crisis. China will still be China even if a real estate crisis occurs. But how do we reestablish the values of a society in an ideological vacuum? In pursuing the "Chinese dream," how can Chinese people better understand other countries? No less, in the process of realizing the "Chinese dream" and gaining a better understanding of other countries, how will other countries view and identify with China? It is not easy to gain another's respect for one's values.

Not all of China's core values need to be universal values, but because certain basic elements of humanity are widely recognized, there must be an element of universality to China's values. Denying this fact would put you on the opposite side of civilization.

Only by rebuilding its values can China become an influential country, an active participant in world affairs, and an envied state — a true great power.

Phoenix Weekly: This is also part of the process of finding out "who I am."

Li: Yes, this means that a country has begun to search for the true meaning of its values. As a major power, China needs to consider both its domestic and global governance. At present, China is doing well domestically in some areas, such as in medical insurance, where reforms have accelerated tremendously over the past five years. The West would view China in a different light if it knew about this progress.

However, China still lags behind in addressing issues related to minority groups, including the protection of women and children, as well as other challenges that stem from existing policies aimed at ethnic minorities and religious groups. Although some Americans have been concerned about and hostile to Muslims after 9/11, as a country of immigrants, the United States has made progress in ensuring freedom of religion, especially in the last few decades. The United States has built an environment of inclusivity and diversity.

Phoenix Weekly: What do you anticipate China's reforms will look like going forward?

Li: China is in need of reforms in many areas. Therefore, the question of which reforms happen first is crucial for decision-makers and strategic thinkers in Chinese research institutions. We need to understand that the leader of such a big country will hesitate to make decisions where he cannot anticipate and control the outcome, or where he will be uncertain as to how to handle a situation should it veer out of control.

It is evident now that the strategy of the new CCP leadership is to reform the economy first and delay or postpone political restructuring. This is understandable, to a certain degree; the leadership may be able to win support from the public, particularly the middle class, by succeeding in its economic reforms. The leadership would then have the political capital to push forward other pieces of its agenda, including possible political restructuring. Down the road, analyzing how the CCP leadership chooses to spend its political capital will be important to charting the path of China's political, social, and diplomatic future.

Notes

This chapter is an edited version of the English translation of the author's Chinese media interview. See Cheng Li, "Zhongguo xuyao jiazhiguan de chongjian" [China needs to rebuild values], *Fenghuang zhoukan* [Phoenix Weekly], July 25, 2014, 48–49. The author thanks Wang Yan for the original Chinese interview and editing, Tina Li for the English translation, and Zach Balin and Lucy Xu for their very helpful comments on early versions of this chapter.

1 Renmin web, July 5, 2014, http://js.people.com.cn/n/2014/0705/c360300-21584757-2.html.

2 For the author's interview on the China-U.S. Strategic and Economic Dialogue, see "Zhong Mei yingyi hezuo lai jianshao fengqi" [China and the U.S. should cooperate to reduce differences], *Fenghuang zhoukan* [Phoenix Weekly], 2014, special issue, 57.

3 Xinhua Newsnet, February 22, 2013, http://forum.home.news.cn/detail/114648529/1.html.

Chapter 11

The Role of Think Tanks in Promoting Mutual Understanding and Preventing Misjudgment in Sino–U.S. Relations

Culture consists of connections, not of separations.

— Carlos Fuentes

This is my first public speech at Tsinghua University. I am not an alumnus, but Tsinghua has meant a lot to my career. Twenty-four years ago, back in 1990, I spent several months at Tsinghua working on my Princeton doctoral dissertation. I was researching the rise of China's technocrats in the post-Mao era, and I used Tsinghua as a case study.

Eight years ago, in 2006, I came here with other Brookings fellows to celebrate the establishment of the Brookings–Tsinghua Center for Public Policy (BTC). The leader of our delegation back then was the co-chair of the Brookings Board of Trustees, Mr. John Thornton, who had also been running Tsinghua's Global Leadership EMBA Program since 2003. As the first overseas center of the Brookings Institution, the BTC is proof of John Thornton's conviction that the rise of China would constitute one of the most significant events of the 21st century, and that the China–U.S. relationship would arguably become the most important bilateral relationship of our age. At the time, the rise of China was merely a prediction, but now it is a reality.

Tensions between China and the U.S. Arise from Misperceptions and Misjudgments

The China–U.S. relationship is not in the best shape. Some would even say that relations are deteriorating, especially in light of rising tensions in the South China Sea and East China Sea, and the U.S. indictment of five Chinese military officials.[1] Promoting mutual understanding and constructive relations between the two countries is crucial — and it is for this reason that the John L. Thornton China Center at the Brookings Institution was established.

My colleagues and I highly value opportunities to interact with our Chinese counterparts. I firmly believe that, should a conflict or war break out between the United States and China, the root cause would most likely be misperceptions and misjudgments on both sides, and not differences in interests or ideology, or changes in international order.

As long as misperceptions exist, they will misinform foreign policies. I think Chinese leaders are sincere and constructive in calling for a "new type of great power relations" — avoiding confrontation and a zero-sum mindset, and seeking cooperation. Their American counterparts hold similar beliefs. While Larry Summers served as Obama's economic adviser, he once said that it was easy to envision a future of common prosperity or shared failure for China and the United States, but hard to imagine how one could prosper while the other fails. I think many Americans would agree.

The Negative Impact of the "Threat Theory" and the "Conspiracy Theory"

Other factors also contribute to current tensions between the two countries: firstly, the "threat theory" (威胁论, *weixielun*) has become amplified by the rapid growth and development of communication technologies, including the emergence and expansion of social media, blogging, and 24-hour TV and radio commentary. Several examples illustrate that changes are needed to prevent the buildup of further tension. According to a recent poll, 87 percent of Americans consider China a major military threat. Most Chinese people view the United States in a similar light.

Secondly, the diversification of political interest groups in both countries has generated a multitude of voices, much of which amounts to noise. Thirdly, U.S.–China relations are not only influenced by domestic political, social, and economic factors, but also by tensions in international geopolitics. In addition, contradictions and inconsistencies in policy-making have deepened misperceptions between the two countries. For instance, the Chinese leadership has often proclaimed that China's focus rests primarily on domestic issues; in the meantime, China has increasingly engaged in the affairs of African, South American, and Asian countries. Similarly, Chinese leaders have often signaled their respect for Deng Xiaoping's "keeping-a-low-profile" policy, yet they have recently started to lay emphasis on "striving for achievements" (奋发作为, *fenfa zuowei*). Likewise, Chinese leaders have reassured the United States that China has no intention of "expelling" it from Asia, but now those leaders claim that Asian affairs should be determined by Asian nations. This "de-Americanization" of Asia worries U.S. leaders greatly.

The American perception of China's foreign policy has increasingly diverged from that of the Chinese. To the United States and many other countries, with China's increasing strength, it is becoming more aggressive — a quality that damages its international image. By contrast, people in China feel that their country is in a defensive posture over issues in the East and South China Seas, and that any tensions are the result of America's attempt to contain China.

The Chinese public considers President Xi Jinping's foreign policy a success. For instance, China finds itself increasingly influential in China–U.S.–Russia relations. Unlike in the Cold War era, when the United States wielded strong influence over this triangle relationship, China now enjoys stronger ties with both the United States and Russia than either of the two countries does with each other. China therefore possesses the greatest leverage at present. Similarly, China has formed deep economic ties with Europe, and it exercises considerable influence in Africa and South America. While China believes that the United States is a power in decline, the United States is not too concerned about close cooperation between China and Russia. Most Americans believe that, sooner or later, China will seek to become a closer partner of the United States.

According to many Chinese scholars and media outlets, the United States will never be able to embrace China's rise and accept its position as the world's largest economy. But, based on my observations, many Americans already do welcome China's ascent. Fact is fact, regardless of whether or not Chinese thought leaders accept it. Americans do not necessarily blame China for their country's own economic problems; instead, they blame the U.S. government for not fulfilling its duties. Although Chinese people tend to believe that the United States is attempting to contain China, I hear little from my U.S. colleagues that would substantiate such a "conspiracy theory" (阴谋论, *yinmoulun*). For example, none of my friends and colleagues in the United States consider the indictment of five Chinese military officials to be a wise move. China worries about the westernization of its system and peaceful political evolution (和平演变, *heping yanbian*), but no American would support a wholesale westernization or Americanization of China. Moreover, China is often irked by the United States' criticism of its human rights record and its lack of democracy, but, in my view, this criticism carries good intentions; malicious racists, on the other hand, would simply think that the Chinese do not deserve human rights and democracy. At times, the United States critiques China out of respect, not disrespect.

How can we avoid misperceptions? More attention needs to be paid to understanding the domestic political, socioeconomic, and cultural factors that influence each country's foreign policy. China's Confucius Institutes have been met with criticism from some American professors. Although I am not one of these professors, this criticism shows that China still lacks a comprehensive understanding of American society and its institutions. That is why exchanges in various fields should be encouraged.

Moreover, I think that China talks a lot about its core interests, but not enough about its core values. This needs to change if China anticipates higher levels of exchange and communication with the world's countries and cultures. In the United States, we pride ourselves on the American dream, and China is certainly entitled to pursuing its own Chinese dream. But let us not forget that a dream for one nation should never be a nightmare for others.

Notes

This chapter is an edited version of the English translation of the author's Chinese media commentary based on his speech at Tsinghua University. See Cheng Li, "Xiaochu wujie, kaiqi Mei Zhong guanxi 'xin huinuanqi'" [Eliminate misunderstandings: Starting a "new warm period" in U.S.–China relations], *Renmin luntan* [People's Tribune], July 2014, 60–61. The author thanks Yuan Qing for the original Chinese interview and editing, Li Yuan for the English translation, and Zach Balin and Lucy Xu for their very helpful comments on early versions of this chapter.

1 David M. Lampton, "A Tipping Point in U.S.–China Relations is Upon Us," US–China Perception Monitor, May 11, 2015, http://www.uscnpm.org/blog/2015/05/11/a-tipping-point-in-u-s-china-relations-is-upon-us-part-i.

Chapter 12

Chinese Think Tanks Go Global

An emerging great power must have great think tanks
(大国崛起必有大国智库, *daguojueqi biyou daguozhiku*)

— Wang Huiyao and Miao Lü

I am pleased that *Global Think Tanks* has been successfully published. I have long been acquainted and worked in partnership with the authors of this fine work, Wang Huiyao and Miao Lü. In 2010, Wang was a visiting fellow at the Brookings Institution, while Miao studied think tanks in Washington, DC, and Boston. Wang, the principal author of *Global Think Tanks*, is now a senior research fellow and a top administrator of a prominent think tank in China. Several years ago, when China lacked systematic studies on and practical experience in developing global think tanks, Wang started examining and exploring approaches to internationalizing China's think tanks.

Wang Huiyao was born in Chengdu, Sichuan Province, in 1958. He was a "sent-down youth" (插队知青, *chadui zhiqing*) during the final year of the Cultural Revolution. When China re-instituted the college entrance examination system in 1977, he passed the exam and enrolled at the Guangzhou Foreign Language Institute, majoring in English. After graduation, he worked as an official in the Department of International Economic Affairs at the Ministry of Foreign Trade and Economic Cooperation for two years (1982–1984). He continued his graduate studies abroad, first at University of Windsor, and then at University of Western Ontario and University of Manchester, where he received an MBA degree and a PhD in international business management respectively. He worked in Canada's business sector for a number of years, serving as chief trade representative for the Quebec Government Offices in China and Hong Kong, director for Asia at SNC–Lavalin, and vice president at AMEC–Agra.

Eventually, he abandoned his business career and pursued his passion for international educational exchanges and think tank development in China. Since 2008, he has served as vice chairman of the Western Returned Scholars Association (WRSA), which in China is known as *Oumei Tongxuehui* (欧美同学会). With over 80,000 members, WRSA is China's largest organization for Chinese scholars who have returned from overseas. In 2015, Chinese Premier Li Keqiang appointed Wang as a counselor to the State Council (国务院参事, *guowuyuan canshi*), a role in which he serves as a consultant alongside several dozen other scholars and professionals.

Wang founded the Center for China and Globalization (CCG) in 2008.[1] Over the past few years, the CCG has emerged as one of the most forward-looking and internationally minded think tanks in China. It houses 80 research and support staff, with headquarters in Beijing and branches in Guangzhou, Qingdao and Shenzhen, as well as representatives in Hong Kong, New York, Washington, Frankfurt, Paris, and Sydney. This think tank publishes approximately 10 books and monographs annually, including authoritative blue books on international human resources, foreign education and returnees, international migration, and Chinese enterprises going global.

China's former chief trade negotiator Long Yongtu and Chairman of Hang Lung Group and Co-Chair of the U.S.-based Asia Society Ronnie Chan serve as co-chairs of the CCG. A number of distinguished scholars serve as academic advisors, including Shing-Tung Yau, William Overholt, Denis Simon, Zheng Yongnian, and Dali Yang. The CCG hosts several dozen public forums and private round tables annually. In 2015, for example, the CCG and the Qingdao municipal government jointly hosted former U.S. secretary of state Condoleezza Rice, who delivered a speech on teaching entrepreneurship.[2] In December 2015, the CCG partnered with the New York–based Council on Foreign Relations (CFR) to host a seminar in Beijing on dealing with environmental health hazards. Other topics featured in 2015 include China's "economic new normal" (经济新常态, *jingji xinchangtai*), an assessment of the "One Belt, One Road" initiative, Chinese outbound investment in South Asia, the improvement of

Sino–Japan relations through think tank exchanges, and U.S. philanthropic practices and law.

I have witnessed the birth and growth of the CCG. I am aware of how difficult it is to develop private or even semi-private think tanks in a Chinese context; the lack of capital, talent, and government support presents a significant long-term challenge. Wang has overcome numerous hurdles to establish the CCG, and we celebrate the fruits of his labor.

Wang is committed to learning about the development experiences of global think tanks in order to internationalize China's own think tanks. He has spent years preparing *Global Think Tanks*, visiting no fewer than 21 U.S. think tanks to study their operations. In 2010, while he was a visiting fellow at Brookings, Wang participated in two public forums and presented on the status of China's "global talent," which includes foreign-educated returnees, as well as those who are still enrolled in programs overseas. His presentations were extremely well received.

Global Think Tanks by Wang Huiyao and Miao Lü is among very few books in Chinese that consider the world's top-tier think tanks from an international perspective while sharing insights based on personal experiences. The authors not only deliver to readers their first-hand observations, but also a holistic assessment of China's think tanks, including the dilemmas and challenges they face. In assessing the current state of the major categories of Chinese think tanks, Wang and Lü observe that government-run think tanks are usually "big but not strong" (大而不强, *da er buqiang*), university-based think tanks tend to be "too academically highbrow" (曲高和寡, *qugao hegua*), and private think tanks are often "weak and weary" (弱而无力, *ruo er wuli*).[3]

The authors of *Global Think Tanks* carefully examine how China's new think tanks can best position themselves in a globalized world. Wang and Lü examine the role of think tanks in a great power government era, and offer various policy recommendations to policymakers. The volume concludes with lessons that Wang and Miao have learned from years of developing think tanks, particularly in China.

I believe the publication of *Global Think Tanks* will contribute to the world's understanding of global think tanks and also spawn a more internationalized school of thought in the think tank sector. For researchers and practitioners at Chinese think tanks, this indispensable volume will also offer guidance on the process of developing truly consequential think tanks in China.

Notes

This chapter is an edited version of the author's foreword to a Chinese book on think tanks. Cheng Li, "Preface," in Wang Huiyao and Miao Lü, *Daguo zhiku* [Global Think Tanks] (Beijing: Renmin chubanshe, 2014), 11–13. The author thanks Yuxin Zhang for the English translation of the original text, and Zach Balin and Lucy Xu for their very helpful comments on earlier versions of this chapter.

1 For the website of the CCG, see http://www.ccg.org.cn.
2 For the full text of Condoleezza Rice's speech, see http://en.ccg.org.cn/Event/View.aspx?Id=1620.
3 Wang and Miao, *Daguo zhiku*, 4.

IV

Toward a More Pluralistic Decision-Making Process

Chapter 13

Interest Group Politics in China: A Paradox of Hope and Fear

A well-functioning society depends on diverse voices.

— Bonnie Angelo

While assessments of China's political development are often remarkably diverse, there is considerable agreement about the critical importance of Chinese interest groups. Scholars both in China and abroad believe that dynamic interest groups will help determine China's future political trajectory. Views on the present and future shape of Chinese interest group politics, however, vary widely, especially regarding their scale and scope, their coordinating mechanisms and the effectiveness of various institutional responses, and their role in China's democratic transformation.

Professor Jing Yuejin's essay "China's Interest Coordinating Mechanism: Challenges and Prospects," published in *China's Political Development: Chinese and American Perspectives*, reflects the mainstream Chinese scholarly community's sophisticated thinking on the ever-growing role of interest groups in the country.[1] Professor Jing's discussion of China's emerging interest groups is well grounded in empirical evidence, links closely to existing debates in the field (both theoretical and policy-based), and sheds valuable light on the major initiatives that are necessary to reform China's political system. Professor Jing is candid and straightforward in acknowledging the daunting political challenges that China faces. He also recommends a set of comprehensive coordinating mechanisms through which the Chinese leadership may be able to reduce or even resolve the tensions and conflicts generated by competing interest groups.

For foreign students of Chinese politics, Professor Jing's article also sets forth data-rich observations and thought-provoking ideas to facilitate a better-structured intellectual dialogue. Such an exchange may not only reveal the areas in which Chinese scholars and their American colleagues agree or disagree, but also help clarify deficiencies in research and analysis on both sides, such as prevalent misperceptions, blind spots, topical obsessions or inadequacies, and methodological missteps. A comparison across countries may also be able to transform deep-rooted fear of interest group politics into hope for the idea that interest groups can foster a more institutionalized, orderly, peaceful, and democratic transition in China. Drawing inspiration from Professor Jing's analysis, I would like to address two questions: First, what is the scale and scope of interest group politics in present-day China? Second, in what direction and through what mechanisms should China institutionalize its interest group politics?

What is the Scale and Scope of Interest Group Politics in Present-Day China?

Just as with think tank development, never in the six-decade history of the People's Republic of China have the Chinese leadership and the general public paid as much attention to interest groups as they have in recent years. Professor Jing notes that, in contrast to the early years of Communist rule, when the concept of interest groups was politically taboo, China's current leadership has come to recognize the validity of individual and group interests. At the same time, the Chinese people have become conscious of their own rights and interests. Thus, interest group politics have gained legitimacy in the eyes of both the Chinese political establishment and the general public.

As Professor Jing observes, Chinese market reforms, particularly the rapid growth of the private sector since the 1990s, have been the primary driver for the emergence of interest groups. As a result of market reforms over the past three decades, every major social class — peasants, workers, intellectuals, entrepreneurs, and cadres — has undergone a profound change. Additionally, substantially different subgroups have emerged from each of these classes. For example, within the traditional category of peasants, some have become rural entrepreneurs, while others have become migrant workers.

In a three-volume landmark study of social stratification in reform-era China, Lu Xueyi and his colleagues at the Chinese Academy of Social Sciences (CASS) propose a ten-stratum framework that conceptualizes and ranks social groups based on economic status, occupational standing, and capacity to access resources. Cadres and managers occupy the top of the ladder, while industrial and agricultural workers and the urban and rural unemployed sit at the bottom.[2] It is interesting to note that workers, previously considered the "masters of the PRC" (共和国的主人, *gong-heguo de zhuren*), are now situated on the bottom rung of Chinese society. They constitute the bulk of the so-called vulnerable social groups (弱势群体, *ruoshi qunti*).

Professor Jing's essay highlights two important aspects of Chinese interest group politics: the role of vulnerable social groups and the growing influence of corporate and industrial interest groups (工商企业利益集团, *gongshang qiye liyi jituan*). In Professor Jing's words, "the former reflects the struggle of the weak when its interests are hurt while the latter, the strong, intends to maximize its profit" through the power-capital nexus.[3] The ways in which these two groups protect or advance their interests are profoundly different. As Professor Jing describes, the vulnerable social groups often express their grievances through petition letters, group appeals, and street protests. These types of activities often receive significant media coverage, may provoke social unrest, and can result in serious government crackdowns. By contrast, corporate and industrial interest groups often exchange favors and make deals at events or occasions such as "dinner banquets, golf courses, or tourist resorts."[4] Not surprisingly, a new term, "black collar stratum" (黑领阶层, *heiling jieceng*), has emerged in China to refer to the increasing number of the rich and powerful who dress in black, drive black cars, have hidden incomes, live secret lives with concubines, have ties to the criminal underground (黑社会, *heishehui*, or black society), and, most importantly, operate their businesses and wield their economic power in an opaque manner.[5] The adoption of this new term reflects widespread resentment toward the increasingly close associations between government officials and the executives of large corporate and industrial firms.

Professor Jing's focus on these two aspects of Chinese interest group politics is analytically appropriate. The growing prominence of these two groups reflects the two predominant tensions in present-day China — that between officials and the masses (官民, *guanmin*), and that between laborers and capitalists (劳资, *laozi*). At the same time, these tensions also represent what are arguably the two most formidable political challenges to the legitimacy of the Chinese Communist regime. Professor Jing is unclear, however, about whether these tensions constitute two long-term challenges or if they are simply temporary problems that have arisen as a result of immediate issues. Professor Jing believes that as the Chinese government acquires greater financial resources and directs them toward social welfare, social protests will gradually decline in number. In my view, resources will remain limited as China faces serious demographic challenges in the years to come. These tensions reflect some of the major defects in the Chinese political structure and its system of resource allocation, which will not be relieved through policy adjustments, but rather will require systemic changes. Without a more representative and more institutionalized political framework, problems of distributive injustice will likely become increasingly acute.

As for vulnerable social groups, their resentment and tendency to protest result from a number of factors, such as growing economic disparity, inflation, social dislocation, political repression, environmental degradation, lack of work safety or job security, inadequacy of consumer rights, problems with internal migration, ethnic tensions, and official corruption. It would be naïve to believe that the Chinese government will come up with an easy solution for any of these problems in the foreseeable future. On the contrary, the financial cost of "maintaining social stability" (维稳, *weiwen*), primarily through the police force, has become astonishingly high. As Professor Jing notes, in 2007 Guangzhou spent as much as 4.4 billion yuan on its police force, a figure that exceeded the total cost of social welfare spending in the city for the year (3.5 billion yuan). According to a recent Tsinghua University study, the total amount of money spent nationwide for "maintaining social stability" in 2009 was 514 billion yuan, which was almost equal to China's total national defense budget for the year (532 billion yuan).[6]

Meanwhile, corporate and industrial interest groups have exacerbated social injustice and public resentment. China's most active business interest groups mainly fall into two clusters. The first includes economic elites who work in state-monopolized industries such as banking, oil, electricity, coal, telecommunications, aviation, and shipping; and the second consists of the lobbying groups who work for state, foreign, or private firms in sectors such as real estate. It has been widely reported in the Chinese media that business interest groups routinely bribe local officials and have formed a "wicked coalition" with local governments.[7] The oligopoly of state-owned enterprises (SOEs) hurts Chinese private enterprises and small businesses. This explains the recent wide use of the phrase, "the state advances and private companies retreat," to criticize the growing trend toward "strong government, weak society." A recent study conducted by Chinese scholars shows that the total profits of China's 500 largest private companies in 2009 were less than the total revenues of just two SOEs, China Mobile and Sinopec.[8] As the distinguished Chinese economist Xu Xiaonian observes, the main beneficiaries of SOE growth are corrupt officials, not the Chinese public.[9]

Various players associated with property development comprise one of the most powerful special interest groups in present-day China. As discussed in Chapter 2, according to Sun Liping, the real estate interest group has accumulated tremendous economic and social capital over the past decade.[10] The huge profits reaped by property developers in China are often likened to those of drug-dealers. The power of this group explains why it took 13 years for China to pass the anti-monopoly law, why the macroeconomic control policy in the mid-1990s was largely ineffective, and why the widely perceived property bubble in coastal cities has continued to grow. In each of these cases, corporate and industrial interest groups have encroached upon the government's decision-making process, either by creating government policy deadlock or manipulating policies in their own favor.

While vulnerable social groups and corporate and industrial interest groups are both crucial players in Chinese interest group politics, there are still many other major actors not adequately discussed or even mentioned in Professor Jing's essay. They include, for example, geographic regions, various bureaucratic institutions, the military, the increasingly commercialized media, NGOs, and local governments. Local governments in the coastal and inland regions are political interest groups that exercise strong influence in Beijing and work to ensure that the central government adopts policies that advance their regional interests. By way of background, 93 of China's 100 wealthiest counties in 2010, including all of the top 40, were located in coastal provinces.[11] According to one recent study, nearly 90 percent of China's exports still come from coastal provinces.[12] In the past few years, provincial and local governments' "liaison offices in Beijing" (驻京办, *zhujingban*), which are region-based Chinese lobbying groups, have rapidly increased in number. In January 2010, the central government issued new regulations to substantially reduce the number of offices permitted to represent local interests. These regulations also require financial auditing of the remaining lobbying groups at the provincial and municipal levels.[13]

However, it would be unfair to say that Professor Jing's essay overlooks the role of local governments in interest group politics. In fact, Professor Jing appropriately links growing local interests to economic decentralization, especially the central-local tax distribution (分税制, *fenshuizhi*) adopted in 1994.[14] It is also obvious that one essay cannot cover all aspects of this complicated subject. Nevertheless, I take issue with Professor Jing's argument that the majority of mass protests by vulnerable social groups in present-day China are "nonpolitical."[15] Although the specific demands of some of these mass protest groups might be economic or financial rather than political, interest group politics are political by nature. Professor Jing may reasonably argue that none of the major socioeconomic groups in China intend to challenge Chinese Communist Party (CCP) rule, but it is not difficult to imagine that the CCP leadership may lose its mandate if it fails to allay public resentments and concerns in this new domestic environment.

The most important interest group that determines China's political future, I would argue, is neither the "black collar" stratum nor "blue collar" workers, but rather the "white collar" members of China's emerging middle class. This interest group is noticeably absent from Professor Jing's analysis. China's new middle class has been a political ally of the CCP throughout its formative years, largely due to a shared interest in maintaining social and political stability.[16] More recently, however, middle-class grievances — directed at rampant official corruption and government policies that favor state-owned enterprise monopolies in several industrial sectors — have become increasingly evident.[17] The rising unemployment rate among recent college graduates (who usually come from middle-class families and are expected to be future members of China's middle class) should also alarm the Chinese government.

A 2008 study conducted by a Chinese scholar at the CASS found that, if a large number of middle-class members feel that their voices are suppressed, their access to information is blocked, or their space for social action is confined, a political uprising is likely to take place.[18] This study implies that what happened in South Korea and Brazil, where members of the middle class in each country demanded direct elections, could also occur in China. Just as yesterday's political target could be today's political ally, so too could today's political ally become tomorrow's political rabble-rouser.

With What Mechanisms Should China Institutionalize Its Interest Group Politics?

Political challenges arising from angry, vulnerable social groups and greedy, bureaucratic-corporate interest groups are not unique to reform-era China. Democracies in the West (and the East) are certainly not immune to these problems. In fact, in many countries, public petitions for social justice and protests against the government's domestic or foreign policies are often considered normal parts of the socioeconomic and political fabric.

As for corporate and industrial interest groups, they are probably equally, if not more, powerful and influential in some Western countries than they are in China. In the United States, for example, hundreds of lobbying groups have flooded Washington, DC, forming an essential feature of American politics. On occasion, powerful business lobbying groups have been caught manipulating the democratic system for a company's commercial gain. As Theodore Lowi, a distinguished political science professor at Cornell University, observes, the U.S. government "expanded by responding to the demands of all major organized interests, by assuming responsibility for programs sought by those interests.... This in turn led to the formulation of new policies which tightened the grip of interest groups on the machinery of government."[19] Lowi uses the term "interest politics liberalism" to describe the pluralistic competition that results from the broad expansion of public programs in the United States.

Robert Dahl, a political science professor at Yale University, expands on Lowi's notion of pluralistic competition. Dahl argues that the development of a Western-style democracy is a process dominated by many different sets of leaders, each having access to a different combination of political resources and representing the interests of different sectors and groups in society.[20] The democratic pluralist system directs power, influence, authority, and control away from any single group of power elites who share the same social background and toward a variety of individuals, groups, associations, and organizations.[21] In a sense, democracy is a matter of establishing rules for mediating conflicting interests among social groups in a given society. Yao Yang, dean of the National School of Development, a top think tank in China, argues along similar lines: "An open and inclusive political process has generally checked the power of interest groups in advanced democracies such as the United States. Indeed, this is precisely the mandate of a disinterested government — to balance the demands of different social groups."[22]

In a democracy, interest group politics are considered neither a threat to sociopolitical stability nor a challenge to the legitimacy of the government, but rather necessary components of democratic governance. The key to coordinating interest group politics — as Lowi, Dahl, and Yao all seem to agree — is to establish certain institutional and democratic mechanisms. Various interest groups can exert their influence over presidential and congressional elections, bureaucratic decision-making, and judicial processes. In response, the independence of the media and the supremacy of the Constitution safeguard the democratic process. Although political crises do occur from time to time, democratic institutions in general and interest group politics in particular are not the source of sociopolitical instability in a given country, but rather a foundation for long-term stability (长治久安, *changzhi jiuan*).

Per the title of his essay ("China's Interest Coordinating Mechanism: Challenges and Prospects"), Professor Jing wisely emphasizes the necessity of establishing a coordinating mechanism to institutionalize Chinese interest group politics. In particular, Professor Jing recommends two sets of mechanisms. The first set is the incremental opening of the public policymaking process, which could involve public hearings, democratic consultation and dialogue, opinion polls, and information disclosure.[23] The second set, which Professor Jing calls "trilateral mechanisms" (三方机制, *sanfang jizhi*), involves consultation and negotiation between government, business groups, and trade unions representing workers.[24] While these mechanisms can be helpful, they are perhaps not strong enough to respond effectively to demands from either vulnerable social groups or corporate and industrial interest groups. The ineffectiveness of the first set of mechanisms has actually driven dissatisfied citizens to make "louder noises" in the public sphere.[25] And as Professor Jing himself acknowledges, China's labor unions are by no means independent; they often speak on behalf of capitalists and managers rather than workers.[26]

Professor Jing is apparently not enthusiastic about adopting the Western democratic system's three branches of government and multiparty elections. This is, of course, a reasonable scholarly position, as each country's political development should be based on its own historical, cultural, and socioeconomic circumstances. But it seems to me that Professor Jing goes too far in endorsing traditional "paternalism" (父爱主义, *fuai zhuyi*) for the political system in present-day China, arguing as he does that the Chinese leadership should seek a "delicate balance between the pressure of interest group politics and benevolent paternalism."[27] In my view, paternalism associated with strongman politics is a political idea unsuited for today's China. The country has for the past two decades been led by a collective leadership with competing factions and coalitions.

I agree with Professor Jing that it is not feasible for China to develop a multi-party political system in the near future. Perhaps the defining characteristic of today's Chinese political system is one-party rule by the Chinese Communist Party, or what Professor Jing candidly calls the "party-state system" (党国体制, *dangguo tizhi*).[28] But this does not necessarily mean — and I believe Professor Jing would agree — that the CCP leadership is a monolithic group of elites with the same socioeconomic backgrounds, career trajectories, policy initiative priorities, and worldviews. I believe that the leadership consists of two informal and almost equally powerful competing political coalitions. These two groups can be classified as the "populist coalition" and the "elitist coalition." Chinese leaders have begun using the term "inner-party democracy" to denote the idea that the party should institutionalize checks and balances within its leadership.

These two coalitions represent two different socioeconomic classes and geographic regions. For example, the elitist group represents the interests of the coastal region (which we might call China's "blue states") while the populist coalition often voices the concerns of the inland region (China's "red states"). The elitist coalition consists of princelings, the Shanghai Gang, entrepreneurs, and foreign-educated returnees, or "sea turtles." In contrast, the populist coalition consists of Chinese Communist Youth League officials (团派, *tuanpai*), and generally claims to represent the interests of farmers, migrant workers, and the urban poor. These two coalitions have advocated contrasting policy initiatives and priorities. Whereas the elitist coalition emphasizes GDP growth, the populist coalition advocates social justice and social cohesion. I call this new dynamic "one party, two coalitions."[29]

These two leadership groups have their own political resources and leadership expertise and can represent different interest groups in the country, thus maintaining a healthy, constructive, and effective coordinating mechanism in the Chinese political system. The relationship between these competing groups is at once competitive and cooperative. A dynamic inner-party bipartisanship can help prevent the situation that Shen Mingmin (as quoted in Professor Jing's essay) describes, wherein the CCP represents only one group of people in Chinese society (presumably the rich and powerful).

As Professor Jing suggests in his essay, the fact that competing coalitions in the CCP leadership can represent different socioeconomic groups and political "constituencies" may also make Jiang Zemin's "theory of three represents" more meaningful.[30] Most importantly, only in such an increasingly representative political system can Hu Jintao's notion of "harmonious society" become intellectually persuasive and practically concrete. One of the most important and urgent tasks for the Chinese leadership, therefore, is to make factional politics more transparent, representative, and legitimate in the Chinese political system.

Notes

This chapter is an edited version of the author's commentary on Jing Yuejin's essay "China's Interest Coordination Mechanism," in Kenneth Lieberthal, Cheng Li, and Yu Keping, eds., *China's Political Development: Chinese and American Perspectives* (Washington, DC: Brookings Institution Press, 2014), 328–339. The author thanks Zach Balin, Ryan McElveen, and Lucy Xu for their very helpful comments on earlier versions of this chapter.

1 Jing, "China's Interest Coordination Mechanism," 328–339.
2 Lu Xueyi, *Dangdai Zhongguo shehuijieceng yanjiu baogao: Zhongguo she-huijieceng congshu* [Research report on social strata in contemporary China] (Beijing: Shehuikexue wenxian chubanshe, 2002); *Dangdai Zhongguo she-hui liudong* [Social mobility in contemporary China] (Beijing: Shehuikexue wenxian chubanshe, 2004); and *Dangdai Zhongguo shehui jiegou* [Social structure of contemporary China] (Beijing: Shehuikexue wenxian chubanshe, 2010).
3 Jing, "China's Interest Coordination Mechanism."
4 Ibid.
5 It is unclear who coined the term "black-collar stratum." Most online postings in China attribute the label to U.S.-educated economist Lang Xianping (Larry Lang), but Lang has publicly denied that he wrote the widely circulated article that popularized the phrase. See "The Black-Collar Class," ChinaTranslated.com, "Commentary and Analysis on China's Economic and Political Situation," June 12, 2009.
6 *Shijie ribao* [World Journal], October 15, 2010, A3.
7 *Zhongguo xinwen zhoukan* [China Newsweek], January 13, 2006, *Liaowang* [Outlook], December 5, 2005; and also see http://www.chinesenewsnet.com, December 12, 2005.
8 *Beijing shangbao* [Beijing Business Daily], August 30, 2010. See also http://news.xinhuanet.com/fortune/2010-08/30/c_12496387.htm.
9 For Xu Xiaoning's views, see http://xuxiaonian.blog.sohu.com/158818651.html. Also see *Lianhe zaobao* [United Morning News], August 1, 2010, http://finance.ifeng.com/opinion/zjgc/20100830/2567934.shtml.
10 Sun Liping, "Zhongguo jinru liyi boyi de shidai" [China is entering the conflict of interests era], http://chinesenewsnet.com, February 6, 2006.
11 See http://bbs.nhzj.com/viewthread.php?tid=377464.
12 Yao Yang, "The End of the Beijing Consensus: Can China's Model of Authoritarian Growth Survive?" *Foreign Affairs*, February 2, 2010. See

http://www.foreignaffairs.com/articles/65947/the-end-of-the-beijing-consensus?page=show.

13 *Liaowang* [Outlook], January 23, 2010.

14 Jing, "China's Interest Coordination Mechanism," 322.

15 Ibid., 316.

16 Jie Chen and Bruce J. Dickson, *Allies of the State: China's Private Entrepreneurs and Democratic Change* (Cambridge, MA: Harvard University Press, 2010).

17 Zhang Yi, "Dangdai Zhongguo zhongchan jieceng de zhengzhi taidu" [Political attitudes of the middle stratum in contemporary China], *Zhongguo shehui kexue* [Chinese Social Sciences] 2 (Summer 2008).

18 Zhang Yi, "Dangdai Zhongguo zhongchan jieceng de zhengzhi taidu" [Political attitudes of the middle stratum in contemporary China], *Zhongguo shehui kexue* [Chinese Social Sciences] 2 (Summer 2008).

19 Theodore Lowi, *The End of Liberalism: The Second Republic of the United States* (New York: Norton, 1979), Dust jacket.

20 Robert Dahl, *Who Governs? Democracy and Power in an American City* (New Haven, CT: Yale University Press, 1961), 68.

21 Ibid., 252 and 270.

22 Yao, "The End of the Beijing Consensus."

23 Jing, "China's Interest Coordination Mechanism," 318–319.

24 Ibid., 320.

25 Ibid., 311.

26 Ibid., 311–312.

27 Ibid., 323.

28 Ibid., 324.

29 For a more detailed discussion of this formula, see Cheng Li, "The New Bipartisanship within the Chinese Communist Party," *Orbis,* Vol. 49, No. 3 (Summer 2005): 387–400.

30 Jing, "China's Interest Coordination Mechanism," 326.

Chapter 14

Shaping China's Foreign Policy: The Role of Foreign-Educated Returnees

It is my belief that extensive contacts and cooperation among nations and increased interchanges and understanding between peoples will make the world we live in more safe, more stable, and more peaceful.

— Deng Xiaoping

Our aim is to make this kind of exchange between our countries no longer the exception, but the norm; no longer a matter of headlines and historians, but a routine part of the everyday life of both the Chinese and the American people.

— Jimmy Carter

"The study of politics," as the distinguished American political scientist Harold Lasswell said, is "the study of influence and the influential."[1] This is true not only of domestic politics, but also of foreign policy. For outside observers, possessing a sophisticated understanding of a given country's domestic circumstances — the interactions among its political leadership, primary bureaucratic institutions, and larger socioeconomic forces — is enormously helpful when analyzing that country's foreign policy process and predicting possible outcomes. For today's students of Chinese foreign policy, one of the most daunting challenges is that "the influential" in the Chinese leadership are no longer limited to a handful of top leaders. At the same time, socioeconomic forces have increased in number and magnitude over the past two decades. An endless variety of domestic constituencies — such as different political factions, regions, industries (including some major state-owned companies), the military, interest groups, think tanks, civil society organizations, commercialized media outlets, and foreign, private, or joint-venture firms — all want to have greater influence on China's foreign policy.

One fast-growing new elite group — consisting of foreign-educated Chinese nationals who returned to China after studying abroad, also known as "sea turtles" or "returnees" (as defined and briefly discussed in Chapter 6) — deserves particular attention.[2] Foreign-educated returnees are, of course, a diverse lot. They differ in terms of their experiences abroad, professional expertise, political affiliations, and worldviews, as well as the means through which they influence Chinese foreign policy. Some of them currently serve as advisors to top leaders; a few hold national leadership positions as ministers of the State Council or senior officials in the CCP; many work in think tanks or universities; and some are considered political dissidents or radicals who exert influence over China's domestic and foreign policy discourse primarily through new media such as the Internet. Over the past decade, the influence of these returnees as a group on Chinese foreign policy has become increasingly pronounced.

Despite the intuitive importance of this new contingent, very few scholars in China or abroad have made it the focus of empirical study.[3] Instead, many generalizations about the returnees, such as the notion that American-educated returnees tend to favor constructive relations with the United States, are anecdotally accepted rather than empirically verified. Many important questions have not been adequately addressed: What are common characteristics of returnees who are now part of China's foreign policy establishment? In what ways do leaders and advisors with experience abroad differ from their homegrown colleagues? What are the major subgroups within the returnee category, and how do they differ in terms of worldviews and policy preferences? What factors contribute to these differences? What are the implications of the growing representation of returnees in the Chinese foreign policy community for China, the United States, and the world? Is international educational exchange a viable way to promote mutual understanding, diffuse global norms, and reduce the chance of violent conflict?

It will take time for full answers to these questions to emerge. As an initial examination, this chapter aims to highlight the dynamic and complex impact returnees are having on Chinese strategic thinking and foreign policy. It begins with a discussion on the background of and impetus for the rise of returnees in the Chinese foreign policy establishment. The chapter then outlines three main channels through which returnees exert influence. The third and final part of the chapter argues that certain well-known contradictions in China's foreign policy and Sino–U.S. relations might be attributable to the paradoxical roles played by returnees. These contradictions include (1) the gap between the Hu Jintao administration's pronounced commitment to "all directional diplomacy" and the actual excessive emphasis placed on China's relations with the United States; (2) the tension between broad Sino–U.S. cooperation in virtually all areas, on the one hand, and the widespread suspicion among Chinese leaders and public intellectuals concerning a "U.S. conspiracy against China" (美国阴谋论, *meiguo yinmoulun*) on the other; and (3) the irony that a sustained, three-decade effort by the United States to promote educational exchanges across the Pacific has instead led to a relationship rife with misunderstanding. A thoughtful discussion of the characteristics of returnees and the roles they play in China's foreign policy establishment may shed light on each of these troubling contradictions.

Factors Contributing to the Growing Influence of Returnees

The official Chinese definition of a returnee, as briefly described in Chapter 6, is someone who was born in China, left to study overseas as a student or visiting scholar for at least one year, and then returned to China to work on either a temporary or permanent basis.[4] According to this definition, returnees do not include foreign-born ethnic Chinese or Chinese immigrants to foreign countries who return without having studied abroad. Three main factors have contributed to the growing influence and power of returnees in present-day China.

The Largest Foreign Study Movement in Chinese History

The first contributing factor is the unprecedentedly large scale of the study abroad movement initiated by Deng Xiaoping three decades ago. Since Deng's landmark decision in 1978 to send a large number of students and scholars to study abroad, approximately 3,518,400 Chinese nationals have pursued their studies in foreign countries, with a large proportion (approximately 37 percent) going to the United States.[5] In recent years China has witnessed a surge in the number of returnees. According to official Chinese data, by the end of 2014, a total of 1,708,800 Chinese students and scholars remained abroad, while 1,809,600 had returned to work in China.[6] Of those who remained abroad, 1,088,900 were still attending educational research programs, with an increasing number expected to return to China.

The heavy presence of returnees in Chinese decision-making circles is not, of course, a new phenomenon. In fact, returnees have played important roles in the Chinese government ever since the founding of the Republic of China in 1911. The founders of the Nationalist and Communist parties, Sun Yat-sen, Chiang Kai-shek, Chen Duxiu, and Li Dazhao, all studied overseas prior to the 1911 Revolution. Tang Shaoyi (first premier of the Republic of China), Liang Tunyen (minister of foreign affairs prior to the 1911 Revolution), and Hu Shih (minister of foreign affairs in the Republic era) were all returnees from the United States, where they studied under the auspices of the Boxer Indemnity. In the temporary cabinet of Sun Yat-sen after the 1911 Revolution, 15 of the 18 ministers and vice ministers — a stunning 83 percent — were returnees.[7]

In the latter half of the twentieth century, several of the most prominent figures in Chinese politics had participated in the "study-abroad movements" of the 1920s and 1930s, including Zhou Enlai, Deng Xiaoping, Liu Shaoqi, and Chiang Ching-kuo. Time overseas allowed the first three individuals to nurture within themselves the Communist ideals and political skills that they later employed to help the CCP seize power. Chiang, for his part, later became the president of Taiwan. Deng and Chiang both rose to preeminent leadership positions in mainland China and Taiwan, respectively, and implemented ambitious economic reforms. The so-called third generation of PRC leaders was dominated by technocrats that had studied in the Soviet Union or Eastern Europe in the 1950s. Among their ranks were Jiang Zemin, Li Peng, Luo Gan, Li Lanqing, and Wei Jianxin, all of whom later served on the Politburo Standing Committee.

While acknowledging this past, it is still clear that the current wave of returnees is the largest foreign study movement in Chinese history and that it continues to gain momentum, partly because a rapidly emerging Chinese middle class can afford to send its children abroad, and partly because the state is steadily increasing its funding for post-graduate education abroad. According to the Chinese authorities, from 2006 to 2008, the State Foreign Studies Fund provided full scholarships for advanced degrees abroad to at least 5,000 students each year. In 2009, the Fund provided scholarships to 12,000 students, half of whom enrolled in graduate programs for masters' or doctorate degrees.[8] The overwhelming majority of these students went to Western countries or Japan to study.

Foreign-educated returnees have now played important roles in virtually every field in the country, and some have emerged as political leaders. Xi Jinping's two confidants, Liu He (director of the Office of the Central Economic Leading Group of the CCP Central Committee) and Chen Xi (executive deputy director of the CCP Central Organization Department), are U.S.-educated returnees. Liu received an MPA degree from Harvard's Kennedy School of Government and currently serves as the chief economic advisor to Xi Jinping. Known as "China's Larry Summers," Liu played a very important role in drafting the pivotal economic reform agenda announced at the Third Plenum of the 18th Party Congress. Chen, who served as a visiting scholar at Stanford University from 1990 to 1992, is now Xi's designee for personnel matters. It stands to reason that the presence of returnees will continue to increase in China's top leadership in the coming years.

Collective Leadership and the Growing Importance of Think Tanks

The end of strongman politics and the emergence of a collective system of leadership have prompted officials to seek legitimacy for their policies through "scientific decision-making" (科学决策, *kexue juece*). The prominent think tanks that returnees populate are the primary venues for this kind of scientific research.

Just as the current wave of returnees has many precursors, think tanks are by no means new to China. On the contrary, one could argue that they have played an important role in Chinese society since the time of Confucius. However, during much of the PRC's history, and especially during its first three decades, the role and influence of think tanks were largely dependent on the preferences and characteristics of the country's top leader (see Chapter 6).

Xi Jinping is the first leader in the PRC's history to publicly affirm the importance of think tanks in enhancing the country's soft power. On a number of occasions in 2013 and 2014, Xi announced the strategic goal of developing new think tanks with Chinese characteristics.[9] Xi has particularly emphasized the need for innovation, diversity, and global outreach in China's new think tanks.

Xi also likes to consult returnees who are experts on global economic and financial development. When he was party secretary of Shanghai, Xi came to know Fang Xinghai, then deputy secretary of the Financial Affairs Committee of the Shanghai Municipal Party Committee and director of the Shanghai Financial Services Office. Fang was born in 1964 and attended Tsinghua University's School of Economic Management from 1981 to 1986, majoring in information systems management.[10] He pursued graduate-level education at Stanford University from 1986 to 1993 under the guidance of Joseph Stiglitz, who was awarded the Nobel Prize in Economics in 2001. After receiving his doctoral degree in economics in 1993, Fang worked in the prestigious young professionals program at the World Bank for several years (1993–1998). He returned to China in 1998 and served as director of the coordination department of the China Construction Bank (1998–2000), secretary general of the Galaxy Securities Regulatory Commission (2000–01), and vice president of the Shanghai Stock Exchange (2001–05) before joining the Shanghai municipal government. Fang has developed a close relationship with Xi and frequently sends him memoranda regarding financial developments in China and around the world.[11] Soon after Xi became general secretary of the CCP, Fang was transferred to Beijing, where he currently serves as bureau chief of the General Office of the Central Leading Group for Financial and Economic Affairs. There, he directly supports Liu He in drafting blueprints of China's financial and economic policy. In November 2015, Fang was appointed vice chairman of the China Securities Regulatory Commission (CSRC). As China grows into a global power, the first-hand knowledge of foreign countries that returnees hold is a vital asset in the political establishment, translating into valuable advice for the top leadership.[12]

The Revolution in Telecommunications and the Demand for Expert Returnees

As in other countries, the revolution in telecommunications and the commercialization of the media have elevated the role of public opinion in foreign policy debates. Over the last decade Chinese media outlets have experienced explosive growth. As of 2009, there were roughly 2,000 newspapers, 9,500 magazines, 257 radio stations, and 277 TV stations in the country.[13] While the newspaper business is shrinking in many parts of the world, China's newspapers continue to prosper, partly because of their international affairs coverage. In 2008, for example, *Reference News* (参考消息, *cankao xiaoxi*) boasted a circulation of 3.1 million, the world's fifth largest.[14] *Global Times* (环球时报, *huanqiu shibao*), a world affairs–focused newspaper known for its ability to fuel nationalistic sentiment, reached a circulation of 2 million.

Social media has achieved a level of pervasiveness that no one could have imagined only a few years ago. According to a Chinese official source, by May 2014 the number of cell phones in China reached 1.26 billion.[15] By mid-2015, internet users in China surpassed 668 million, including 594 million mobile Internet users, and as much as 48.8 percent of the population had Internet access.[16]

Foreign-educated experts from various walks of life are often in high demand as commentators on world affairs. Some of them have served as anchors on TV and radio talk shows, some have become regular guest experts on programs, and others have run many of the country's most popular websites, magazines, newspapers, and blogs. To a profound degree, returnees initiate intellectual and political discourse, influence government policy, educate younger generations, and shape public opinion in the PRC.

Returnees' Primary Channels of Influence

China's foreign-educated returnees have exerted influence over the country's foreign and domestic policymaking through many channels. A select few have already emerged as decision-makers in the party and government, expert advisors to top leaders, and opinion leaders who shape the media discourse on world affairs and China's foreign policy.

Returnees as Decision-Makers

The proportion of returnees at high levels of party leadership is still very small. Returnees usually serve in administrative fields such as education, finance, foreign trade, and foreign affairs. However, their presence in the national and provincial leadership has steadily increased. In the 18th Central Committee of the CCP, formed in 2012, returnees occupied 14.6 percent of seats, 4 percent higher than their representation in the 17th Central Committee in 2007, and 8.2 percent higher than their representation in the 16th Central Committee in 2002 (see Table 14.1). In contrast to the 15th Central Committee in 1997, in which most returnees were trained in the former Soviet Union or other Eastern European countries, an overwhelming majority of returnees in more-recent central committees were educated in the West or in Japan.

Western-educated returnees in the 17th Central Committee include several prominent decision-makers, such as then member of the Secretariat and director of the Central Policy Research Center of the CCP Wang Huning (visiting scholar at University of Iowa and University of

Table 14-1:   Foreign-Educated Returnees in the Memberships of the 16th, 17th, and 18th Central Committees of the CCP.

Membership	16th Central Committee (2002) No. of Returnees/ Total No.	%	17th Central Committee (2007) No. of Returnees/ Total No.	%	18th Central Committee (2012) No. of Returnees/ Total No.	%
Full Members	9/198	4.5	17/204	8.3	20/205	9.8
Alternate Members	13/158	8.2	22/167	13.2	35/171	20.5
Total Members	22/356	6.2	39/371	10.5	55/376	14.6

Source: Cheng Li, "Shaping China's Foreign Policy: The Paradoxical Role of Foreign-Educated Returnees," *Asia Policy*, No. 10 (July 2010): 73. The data on the 18th Central Committee has been updated by the author.

California at Berkeley), then minister of education Zhou Ji (PhD in engineering, State University of New York at Buffalo), then chairman of the China Banking Regulatory Commission Liu Mingkang (MBA, London University), then procurator-general of the Supreme People's Procuratorate Cao Jianming (visiting scholar at Ghent University of Belgium and the University of San Francisco), and then president of the Chinese Academy of Sciences Lu Yongxiang (PhD in engineering, RWTH Aachen University).

Of the 27 people who served as ministers of the State Council between 2008 and 2013, there were five returnees, and three of them served on the 17th Central Committee: then education minister Zhou Ji, then foreign affairs minister Yang Jiechi (visiting student, University of Bath and the London School of Economics and Political Science) and Governor of the People's Bank Zhou Xiaochuan (visiting scholar, University of California, Santa Cruz). Two ministers in the State Council who are not CCP members — Minister of Science and Technology Wan Gang and then minister of health Chen Zhu — each spent many years in the West. Wan received his PhD in physics from Technische Universität Clausthal in Germany and worked as a senior manager at the Audi Company in Germany for over a decade. Chen received his PhD in medicine from Université Paris 7 in France. He is one of the world's leading hematology experts and is a member of several prestigious academies, including the Academy of Sciences for the Developing World, the United States National Academy of Sciences, and the French Academy of Sciences. Chen currently serves as vice chairman of the NPC. The growing presence and power of Western-educated elites in the Chinese leadership is an important indicator of increased openness and political progress in the country.

Returnees have dominated the financial leadership of the country for quite some time. In addition to Liu He, Fang Xinghai, and Zhou Xiaochuan, who were mentioned above, other senior decision-makers in the Chinese financial administration include: former chairman of the Industrial and Commercial Bank of China Jiang Jianqing (visiting scholar, Columbia University), former chairman of China Construction Bank and current governor of Shandong Guo Shuqing (visiting scholar, Oxford University), former director of the State Administration of Taxation and current minister of finance Xiao Jie (visiting scholar in Germany), former director of the State Council's Research Office and current party secretary of Henan Xie Fuzhan (visiting scholar, Princeton), Vice Governor of the People's Bank Yi Gang (PhD in economics, University of Illinois), and former vice governor of the People's Bank and former deputy director of the IMF Zhu Min (MPA, Princeton University; PhD in economics, Johns Hopkins University).

Table 14.2 presents the members of the current (i.e., 18th) Central Committee of the CCP who have received advanced degrees overseas. They include Minister of Commerce Gao Hucheng (PhD in sociology, Université Paris 7), Vice President of CASS Li Peilin (PhD in sociology, Université Paris 1), Shaanxi Governor Hu Heping (PhD in engineering, Tokyo University), and Vice Minister of Agriculture Li Jiayang (PhD in genetics, Brandeis University). It is interesting to note that leaders who received degrees from Russia or from formerly Communist countries in Eastern Europe have also reappeared in the CCP leadership. They include governor of Sichuan Yin Li (PhD in medicine, Public Health, Economic and Health Service Institute in Russia) and former chief of staff of the People's Liberation Army Nanjing Military Region Yang Hui (PhD in literature, University of Belgrade, Yugoslavia). Both were born in the 1960s and thus are regarded as rising stars in the CCP leadership.

My 2005 study of Western-educated returnees at the vice ministerial level and higher shows that, in terms of destination countries for foreign studies, the United States ranks first for Chinese leaders in the categories of "foreign study in general" and "foreign study resulting in an advanced degree" (see Table 14.3). There is a considerable spread between the total number of Chinese students who studied in the United States and the number who studied in England, which is ranked second in both categories. My 2015 study of the country's distribution of returnee members of the 18th Central Committee of the CCP discerns a similar pattern (see Table 14.4).[17]

Returnees as Think Tank-Based Advisors

The fact that foreign-educated returnees play dominant roles in China's think tanks, especially in relation to economic issues and foreign affairs, is truly remarkable. Tsinghua University and Peking University (北大,

Table 14-2:   Selected Members of the 18th Central Committee Who Received Foreign Advanced Degrees.

Name	Born	Current Position	Country	Foreign School	Years	Degree	Academic Field
Gao Hucheng	1951	Minister of Commerce	France	Université Paris 7	1982–85	PhD	Sociology
Zhou Ji	1946	President of the Chinese Academy of Engineering	USA	SUNY, Buffalo	1980–84	PhD	Engineering
Hu Heping	1962	Shaanxi Governor	Japan	Tokyo University	1992–95	PhD	Engineering
Li Jiayang	1956	Vice Minister of Agriculture	USA	Brandeis University	1985–91	PhD	Genetics
Li Peilin	1955	Vice President of the Chinese Academy of Social Sciences	France	Université of Lyon; Université Paris 1	1983–87	Master's/ PhD	Sociology
Wan Lijun	1957	President of University of Science and Technology of China	Japan	Tohoku University	1996–99	PhD	Chemistry
Yin Li	1962	Sichuan Deputy Party Secretary and Governor	Russia (Soviet Union)	Public Health, Economic and Health Service Institute	1988–93	PhD	Medicine
Gong Ke	1955	President of Nankai University	Austria	Technical University of Graz	1983–86	PhD	Engineering
Yang Hui	1964	Former chief of staff of Nanjing Military Region	Yugoslavia	University of Belgrade	1985–88	PhD	Literature

(*Continued*)

Table 14-2: *(Continued)*

Name	Born	Current Position	Country	Foreign School	Years	Degree	Academic Field
Cao Shumin	1967	President of the Telecommunications Research Institute in the Ministry of Industry and Information Technology	Hong Kong	The Hong Kong Polytechnic University	2003–07	PhD	Management
Liu He	1952	Office Director of the Central Economic Leading Group	USA	Seton Hall University; Harvard Kennedy School	1992–95	Master's	Business/Public Administration
Lan Tianli	1962	Vice Governor of Guangxi	Singapore	Nanyang Technological University	2006–07	Master's	Public Administration
Li Qun	1962	Party Secretary of Qingdao	USA	University of New Haven	2000	Master's	Public Administration
Song Liping	1962	President of Shenzhen Stock Exchange	USA	University of Dallas	1986–88	Master's	Business Administration

Source: The author's database.

Table 14-3:   Foreign Countries in Which Chinese Leaders Studied.

Country	Foreign Study in General		Foreign Study Resulting in an Advanced Degree	
	Number	Percentage (%)	Number	Percentage (%)
USA	29	43.9	11	37.9
England	13	19.7	6	20.7
France	4	6.1	4	13.8
Germany	4	6.1	3	10.3
Japan	4	6.1	1	3.4
Canada	3	4.5	0	0.0
Australia	2	3.0	1	3.4
Sweden	2	3.0	0	0.0
Denmark	1	1.5	1	3.4
Ireland	1	1.5	1	3.4
New Zealand	1	1.5	0	0.0
Singapore	1	1.5	0	0.0
Switzerland	1	1.5	1	3.4
Total	66	100.0	29	100.0

Source and Notes: Cheng Li, "Foreign-Educated Returnees in the PRC: Increasing Political Influence with Limited Official Power," *Journal of International Migration and Integration*, Vol. 7, No. 4 (Fall 2006). All countries are counted if a leader studied in more than one country. Individual percentages may not add up to 100 due to rounding.

Beida) are now home to some of the most influential think tanks in the country. There are, for example, more than two dozen prominent research centers and institutes at Tsinghua, including the Center for China Studies (CCS), the Center for the Study of Contemporary China (CSCC), the National Center for Economic Research (NCER), the Institute of International Studies (IIS), and the Institute of International Strategy and Development (IISD). The most important resources for think tanks, of course, are research scholars and thinkers. For this reason it is not surprising that research centers and institutes are often "built around a single, strong-minded individual," as Barry Naughton observes in his study of China's economic think tanks.[18] Hu Angang (CCS), Hu Zuliu (NCER),

Table 14-4: Foreign Countries in Which Members of the 18th Central Committee Studied.

Country	Foreign Study in General		Foreign Study Resulting in an Advanced Degree	
	Number	Percentage (%)	Number	Percentage (%)
USA	25	37.9	5	27.8
England	11	16.7	2	11.1
Japan	6	9.1	3	16.7
Germany	4	6.1	1	5.6
France	3	4.5	2	11.1
Russia	3	4.5	1	5.6
Canada	2	3.0	0	0.0
Netherlands	2	3.0	0	0.0
Italy	2	3.0	0	0.0
Austria	1	1.5	1	5.6
Yugoslavia (fmr.)	1	1.5	1	5.6
Singapore	1	1.5	1	5.6
Sweden	1	1.5	0	0.0
Belgium	1	1.5	0	0.0
New Zealand	1	1.5	0	0.0
North Korea	1	1.5	0	0.0
Zaire (fmr.)	1	1.5	1	5.6
Total	66	100.0	18	100.0

Source and Notes: Cheng Li, *Chinese Politics in the Xi Jinping Era: Reassessing Collective Leadership* (Washington, DC: Brookings Institution Press, 2016), Chapter 4. The author's database. If a leader studied in more than one country, each country is counted. Individual percentages may not add up to 100 due to rounding.

Li Qiang (CSCC), Yan Xuetong (IIS), and Chu Shulong (IISDS) are good examples, and they are all returnees who either received PhDs from foreign universities or spent many years abroad as visiting scholars. Chapter 6 describes the pivotal role certain prominent scholars play in various leading think tanks. To a great extent, these individuals are the faces, brains, and souls of their respective institutions.

Returnees now regularly help shape the research agendas and research methods employed in the fields of economics, management, international relations, and demography. They are also leaders in China's intellectual and policy discourses. They often contribute to international academic exchanges, which can greatly improve the quality of think tank work in China and broaden Chinese perspectives on issues of global significance (see Chapter 6).

Returnees as Opinion Leaders

Returnees in think tanks and academic institutions not only provide policy recommendations and other advice to the Chinese leadership, but also influence foreign and domestic policy discourse through media outlets by way of their roles as anchors, talk show hosts, columnists, and commentators. For example, Lang Xianping, a Taiwan-born, University of Chicago–educated, Hong Kong–based economist also known as Larry Lang, is a household name in China because of his popular talk show, on which he discusses issues around China's role in an era of economic globalization. Yang Lan, who holds an MPA degree from Columbia University, has her own studio at both the Hong Kong–based Phoenix TV headquarters and in Beijing's CCTV building. In 2010 she interviewed a number of U.S. leaders, including former president George H. W. Bush, then secretary of state Hillary Clinton, and former secretary of state Henry Kissinger.

Opinion leaders with backgrounds in foreign studies differ greatly in their views, values, and strategic thinking regarding China's foreign relations. It is notable, however, that several of the best-selling books in the PRC over the past decade, especially in recent years, take ultra-nationalistic and anti-U.S. positions. Most of these books were actually written by returnees. For example, Wang Xiaodong, a co-author of both *China Can Say No* (1996) and *China is Unhappy* (2009), studied in Japan for several years early in his career.[19] According to the Chinese media, *China is Unhappy* sold 600,000 copies in its first month of publication.[20]

Fang Ning, a prolific writer and director of the Institute of Political Science at CASS, is another best-selling author who has been extremely critical of U.S. foreign policy for over a decade. In 1995, through the popular newspaper *China Youth,* Fang Ning and two of his colleagues conducted a public opinion survey of young people in China, assessing their views of the world. This was considered to be China's first large-scale, open public opinion survey, as well as its first survey on attitudes towards international affairs.[21] One of the survey's most astonishing findings — for people in both China and abroad — was that about 75 percent of some 120,000 respondents were very critical of the United States.[22]

Fang Ning was born in Beijing in 1957 and grew up on the campus of People's University. In 1975, at the age of 18, Fang was sent to the outskirts of Beijing, where he worked as a farmer for a few years. In 1978 he enrolled in the department of politics at Beijing Normal University. After graduation he stayed on as an instructor and then, in 1987, spent a year in the United States as a visiting scholar. In the 1990s, while working as a professor at Beijing Normal University, Fang also worked as an advisor and speechwriter for Li Tieying, who was at the time a member of the Politburo and the president of CASS. Fang was transferred to CASS in 2001.

Fang is one of the most prominent thinkers of the so-called "new left" (新左派, *xinzuopai*). He was probably also the scholar who first developed the now-ubiquitous concept of "harmonious society." In an article published in 1997, Fang argued that the fundamental flaw in the conventional understanding of socialism was that socialism would give rise to higher productivity than capitalism had historically. According to Fang, this catch-up mentality led to the failure of Stalin's Soviet Union and Mao's China (and perhaps, ultimately, Deng's and Jiang's modernization programs as well).[23] In Fang's view, socialist countries' concentration on productivity was actually the "pitfall of the catch-up" (赶超的陷阱, *gan-chao de xianjing*). In Fang's view, socialism should not share with capitalism the goal of high productivity. Instead, socialism should set out to create a harmonious society leading ultimately to complete balance between man and nature. According to Fang, "socialism is eventually a form of harmony."[24] It certainly does seem that Fang's concept of harmonious society laid the philosophical foundation for Hu Jintao's new developmental strategy, and one may reasonably suspect that Hu even adopted the very phrase from Fang Ning.[25]

The 1999 book *China's Road in the Shadow of Globalization*, co-authored by Fang Ning, Wang Xiaodong, and Song Qiang, was one of the most influential and representative works of the "new left" on the subject of international affairs.[26] The book was published at a time when Chinese leaders, public intellectuals, and the general public were enthusiastic about China's upcoming accession to the WTO. The book offers a very critical account of economic globalization. Fang's most famous line regarding globalization is: "Capital flows all over the world, but profits only go to the West."[27] Fang argues that economic globalization will increase economic disparity in the world, causing more conflicts and wars in the future. He also believes that the so-called "international division of labor" and "comparative advantage" will make developing countries such as China more dependent on the West. To avoid this "trap of development," Fang argues that China should more aggressively develop its heavy industry and high-tech sectors. The book also contends, implicitly if not explicitly, that the United States' policy towards China had the evil intention of dividing the PRC by supporting independent movements in Taiwan, Tibet, and Xinjiang.[28]

In 2003, Fang further developed his critique of globalization in a new book, *The Era of New Imperialism and China's Strategy*. In it, he challenges Deng's notion of "peace and development" in international relations and argues that the new American imperialism is the defining characteristic of the world. According to Fang, the era of new American imperialism has five components: military dominance, political power, cultural imperialism, the imposition of democratic ideology, and preemptive attack. Fang argues that no matter how obedient China may be, American imperialists will never change their strategy to contain China. In Fang's view, the only way for China to break the American encirclement is to develop military technology.[29]

From a Chinese nationalist's perspective, Fang's conceptions of domestic and international affairs — "a harmonious society" and "a new imperialist world" — are not necessarily contradictory. His perspective on world affairs, however, has received much more criticism from the scholarly community in China than his view of domestic policies. At the same time, Fang's ultranationalistic views and, especially, his direct appeal to Chinese youth have made him an "intellectual mentor of the angry youth generation."[30] The 2009 global financial crisis, fans of Fang Ning argue, has proved many if not all of Fang Ning's predictions.[31]

Fang Ning's theory of a U.S.-led anti-China conspiracy is echoed in another best-selling book by a returnee from the United States. Song Hongbing became a celebrity in the PRC almost overnight after the publication of *Currency War*.[32] His blog is now the most popular blog in the country for public intellectuals. Song went to the United States in the early 1990s and received a master's degree in information engineering and education from American University. He also worked as a senior consultant for Fannie Mae and Freddie Mac. In Song's view, the U.S. pressure on China to appreciate its currency is part of a grand conspiracy to stymie China's rise. The book is not widely regarded as a serious academic study, but its successful prediction of the global financial crisis made Song Hongbing more credible than many other U.S.-educated economists who had long painted a rosy picture of economic globalization.

Contradictions in Foreign Relations and the Paradoxical Roles of Returnees

The addition of returnees — with their dynamic, diverse, and complex views and experiences — to the Chinese discourse on foreign affairs, especially as it relates to China's relations with the United States, helps explain three major contradictions in China's foreign policy posture in general and Sino-U.S. relations in particular. Specifically, these contradictions exist between vision and implementation, means and end, and objective and outcome.

"All Directional Diplomacy" and "Counting on No One but the United States"

Each generation of Chinese leaders has its own foreign policy legacy. Jiang Zemin placed tremendous emphasis on building a good relationship between China and the United States. Under his leadership, China's foreign policy was mostly oriented around "major powers diplomacy" (大国外交, *daguo waijiao*), with a particular focus on the United States. Despite many unfortunate incidents and perceived slights by the United States — such as the accidental bombing of the Chinese embassy in Yugoslavia, the Cox report accusing China of technological espionage, the

U.S.-led opposition to Beijing's bid to host the 2000 Olympics, the crisis in cross-Strait relations stemming from the Taiwan election, and the "hectoring of China over human rights" — Jiang did not alter his strategic thinking. Some public intellectuals felt China made too many concessions to the United States in order to gain entry into the WTO, and Jiang was sometimes criticized for being too "soft" on U.S. leaders.[33]

When Hu Jintao rose to power in 2002, many expected that he would be much firmer than Jiang in protecting China's national interests. His pronounced "all directional diplomacy" was seen as a strategic departure from Jiang's "major powers diplomacy." Hu's foreign policy priority seemed to be improving China's relationships with neighboring countries, particularly in Southeast Asia. His visits to Vietnam and Russia soon after succeeding Jiang appeared to be in line with this new approach. But in his second term, Hu Jintao became very actively engaged in seeking a good relationship with the United States. In 2009 alone, Hu met with U.S. president Obama four times. Other senior Chinese leaders in the Hu-Wen administration frequently visited the United States. Although most Chinese leaders of the fourth generation did not use the concept of "the G2" to refer to China and the United States, they often emphasized that the Sino–U.S. relationship was the most important bilateral relationship of the 21st century. For many Chinese, the United States is the only other country in the world more powerful than the PRC, and therefore it is the only other country worth paying attention to. China's excessive interest in the United States is evident in many respects, one of which is that China's foreign policy lobby now concentrates disproportionately on the United States.

There are perhaps several reasons that "all directional diplomacy" yielded few concrete results. One can argue that the trends toward collective leadership and factional checks and balances helped to institutionalize China's foreign policy and make it less sensitive to individual leaders' idiosyncratic preferences. Because of the restraints on his power, Hu might have found it difficult to implement his policy initiatives. Probably the most important reason for this contradiction between words and deeds is the fact that U.S.-educated returnees have dominated China's foreign policy establishment. It was in their best interest — and happened to be their area of expertise — to promote all sorts of engagements and exchanges with the United States. Returnees from elsewhere were not strong enough to compete for attention and priority over the U.S.-educated returnees in the foreign policy establishment. Chinese experts on certain countries and regions, including India, Indonesia, Pakistan, the Middle East, South America, and Africa, are woefully small in number, especially considering China's aspiration to become a great power.

Similarly, Xi Jinping has frequently met with Russian president Vladimir Putin and significantly consolidated Sino-Russian relations since taking the top leadership post in 2012. But Xi is chiefly focused on the Sino–U.S. relationship, in which the Chinese seek a "new type of major power relations" (新型大国关系, *xinxing daguo guanxi*) between China and the United States.

"The Best Time in Sino–U.S. Relations" and "the U.S. Conspiracy against China"

China's emphasis on its relationship with the United States does not necessarily contradict its concern about a U.S. conspiracy against China. It is, nevertheless, strange that Chinese leaders and public intellectuals assert two contrasting views of U.S.–China relations simultaneously (not just as a group, but often the individuals themselves). The first stipulation is that this is the best Sino–U.S. relations have been since the 1989 Tiananmen incident, if not since the founding of the PRC. This is evident in the broad contact and cooperation between the United States and China over a wide range of issues, including global economic rebalancing, climate change, anti-terrorism, and nuclear nonproliferation. Cultural and educational exchanges between China and the United States have never in the long history of relations between the two countries been as dynamic as they are at present. The second notion is the strangely incompatible but widely held belief that the "U.S. conspiracy against China" is still in process.

To a certain extent, these contrasting views and their possible policy implications reflect the growing diversity and sophistication of the Chinese foreign policy establishment. In recent years, foreign policy questions have been debated more openly by the Chinese public and in scholarly circles. For example, Shi Yinhong and Yan Xuetong, two distinguished returnee scholars of international relations who serve as advisors to Chinese policymakers, have expressed sharply differing views on how the Chinese government should handle the possible independence of Taiwan.[34] This diversity notwithstanding, it is fair to assert that the enduring obstacles in this most important bilateral relationship are the lack of mutual trust between the United States and China, China's worry (often reinforced by U.S.-educated returnees) about a supposed U.S.-hatched conspiracy against China, and the United States' concern over the "China threat."

Part of China's mistrust of the United States stems from the arrogance and ignorance of several American politicians and opinion leaders who, driven by narrow perspective, have incessantly criticized China over the past two decades. In fact, U.S. leaders' policies towards China have not been consistent, either. For example, in 2008, in the heat of the presidential primaries, Secretary Clinton made headlines by calling for a boycott of the Beijing Olympics. Two years later, she became a chief spokesperson for the American pavilion at the 2010 Shanghai Expo. Former speaker of the House of Representatives Nancy Pelosi was the world's leading critic of China's human rights record for almost two decades. After a trip to China in 2009, however, she declared that economic well-being and environmental protection should also be seen as human rights and acknowledged that China has made very impressive progress in these areas.[35]

Ironically, despite evidence of U.S. goodwill toward China, and despite the United States' new strategic formulation of "strategic reassurance," Chinese leaders and the public simply do not trust the United States. The fact that some U.S. policymakers have quickly changed their tune has actually reinforced the perception among many Chinese that the United States is seeking to cleverly manipulate China.

U.S.–China Education Exchanges: Areas for Improvement?

The suspicions about the United States that are widely held by Chinese leaders and public intellectuals should give the United States pause, and should encourage creative solutions to reduce Chinese misperceptions. The United States' three decades of helping to train China's best and brightest has of course been driven, at least partially, by self-interest. Policymakers in China and the United States had different agendas when planning these far-reaching educational exchanges. For Deng Xiaoping, the primary goal was to "make up for the years lost" during the Cultural

Revolution, when China was almost completely cut off from the international academic community.[36] Today, it is clear that Deng's goal has been achieved.

For the United States, educational exchanges with non-Western countries were considered by some U.S. decision-makers (especially during the Cold War era) to be a form of cultural diplomacy — a "fourth dimension" of foreign policy that would complement the political, economic, and military dimensions.[37] In the words of a former U.S. president, "Just as war begins in the minds of men, so does peace."[38] Education, U.S. policymakers reasoned, could be a vital channel through which future leaders of foreign countries would be exposed to American values and ideas.[39] This also reflects the long-standing assumption underlying American foreign policy toward China: that the country that is able to educate China's young generation will eventually influence China's development.[40] As Jonathan Spence observes, for many Western internationalists, China offers a hope — a "chance to influence history by the force of personality."[41] This educational endeavor "would do a far better service than guns and battleships in keeping a peaceful world."[42]

The United States certainly cannot say that its goal for American-Chinese educational exchanges has succeeded if a significant number of U.S.-educated Chinese returnees continue to believe in a U.S. conspiracy against China. There are multiple plausible explanations for the persistence of this misunderstanding. One possible explanation may have to do with the way Chinese nationals have studied in the United States. Among the returnees who serve in the government, most were one-year-long visiting scholars in educational institutions rather than degree candidates. An overwhelming majority of returnees spent all of their time in the United States at educational institutions. Very few had the opportunity to stay and work beyond school.[43]

As Wang Jisi recently observed,

> Chinese scholarly works on U.S. domestic politics and society are woefully inadequate.... The lack of understanding of American politics, spiritual life, and mindset leads to misperceptions of U.S. international strategy in general and its China policy, in particular. A daunting task is

how institutions and scholars of American Studies can be encouraged to look below the surface and fully grasp what is happening in the "heart" of America.[44]

One possible remedy is for both the United States and China to encourage more exchanges that allow Chinese post-graduate professionals to come to the United States for one or two years as observers or trainees in various fields. Instead of being confined to educational institutions, they would experience real work environments in local governments, courts, law firms, media outlets, public relations firms, non-governmental organizations, neighborhood associations, foundations, think tanks, and so on.

At a time when tensions, prejudices, misunderstandings, and wars abound throughout the world — and when policymakers and the general public in the United States are concerned about America's own educational "Open Door Policy" — we must evaluate whether or not sweeping educational and professional exchanges between two profoundly different countries can truly contribute to mutual reassurance and, most of all, mutual trust. Phenomena such as Western-educated Chinese nationals taking over leadership positions in their country, the growing political influence of returnee-led think tanks, and widely divergent views held among the opinion leaders with foreign educational backgrounds all indicate how vastly the underpinnings of China's foreign policy have changed. Returnees' confidence that they can help shape their country's foreign policy has grown in parallel with the importance of think tanks in policy discourse and the Chinese public's aspiration for great-power status in today's world. Time will tell whether or not the returnees' foreign experiences can truly make a difference.

Notes

This chapter is an edited version of the author's article that appeared previously in Allen Carlson and Ren Xiao, eds., *The New Frontiers of Chinese Foreign Policy* (Lanham, Maryland: Lexington Books, 2011), 41–62. The author is indebted to Yinsheng Li for research assistance. The author thanks Zach Balin, Eve Cary, Jordan Lee, Ryan McElveen, Robert O'Brien, and Lucy Xu for their very helpful comments on earlier versions of this chapter.

1 Harold Lasswell, *Politics: Who Gets What, When, How* (New York: Meridian Books, 1958), 13.

2 In Chinese, the words for "returnee" and "sea turtle" have the same pronunciation.

3 There are, however, a few exceptions. See David Zweig, *Internationalizing China: Domestic Interests and Global Linkages* (Ithaca, NY: Cornell University Press, 2002); and Cheng Li, ed., *Bridging Minds across the Pacific: U.S.-China Educational Exchanges, 1978–2003* (Lanham, MD: Lexington Books, 2005).

4 *Renmin ribao* [People's Daily], January 7, 2003, 10.

5 Wang Yucheng and Shi Rui, "2014 Zhongguo chuguo liuxuerenyuan zaizeng" [Continuing increases in the numbers of Chinese students and scholars studying abroad], Caixin Newsnet, March 6, 2015, http://china.caixin.com/2015-03-06/100788923.html; and also "2014 nian chuguo liuxue qushi baogao" [Report on the Status and Trends of Study Abroad in 2014], *Zhongguo jiaoyu zaixian* [China Education Online], October 12, 2014, www.eol.cn/html/lx/2014baogao/content.html. The total number of Chinese students and scholars who have studied in the United States is based on a speech delivered by China's ambassador to the United States, Zhou Wenzhong, in Seattle on June 1, 2005. See www.chinesenewsnet.com, June 6, 2005.

6 Wang and Shi, "2014 Zhongguo chuguo liuxuerenyuan zaizeng."

7 *Nanfang Zhoumo* [Southern Weekend], April 15, 2005; also see news.xinhuanet.com/report/2005-04/15/content_2833349.htm.

8 See www.taisha.org/abroad/topic/gongpai, October 17, 2009.

9 Zhang Guozuo, "Zuoqiang xinxing zhiku tisheng guojia ruanshili" [Building a New Type of Think Tanks to Enhance China's Soft Power]. Also see *Renmin ribao*, October 14, 2014, www.chinanews.com/sh/2014/10-14/6675278.shtml.

10 For Fang's early career, see Sun Tao, "Guogan Fang Xinghai" [Bold Fang Xinghai]. Also see *Jinrong shijie* [Financial World], August 2012, http://blog.sina.com.cn/s/blog_695557320101d583.html.

11 George Chen and Daniel Ren, "Shanghai booster Fang Xinghai lands Beijing financial advisory role," *South China Morning Post*, June 18, 2013.

12 Cheng Li, "Shaping China's Foreign Policy: The Paradoxical Role of Foreign-Educated Returnees," *Asia Policy*, No. 10 (July 2010): 65–85.

13 See news.xatvs.com/newshtml/15/10/1008101012.html, October 8, 2009.

14 See news.xinhuanet.com/newmedia/2008-10/14/content_10192574.htm, October 14, 2009.

15 Shen Changchang, "Zhongguo shouji yonghu shuliang jiejin 13 yi ren" [The total number of cell phones users in China is nearing 1.3 billion], Renmin Net, June 25, 2014, http://mobile.people.com.cn/n/2014/0625/c183175-25195976.html.

16 Gao Kang, "Zhongguo wangmin shuliang yida 6.68 yi ren" [China's netizens reach 668 million], Xinhua Net, July 23, 2015, http://news.xinhuanet.com/fortune/2015-07/23/c_1116022351.htm.

17 Cheng Li, *Chinese Politics in the Xi Jinping Era: Reassessing Collective Leadership* (Washington, DC: Brookings Institution Press, 2016), Chapter 4.

18 Barry Naughton, "China's Economic Think Tanks: Their Changing Role in the 1990s," *China Quarterly*, No. 171 (September 2002): 629.

19 Song Qiang, Wang Xiaodong, and others, *Zhongguo keyishuobu* [China Can Say No] (Beijing: Zhonghua gongshang lianhe chubanshe, 1996); and Song Xiaojun, Wang Xiaodong, and others, *Zhongguo bugaoxing* [China is Unhappy] (Nanjing: Jiangsu renmin chubanshe, 2009).

20 See product.dangdang.com/product.aspx?product_id=20510131.

21 Zhang Xiaoming. *Hou Jiang Zemin shidai de Zhongguo xinzheng zhinang* [Think Tanks for China's New Deal in the Post-Jiang Zemin Era] (Hong Kong: Gonghe chuban, 2004), 59–60.

22 Approximately 75 percent of respondents chose the United States when answering each of the following three questions: "Which country is the most hostile toward China?", "Which country has influenced China the most?", and "Which country do you dislike the most?" Ibid., 60.

23 For Fang's article, see ufca61.chinaw3.com/sc34.htm.

24 Ibid.

25 Zhang, *Hou Jiang Zemin shidai de Zhongguo xinzheng zhinang*, 55.

26 Fang Ning, Wang Xiaodong, and Song Qiang, *Quanqiuhua yinyingxia de Zhongguo zhilu* [China's Road in the Shadow of Globalization] (Beijing: Zhongguo shehui kexue chubanshe, 1999). Wang and Song were also the authors of *China Can Say No*.

27 Zhang, *Hou Jiang Zemin shidai de Zhongguo xinzheng zhinang*, 58.

28 The cover of the book is a map of China, showing how the outside world's anti-China forces intend to divide the country.

29 Fang Ning, *Xin diguozhuyi shidai yu Zhongguo zhanlue* [The Era of New Imperialism and China's Strategy] (Beijing: Beijing chubanshe, 2003).

30 Fang Ning, *Chengzhang de Zhongguo: Dangdai Zhongguo qingnian de guojia minzhu yishi yanjiu* [Growing China: Study of National Consciousness of the Chinese Youth in the Contemporary Era] (Beijing: Renmin chubanshe, 2002).

31 See www.chinathinktank.cn. October 7, 2009.

32 Song Hongbin, *Huobi Zhanzheng* [Currency War] (Beijing: Zhongxin chu-banshe, 2007).

33 Thomas L. Friedman, "The Five Myths: How America Misreads China," *The New York Times*, October 27, 2000, A31.

34 Shi Yinhong, "Taiwan wenti shangde yanzhong weixian he zhanlue bixu" [Severe Danger and Strategic Necessity in Dealing with the Taiwan Issue], *Zhanlue yu guanli* [Strategy and Management], No. 1 (2004), 101–6; and Yan Xuetong, "Wuli ezhi Taiwan duli de libi fenxi" [Pros and Cons on the Use of Force to Deter the Legal Independence of Taiwan], *Zhanlue yu guanli* [Strategy and Management], No. 3 (2004), 1–5.

35 Remarks by Speaker of the House of Representatives Nancy Pelosi at the Brookings Institution, "The Recent Congressional Delegation's Trip to China," Vote Smart Website, June 5, 2009, http://votesmart.org/public-statement/429480/remarks-by-speaker-of-the-house-of-reps-nancy-pelosi-d-ca-at-the-brookings-institution-the-recent-congressional-delegations-trip-to-china#.VqoVZygQifQ.

36 David Zweig, Chen Changgui, and Stanley Rosen, *China's Brain Drain to the United States: Views of Overseas Chinese Students and Scholars in the 1990s* (Berkeley, CA: Institute of East Asian Studies, University of California at Berkeley, 1995), 7.

37 Philip Coombs, *The Fourth Dimension of Foreign Policy: Educational and Cultural Affairs* (New York: Harper and Row, 1964), 6–7, 17.

38 Remarks by Dwight D. Eisenhower at ceremony marking the tenth anniversary of the Smith-Mundt Act, January 27, 1958.

39 Bu Liping, *Making the World Like Us: Education, Cultural Expansion, and the American Century* (Westport, CT: Praeger, 2003), 7.

40 Zhang Hongjie, *Jituo de yidai: Qinghuaren he Beidaren liumei koushu de gushi* [A Generation of GRE and TOEFL: Oral Accounts of the U.S.-Educated at Tsinghua and Peking Universities] (Shenyang: Chunfeng wenyi chubanshe, 1999), 3.

41 Jonathan D. Spence, *To Change China: Western Advisers in China, 1620–1960* (Boston, MA: Little, Brown Publishers, 1969), 292.

42 Bu, *Making the World Like Us*, 86.

43 Among the 61 Western-educated returnees in China's ministerial level of leadership, only one, Yi Gang, the vice governor of the People's Bank of China, taught in the United States after finishing his PhD degree. He began his studies in the United States in 1980 as an MBA student at Hamline University and then continued to study for a PhD in economics at the University of Illinois. After receiving his PhD in 1986, he began teaching at

Indiana University, where he received tenure and became an associate professor in 1992. In 1994, after studying and teaching in the United States for fourteen years, he returned to China.

44 Wang Jisi, "Foreword," in Julia Chang Bloch, *All-China American Studies Directory: An Overview of American Studies in China* (Washington, DC: U.S.-China Education Trust/FY Chang Foundation, 2008), iv.

V

Conclusion: Top-Level Design of Reform and China's Political Future

Chapter 15

Will China's "Top-Level Design of Reform" Prevent a "Bottom-Up Revolution"?

Why do they call it rush hour when nothing moves?

— Robin Williams

If one does not know to which port one is sailing, no wind is favorable.

— Lucius Annaeus Seneca

A host of troubles have plagued the People's Republic of China (PRC) as of late: widespread social unrest, slowing economic growth, and rampant official corruption, as revealed by the Bo Xilai scandal and the purges of Zhou Yongkang, Ling Jihua, Xu Caihou, and Guo Boxiong.[1] Less obvious to the outside world, however, has been the battle between two sharply contrasting and controversial perspectives on the country's near- to medium-term future. These two rival scenarios reflect fundamentally different assessments of the socioeconomic health and anticipated political trajectory of the world's most populous country.

The first scenario envisions an abrupt bottom-up revolution. This assessment has generated heated intellectual and political debate in the PRC. In December 2011, thirty-year-old, best-selling author Han Han (China's most popular blogger, whose site has registered well over 580 million hits) posted a now-famous essay titled "On Revolution."[2] Although Han argues that "revolution is hardly a good option for China," his intriguing view of the choice between reform and revolution pointedly reflects — and greatly enhances — the public's awareness of the risk of revolution in the country.

Additionally, one of the most popular books in PRC intellectual circles today is the Chinese translation of Alexis de Tocqueville's 1856 classic, *The Old Regime and the Revolution*. One frequently quoted passage is Tocqueville's argument that revolutions typically occur not when an old regime resists change, but rather when it begins to attempt reform, only to find that expectations outstrip any possible rate of improvement.

The second scenario is reform from above, which Chinese Communist Party (CCP) elites often refer to as "top-level reform" or the "top-level design of reform" (改革的顶层设计, *gaige de dingceng sheji*). This latter term was first introduced at a top CCP leadership meeting in October 2010.[3] It reflects the leaders' newfound understanding that China is now in "deep water" with regard to reform, and can no longer afford to "cross the river by feeling the stones," as the Chinese expression goes. In short, improvised reform needs to give way to a more methodical and profound set of changes. Moreover, with so many of present-day China's socioeconomic problems growing out of gridlock and obstacles within the political system, basic political and legal reforms will have to be part of any agenda as well.

According to those calling for top-level reform, China needs better coordination between socioeconomic policy and political development, along with structural changes that are more coherent. The older, bottom-up approach that stresses grassroots elections must yield, they say, to a new roadmap that includes intra-CCP elections of national-level party leaders; enhanced institutional checks and balances; structural changes to China's economy, including bold state-owned enterprise reforms; and judicial reform.[4] The "top-level design of reform" naturally calls for think tanks to play greater roles in assessing the feasibility and risks of new reform initiatives.

It is critically important for foreign analysts to grasp the ongoing Chinese discourse in three key areas: (1) the impact of the Bo Xilai crisis and other corruption scandals on China's political trajectory; (2) possible triggers for sociopolitical uprisings and initiatives; and (3) institutional safeguards through which the CCP leadership may open the way to systemic change. Foreign analysts need to reevaluate the concept of "authoritarian resilience," a commonly held view in overseas studies of Chinese politics, which argues that Chinese authoritarianism is "resilient" or "strong."[5] This notion underestimates both the inherent vulnerability of the one-party system and the public's growing resentment over the enormous wealth and power that some senior officials (and their families) have accumulated.

Bo Xilai and the Illusion of CCP Meritocracy

In 2012, the Bo Xilai affair put the political system's deep flaws on display. Although the CCP has been guilty of political repression and grave mistakes during its long rule, its senior leaders had generally not been known for gangland-style murders. But now Bo's wife has been convicted of plotting the murder of a British business associate, and Bo's former lieutenant, the police chief of Chongqing, has been found guilty of abusing his power. The public is left to wonder: What expectations of impunity moved Bo, well known as party chief of Chongqing and a rising star in the CCP's top ranks, to engage in the misdeeds alleged on his lengthy charge sheet? How could this iron-fisted leader, famous for cracking down on organized crime in Chongqing, have run the city's police force in a lawless and at times outright criminal fashion?

The current CCP leadership dismisses these incidents as "isolated and exceptional," but many PRC intellectuals argue that rampant official corruption, especially involving relatives of senior party leaders, exemplifies an especially decadent form of crony capitalism that of late has become more the rule than the exception.[6] In addition to the Bo scandal, another separate and pending corruption case — involving former top officials of the Railways Ministry taking bribes totaling several billion U.S. dollars — has vividly exposed to the public that national level elite corruption is occurring at a scale never seen before.[7]

The recent purges of other senior leaders have further enhanced public awareness of the fundamental flaws in the Chinese political system. These leaders, purged on corruption charges, include some of the most formidable power brokers in Chinese politics: former Politburo Standing Committee member Zhou Yongkang, who was in charge of China's security apparatus for a decade; former director of the General Office of the

CCP Central Committee Ling Jihua, who was the most important confidant of former general secretary Hu Jintao and the person in charge of daily affairs in the top leadership operation; and former vice chairs of the Central Military Commission Guo Boxiong and Xu Caihou, the two highest-ranking military officers from the previous administration.

As for Bo Xilai, one of the official charges against him is that "he made erroneous decisions in the promotion of personnel, resulting in serious consequences." Chinese critics find this charge particularly ironic, asking why those who promoted Bo should not also be held accountable for their even greater "erroneous decisions." In a dramatic and astonishing way, the Bo imbroglio undermines the notion — so central to the authoritarian resilience thesis — that the CCP elite is in any way a meritocracy. In the eyes of the Chinese public, the current method of selecting PRC leaders — through nepotism, patron-client ties, "black-box" manipulation by political heavyweights, fake academic credentials, and even the use of bribes to "purchase office" (买官, *maiguan*) — looks to be based on anything but merit.[8] The legitimacy of the CCP leadership as a whole is now in doubt.

It should be noted that Bo still has a significant number of supporters in China. His strongly nationalistic views, his tendency to use violence to resolve socioeconomic conflicts, his pronounced hatred of the rich, and his reputation as a leader who can get things done are traits that resonate deeply with some groups in Chinese society. Furthermore, unless China profoundly changes its method of governance, demagogues even more brazen and despicable than Bo may well arise in the future.

A Bottom-Up Revolution in the Making?

The CCP legitimacy crisis that the Bo incident has sparked is, of course, not the only factor that could lead to a sociopolitical uprising. After more than two decades of remarkably rapid economic growth, China has recently experienced a slowdown. This downturn, partly born of political bottlenecks, will reveal further flaws in the PRC's authoritarian system and thus become a trigger for political crises. The growing oligarchic power of state-owned enterprises (SOEs), especially gigantic flagship companies, is widely viewed as driving massive corruption, crowding out private investment, shrinking the middle class, and stalling the innovation that China must achieve if it is to transition from an export-led economy to one oriented around consumption and innovation.

A sense of political uncertainty — and fear of socioeconomic and other disasters — is on the rise in China. Many worry about environmental degradation, public-health hazards, and all manner of public-safety problems. Anxiety and discontent touch all socioeconomic classes. The large flow of capital out of China in recent years signals that the elites themselves lack confidence in the country's political stability. According to a 2011 report by Global Financial Integrity (GFI), from 2000 to 2009, China's illegal capital outflow was the world's highest at US$2.7 trillion.[9] The latest GFI report, released in October 2012, shows that cumulative illicit financial outflows from China totaled a massive US$3.8 trillion for the period from 2000 to 2011.[10]

Middle-class anger at government policies has become increasingly evident in recent years. An unemployment rate of about 20 percent among recent college graduates (who usually come from middle-class families and are presumed to be members of China's future middle class) should alarm the Chinese government. Given the difficulty of getting a small-business loan, the opaque and poorly regulated nature of the Chinese stock market, and the general lack of investment opportunities, middle-class savings have flowed heavily into real estate. The nightmare of a bursting property bubble is a real possibility: Some regions are dotted with massive but tenantless areas of new construction known as "ghost cities." A study conducted by the Beijing Municipal Security Bureau in 2012 revealed that there were 3.8 million vacant housing units in the capital alone.[11]

Lower down the socioeconomic scale, the manual-labor shortage that has hit some coastal cities in recent years reflects a growing awareness of individual rights among "vulnerable social groups" (see Chapter 13). Migrant workers, in particular, move from job to job seeking better pay. Yet China's urbanization policy is strikingly unaccommodating to migrants. Such workers resent the middle-class families who own multiple homes and the corrupt officials or rich entrepreneurs who buy costly villas for their mistresses.

Given the CCP elite's interest in maintaining its own grip on power, it is no surprise that the police have become more powerful, with their influence over socioeconomic policy growing alongside their budgets. The sum of spending on "maintaining social stability" now exceeds the amount spent on national defense (see Chapter 13).[12] The growing power of the police has also created a vicious cycle in which the more fiercely the police suppress unrest, the more violent and widespread unrest becomes. With so many sources of social resentment, potential triggering factors, and other disturbing trends, one should not be too quick to discount the possibility of a bottom-up revolution.

Will Intra-Party Democracy Work?

In the wake of the Bo Xilai crisis and the ominous airing of the CCP's dirty laundry, and the emergence of so many other factors that could trigger a bottom-up revolution, what is the likelihood that the CCP leadership will act to save itself by undertaking systemic political reform? Does the party have a chance?

Since the era of Deng Xiaoping, several institutional reforms designed to promote intra-CCP democracy have been gradually adopted. Authorities and the state-run media often speak of "intra-party democracy" (党内民主, *dangnei minzhu*) as a byword for institutional checks and balances within the CCP. In September 2009, at the Fourth Plenary Session of the 17th Central Committee, CCP leaders called for promoting democracy within the party and characterized intra-party democracy as the "lifeblood of the party" (党的生命, *dangde shengming*) and the principal determinant of whether or not the CCP would be able to maintain its position of primacy in the future.

It is understandable that CCP leaders and their advisors are inclined to pursue democratic experiments within the party or, in other words, to carry out political reform in a way that is incremental and manageable. The CCP is the world's largest ruling party, consisting of 4.3 million grassroots branches and almost 88 million members.[13] In the absence of any organized opposition, one can hardly expect China to suddenly adopt a multiparty political system. Under these circumstances, a form of intra-party democracy — one characterized by elite competition, balance of power among factions, and links to distinct interest groups in Chinese society — may well be a more realistic way to promote democracy in the country.

The path to democracy varies from nation to nation, and depends largely on a country's historical and sociopolitical circumstances. Chinese leaders and public intellectuals have every right to argue that the PRC's version of democracy will, and should, have its own distinct (or even unique) features. After all, the democratic regimes that one finds in India, Indonesia, the United Kingdom, and the United States are different from one another in significant ways. Moreover, it is even possible for a government — Japan and Mexico are examples — to undergo lengthy stretches of one-party control without losing its status as a democracy.[14] The interplay of checks and balances among ruling-party factions is often key to this dynamic.

In China today, intra-CCP democracy is more than just rhetoric. A number of important institutional developments have already changed the way that China's political elite does business. Holders of top posts in both the party and the state now serve terms capped at five years, and no official may serve more than two terms. Leaders above a certain level cannot exceed a set age limit. For example, all CCP Central Committee members who were born before 1940 retired from that body at the 2007 Party Congress. Similarly, all Central Committee members who were born before 1945 retired from that body at the 2012 Party Congress. The CCP has endorsed a method known as the "more candidates than seats election" (差额选举, *cha'e xuanju*) when selecting members of the Central Committee and other higher bodies. These rules and norms not only establish a sense of consistency and fairness in the selection of leaders, but also speed up turnover within the elite.[15]

Such experiments in intra-party democracy, however, have made little progress since 2009. The scope and scale of intra-party competition have not increased much over the past two decades. Despite promises to the contrary, top posts at various levels are still not filled by means of multi-candidate elections. Yet it remains noteworthy that the CCP leadership is now structured around two informal coalitions or factions that check and balance each other. This is not the kind of institutionalized system by which, say, the U.S. government's executive, legislative, and judicial branches check and balance one another. But it does represent a major departure from the strongman traditions of the Mao and Deng eras, and it is reshaping the inner workings of high-level intra-party politics in China.

The two groups can be labeled the "populist coalition" (民粹同盟, *mincui tongmeng*), led by outgoing president Hu Jintao, and the "elitist coalition" (精英同盟, *jingying tongmeng*), which emerged during the Jiang Zemin era and is currently led by Jiang's top protégés. At the 18th Party Congress in November 2012, Xi Jinping, from the elitist faction, became the general secretary of the party, and Li Keqiang, from the populist faction, was designated to become China's premier. This division of power is sometimes referred to as the "one party, two coalitions" political mechanism.[16]

These two coalitions represent different socioeconomic and geographical constituencies. Most of the top leaders in the elitist coalition, for instance, are "princelings" from families of veteran revolutionaries and high-ranking officials. These princelings typically began their careers in rich and economically well-developed coastal cities. The elitist coalition usually represents the interests of China's entrepreneurs.

Most of the populist coalition's leading figures, by contrast, come from less-privileged families. They also tend to have accumulated much of their leadership experience in less-developed inland provinces. Many of these leaders began their respective climbs up the political ladder through leadership roles in the Chinese Communist Youth League and are therefore known as *tuanpai* (团派). The populists often voice the concerns of vulnerable social groups such as farmers, migrant workers, and the urban poor.

Leaders of these two competing factions differ in expertise, credentials, and experience. Yet they understand that they must find common ground in order to coexist and govern effectively, especially in times of crisis — and now is such a time. A factional leader such as the princeling Bo Xilai may fall due to scandal, but the factions themselves are too strong to be dismantled.

The rise of a subdued form of Chinese "bipartisanship" within the leadership may, however, still not be enough to save the CCP. Cutting deals, sharing power, and arriving at compromises can be hard. Moreover, having more candidates for positions than there are seats to fill naturally creates a sense of winners and losers. There is no shortage of contentious issues: serious disputes are brewing over how best to distribute national resources, the optimal methods for fighting corruption, the establishment of a public health care system, the construction of more affordable housing in cities, and the reform of finance and rural land ownership. Can a consensus wide and strong enough to support effective governance be achieved? This remains an open question.

China's much-needed political reform may be delayed due to strong resistance from some conservative leaders and vested interest groups such as large, state-monopolized firms. However, public demand for a more competitive, more institutionalized, and more transparent political system will only grow stronger. Factions in the top leadership mirror the desires of new stabilizing forces in Chinese society, none of which existed in 1989, so the degree to which top leaders cooperate or compete may play a decisive role in determining China's political future. Along with a larger middle class, the country has a more assertive community of legal professionals that argue for constitutionalism and strong measures to curb corruption and abuses of power. The media, too, are more commercialized and influential, and social media have achieved a level of pervasiveness that no one could have imagined only a few years ago. It will also be interesting and important to see how Xi Jinping's ongoing consolidation of power and drive against bureaucratic inaction might undermine or improve collective leadership in the years to come.

Various other interest groups, including foreign business lobbies, have grown in number. Most importantly, there is a widespread perception that China, its current economic problems notwithstanding, is on the rise rather than on the decline. All these factors should increase the public's confidence that a political transformation could go well and may point in the direction of a freer and more open China.

The competitive dynamics within the collective CCP leadership, meanwhile, should serve to make lobbying more transparent, factional politics more legitimate, rules and laws more respected, elections more genuine, and elites more accountable and representative. Could the CCP itself formally split into elitist and populist camps? It is not difficult to imagine this happening. In the best-case scenario, the split will be incremental rather than sudden, violence will be absent or minimal, and the example of elections and competition within the CCP will, through a classic "demonstration effect," promote the cause of general elections for the whole country.

Over the next decade or so, the Middle Kingdom's future will hinge on the dynamic between the fear of revolution and the hope for political reform. The threat of revolution from below may push the elite to pursue incremental yet bold political reform. Should reform fail, however, revolt may well be the upshot. And the unfolding drama, wherever it leads, will undoubtedly have profound ramifications far beyond China's borders.

Notes

This chapter is an edited version of the author's article that appeared first in *Journal of Democracy*. See Cheng Li, "Top-Level Reform or Bottom-Up Revolution?" *Journal of Democracy*, Vol. 4, No. 1 (January 2013): 41–48. The author is indebted to Yinsheng Li for research assistance. The author thanks Zach Balin, Ryan McElveen, and Lucy Xu for their very helpful comments on earlier versions of this chapter.

1   Cao Yin, "Top leadership expected to discuss high-level vacancies," *China Daily*, October 21, 2015, http://europe.chinadaily.com.cn/china/2015-10/21/content_22237778.htm.

2   "On Revolution" was one of the three articles in Han Han's series, which he wrote in the lead-up to 2012; the other two were "On Democracy" and "On Freedom," http://blog.sina.com.cn/s/article_archive_1191258123_201112_1.html. For further discussion, see Eric Abrahamsen, "Han Han's U-Turn?" *International Herald Tribune*, January 26, 2012, http://latitude.blogs.nytimes.com/2012/01/26/blogger-han-han-controversy-on-democracy-in-china.

3   Zou Dongtao, Zhou Tianyong, Chi Fulin, and Li Zhichang, "Dingceng sheji: Gaige fanglue de yige zhongda fazhan" [Top-level design: An important development in the reform strategy], *Beijing ribao* [Beijing Daily], January 24, 2011, http://theory.people.com.cn/GB/13796713.html.

4   Liu Junxiang, "Jingying minzhu: Zhongguo dingceng zhenggai xiwang" [Elite democracy: The hope for China's top-level political reform], *Wenzhai* [Digest], October 22, 2012, www.21ccom.net/articles/zgyj/xzmj/article_2012102269487.html.

5   David Shambaugh, for example, observes that the CCP is a "reasonably strong and resilient institution." See *China's Communist Party: Atrophy and Adaptation* (Washington, DC: Woodrow Wilson Center Press, 2008), 176. See also Andrew J. Nathan, "China's Changing of the Guard: Authoritarian Resilience," *Journal of Democracy*, Vol. 14 (January 2003): 6–17; and Alice Miller, "Institutionalization and the Changing Dynamics of Chinese

Leadership Politics," in Cheng Li, ed., *China's Changing Political Landscape: Prospects for Democracy* (Washington, DC: Brookings Institution Press, 2008), 61–79.

6 In March 2012, for example, Renmin University political scientist Zhang Ming launched a strong critique of widespread official corruption. It would take the foreign media another few months to begin tracing the "family trees" of crony capitalism among the Chinese leadership. See Zhang Ming, "Zhongguo xiang he chuqu?" [Whither China?], *Ershiyi shiji* [Twenty-first Century], March 3, 2012. For the CCP authorities' effort to present the Bo case as "isolated and exceptional," see Sina News, May 25, 2012, http://news.sina.com.hk/news/1617/3/1/2673095/1.html.

7 See Evan Osnos, "Boss Rail: The Disaster That Exposed the Underside of the Boom," *The New Yorker*, October 22, 2012, http://www.newyorker.com/magazine/2012/10/22/boss-rail.

8 See Minxin Pei, "The Myth of Chinese Meritocracy," *Project Syndicate*, May 14, 2012, www.project-syndicate.org/commentary/the-myth-of-chinese-meritocracy.

9 *Shijie ribao* [World Journal], April 20, 2012, A4.

10 Dev Kar and Sarah Freitas, *Illicit Financial Flows from China and the Role of Trade Misinvoicing* (Washington, DC: Global Financial Integrity, 2012), iv.

11 Jia Lynn Yang, "As China's Growth Lags, Fears of a Popping Sound," *Washington Post*, October 3, 2012, A16.

12 In 2009, the regime spent 532 billion yuan to defend against foreign threats, and 514 billion to keep domestic order. In 2012, the figures were 670 billion yuan for the military and 702 billion for "stability maintenance." See "Kanshou Chen Guangcheng" [Watching Chen Guangcheng], *Shijie ribao* [World Journal], May 3, 2012, A4.

13 See Xinhua News, http://news.xinhuanet.com/ziliao/2004-11/24/content_2255749.htm.

14 Gerald L. Curtis, *The Logic of Japanese Politics: Leaders, Institutions, and the Limits of Change* (New York: Columbia University Press, 1999); and Steven T. Wuhs, "The Legacies of Transition from One-Party Rule: Mexico in Comparative Perspective." *International Studies Review* 9, No. 2 (2007): 348-356.

15 On these political experiments, see Cheng Li, "Leadership Transition in the CPC: Promising Progress and Potential Problems," *China: An International Journal*, Vol. 10 (August 2012): 23–33.

16 Cheng Li, *Chinese Politics in the Xi Jinping Era: Reassessing Collective Leadership*. (Washington, DC: Brookings Institution Press, 2016).

Chapter 16

Xi Jinping's Reform Agenda: Promises and Risks

When feet meet a dead end road, the head may help go through.

— A Slavic proverb

God give me the courage to accept the things that I cannot change;
the power to change the things which I can; and the wisdom
always to know the difference between the two.

— Reinhold Niebuhr

For foreign stakeholders, China's socioeconomic environment inspires a mix of hope and fear. This is truer today than at any point since the 1990s. On the side of *hope*, several recent developments in China are encouraging. During his first few years as China's top leader, Xi Jinping has launched a bold anti-corruption campaign resulting in the arrests of over 130 ministerial and provincial level senior leaders — including leaders within the country's most formidable special interest groups like the oil, coal, railways, and telecommunications industries.[1] The campaign has already significantly altered the behavior of Chinese officials at various levels and has greatly enhanced public confidence in Xi's leadership.[2]

Equally important is that at the Third Plenum of the 18th Central Committee of the CCP, held in the fall of 2013, Xi and his team presented to the nation and the world a blueprint for the next phase of China's economic reform, which the official media has characterized as "version 2.0" of China's reform and opening. This plan promises to be as consequential as Deng Xiaoping's landmark decision to embark upon economic reform in 1978.[3] With a new mission to bring about "the Chinese dream," Xi has embraced the market as the "decisive force" propelling the country's future economic development, and he has highlighted the expansion of China's middle class as the main objective of reform. This well-articulated plan — encompassing 15 areas, 60 tasks, and over 300 policies — also includes a clear timetable: the Shanghai Free Trade Zone and interest rate liberalization, for example, will be fully implemented within three years and the entire agenda will be completed by 2020.

But *hope* for China's development is counterbalanced by *fear* of failure in the face of significant challenges. China's economy is beset by serious and interrelated problems, including mounting local debt, shadow banking, overcapacity, and a property bubble. The old development model that relied on exports and cheap labor for growth has already come to an end, yet a new consumption-driven, innovation-led, and service sector–centric model has yet to fully take flight. The Chinese leadership is deeply concerned about the outflow of capital and the vulnerability of the Chinese financial system. Meanwhile, the potential negative side effects of China's urbanization drive — vis-à-vis the environment, employment, and social stability — have become increasingly evident.

Xi's anti-corruption campaign has not been without serious political risks. Though the campaign is popular among the Chinese public, President Xi and his main political ally Wang Qishan (who is known as the czar of the anti-corruption campaign) may be alienating the officialdom — the very people on whom the system relies to function effectively.

How can we reconcile the potentially fantastic opportunities with the enormous risks that lie ahead for the world's second-largest economy? Contrary to the pessimism that currently prevails, I am optimistic for several reasons.

First and foremost, Xi's economic reform agenda wisely addresses some of the country's most urgent economic problems. The new leadership unambiguously aims to tackle these in a forceful manner.

Second, Xi not only took control of all the supreme institutions in the party, state, and military during the last political succession, but he also now chairs the newly established National Security Commission and the Central Leading Group for Comprehensively Deepening Reforms. The lower levels of the Chinese government have also established leading groups on economic reform, headed by party secretaries and governors or mayors. All of these bodies provide institutional mechanisms through which Xi and his team can more effectively implement reform policies.

Third, Xi has been supported not only by experienced economic reformers in the top leadership but also by a group of world-class financial technocrats, including Harvard graduate Liu He and Stanford-trained economist Fang Xinghai. Recently, Ma Jun, Deutsche Bank's former chief economist for Greater China, was appointed chief economist of the People's Bank of China. Huang Yiping, former chief economist on Asia at Barclays, also joined the top leadership's advisory team.

Finally, the timetable for President Xi's bold reform agenda reflects his politically minded goal of stabilizing the Chinese economy before the fall of 2017, when the party leadership will experience another major turnover (because of age limits, five of the seven members of the Politburo Standing Committee will retire that year). Xi needs to consolidate power for his second term by unequivocally succeeding in implementing his economic reform agenda.

To minimize political risks, President Xi needs to delicately balance several key issues. While it is strategically sound for him to prioritize economic reforms, he must also, at the appropriate time, make bold moves to implement much-needed political reforms — like increasing political openness and the role of civil society — without which China can never become a true innovation-driven economy. The ongoing anti-corruption campaign is crucial to increasing public confidence in the short term, but it should not serve as a replacement for developing the rule of law or taking concrete steps toward establishing an independent judicial system in the country. It makes sense that President Xi wants to initially consolidate his power by taking over all important leadership posts and by promoting his confidants and allies. But he should also broaden his political coalition to incorporate some of the prominent leaders in the competing faction (notably, Premier Li Keqiang's "youth league" officials). At the very least, the broad public support that Xi has earned, especially from the People's Liberation Army in light of the ongoing large-scale structural transformation of the Chinese military, should allow him to concentrate on a

332   *The Power of Ideas*

domestic economic reform agenda and avoid being distracted by foreign disputes and tensions that might otherwise give rise to ultra-nationalism in the country.

The degree to which Xi and his team successfully manage the delicate balance between economic and political measures will be the key determinant of risk at this critical juncture in China's development. This will not only be a test of Xi's vision, guts, and political might, but also of his capacity to absorb and judge the creative ideas that China's dynamic think tanks provide and to distill them into effective initiatives.

Broadly speaking, Chinese think tanks are in the throes of far-reaching change. Further transformation is inevitable as a more diverse array of committed, globally minded thought leaders in China vigorously seek to play greater roles in governance and to enhance their influence over public policy, both domestically and internationally.

Notes

This chapter is an edited version of the author's article that first appeared in the online journal *China-U.S. Focus*. See Cheng Li, "Xi's Reform Agenda: Promises and Risks," March 3, 2014, http://www.chinausfocus.com/political-social-development/xis-reform-agenda-promises-and-risks. The author thanks Zach Balin, Ryan McElveen, and Lucy Xu for their very helpful comments on earlier versions of this chapter.

1 See Sina Web, November 19, 2015, http://news.sina.com.cn/c/sz/2015-11-19/doc-ifxkwuwy6977243.shtml.
2 The GDP of Macau, a city famous for its casinos and a popular destination for corrupt Chinese officials, dropped by 30 percent in 2015, and the revenue of its casinos dropped by 40 percent. The author's interview in December 2015.
3 "Communiqué of the Third Plenary Session of the 18th Central Committee of the Communist Party of China," China Newsnet, January 15, 2014, http://www.china.org.cn/china/third_plenary_session/2014-01/15/content_31203056.htm.

Index

About the Author

Cheng Li is director and senior fellow at the Brookings Institution's John L. Thornton China Center. Dr. Li is also a director of the National Committee on U.S.–China Relations, a member of the Academic Advisory Team of the Congressional U.S.–China Working Group, and a member of the Council on Foreign Relations.

He is the author/editor of numerous books, including *China's Leaders: The New Generation* (Rowman and Littlefield, 2001), *China's Changing Political Landscape: Prospects for Democracy* (Brookings, 2008), *China's Emerging Middle Class: Beyond Economic Transformation* (Brookings, 2010), *The Road to Zhongnanhai: High-Level Leadership Groups on the Eve of the 18th Party Congress* (Mirror Books, 2012, in Chinese), *China's Political Development: Chinese and American Perspectives* (Brookings, 2014, co-editor), and *Chinese Politics in the Xi Jinping Era: Reassessing Collective Leadership* (Brookings 2016). Dr. Li is also the principal editor of the Thornton Center Chinese Thinkers Series published by the Brookings Institution Press.

Li grew up in Shanghai during the Cultural Revolution. In 1985, he came to the United States where he later received an MA in Asian Studies from the University of California and a PhD in Political Science from Princeton University.

www.ingramcontent.com/pod-product-compliance
Lightning Source LLC
Chambersburg PA
CBHW050331270326
41926CB00016B/3405

9789813232181